Queer for Fear

HORROR FILM AND THE QUEER SPECTATOR

HORROR STUDIES

Preface

Horror Studies is the first book series exclusively dedicated to the study of the genre in its various manifestations – from fiction to cinema and television, magazines to comics, and extending to other forms of narrative texts such as video games and music. Horror Studies aims to raise the profile of Horror and to further its academic institutionalisation by providing a publishing home for cutting-edge research. As an exciting new venture within the established Cultural Studies and Literary Criticism programme, Horror Studies will expand the field in innovative and student-friendly ways.

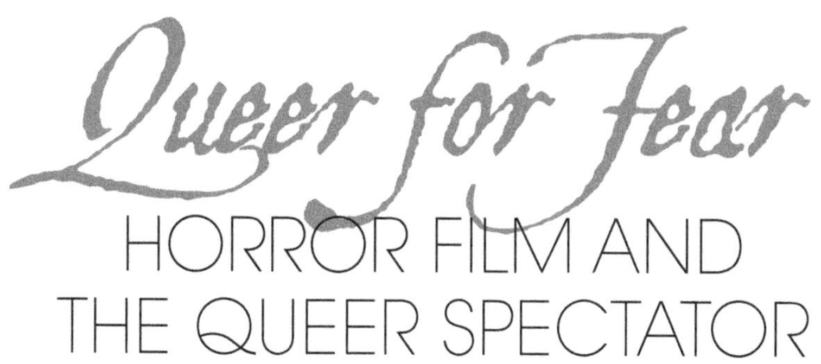

HORROR FILM AND THE QUEER SPECTATOR

HEATHER O. PETROCELLI

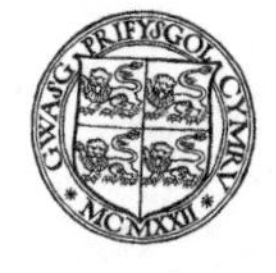

UNIVERSITY OF WALES PRESS
2023

This work is dedicated to all the horror queerdos, gay ghouls and queer creatures of the night – what music we make.

For Amie.

Reprinted 2025 (three times), 2026

www.uwp.co.uk

British Library Cataloguing-in-Publication Data

A catalogue record for this book is available from the British Library.

ISBN 978-1-83772-309-6
eISBN 978-1-83772-052-1

For GPSR enquiries please contact:
Easy Access System Europe Oü, 16879218
Mustamäe tee 50, 10621, Tallinn, Estonia. gpsr.requests@easproject.com

Typeset by Chris Bell, cbdesign
Printed and bound by CPI Group (UK) Ltd, Croydon, CR0 4YY

Contents

List of Figures ix

Acknowledgements xi

Prologue xiii

1. **Horror is Queer: Theoretical and Ontological Foundations** 1

Queer Identity and Community 6

The Ontological Queerness of Film and the Horror Genre 10

Queer Theory, Queerness and Queer Scholarship 16

Centring Queers and Queerness in Horror Studies 26

A Note on Statistics 44

2. **Portrait of a Queer Horror Fan: the Opinions, Habits and Tastes of the Queer Spectator** 55

Queer Heterogeneity and Consensus 57

Gender and Sexual Orientation Diversity of Queer Spectators 59

Racial/Ethnic Identifications 62

Educational Attainment and Age 64

The Othered Lens of Queerness 67

Monsters, Victims and the Final Girl 75

Women and Queers Represented in Horror 79

Fan Status of Queer Spectators 81

Childhood Introduction to Horror 83

Horror as Interpersonal Connection 86

Queer Spectators' Horror Genre Knowledge 88

Queer Identities and Identifications as Queer 90

Queer Horror Spectators Compared with Female Horror Fans 94
Non-Cinematic Modes of Horror Consumption 98
Queer Spectators and International Horror 98
Cinemagoing and Queer Spectators 100
Horror Habits Beyond Film Spectatorship 100
Violence, Gore and Tension 102
Horror Subgenres 103
The Favourite Horror Films of Queer Spectators 107
Summarising the Queer Spectator of Horror Film 111

3. Trauma and Camp: Queer Connections to Horror 121
Queer Trauma, the Horror Genre and Traumatic Expressions 122
Evidencing Queer Trauma, Affect and Catharsis 134
The Camp Relationship to Horror 145
Evidentiary Data on Queerness, Camp and Horror 152
Camp Laughter as a Trauma Processor 161

4. Drag Me to Hell: Queer Performance and Live Cinema 175
Establishing Queer Performance as Live Cinema 177
The Phenomenology of Queer Live Cinema 182
The Cult of Queer Live Cinema 190
Drag as Queer Performance and Drag Performers as Horror Hosts 197
Midnight Mass with your Hostess Peaches Christ 201
Welcome to Queer Horror 205
When Live Cinema Becomes a Significant Queer Event 208
Evidencing Queer Live Cinema with Empirical Data 212
Film as the Cinematic Church of Queer Community and the Future of Queer Live Cinema 217

Conclusion 233

Appendix 243
Oral History Bibliography 251
Works Cited 255
Index 275

List of Figures

Chapter 2

2.1	Graph of survey participants' gender identities	60
2.2	Graph of survey participants' sexual orientations	62
2.3	Graph of survey participants' racial and/or ethnic identities	63
2.4	Chart of country of residence by racial and/or ethnic identity	63
2.5	Chart of survey participants' level of education	65
2.6	Chart of survey participants' age	66
2.7	Graph of survey participants' identification in horror films	76
2.8	Chart comparing survey participants' identification in horror	77
2.9	Graph of survey participants' level of horror fandom	81
2.10	Graph of survey participants' length of horror fandom	83
2.11	Graph of what started survey participants' interest in horror	87
2.12	Graph of survey participants' international horror habits	99
2.13	Chart comparing queers' top horror subgenres with women	103
2.14	Chart of survey participants' top twenty-five favourite horror films	109
2.15	Gendered breakdown of survey participants' top ten horror films	110

Chapter 3

3.1	Graph about horror films helping work through trauma	135
3.2	Graph about horror films and catharsis	140
3.3	Graph about enjoying 'camp-y' horror films	153
3.4	Graph about horror films and laughter	160

Chapter 4

4.1	Portrait of Peaches Christ	179
4.2	Portrait of Carla Rossi	181

Acknowledgements

THIS PROJECT was completed where I live, the unceded and stolen traditional and ancestral lands of the Multnomah, Wasco, Cowlitz, Kathlamet, Clackamas, Watlala bands of the Chinook, the Tualatin Kalapuya, Molalla, Tumwater and other Tribes and Bands who have lived and continue to live on and steward the lands that are now known as the Portland metropolitan area in the United States. Acknowledging and rendering visible the ongoing traumas of white settler colonialism on Indigenous peoples everywhere is an initial step towards a more equitable future.

This project is marked by personal, familial, national and international traumas that also demand acknowledgement, as all cultural production is sociopolitically situated. As for many, the past few years were personally very difficult and painful. My brother's death punctuated the beginning of this research endeavour. Throughout this research project, the United States further fractured under a hateful leader and a fraught presidential election. Since spring 2020, life has been permeated by the death and illness of the coronavirus pandemic and the reality of and reckoning with racism in America. This work was written against the odds in a society facing the increasing effects from misogyny, racism, homophobia, transphobia, ableism, Islamophobia, antisemitism, colonialism and neoliberal capitalism.

This study would not exist in its current form without the love, support and guidance of numerous people, manifested in numerous ways. Anyone who helped me on this journey in any capacity, from sharing my queer horror survey to providing feedback on my work, I thank you.

Enthusiastically and specifically, I thank each and every one of the 4,107 survey participants and all of the oral history narrators: Gabe Castro, Harmony Colangelo, Lana Contreras, Jason Edward Davis, Mark Estes, Joe Fejeran, Joshua Grannell, Alex Hall, CJ Hodges, Anthony Hudson, Stacie Ponder, Kaitlyn Stodola, Kim Thompson, Michael Varrati and Christopher Velasco. I am grateful that you each took the time to share your knowledge, experience and love of horror with me. This research would not exist without you.

Prologue

LANGUAGE SHIFTS, word meanings change, and social sensibilities evolve; therefore, the queer identifying words, terms and markers used in this study may become outdated with time or even may not be preferred by some members of the queer community today. Due to being focused on non-normative subjectivities, this study and document could potentially present demographic or community terms that do not feel right or appropriate for (or that even feel offensive to) some individuals. My approaches that informed this study and my actions that created it are founded on respect for individual subjectivities and differences in the words that we choose to describe ourselves. My intentions and attention are focused squarely on dismantling the misogynistic, racist, homophobic, transphobic, classist and ableist societal institutions and systems that hurt our communities. I believe this focus (rather than solely attending to individual words and behaviours) to be most productive because the culture wars and 'cancel culture', which run rampant at the time of this study and writing, reflect the fracturing function of neoliberal identity politics. About this, Jack Halberstam astutely remarks:

> In queer communities today, while we fight about words like 'tranny,' worry about being triggered, and 'call each other out' for our supposed microcrimes of omission/inclusion/slang, we are, like the People's Front of Judea, trying to fight power by battling over the relations between signifiers and signifieds while leaving the structures of signification itself intact. (2018, p. 16)

I remain sensitive to others in my community while being resolutely focused on deconstructing the systems that ultimately harm us. The COVID-19 pandemic, disproportionately harming numerous marginalised communities, has ravaged the world throughout the writing of this book. Instead of trying to be 'business as usual', with ongoing attempts to return to the pre-pandemic 'normal', I hope that we work together to create a different and more equitable way forward.

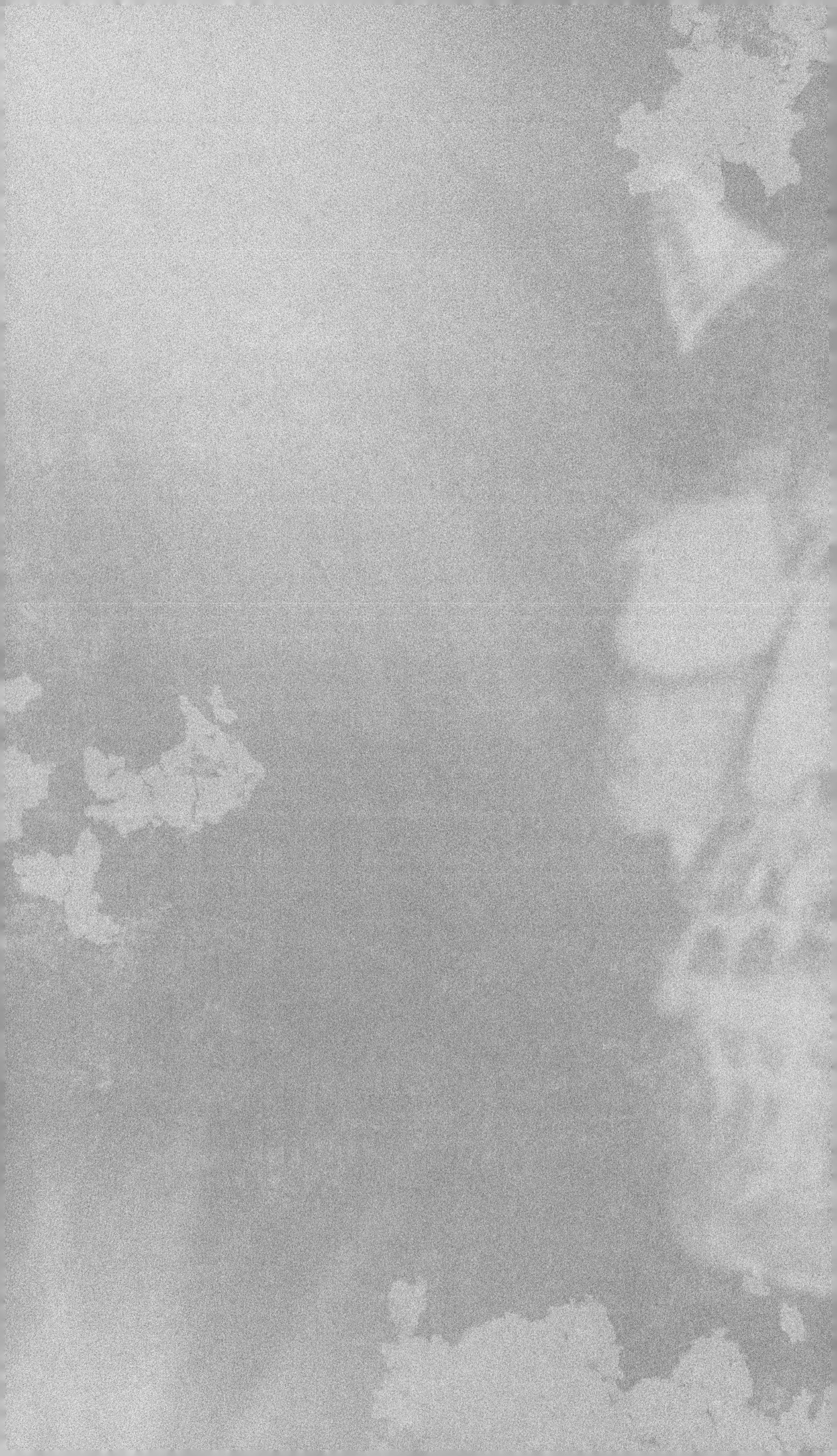

1

Horror is Queer

Theoretical and Ontological Foundations

I believe horror is queer because it's always the perspective of an outsider. As queer people, we've always been on the side. Y'all are not us. We haven't been part of the majority culture. So, in essence, we do see a lot of our perspective in the main characters trying to survive, you know, and that's what I find very appealing. And I think that there's a lot of parallel between the reality of a queer person and the reality of someone in a horror film.
(Contreras, 2020, pp. 20–1)

Without queerdom – which includes drag, camp, and being Othered – you don't have a lot of the horror that the straight horror bros tend to take for granted. It's the fact that they just don't like to take their claws off what they feel has been theirs, but it's *always* been ours and we're clawing back and our claws are sharper 'cause we've had years to grind them up on our anger, our frustration, and our denial of just being who we are. So we're coming out of the shadows. We're coming out of closets. We're coming from under the beds. We're coming to take back what's ours and y'all just need to be ready for it.
(Estes, 2020, p. 37)

I think queers engage with horror in a way that's different from heterosexuals in that we inherently understand that this is *our* genre.
(Varrati, 2020, p. 17)

IN 'PROUDLY SETTING TRENDS: The 2015 LGBT Consumer Report', the internationally recognised global information, data and measurement company Nielsen revealed that 43 per cent of Lesbian, Gay, Bisexual and Transgender (LGBT) moviegoers report that horror movies are a favourite genre to see in movie theatres, which is nearly 50 per cent more than non-LGBT moviegoers. The report states, moreover, that LGBT moviegoers were 50 per cent more likely than their heterosexual counterparts to name horror as a favourite film genre (Nielsen, 2015, pp. 5–6). While this confirms the anecdotal truism that a statistically significant number of queer[1] community members both enjoy and actively seek out horror films, little else is known about the viewing patterns, practices, tastes, appropriations and relationships of the queer spectator with regard to horror film. Certainly, the queer community has had a relationship with the horror genre – both in the production and consumption of horror film – for as long as the horror genre has existed. Although biographies and documentaries about queer horror icons, from James Whale to Mark Patton, have established a sense of queered horror history, almost nothing is known about queer horror spectators. This study is predicated on the assertion, therefore, that even though 'doing empirical audience studies is cumbersome, time consuming, and it requires resources' (Kjeldsen, 2018, p. 4), engaging queer horror spectators directly is imperative to understanding the importance of the horror genre to queer people and, in turn, to foregrounding queer voices in academic critique of the genre. For 'whilst socio-political readings of Horror are necessary', as Xavier Aldana Reyes claims, 'they hardly ever cover the experiential side of Horror' (2016, p. 134). And while 'audience studies are inordinately time consuming and labor-intensive' (Brunt, 1992, p. 69), they are, I will argue, the pre-eminent means of understanding both the horror genre and its significance to its spectators.

To have the substantial and adequate data set – quantitative and qualitative (mixed method) results – that is necessary to study and subsequently to understand queer spectatorship of horror film, I created a sixty-six-question survey that garnered thousands of participants, producing the largest study on horror spectators and the largest audience study of the horror genre.[2] In order to extend understanding about both horror film and queer audiences, my work here centres the quantitative and qualitative empirical data of 4,107 queer people. This survey response rate is all the more noteworthy when considering that 'people are less willing to answer a lengthy questionnaire than a brief one'

(Austin, 1989, p. 10). Indeed, the overwhelming success of this in-depth sixty-six-question survey speaks volumes about the significant relationship between queers and horror.

Throughout this study, in a direct and purposeful act to elevate queer horror spectators' voices, I present and analyse quantitative and qualitative data from queer survey participants and queer oral history narrators[3] who provided in-depth interviews that uncover understandings of and meanings behind their relationship with the horror genre.[4] Since the queer community exists at the periphery of mainstream society, this choice to centre queer voices and perspectives in this study is an explicit and political decision. The Queer for Fear Oral History Collection functions as a resource for better understanding how queers create meaning and make sense of their love of horror and how horror is integrated into their queer identity. While there may be as many queer identities as there are research participants, this project congregates members of the LGBTQ+ population into one, a queer community centred on its love of horror that is rooted in 'a queer world that affirms the non-normative, the odd, and the deviant' (Carnes, 2019, p. 12). Taken together, this collected data set creates the most complete portrait of queer spectators of horror to date, based on their opinions, habits and tastes, and serves as evidence of the *sui generis* nature of the relationship that queers have to the horror genre. This study, therefore, fills a gap in academic and theoretical discourse by creating a research project that focuses on queer spectatorship of horror film in a viewing context in which queer fandom itself occupies 'a liminal position on the fringes of both gay culture and the horror community' (Scales, 2015, p. 201). This research does so by building on, and moving beyond, the spectator scholarship of academics such as Brigid Cherry who, in 1999, examined the viewing pleasures and fan practices of female horror film audiences.

My addition to the limited scholarship on horror spectatorship is both felicitous and vital due to the queer community's increased visibility in horror, as well as horror film's growing legitimacy. Films such as *The Babadook* (2014), *It Follows* (2014), *The Witch* (2015), *Get Out* (2017) and *Hereditary* (2018) brought a renewed era of critical acclaim to the genre, a period that also saw the release of explicitly queer horror films such as *Rift* (2017), *Thelma* (2017), *The Perfection* (2018), *Knife+Heart* (2018) and *Bit* (2019).[5] This study eschews the mainstream critical terminology 'elevated horror' because the term ignores 'horror film's long history of critically engaging with social issues' (Pinedo, 2020, p. 96) and it obscures an important reason why audiences are further consuming horror at the box office: the increasingly inclusive representation of women, Black, Indigenous and People of Colour (BIPOC),[6] and/or queers as actors, directors and producers. Oral history narrators Gabe Castro and Kim Thompson speak directly to this inclusive era of horror, stating:

> We're in, luckily, this time where people are confronting the way that they're being seen or portrayed, we're trying to be a little more purposeful in representing certain voices and elevating them . . . Having someone like Jordan Peele who can create *Get Out* which is just phenomenal in itself and in being a social-horror piece. But to also be able to back that up with *Us*, which is a film about classism, but featuring a Black family who just exists as a family. Like it doesn't have to be about race . . . And, you know, seeing more women popping up, even seeing some Latinx people popping up, and getting that support and to be able to tell those stories . . . We've had enough white men telling those stories – and they've done a pretty bad job in the past trying to tell the stories of others. (Castro, 2020, pp. 9–10)

> There's a message in the fact that there are these very incredible women who are directors coming to the forefront – or anybody who is directing horror who isn't a cishet white male who is making a film now – who is making a film that people are excited about because it's something we've never seen before. I think what that is communicating is that perhaps it's time to give a platform to those communities that haven't really had the opportunity to tell horror from their perspective. And the reason that we're interested in and excited is because these peoples' perspectives are completely different because they don't exist at the top of the food chain of the patriarchy and will not make a film in the way that a cishet white dude's going to make a horror film. We're not talking about the same thing because the same things aren't horrific to us. (Thompson, 2020, p. 16)

Oral history narrator CJ Hodges directly foregrounds the queer spectator's passion for horror's growing inclusivity, stating: 'I'm very attached to these new movies' (2020, p. 22). The rise of inclusive horror not only engages and renders visible an ever-increasing number of queer horror makers, but also provides more filmic content embraced by queer spectators, all of which demonstrates that queer spectators of horror are positively responding to the shifts and changes within horror in the twenty-first century.

Although the definition of what, precisely, constitutes a horror film has lain at the heart of horror criticism since its inception, the transgressive and affective nature of the horror genre has made it resistant to 'water-tight definitions' (Neale, 2000, p. 85). Regardless of any strict or collective consensus on the definition of what constitutes a horror film, the genre, nonetheless, has a communicative shorthand, which is an 'implicit conception of the language of the genre' (Tudor, 1989, p. 4). The generic language of horror, therefore, is not a strictly codified process, but instead an inferred understanding by the spectator. Tudor theorises genre as a reception concept when he argues that 'genre is what we collectively believe it to be' (2003, p. 7). Someone recognising the language of horror in a film is, I argue, viewing a horror film. The aim of this study is not, therefore, to define horror. Neither will this study play gatekeeper on research participants' individual definitions or understandings of horror. Such restrictions and boundaries serve only to undermine the transgressive, queer nature of horror itself, which this study investigates more in detail. In a study such as this one, that privileges the audience over the text, I follow Cherry in asserting that 'any definition of the genre is bound to be irrelevant since the individual viewers taking part in study [*sic*] will undoubtedly hold their own ideas of what films constitute the boundaries of horror' (1999, pp. 29–30). Distilled down to its simplest form, empirical evidence is about engaging audiences, individual people who form a community of interest, to discuss and collect data about their embodied experiences as horror spectators. As such, this study is grounded in the experiential side of horror – my own experiences, the survey participants' experiences, the interview narrators' experiences, and the experiences of this book's readers. For while critics such as Harry Benshoff and Sean Griffin may observe that 'for generations, queer audiences have also been fascinated with horror films' (2006, p. 75), there had never been a large-scale study that engages the full spectrum of queer horror spectators and documented their opinions, habits and tastes. Heeding Amin Ghaziani and Matt Brim's 'call to action', I have built 'a productive, plentiful, powerful, and pleasurable queer worldmaking and livability project' of my own to do so (2019, p. 23). Beyond presenting the most complete picture to date about queer horror spectators, this study additionally and importantly helps to queer the burgeoning field of live cinema. As defined by Sarah Atkinson and Helen W. Kennedy, live cinema is 'an umbrella term through which to capture the broad range of emergent creative art practices and novel commercial strategies' (2018, p. x). This study situates case studies on Peaches Christ's

Midnight Mass and Carla Rossi's Queer Horror in the appropriate cultural context and within live cinema studies, underscoring queer contributions to this mode of cultural engagement. This expansion demonstrates how Midnight Mass and Queer Horror are acts of 'queering' heterosexual spaces with horror film exhibition that include live pre-shows and consider the audience experiences at these screenings. Live cinema studies is a nascent academic field that, until this study, had yet to explicitly and empirically engage with queer individuals and reckon with queer identity.

Queer Identity and Community

Any work centred on identity needs to confront the use of identity politics as a tool of neoliberalism to erode people's sense of class consciousness. This fact does not invalidate identity-based research; it just means that, as the work's author, I must acknowledge that identity politics do not encapsulate the complete human subjective experience in society or, indeed, the economic determinants that shape both experience and identity.[7] Regardless, identity does matter, for '[i]dentities and memories are not things we think *about*, but things we think *with*' (Gillis, 1994, p. 5; italics in the original). While individualistic neoliberal capitalism erodes the function of the collective and communities, this study aims to create a sense of community, even if it is an 'imagined community', a perceived grouping based on a collective identity that is always intertwined with sociopolitical and historical forces (Anderson, 2006, p. 6). My imagined community of queer horror spectators functions in opposition to both the destructive forces of the cisheteropatriarchy[8] and the fracturing tide of neoliberal capitalism. To borrow Jack Halberstam's sharp rationale: 'rather than remaining invested in an identitarian set of conflicts that turn on small differences and individual hurts, let us rather wage battle against the violent imposition of economic disparity and forcefully oppose a renewed and open investment in white supremacy and American imperial ambition transacted through the channels of globalization' (2018, p. 126). My imagined queer horror community is filled with difference yet still united in our queerness, with our differences as a source of strength. In other words, this study privileges the collective community of queer horror spectators over the individual queer horror fan, emphasising the value of community over the goals and gains of the individual. As Henry A. Giroux heeds: 'Neoliberalism produces a notion of individualism and anti-intellectualism that harbors a pathological disdain for community'

(2021, p. 91). This research, thus, philosophically holds an anti-neoliberal praxis that maintains the positive power of community by centring the collective consensus evidenced by the data, while, at times, highlighting intersectional individualisms in order to underscore simultaneously that distinct facets of our identities are socially and historically relevant. This study dispels ideological tensions arising between a collective community consensus and individual identity differences by discerning that a disparate group of queer people from various intersectional embodiments can still find 'social solidarity and collective obligation' within the queer horror community and thereby undermine the fracturing effects of neoliberal individualism (Giroux, 2021, p. 35). As theorist David M. Halperin declares: 'Queer is by definition *whatever* is at odds with the normal, the legitimate, the dominant. . . . a positionality vis-à-vis the normative' (1995, p. 62; italics in the original). Relatedly, narrator Stacie Ponder reflects on queerness as an existence created outside the norm:

> Queerness puts you out of step with society because we're told that there's a certain path that we're supposed to take from birth to grave basically. Queerness automatically puts you out of step with that and therefore it kind of changes everything around you because you just see things differently. You have to figure out how you fit into life when the prescribed life path doesn't work for you. (2020, p. 19)

While there are various ways to designate and name the community under study, I employ and embody the term 'queer', a labelling that is in direct opposition to the exclusionary limitations of gay and lesbian and the disembodied sterility of the acronym LGBTQA+ (Case, 1991, p. 3).

Reclaiming the word queer is not only personal and political, but also perfectly suited for the horror spectator, for the 'queer is the taboo-breaker, the monstrous, the uncanny' (Case, 1991, p. 3). This research employs the term queer to represent embodied subjectivities that transgress cisheterosexual norms, most specifically but not exclusively non-normative sexualities (not heterosexual) and/or genders (not cisgender or binaristic genders) and their intersections. Queer – as a noun, an adjective and a verb – continually foments transgression and multiplicity, thereby offering non-normative alterity. The use of the term queer in a disembodied context (usage not related to non-normative sexuality or gender variances) is to represent the broader existence that transgresses cisheteronormative norms. As Gust Yep explains: 'Heteronormativity, as the invisible center and the presumed bedrock of society, is the quintessential force creating, sustaining, and perpetuating the erasure, marginalization, disempowerment, and oppression of sexual others' (2003, p. 18). For as long as cisheteronormativity is the enforced dominant societal state and queers are forced to exist within cisheteronormative power structures,[9] queer theory (and queer embodied realities) not only retains its sociopolitical charge, but also offers possibilities for legitimacy outside the norm. While research participants may express their queerness or understanding of queerness differently, they fundamentally share that misalignment with normative society, a society in which '[h]eteronormativity makes heterosexuality hegemonic through the process of normalization' (Yep, 2003, p. 18). The queer community's sense of unity in part stems from growing up in a cisgender, heterosexual dominant society, not in a queer community (unlike common upbringings within ethnic and racial communities). As Ghaziani notes, with respect to Eve Kosofsky Sedgwick: 'Compared to racial and ethnic groups, queer communities lack a clear sense of ancestral linearity (Sedgwick 1990). The absence of awareness – who are my people? – induces collective amnesia about our lives. This is one of the most insidious and painful forms of homophobia' (2019, p. 114). Richard Dyer further explains, 'as gays, we grew up isolated not only from our heterosexual peers but also from each other' (1977, p. 1); since most queers grow up in binaristic cisheterosexual familial units, we must either make our own or find our own way to queer community.[10] We have to construct our community, our chosen family. Queers are further bonded by the fact that we 'are understood as belonging to a permanent minority that perpetually replenishes but never comes close to a majority' (Schoonover and Galt, 2016, p. 167).

While queers will always be a small minority,[11] we are everywhere and nowhere. We are visible and invisible. Gloria Anzaldúa developed thinking on this, writing that: 'Being the supreme crossers of cultures, homosexuals have strong bonds with the queer white, Black, Asian, Native American, Latino, and with the queer in Italy, Australia and the rest of the planet. We come from all colors, all classes, all races, all time periods' (1987, pp. 84–5). Anzaldúa's words reiterate how queerness is a diverse yet unifying identity marker. Queers' very existence is a threat to the cisheteropatriarchy – to cisheteronormativity – 'a world system that naturalizes its own dominance and far-reaching proliferation as a theory of human life' (Schoonover and Galt, 2016, p. 23), a system that is intrinsically linked to and the creator of neoliberal capitalism. Indeed, the establishment and dominance of cisheterosexuality is predicated on the constructed societal fear of the queer, a subjectivity that needs to be abjected in order for the normative to be instated and affirmed. This exact dynamic upholds the structure of white supremacy, which normalises whiteness and renders the non-white as the feared and subjugated Other. This study's goal is to simultaneously highlight the data about queer horror spectators and create initial space to discuss how intersectional differences within the queer community shift data results and embodied experiences. Since this research has created and presents the first empirical understanding of queer spectators of horror film, I purposefully and actively centre the cohesive narrative of queer horror spectatorship. This cohesive narrative focuses on and explicates the majority findings and shared stories found in the quantitative and qualitative data, rather than examining more nuanced intersectional differences. Yet, indisputably, the queer community is certainly not devoid of racism, misogyny, classism and ableism, with race particularly informing intersectional perspectives and experiences. In other words, queer BIPOC horror fans are subject to society's, and certainly fandom's, white supremacist structures. Kevin Leo Yabut Nadal pointedly explains: 'For decades, LGBTQ people of color (LGBTQPOC) have described how experiences of racism within mainstream LGBTQ communities are often dismissed or invalidated and how racial hierarchies within White-dominant LGBTQ communities are pervasive, but unspoken about' (2020, p. 41). While this study privileges queerness – whereas Cherry 'privileged gender' (1999, p. 213) – that privilege will not 'override difference in the pursuit of sameness' (Whatling, 1997, p. 12). To that end, this research, based on a diverse spectrum of survey participants and narrators, not only amplifies our voices and legitimises our experiences, but also provides a rationale for the understanding that horror itself is queer. To emphasise this claim on the genre, Shudder's 2020 Comic-Con@Home panel, on 23 July, was aptly titled 'Horror is Queer'. This study demonstrates that horror is resoundingly queer, with the ways in which queer spectators connect to the genre being distinctive, and that horror acts, in narrator Jason Edward Davis's words, as an 'access to queerness' (2020, p. 11). Narrator Joe Fejeran clarifies how horror can be part of identity formation: 'Horror has been a way for me to know more about myself. It's been a way for me to know more about the rest of the world' (2020, p. 40). Repeatedly, the words of the survey participants and oral history narrators collectively and directly shed light on this emotional connection between genre and identity. As narrator Mark Estes explains, 'It seems like there's some type of freedom within horror for us queer people. It's some type of freedom' (2020, p. 16).

The Ontological Queerness of Film and the Horror Genre

Identifying the ontological nature of film as being queer explains the queer spectator's distinctive relationship to the horror genre and augments further understanding of that relationship. Stated differently, this study clarifies the queer nature of film and recognises the significance of this shared connection for queer spectators in their relationship to horror. The idiosyncratic and interconnected relationships between film, horror and queerness is an undelineated interconnectivity that illuminates film as a queer medium and horror as the queerest film genre.[12] As argued by Galt and Schoonover: 'It is crucial to affirm that cinema is not simply a neutral host for LGBT representations but is, rather, a queerly inflected medium. To adapt Jasbir Puar's terminology, we understand cinema as a queer assemblage' (2016, p. 6). Succinctly restated, film is a queer medium. The ontological nature of film specifically speaks to the queer experience in a way that differs from how it may speak to and for other Others in our society: workers, women and BIPOC, as Robin Wood defines, with queer people, as the Others 'of white patriarchal bourgeois culture' (2003, p. 160).[13] A primary claim of this study is not only that horror is a queer genre, then, but is in fact the queerest genre in cinema because both the aesthetics of horror and its representation of the Other are intrinsically transgressive. Queers find kinship in horror since their individual queerness transgresses societal taboos and, as Cyndy Hendershot confirms, 'horror film is a genre that operates within a framework of taboo and transgression' (2001, p. 25). Indeed, both queer people and horror films are 'punished' for their non-normative transgressions. Queers suffer personal abuses, institutional discrimination and anti-queer legislation, among other societal aggressions. Similarly, horror films are not only censored and banned at familial/community and national levels, but also considered by film scholars and critics to form a lowly genre. Queers identify with 'transgressive behaviour' (47108917)[14] represented in the horror genre since 'queer identity is transgressive' (47112447). As a survey participant writes, 'growing up queer gives me more of a natural appreciation for the transgressive and monstrous in horror' (47121814). These participants' comments explicitly illustrate how queers directly identify with 'horror's violation of taboos' and recognise that 'the power of horror lies in its transgressive nature' (Jones, 2018, p. 13). The claim that horror is queer is strengthened by the words of this study's oral history narrators, who unequivocally hold ideas that connect queerness with the spaces, themes and motifs in horror films and, indeed, the horror genre itself. I posit that a significant number of queer spectators of horror films understand the horror genre to be a queer genre, based on the unequivocal declaration by all fifteen of the oral history narrators, including the following quotes from Alex Hall, Anthony Hudson, Gabe Castro, Jason Edward Davis, Michael Varrati and Joe Fejeran:

> Because it explores the Other, obviously, in that regard, horror has been always super, super queer. The fact that the monster is always subjugated to dark small closet-y spaces – the basement, the attics, the closet. And just the fear of the monstrous body, too, speaks to queerness in a very visceral way. (Hall, 2020, p. 14)

> Horror is a queer art form, not a subgenre. Horror is . . . the entire genre of horror itself is the queerness. You know this, but it is a site, and it is a genre, and it is a theme, and an aesthetic that was created by queer makers. And it's all about longing for the Other, or identifying with Other, or being made Other, like Frankenstein. I mean this is so basic, so 101, but Frankenstein is born a monster. It's outside of his will. Society has named him a monster and made him a monster. (Hudson, 2020a, p. 12)

> I think horror is queer. And I also think it's a home for any of us who consider ourselves the Other or different – and needing to live through that or feel like you're not the only one who's living through that. Because you can kind of see yourself on either side of that story of the protagonists and the villain and live through all the emotions that we're going through. (Castro, 2020, p. 7)

> I mean, horror *is* queerness. From the very first horror films, it was about queerness, and it'll always be about the Other. It'll always be about destroying the nuclear family, the status quo, structures that are in place. It'll always be about something being outside of that, breaking shit up. It is queer. The physical intimacy of it is queer. Even in the violence people are being penetrated in ways that they have not defined as the way they thought they would be penetrated. (Davis, 2020, pp. 29–30)

> I think everybody who loves horror loves horror, and that's never in question. But I think our [queer] connection with it is different

> because we feel it baked in somehow – it's like it is baked into our essence. If you are a queer horror fan, it is because we love horror, but it's also because we're queer, because we get both of those things and the DNA of both of them is intertwined. (Varrati, 2020, p.18)

> Horror is intrinsically queer. And, at that time, I didn't know about the early directors – like *Frankenstein* – I didn't know about James Whale. I didn't know about that. I didn't know about those men. And it's been really interesting to kind of discover that and be like, yeah, this is *very* queer. It *is* very queer; the queerness as a genre is talking about very politically, very queer things and dealing with isolation and being an outsider and all of that. (Fejeran, 2020, p. 20)

The interviews, combined with the survey results, evidence that queers understand horror to be a queer genre, engage with horror as a queer genre and claim horror as a queer genre. As a survey participant notes, 'so much of the gothic/horror genre has been *born* from queerness, outsiderness, and queer creators in general. The genre is fundamentally built on a queer foundation' (47085220). Queer spectators connect to horror through shared status as societal transgressions and the figurative Other, as well as through a queer trauma and a camp relationship. When this study attends to the Other, it attends to the worlds of both queerness *and* horror; to be queer is to be an Other who exists in opposition to the mainstream, causing societal unease, which is reflected in horror films.[15] Horror 'fashions a space in which challenges to the status quo and non-normative bodies, identities, expressions and affects are actively centralised' (Harrington, 2018, p. 28). Horror's centring of the non-normative in its fictional narratives provides an important space for queer spectators to experience catharsis, find connection or feel seen since their non-normative lives exist oppressed, judged and unseen at the periphery of society. Noël Carroll writes 'that what horrifies is that which lies *outside* cultural categories' (1987, p. 57; italics in the original), which Benshoff summarises as being 'in short, the queer' (1997, p. 26). To the cisheteropatriarchal norm, the queer is horrific and the representation of that horror in the filmic medium is often queer in return.

The queer connection to the horror genre can be better understood through recognition that the nascent, ontological nature of the film medium and the embodied experience of queerness are uncanny. In other words, the nature of queerness, in individuals and film, is uncanny. When

Freud discussed the uncanny in 1919, he restated F. W. J. Schelling's definition of the uncanny as 'that ought to have remained secret and hidden but has come to light' (p. 225). This definition not only inadvertently confronts the historic queer experience of being expected to remain hidden in the shadows, but also simultaneously underscores the uncanny nature of queerness – queers are the uncanny (un)seen. Theorists such as Sue-Ellen Case (1991), Paulina Palmer (2012) and Nicholas Royle assert that the 'uncanny *is* queer. And the queer is uncanny' (Royle, 2003, p. 43). As a survey participant indicates:

> Most horror films have two motifs that queer folks identify with. The first is acts of transgression, the second is the unheimlich or the uncanny. Uncanny: that which is like us but not like us. This is something that a lot of queer people identify with due to feeling alienated from our own bodies or society. (47181591)

Combined, the above establishment of the preternatural nature of queerness and the 'queer nature of cinema itself as a medium' (Schoonover and Galt, 2016, p. 90) denote how '[c]inema can be uncanny' (Hubner, 2018, p. 50).

In 1896, Maxim Gorky, on first seeing a projection of the Lumière Cinématographe, famously wrote in a Russian newspaper of this new filmic experience: 'It is terrifying to watch but it is the movement of shadows, mere shadows. Curses and ghosts, evil spirits that have cast whole cities into eternal sleep come to mind' (Gorky quoted in Skakov, 2012, p. 220). Gorky's deployment of the words 'curses', 'ghosts' and 'evil spirits' illustrates the 'uncanny' and haunting nature of cinema (Newton, 2019, p. 17). In fact, through his filmic experience, Gorky believed that 'he had had an encounter with the undead' (Jones, 2018, p. 44) – and, in a way, he had; '[t]here is something *spectral* about the experience of cinema', and that 'to enter the cinema is to cross a boundary, a threshold into the supernatural world' (Jones, 2018, p. 45; italics in the original). The capture and projection of images and sound are a ghostly manifestation. Furthermore, since 'all motion pictures become ghost stories' (Frayling, 2013, p. 5), film can be understood to be the reanimated past haunting the present. The cinema experience creates a liminal space between the audience and the projected image, images which are of 'the past' and are captured in ghostly light and shadow, animating in and for the present through the medium of film, which itself queers time. Film is a victory over and a disruption of linear time through this ghostly and uncanny queer intrusion of the past in the present. Film is a present-embodied experience of the past, with a spectator sometimes viewing dead actors brought back to life on the screen. The cinema experience is 'a kind of semi-private séance' (Winter, 1998, p. 138) and 'a medium giving life and spirit to dead forms' (Hubner, 2018, p. 45). In 1960, André Bazin spoke of film's ontology as 'change mummified' (1967, p. 15), further underscoring the queered uncanny nature of film, since change is active and unending, yet mummification speaks to the ossification of ghosts, in this case on screen. Therefore, the unsettling abnormality, or otherworldliness, of both the cinematic experience and queer individuals' existence are a lurking reminder of possibilities beyond the enforced cisheterosexual norm. Film is simultaneously queer and uncanny, possessing a haunted quality that circuitously resonates with queer identity since 'queerness can be understood in terms of haunting' (Boellstorff, 2007, p. 185) and 'being haunted and being a monster are queer narratives' (47121426).

Explicating the intrinsic haunted nature of queerness generates a greater understanding of the queer connection to horror film. If film is a haunted medium, so, too, is queer embodiment. Queer, as both a term and an identity, is imbued with the painful ghosts of our collective traumatic past – a past that still haunts the present and future – which is, as Laura Westengard states, 'the trauma of being queer in a system built to invalidate and destroy anyone who strays from the norm' (2019, p. 3). The experience of being queer, and even the formulation of queer theory, therefore, is imbued with ghosts, hauntings, possessions and conjurings. So much so that Rommi Smith, in *Imagining Queer Methods*, declares that the 'academic engaged in resurrecting repressed knowledge is like the medium: we speak to (and narrate) the ghost – the thing that is culturally, or intellectually, invisible' (2019, p. 214). Cisheteronormative society both renders queers as societal spectres and leaves the queer person haunted. To comprehend the spectral queer identity that is beyond the visible social norm, queerness (from the past, present and future) should be considered haunted and thus studied accordingly. One theoretical tool that can be utilised in order to see and understand the haunted nature of queerness is hauntology. Jacques Derrida's concept of hauntology addresses a haunting which precedes ontology (1994, p. 10). Distilled down to its most comprehensible essence, hauntology is 'a shorthand for the ways in which the past returns to haunt the present' (Coverley, 2020, p. 7). Accordingly, hauntology will have always already haunted our understanding of the nature of queerness (as with film). Indeed, the 'queer past that haunts queers in the present' is inextricable from queer embodiment (Muñoz, 2009, p. 88). The haunted queer consequently experiences an asynchronous temporality in which the past simultaneously haunts the present and future. This is one reason why queer potentiality within a cisheteronormative cultural ecology becomes rejected (Edelman, 2004) or unrealised (Muñoz, 2009), leaving the embodied queer in a state of liminal precarity. Queer liminal precarity is multiplicitous; the liminality is caused and perpetuated by cisheteronormative society, which grants queer acceptance conditionally based on homonormative assimilation (as when queer people adopt heteronormative institutions, such as marriage), with the rights or acceptance that cisheteronormative society decides to extend always already being threatened to be controlled or taken away at any moment. When a critical eye is focused on these liminal spaces, hauntology is a useful, intrinsically queer theoretical lens, a tool and 'a transgressive process' that 'attempt[s] to articulate an 'otherness' that has effects in the present' (Connor, 2017, pp. 14–15). Hauntology, at its core, challenges binary oppositions, concentrating on the in-between spaces of the 'past and the present, being and non-being, presence and absence' (Connor, 2017, p. 15). Hauntology, then, offers queers a framework to embrace their ghostly state, an (in)visible and non-binaristic liminal state of being. As cultural theorist Mark Fisher states: 'Hauntology is the proper temporal mode for a history made up of gaps, erased names and sudden abductions' (2014, p. 130). This understanding of hauntology even applies to the omissions, eliminations and removals of queers throughout history: queer history as spectre – invisible, neglected, feared.

To be queer is to be haunted by not only the invisibility of our shared collective history, but also the dominance of cisheteronormativity. Queerness 'remains haunted by the political and transgressive charge of the early 1990s moment, and that this haunting orients it toward particular political and intellectual projects in the present' (Amin, 2019, p. 286). The anger that underlies much of queer theory is its power, for queer theory emerged from queer activism spurred by pain, death and rage. As Kadji Amin points out, queer 'is a term *sticky* with history' (2019, p. 285; italics in the original). In fact, the term queer is haunted by its homophobic deployment as a long-time verbal weapon by 'straight' people, as well as from its queer community reclamation during the AIDS crisis, one of the times when wilful inaction from cisheteropatriarchal institutions killed many in a generation of queer men and trans women (Nadal, 2020, p. 29).

While joyous celebration is part of the queer community, there also exists a haunted undercurrent with a long history of invisibility, suppression, persecution, punishment and death. Queer spectators comprehend, both consciously and unconsciously, the haunted nature that they represent and that they are drawn to see reflected back in their cinematic experiences with the horror genre.

Queer Theory, Queerness and Queer Scholarship

Queer is a verb, an adjective, a noun, a pejorative, an identity, a sexual orientation and a gender identity. And, like the horror genre itself, queer theory is a complex umbrella term that is difficult to define; queer theory is plural and fluid, not singular and static (Browne and Nash, 2010, p. 7). Vitally, queer is not gender specific (Case, 1991, p. 2), opening research to any and all queer embodiment. Queer, moreover, is not a biological designation but a sociopolitical definition that carries a spirit of solidarity. Yet, my employment of the umbrella term queer in this research is not to collapse and conflate the heterogeneous queer community into a single monolithic and marketable community; my aim is to create space for diversity within the queer community, while simultaneously highlighting how these differences are formed in a nameable opposition to the cisheteronormative mainstream. 'Universalizing thinking can erase vulnerable queers, while minoritizing thinking can foreclose on connections and alliances' (Schoonover and Galt, 2016, p. 77); therefore, I will analyse both the connections and salient differences of the aggregate data. Overall, my argument is that queer spectators have a distinctive relationship with horror, but individual intersectionality can definitely shift perspectives and experiences with horror fandom, narrative content and access.[16] Furthermore, 'queer is a term that can and should be redeployed, fucked with and used in resistant and transgressive ways' (Browne and Nash, 2010, p. 9). When I use the term queer, I draw on the neglected power of all queers silenced before me, all those silenced now and all those who will be silenced in the future. I draw on queer theory's potential to destabilise the norms of time, space, society and certainly academia.[17] Rosalind Galt's and Karl Schoonover's assertion in *Queer Cinema in the World* that they 'are unwilling to relinquish the category of queer to charges that openness equals conceptual looseness and a dissipation of power' (2016, p. 14) is particularly empowering in this respect. In addition to Galt and

Schoonover and the scholars featured in *Queer Methods and Methodologies: Intersecting Queer Theories and Social Science Research* (2010) and *Imagining Queer Methods* (2019), the works of Eve Kosofsky Sedgwick, Judith Butler, Jack Halberstam and José Esteban Muñoz inform my analysis of identity formation outside of the cisheteronormative majority, as well as queer world-making and performance. In *Queer Theory and Communication: From Disciplining Queers to Queering the Discipline(s)*, Gust Yep, Karen Lovaas and John Elia ask, 'What does queer theory mean to scholars personally, theoretically, methodologically, and pedagogically?' (2003, pp. 335–6). Personally, theoretically, methodologically and pedagogically, queer theory liberates scholars from the academy's adherence to white cisheteropatriarchal norms. Importantly, this queer liberation is not to be confused with or equated to a lack of rigour; in fact, queer theory as liberator aids queer academics like myself to see beyond the normative, the standard, the status quo, all of which is a boon to academic research and thinking.

Queer theory encourages paying attention to the embodied, living experiences of queer people. Browne and Nash refuse to clarify and define the terms queer and queering because they argue that 'to clarify and define these terms is to limit their usage just to these understandings' (2010, p. 8). Categorisation and definition is the work of the white cisheterosexual male coloniser that aims to limit existence into what *he* can understand and what *he* will legitimise. Instead of limiting, Browne and Nash opted for the scholars in the collection to adopt their own usage and definition of queer. Hence, my uses and definitions here follow this lead. Queer theory seeks to resist, reframe, recycle, negotiate and subvert the cisheteronormative status quo. 'A consciously cultivated multidisciplinarity', Halberstam asserts, 'encourages queer scholars to use the methodologies that best match their projects rather than finding projects that allow them to use the discipline-appropriate methods' (2003, p. 363). This research project is, therefore, rooted in my own 'scavenger methodology', which incorporates differing methods in the research production process, and furthermore adopts Halberstam's position that queer methodology 'refuses the academic compulsion toward disciplinary coherence' (1998, p. 13). Apropos of the transdisciplinary nature of the horror genre, this research project situates an original data set from queer horror spectators in a critical framework at the nexus of horror studies, queer theory, cultural studies, film studies, reception studies, live cinema studies, ethnography, history and social science. Therefore, following Andrew Scahill, this study's textual promiscuity 'will flirt with many bodies of theory but ultimately not be married to any of them. This critical nonmonogamy is useful in examining a figuration that touches so many areas, and this work will scavenge theoretically to provide a multidimensional portrait' (2015, p. 6). Decades ago, Judith Butler warned that 'normalizing the queer would be, after all, its sad finish' (1994, p. 21). Built into the construct of queer theory being accepted as an academic tool is the paradox that, if it were ever to become academically institutionalised, queer theory would be rendered inefficacious. To maintain queer theory's distinct function as the undisciplined discipline, scholars must resist 'the institutional domestication of queer thinking' (Butler, 1994, p. 21). One large threat to the progress of queer theory is the academy's siloed university structure; to silo queer theory or studies into one department is to put it in a suffocating box, a coffin of sorts. In fact, as Halperin warns, 'the more it verges on becoming a normative academic discipline, the less queer "queer theory" can plausibly claim to be' (1995, p. 113). A part of the process of resisting normalisation is resisting institutionalisation; queer theory needs to continually question, push, radicalise and look forward in order to remain queer. Looking forward also includes looking back to acknowledge the past, to respect and honour our elders; queer theory is deeply indebted to BIPOC feminist thinking including, but not limited to, the works of Gloria E. Anzaldúa, Audre Lorde, bell hooks, Patricia Hill Collins, Cherríe Moraga, Angela Davis and Kimberlé Crenshaw. Moreover, queerness is infused into intersectional BIPOC feminist theory and work; indeed, the majority of the above-named women are queer. Given the aforementioned theorists' intersectional embodiment in which race, sex, gender, sexuality and class all exist in varying degrees of simultaneous oppression, there is little surprise that '[t]o interrogate heteronormativity *is* to critique colonial power' (Schoonover and Galt, 2016, p. 241; italics in the original). When I employ queer theory, I am invoking the multiple queer theories embodied in the singular, and, furthermore, signalling that queer theory exists as an amalgam of critical theory, art and activism.

While queer theory can seemingly appear complicated, amorphous and elusive, at its foundation, queer theory is a simple and distinctive tool to continuously question cisheteronormativity since 'queer worldmaking and livability require us to embrace multiplicity and pluralism, not binaries and dualisms' (Ghaziani and Brim, 2019, p. 12). To be clear, queer theory does not vacillate in its definition; integral to the theory itself is a fluidity and transgression. Even while queer theory questions and challenges essentialist identity and binarism, I acknowledge that, by framing this study around queerness being both an identity and a methodological tool, I have thus constructed a binary between those who are queer and those who are not; however, even this binary is a false dichotomy. While the focus of this research is on those who identify as queer, this study is purposefully not structured in opposition to those who are not. This research instead creates space for a heterogeneous population of queer people, one that shares a similarity in how we exist in opposition to the cisheteronormative world. Importantly, however, the focus remains fixated on the unique relationship that self-identified queers have with the horror genre, not on a sustained comparison or opposition to (or need to legitimise against) any cisheterosexual norms or populations, with the goal of adding to the small body of research that illustrates the 'deep relevance of the horror film to queer audiences and queer scholars' (Miller, 2011, pp. 220–1).

I position this project as deliberately and decisively queer, as one that queers methodology to render visible a segment of the queer population that has a special relationship to horror film. Queerness – personally, ontologically, epistemologically, phenomenologically, methodologically and theoretically – underpins every aspect of this study, and queer theory will function as a tool, an infused method, to root my thinking and challenge the dominance of cisheteronormativity in academia. Since my thinking and decisions will be always already queer, I queered the data collection process, thereby making 'queer' both a methodology and a method. 'An essential component of queer methods', argues David Rivera and Kevin Nadal, 'is the recentering of academia on the lived experiences of LGBTQ people' (2019, p. 192). To do just that, I centre the voices of my survey participants and interview narrators as the core of this study. Moreover, in the tradition of numerous queer theorists (see, e.g., Stryker, Halberstam, Muñoz and Ahmed), I will be visible throughout. I am a horror-loving queer and that is inseparable from my research and central to its existence. Like other queers before me, I am unable to 'remove my analysis from my own situation, my own attitudes towards and hopes for the genre, and this includes the act of (gendered, embodied) spectatorship' (Harrington, 2018, p. 24). I identify as queer, gay, as a dyke, a lesbian and, while society polices, regulates and objectifies my self and my body as being 'woman', I understand and represent myself to be post-binary and gender non-conforming. My declaration and visibility as a queer scholar here is important because of the 'shortage of critical engagements with quantitative methods and methodologies by queer and sexualities researchers' (Browne, 2010,

p. 231). The self-reflective nature of this work functions as an act of excavation and reclamation for myself and the queer community. My own knowledge of horror and experiences being a horror-loving queer further function as 'a legitimate data point in this research' (Robinson and Hunter, 2019, p. 178). For example, in my role as a participant observer of the Queer Horror experience, I functioned as a 'subcultural analyst [who] not only observes and records the behavior of the group under study, but also participates in the community' (Marchetti, 2008, p. 417). All the privileges and understandings that come from my years of academic training are now inseparable from my lifetime of passion for the horror genre and participation in queer horror communities. I further proclaim that queer embodiment is, in fact, necessary for studies about the queer community. Thus, both my queerness and my love of horror are explicitly and necessarily a part of this study.

I came of age during the AIDS epidemic, losing both my father (d. 1983) and uncle (d. 1991) to AIDS, and I came into adulthood as an active participant in Queer Nation and AIDS Coalition to Unleash Power (ACT UP). For me, the personal *is* political; therefore, I invoke this phrase from the politics of disenfranchised experience not to uphold the fracturing outcomes of neoliberal identity politics, but instead to wield a tool for collective action, 'for challenging illegitimate forms of power and dominance' (Heberle, 2016, p. 594). Academic obfuscation contributes to the upholding of class distinctions and ossification of academic privilege; therefore, my conscious intention to make this study an approachable document should be understood as a queered political act.[18] Since queer scholars 'are subject to heightened scrutiny of their research topics, accusations of being biased in their work, and charges of an overall lack of academic rigor' (LaSala et al., in Rivera and Nadal, 2019, p. 201), I not only challenge those practices but also make my queer subjective intentions and theoretical groundings explicitly clear.

This study offers interventions in queerness, horror, camp and trauma, all of which evade a consensus on exact definitions – and are intricately interconnected. Similarly, I deliberately do not anchor this research to one traditional centre; instead, this research experience consciously 'has been rhizomic, anarchic, queer' (Heckert, 2010, p. 48). As Deleuze and Guattari write, 'any point of a rhizome can be connected to anything other, and must be' (2004, p. 7), which is illustrated by the connections between queerness, horror, camp and trauma, all manifesting in multiple ways and multiple combinations. I remain committed to 'nonlinear, open knowledges from the borders and margins' (Eversley and Hurson, 2019, p. 252). For example, I value the expressions of theory from my narrators as much as I do those from established academics. I not only value the contributions of all my research participants, but also explicitly understand that 'citation is a political act' and bibliographies operate as political documents (Schottmiller, 2018, p. 5). Particularly for marginalised communities, '[a]cademia has a long history of gatekeeping that prizes the doctoral degree as an essential qualification for inclusion in traditional academic circles' (Rivera and Nadal, 2019, p. 199).[19] While I am doing a culturalist reading that is grounded in queer theory, my research into queer spectators of horror film will also be theoretically and methodologically rooted in *my* embodied and active queerness – my non-normative gender and sexuality.

As both the medium of film and the horror genre have intrinsically queer qualities, the development of horror studies, the academic discipline that investigates and theorises horror, is indebted to queer scholars and theorists. Not coincidentally, film took quite some time to gain a foothold in the academy (while film was first publicly screened in 1895, film studies was not widely established until the 1960s) and the horror genre has been plagued historically by critical disapproval and disparagement. While there are multiple reasons for the slow acceptance of film studies, the primary reason distils down to the fact that 'film was thought too trivial a subject to be taken seriously' (Chapman, 2013, p. 2). Similarly, the 'lowbrow' populist appeal of horror films often led critics to pan the genre. Correspondingly, the 'horror genre itself' has 'been treated like a second-class citizen' (Browning, 2017, p. 97). Although academics and critics never cited a specific rationale for their beliefs, for keeping film and horror specifically at the margins of academic and critical respectability, one must question whether the intrinsic queerness of both film and horror could be an underlying reason why film and horror took so long to gain both critical and academic respect. Although tracing the development of cinema studies as an academic discipline is outside the purview of this research, focusing on the development of horror studies reveals the outsized contributions of queer academics to this discipline, starting with Robin Wood's 'pioneering studies of the horror film' (Hubner, 2018, p. 6).

The birth of horror studies can be traced back to 1979 when Wood, along with his partner Richard Lippe, organised 'The American Nightmare', a special retrospective held at the Toronto International Film Festival (Grant, 2018, p. vii). Until this retrospective, 'the study of horror cinema' was 'a subject area that, until the 1970s and 1980s, made only sporadic appearances in film studies journals and other discourses' (Browning, 2017, p. 97). From this horror film retrospective (which included screenings and interviews with prominent horror directors such as Wes Craven, John Carpenter, Brian De Palma, George A. Romero, Tobe Hooper, Stephanie Rothman and David Cronenberg) came Robin Wood's essay 'An Introduction to the American Horror Film', often credited with 'jumpstarting' the discipline (Browning, 2017, p. 97). Wood, an 'out' gay man, even wore t-shirts that brandished gay rights messages on stage, a daring political move for the era (Wood, 2002, p. xxix). If Wood gave the formation of the discipline its first jolt of electricity, queer scholars throughout the 1980s and 1990s furthered the field with groundbreaking works that continue to influence and shape discourse today. These queer scholars include Bonnie Zimmerman ('*Daughters of Darkness*: The Lesbian Vampire on Film', 1981), Barbara Creed ('Horror and the Monstrous-Feminine: An Imaginary Abjection', 1986), Richard Dyer ('Children of the Night: Vampirism as Homosexuality, Homosexuality as Vampirism', 1988), Rhona J. Berenstein ('Mommie Dearest: *Aliens*, *Rosemary's Baby* and Mothering', 1990), Sue-Ellen Case ('Tracking the Vampire', 1991), Ellis Hanson ('Undead', 1991), Andrea Weiss (*Vampires and Violets: Lesbians in the Cinema*, 1992), Terry Castle (*The Apparitional Lesbian: Female Homosexuality and Modern Culture*, 1993), Susan Stryker ('My Words to Victor Frankenstein Above the Village of Chamounix: Performing Transgender Rage', 1994), J. Halberstam (*Skin Shows: Gothic Horror and the Technology of Monsters*, 1995), Harry Benshoff (*Monsters in the Closet: Homosexuality and the Horror Film*, 1997) and Patricia White (*Uninvited: Classical Hollywood Cinema and Lesbian Representability*, 1999). All of them continue to be among the most cited academics in horror studies, indicating some measure of how difficult it is to overstate queer contributions to the development of the horror discipline. Even a cursory 'horror studies' search online quickly yields Wood's 'return of the repressed' and Creed's theory of the 'monstrous-feminine'. In fact, in myriad ways, the contributions of these queer academics functioned, and continue to function, as personal and political acts from our academic queer elders.

A direct link exists between the queer scholars whose work helped shape the discipline of horror studies and the work of the queer scholars continuing to shape the field today. To clarify, this queer inheritance does not stipulate an intellectual consensus; this academic lineage speaks to a way of framing thoughts and arguments about the function of the horror genre, as well as how discourse is in a constant state of conversation with the past. Yet, conceivably and most importantly, all the aforementioned foundational queer scholars deliberately and explicitly embed queerness into horror studies. While an in-depth discussion of every queer scholar's works that helped to galvanise horror studies as a respected discipline would distract focus, for not all those works directly relate to this study, it is important to indicate how this queered thinking influences mine. For example, work by Ellis Hanson, Richard Dyer, Terry Castle and Patricia White indicates the impossibility of disentangling or extricating the personal from the political and the theoretical. Moreover, each teaches me that my queerness exists at the core of this research. My study contributes to this long tradition by placing queer spectators, often ignored or sidestepped, at the centre of the horror experience.[20]

Robin Wood argued for the genre to be taken as a serious subject worthy of analysis, stating that horror was 'the most important of all American genres and perhaps the most progressive, even in its overt nihilism' (2003, p. 76). Wood mixed Marx with Freud, and it would be difficult to overstate the influence of both Marxism and psychoanalysis in horror studies. Hence, the earliest contributions from queer scholars were steeped in Freudian and Lacanian psychoanalytic thought, as was vogue throughout the academy; in fact, this era was the 'Golden Age of psychoanalytic film criticism' (Dumas, 2014, p. 32). Wood's permanent ideological marks on the discipline are his focus on the figure of the monster, the Other and on how 'normality is threatened by the Monster' (2003, p. 71). While myriad scholars have employed Wood's 'return of the repressed' theory when analysing horror, my use here will take it beyond textual analysis to embodied experience. My study is centred on the unique relationship that queers have with the horror genre and builds the argument that the horror genre is intrinsically queer. This declaration can, and arguably should, be understood as a societally repressed population returning to stake their claim on, instead of within, horror film.

The act of acknowledging and naming the contributions of queer scholars to the development of horror studies is a political act. When cisheterosexual academics analyse horror films, they unwittingly privilege cisheterosexual experiences, thereby inadvertently excluding or bypassing queer ones. One salient example is Carol J. Clover's work on the slasher subgenre and its 'final girl' because of the groundbreaking and enduring impact that this work has had on the field.[21] In her book *Men, Women, and Chain Saws: Gender in the Modern Horror Film* (1992), Clover theorises the final girl and represents the audience as being predominantly adolescent and heterosexual male, both for the slasher film in particular and the horror genre in general.[22] In her theorisation of the final girl, Clover roots the concept in fixed and binaristic gender norms, which explains the presumed cisheterosexual male spectator's cross-gender identification with the film's heroine. What Clover's 'account leaves out', Halberstam notes, however, 'are the powerful potential identifications to be made between queer female viewers and the queer monster killer final girl' (2000, p. 341). Building on Halberstam's point, Darren Elliott-Smith emphasises the importance of queer considerations for slasher films, being that the 'heterosexual assumption placed upon the horror spectator limits the possibility of the gay male spectator identifying with the female Final Girl figure in a non-heterosexual way' (2016, p. 28). Clover's declaration that '[y]oung males are also, I shall suggest, the slasher film's implied audience, the object of its address' (1992, p. 23) was a long-standing premise in early horror scholarship. However, in my survey of more than 4,000 queer individuals, the slasher film ranks as a top ten favourite subgenre across *all* gender identities surveyed (see Chapter 2).[23] In other words, queer people are ardent slasher film spectators and queer men do not dominate the queer fanbase of slasher films. This finding does, then, validate Clover's declaration that 'horror is a marginal genre that appeals to marginal people' (1992, p. 231), even if she does not directly name queer people as being part of that marginal group. The popularity of the slasher film with a range of queer spectators, despite previous cisheteronormative assumptions, underscores the obligation for horror scholars to actively consider the queer spectator, for the white cisheteropatriarchy has been allowed to be singularly assumed and unchallenged for too long. Conversely, since queer scholars experience a non-normative reality, they inevitably and importantly challenge the heteronormative binaristic paradigms and, thus, further scholarship. For example, Rhona J. Berenstein, in *Attack of the Leading Ladies: Gender, Sexuality, and Spectatorship in Classic Horror Cinema*, disputes Clover's model of the masochistic female spectator and discusses how Clover actively bypasses the analysis of women viewers altogether (1996, pp. 36–7). Berenstein, furthermore, not only challenges the presumptive idea that classic Hollywood horror film narratives centre heterosexual desire, but also rejects typical masculine/feminine, sadistic/masochistic, spectator/spectacle gendered binaries. In doing so, Berenstein creates academic space in the field of horror for non-normative desires, sexualities and identities. Berenstein herself explicitly states: 'As a lesbian film scholar and spectator living in a late twentieth-century culture in which heterosexuality is the norm, I delight in classic horror's transgressions of sexual difference and gender traits' (1996, p. 37). This quote underscores the importance of Berenstein's identity to her work, intimates how her queerness is essential to her research and findings, and informs this study's praxis.

Berenstein was also the first scholar to excavate and reanimate the female horror spectator from historical sources. Working within a focus on Hollywood horror films from the 1930s, Berenstein used archival research to (re)insert the female spectator into horror's audience, while simultaneously challenging James B. Twitchell's sadistic male/passive female binaristic spectatorship model (Berenstein, 1996, p. 36). Berenstein writes that classic horror shapes 'gender as a malleable feature of identity, as well as a stable role. To see it otherwise is to impose a familiar, but reductive, model of gender and genre relations' (1996, p. 203). Echoing Berenstein, this study positions queerness as both a fluid state and a stable identity – queer spectators cannot remove their queerness, yet that queerness does not exist in a fixed state. While Berenstein's concept of 'spectatorship-as-drag' releases gender roles to be more fluid, acknowledging that horror audiences temporarily 'wear their spectatorship as a costume that offers temporary release from everyday identities', her concept does not account for those whose identity is given release through horror film consumption (1996, p. 204). While my survey results reveal that queer horror spectators do find temporary release through horror film consumption, there is no indication that this release is predicated on donning an ideological spectatorial costume that cloaks queerness. In fact, a spectator's queerness is not only inseparable but intrinsic to their relationship to the horror genre. More than 57 per cent of survey participants report that they have a different reaction to horror films as compared with heterosexual spectators (see Chapter 2). While Berenstein focuses on spectatorial gender identity, Rob Latham instead asks, 'what if the spectatorial system is a contingent historical artifact rather than an essential psychic structure?' (1998, p. 88). Here Latham's binarist thinking overlooks how spectatorship is simultaneously rooted in film as a cultural historical artefact *and* a psychic function. A horror spectator's engagement with horror films is historically and sociologically contingent on multiple factors, such as release dates, developments within the genres and modes of viewing (movie theatre/cinema, television, streaming and so on), with the viewer's queerness also being essential and inextricable to their viewing experience and how they decode that artefact.

The aforementioned landmark books by Creed and Berenstein functioned to belatedly incorporate women, gender and queerness into horror studies. In 1993, Creed was able to 'justifiably complain about the dearth of previously published scholarship on the role of women in the horror genre', underscoring the lack of attention paid to the role of women in horror both on screen and as spectators (Humphrey, 2014, p. 39). Creed's scholarship expanded the function of women in horror, raising them from passive victim to active monster (1993). And since that insertion of women into horror studies, '[g]ender has been one of the most important and productive areas of debate in Horror Studies' (Aldana Reyes, 2016, p. 29). By the late 1990s, books began to be focused solely on homosexuality and horror. However, even though Patricia White, in one such text *Uninvited: Classical Hollywood Cinema and Lesbian Representability* (1999), analyses Gothic horror films such as *Rebecca* (1940), *The Curse of the Cat People* (1944), *The Uninvited* (1944), *The Innocents* (1961) and *The Haunting* (1963), she only speaks about a theoretical lesbian spectator. While the contributions of these queer scholars stepped horror studies in new queer directions, a larger push came in 1997 when Harry M. Benshoff, a queer academic, theoretically argued the direct connection between the queer spectator and the horror genre.

Centring Queers and Queerness in Horror Studies

I now turn to one queer scholar's canonical work that centres its discourse on the intersection of queerness and horror: Harry M. Benshoff's *Monsters in the Closet: Homosexuality and the Horror Film*. First published in 1997, Benshoff's book brought the queer monster out of the closet, 'showing convincingly that one can produce a thorough history of horror cinema by focusing on its "queer" moments' (Latham, 1998, p. 100). Specifically, and most pertinently, Benshoff argues that 'the figure of the monster throughout the history of the English-language horror film can in some way be understood as a metaphoric construct standing in for the figure of the homosexual' (1997, p. 4). Benshoff, with great detail, delineates how this 'monster queer' functions to oppress queer people while simultaneously acting as a beacon for queer spectators, specifying that queer viewers are 'more likely than straight ones to experience the monster's plight in more personal, individualized terms' (1997, p. 13). My survey participants support Benshoff's allegorical reading of the monster as homosexual, with

73.3 per cent identifying with either the monster, the victim or both (see Chapter 2). Building on Benshoff's metaphorical 'monster queer', Sam J. Miller, in 'Assimilation and the Queer Monster', argues that the post-9/11 political and cultural of assimilation of the queer community has all but killed the queer monster (2011). Miller states 'that the death of the queer monster provides an analogy for the normalization of queer identity' (2011, p. 222). Even though queers have gained increased societal acceptance, as Miller notes, queer identity is far from normalised and, in fact, as will be discussed, queer subjectivity exists in a state of precarious liminality.[24]

As an empirical research project, this study is less concerned with the symbolic and allegorical construct of the queer monster and more interested in how queer spectators identify with the central figures in horror films – both the monster and the victim – supplementing the theory of Benshoff and Miller with the evidenced experiential. This study, therefore, investigates and provides data on '[h]ow actual practices of spectatorship interact with the narrative patterns of a genre system', which Benshoff urges 'must then be considered when discussing the queer pleasures of a horror film text itself' (1997, p. 11). Benshoff sets out four distinct paths for a film to be queer: textual, extratextual, subtextual and the queer gaze, which means that any film viewed by a queer person 'might be considered queer' (1997, pp. 13–15). The queer gaze is most applicable to this research. Benshoff argues, as Vito Russo and Alexander Doty did before him, that a queer audience member can queer a text through a queer reading, a method that 'crucially unhitches queer film from intentionality' (Schoonover and Galt, 2016, p. 169). While explicit queerness, coded queerness and the queerness of the filmmakers matter, the queer gaze ultimately sets its sights beyond the singular film; a queer person views a film and then 'forge[s] deep emotional connections with horror' (Scales, 2015, n.p.) as an entire genre, ingesting it whole.

The twenty-first century's queer horror scholars, advancing and expanding the works of our queer academic elders, are centring queerness and the queer experience in horror studies; however, even still, these works remain focused on the queer male experience. For instance, the primary focus of Darren Elliott-Smith's *Queer Horror Film and Television: Sexuality and Masculinity at the Margins*, 'rests on representation of masculinity and *gay* male spectatorship in queer horror films and television post-2000' (2016, p. 2; italics in the original). Elliott-Smith shifts the focus from the queer monster as a threat to heteronormativity to 'the anxieties *within* gay subcultures'

(2016, p. 3; italics in the original). Similarly, Adam Scales expands beyond the representational to examine the reading receptions and online subjectivity of queer horror fans in 'Logging into Horror's Closet: Gay Fans, the Horror Film and Online Culture'; however, he too focuses narrowly on gay men. Even still, the queer horror spectator study I conducted for this research affirms Scales's argument that 'gay fans hold vastly different investments in and emotional connections to horror' (2015, p. 242). And while Scales argues that gay male horror fans want 'to "out" what they perceive to be "closeted" horror texts' (2015, p. 24), I argue that queer horror fans overall have less concern with 'outing' specific texts and greater interest in claiming the entire horror genre as queer. Overall, this study and research creates a more complete understanding of the queer experience with and through the horror genre, changing 'the significant lack of empirical research on horror's audiences' (Scales, 2015, p. 20). This work encompasses the vast queer spectrum of sexual orientation and gender identity[25] while emphatically declaring that queerness exists in horror not only representationally but also ontologically and phenomenologically.

In a 2019 introduction to the journal *Horror Studies*, Mark Jancovich 'was struck both by how much has changed in horror scholarship since the late 1980s and, depressingly, by how little has changed' (2019, p. 3). From Freud to Lacan and Kristeva to Creed, Freudian psychoanalysis has long held sway over horror studies.[26] Even in the twenty-first century, psychoanalysis still held such an influential hold over the discipline that Reynold Humphries chastised Steven Shaviro's 'silly and counterproductive injunction to "avoid Freud"' (2002, p. 168).[27] In usage, psychoanalytic readings centre the film text and do not take 'into account the film's impact on audience' (Fischer and Landy, 1987, p. 62).[28] In fact, because horror studies has spent so much time looking to 'Freud and his heirs', some scholars such as Jonathan Lake Crane actively work against 'the unconscious unilaterally determin[ing] the meaning of terror' (1994, p. vi). In other words, there must be more to terror than the universally applied psychoanalytic theories of repression, libidinal urges, phallic and castration obsession, and other psychic disturbances, all of which render the spectator a passive or unnecessary subject. This study moves beyond such psychoanalytic paradigms by privileging embodied experiences, rather than by centring on unconscious biases or unreachable psychosexual drives. The slow theoretical shift away from Freudian and Lacanian psychoanalytic theories of spectatorship began to invigorate methodological investigations, starting with the hypothetical active spectator. Furthermore, this research actively disengages from Freudian psychoanalytic theory not only because his 'work on homosexuality is peppered with misogyny and homophobia' (Westengard, 2019, p. 37), but also due to the fact that the theoretical framework 'has crumbled under more than a century of scientific scrutiny, which has falsified or failed to find evidence for the psychological mechanisms and processes that Freud posited' (Clasen, 2017, p. 3). Furthermore, this study does not engage with disembodied theories like psychoanalysis (the authority of the white cisheteropatriarchy that aims to dictate what something means), but with embodied experiences and queered meaning-making (meaning determined by distinct non-normative individuals for themselves). This work fluidly engages with a transdisciplinary queered theoretical framework, in part driven by the fact that, in aggregate, the theoretical and methodological developments – from the abject to affect and from psychoanalysis to neurocinematics – in horror studies over the past forty years were born from a wide range of analytical perspectives and frameworks, including cultural (Blake, 2008), historical (Dixon, 2010), philosophical (Carroll, 1990), sociological (Clover, 1992), psychological (Creed, 1993), physiological (Aldana Reyes, 2016), biological (Morgan, 2002) and phenomenological (Hanich, 2018). With the ever-increasing institutionalisation of horror studies in the academy, it remains pertinent to remember that this discipline was forged from the work of scholars who crossed academic departments and came from various disciplines to engage with the horror genre, which should compel contemporary scholars to continue to approach the genre from a similarly fluid, transdisciplinary queered position. As scholars engage across various disciplines, key shared frameworks and methods are still foundational. For example, film, regardless of genre, is a cultural project that should not be removed from its historicised sociopolitical contexts. However, horror is a genre designed to elicit a biophysiological response; thus, horror studies must continue to embrace biopsychological and quantitative investigations to specifically understand responses to the specific affect as well as the unique genre. Even still, any focus on horror through biological and clinical psychology lenses should not come at the cost of theoretical perspectives that lie outside the biopsychological. Since horror shares an epistemological, transgressive core with queer theory, it is no surprise that numerous queer theorists have seamlessly engaged with horror. In fact, Westengard argues 'that queer theory is *itself* expressly gothic' (2019, p. 63; italics in the original), further illustrating the inextricable connection between the queer, the Gothic and horror film.[29]

Evidencing this interconnectivity, the work that follows examines the unique relationship that queer spectators have with the horror genre, using queer theory as my main tool of intellectual inquiry. Simply stated, if horror studies is the 'what' of my investigation, queer theory informs my analytical 'how'. While I previously situated myself within a queer theory framework, I need to be explicit that this queer framework also exists throughout my work here. Queer theory is the theoretical, ontological, epistemological, phenomenological and methodological scaffolding from which this work will frame itself. Examining the queer is crucial to understanding horror; as Halberstam states: 'Homosexuality haunts the gothic in all of its manifestations' (2000, p. 340). This is equally true of horror, as this study demonstrates. Hence, the homosexual haunts horror in all of its manifestations. Horror film was born from Gothic literature, with both being capable of functioning as tools of transgression.[30] Taking this further, the homosexual haunts more than merely the horror genre, for, as Ken Gelder states, 'the figure of the homosexual "haunts" heterosexuality. The latter earnestly goes about exorcising the former from its domain, even though the achievement of its self-definition depends upon the homosexual's unceasing presence' (2000, p. 187). Heterosexuality needs homosexuality to exist, whereby the cisheteropatriarchy frames the queer as the monstrous Other in order to preserve the heterosexual as the 'natural' centre of society. George E. Haggerty, in fact, theorises how the Gothic and the queer actually operate similarly in terms of undermining consensual epistemologies, explicitly stating that we can understand Gothic affect as a queer mode. Laura Westengard emphasises this point when she asserts, as with queer theory, that 'queer culture is gothic at its core' (2019, p. 191). Haggerty states, a 'wide range of writers, dispersed historically and culturally, use "Gothic" to evoke a queer world that attempts to transgress the binaries of sexual decorum' (2006, p. 2). With this evocation, Haggerty directly addresses how affect, the objective of both the Gothic mode and the horror genre, is deployed to elicit a reader/spectator response to queer transgression.

The intertwined connection between the Gothic and horror has existed ever since the horror genre was developed through Gothic fiction. As Aldana Reyes argues, the 'collapse of Gothic into horror, or vice versa, is understandable: both the horror genre and Gothic aesthetics are invested in darkness and in negative affect' (2020a, p. 7). While not all gothic is horror, nor is all horror gothic, both the Gothic and horror ontologically share a transgressive, non-normative, affective core – a distinction and relationship that warrants further explication and analysis here. This study emphasises and employs the shared affective nature of both the Gothic mode and horror genre, thereby deploying and incorporating theories that detail Gothic affect to examine horror film affect and its queer spectatorship. To this end, Westengard traces 'the unspeakability of [Gothic's] affective register' and outlines how Gothic aesthetics function to create an 'experience of heightened and disorganized emotion' (2019, p. 7). Given that both the Gothic mode and horror genre are fundamentally affective, then Gothic affect (in its terminology, sentiment and employment) should be understood as a primogenitor to horror film affect. Both primarily and primally trigger emotional and physical reactions to possess their readers and spectators. While 'the Gothic and horror remain strange, associative bedfellows' (Aldana Reyes, 2020a, p. 8), the Gothic, as an aesthetic and affective mode that investigates terror and fear, is employed to be and should be understood as synonymous with horror for the purposes of this study. This framework specifically engages Gothic theory that elucidates the mode's affective nature – both aesthetically and representationally – since this study exists at the nexus of that affect and its queer reception. Indeed, the mode of both the Gothic and horror is 'most effective when it is most affective' (Clemens, 1999, p. 1).

Queer theorists have influenced horror studies and horror has influenced queer theory, even if to a lesser degree.[31] Even though queer scholars were instrumental to the establishment of horror studies as a discipline, few queer theorists actively engage with horror studies. To date, when queer academics have engaged with queer spectators of the horror genre, the focus has been almost exclusively on gay men. Until now, both horror studies and queer theory have neglected to interact with the full spectrum and reality of queer horror spectators – which, considering the transgressive nature of horror and queerness, is a glaring oversight that results in an erasure. This project presents itself as a timely and critically significant corrective by actively working to amplify the voices of a diverse range of queer horror fans, based on embodied research and through their lived experiences. 'Audience research is *hard*, in many ways. Not doing it, however', as Martin Barker states 'is becoming inexcusable' (2011, p. 115; italics in the original). I worked 'in a theoretically engaged way by grounding analysis in materiality, lived experience and empirical research' (Rooke, 2010, p. 26). My focus is not the deconstruction and analysis of the *object* of the fandom (the horror film), but the subjective experiences and meaning making of the spectators (audience/fans) themselves. As Matt Hills states:

'Audience studies focuses on *what* texts mean *for their viewers/fans*' (2014, p. 91; italics in the original). If horror studies represents *what* I am thinking about and queer theory is the tool that frames *how* I think, empirical audience studies makes visible about *whom* I am thinking: horror-loving queers.

Bruce A. Austin, echoing Roland Barthes's restoration of the reader, writes: 'The message and its meaning are not synonymous; the meaning of a film is created by those who view it. What the meaning is and how it is created, therefore, fall within the purview of audience research' (1989, p. x). Direct engagement of horror audiences is the only route that allows researchers to understand the *meaning* of the horror genre to queer individuals. Therefore, the distinctive relationship that queer spectators have with the horror genre will be elucidated through both quantitative and qualitative research methods. For the purposes of this study, I designed and created an original data set devoted to the queer horror spectator that goes well beyond the assumed genre audience – young, heterosexual males (see, e.g., Handel, Twitchell and Clover) and that aims very specifically to gauge the relationship that queer spectators have with horror film. While a small number of scholars have analysed women spectators and the horror film (see, e.g., Creed, Berenstein, Cherry, Pinedo and Harrington), the vast majority of horror spectator scholarship remains focused on the young, heterosexual male viewer, perpetuating an assumed dominate viewer and a binary division across gender and sexual orientation. Further, when scholars discuss the intersection of homosexuality and horror film (see, e.g., Benshoff, Skal, Scales and Elliott-Smith), the focus is most often textual analysis centred primarily on gay (cis) men. Scholarship has also largely dismissed women from being considered horror enthusiasts, with lesbians predominantly discussed in the context of vampire films (see, e.g., Zimmerman, Weiss and Auerbach). Even more, analysis about trans*,[32] non-binary, asexual and other queer identities is scant. Consequently, the full spectrum of the diverse, engaged and creative horror audience and fanbase has not been entirely visible or understood. This study remedies that by staging an inclusive empirical intervention, thereby becoming both the largest horror study and most inclusive queer horror study to date.

In 1996, James B. Weaver, III and Ron Tamborini edited *Horror Films: Current Research on Audience Preferences and Reactions* as a way to 'put the study of audience responses to frightening fiction on the map as a significant research venture' (1996, p. ix). Yet, nearly a quarter of a century later, this volume remains the only organised effort to bring together distinct empirical studies on horror audiences into one collection, even as the scholarship included does not directly address queer audiences. Brigid Cherry, in 'The Female Horror Film Audience: Viewing Pleasures and Fan Practices' (1999), concludes not only that female horror fans 'refuse to refuse to look' (p. 204), but also that 'female viewers of the horror film do not adopt purely masculine viewing positions' (p. 213). While I incorporate Cherry's empirical research techniques by using data primarily collected from both questionnaires and in-depth interviews that are quantitatively and qualitatively analysed, my research has been able to expand on Cherry's methods by utilising online engagement tools, which helped me to increase massively my *n* number (my usable sample size, which is 4,107) from Cherry's 109 questionnaire respondents (1999, p. 72). In the conclusion to 'Questioning Queer Audiences: Exploring Diversity in Lesbian and Gay Men's Media Uses and Readings' (2012), Alexander Dhoest and Nele Simons challenge the application of queer theory's more radical notions to the entire LGBTQ+ community, arguing that the general queer masses do not actualise those extremes. In fact, they explicitly state that their findings 'strongly support the necessity to further explore the claims of queer theory in empirical research' (Dhoest and Simons, 2012, p. 274). Based on data from my empirically engaged queer spectators, I challenge Dhoest and Simons's findings that 'most respondents sounded anything but queer in their approach to representations' and that 'none commented on the heterocentrism that is such a central issue in academic criticism' (2012, p. 273). In other words, Dhoest and Simons state that their research indicates that most queers do not centre their queerness in their media uses and readings. In direct opposition to that claim, my empirical research clearly illustrates that the majority of queer horror spectators centre queerness in their relationship to horror. As examples, these direct quotes from anonymous survey participants emphasise their queerness and/or comment on being queer in a straight world:

> I have way less tolerance for heterosexual tropes and cliches. And I prefer camp and intelligence out of horror films, whereas I think the average viewer is happy with lazy films that perpetuate their heteronormative reality. (46764770)

> I feel differently from heterosexual people about MOST things, and Horror as a genre is no different. I think that het folks may not read queer subtext or nuance into things the way that I do, and that het

> folks react differently than queer viewers do to themes such as rape, possession, impregnation, brainwashing, torture, home invasion, and body horror – all of which can hit much closer to home. (47119978)

> My being queer influences my tastes in everything. However, beyond this overarching influence, I feel myself often drawn to horror films that disrupt heterosexual relationships, family units, or romances. Because of this, I am often drawn to horror that contains a physical monstrous presence, though ghosts and incorporeal demons might also serve to disrupt normative behavioral models. I especially like horror films that do not have a clean resolution, where the norm cannot be returned to, often because patriarchal, heterosexual, cisgendered norms have caused the calamity in some way in the first place, and a return to these norms really just represents another moment of terror and disquiet. (47725637)

> My favorite thing about horror is its disruption of heteronormativity. Whereas I think straight people sometimes thrill in the scare of that threat, I rarely identify with the 'normal' characters and revel in their plight. (47112178)

> When what is threatened is a sort of heteronormative way of life or society, I'll tend to side with the monster. (47716725)

> I feel LGBTQ people are constantly having to adjust themselves to navigate around heterosexual society so it's easier for us to enjoy horror as we are in scary situations and live in a type of fear daily that heterosexuals don't have to deal with. (48766870)

The survey participants explicitly comment, as well, on the horror genre's representational heterocentrism, with 61.4 per cent strongly agreeing or agreeing that 'there is too much heterosexual sex in horror films'.[33] This and additional mixed-method data from queer survey participants and narrators emphasise that their queerness is centred in not only their media uses and readings, but also their identities.

Historically, horror studies has barely engaged horror audiences and, moreover, the majority of the few studies that have been conducted did not directly engage queer audiences. As prime example of that exclusion, Weaver and Tamborini's *Horror Films*, the only empirical collection about horror to date (and now dated itself), ignores the potentialities and possibilities of queer audiences. Instead, the collected empirical studies featured in *Horror Films* reach conclusions such as this: horror 'provide[s] a forum, akin to rites of passage, for male and female adolescents to practice and demonstrate mastery of societally defined gender-specific expressive displays' (Zillmann and Weaver, 1996, p. 83). Zillmann and Weaver further report that male enjoyment of a horror film nearly doubles when accompanied by a female peer who displays acute distress as compared with a female peer who does not display fear, and that 'female respondents enjoyed horror the least in the presence of a fearful, distressed male' (1996, p. 93). This perpetuates an extreme heteronormative binaristic sociopolitical structure. Similarly, in another study, Zillmann and Gibson state that male enjoyment of horror is predicated on mastering any form of distress and, conversely, that female enjoyment is predicated on displaying distress; this underscores a 'gender-specific socialization of fear and its mastery' (1996, p. 25). Yet another chapter finds: 'Watching horror films is said to offer viewers a socially sanctioned opportunity to perform behaviors consistent with the traditional gender stereotypes' (Tamborini and Salomonson, 1996, p. 184). Furthermore, Tamborini and Salomonson, in their study, discuss how 'cultural norms provide males with few situations where they can practice fear mastery behaviors, and females have few occasions to display distress or to seek male protection apart from viewing graphic horror presentations' (1996, p. 184). Quite simply, the research featured in *Horror Films* does not seek, and consequently the findings leave no room for, the experiences of non-normative genders, sexualities and relationships. While Zillmann and Weaver point out that the 'all-inclusiveness' of their findings are 'certainly open to challenge' because of the existence of 'meek and mild-mannered boys and tough tomboys', this disclaimer hardly constitutes a theoretical reckoning with the queer spectrum and, additionally, is based in coded stereotypes (1996, p. 98). Moreover, Zillmann and Weaver, reporting R. H. Weiss's (1990) findings that were based on a study of fourteen-year-old and fifteen-year-old teens, write that there is 'no doubt that females respond unfavorably to horror' (1996, p. 89). In contrast to that finding, while my survey participants all were over the age of eighteen, more than 56 per cent of my cisgender women survey participants report that they were under twelve when they first started watching horror films and 89 per cent were seventeen and under when they first started watching horror films, indicating that Weiss's findings likely excluded queer teenage women.[34] In summary, to date, the only empirical collection focused exclusively on horror, *Horror Films*, renders the queer horror spectator invisible and presents evidentiary data in conflict with my current data and findings, demonstrating glaring omissions and a resounding need for future empirical research to include the full spectrum of genders and sexualities.

While the collected scholars in *Horror Films* ignore the queer spectator, the scholars featured in *Making Sense of Cinema: Empirical Studies into Film Spectators and Spectatorship* (2016) largely ignore the horror film in their important contribution to film studies: empirically investigating film audiences. While *Making Sense of Cinema* functions to highlight various empirical approaches to film studies, it also offers via the editors' introduction a succinct and informative review of the theoretical development of spectator, audience and reception studies. Even though my work is not in direct engagement with a particular chapter, study or scholar in *Making Sense of Cinema*, the entire collection presents a range of methodologies and methods – from observational research to eye-tracking technologies and from think-aloud protocols to online questionnaires – all from an interdisciplinary group of scholars engaged in empirical studies. Moreover, the aforementioned introductory overview enables me to better situate my work within the development and discourse of film spectatorship and empirical audience studies. In agreement with the collection's editors, CarrieLynn D. Reinhard and Christopher J. Olson, I understand film spectatorship as 'the process of engaging with a film text' (2016, p. 2). Hence, throughout this study, my research participants are designated as horror film spectators when viewing horror individually and comprise horror film audiences when viewing together in various group sizes. And to avoid the 'the trap of textual determinism' (Waldron, 2016, p. 62), I am less concerned with the queer relationship to individual horror texts, and instead focus largely on the queer relationship to the horror genre. Film studies, while vying for institutional respectability, centred the power of the cinematic apparatus and its filmic texts to underscore the academic worthiness of the medium, unfortunately leaving the active spectator under-theorised and disempowered. In the 1960s and 1970s, as film studies was working to establish itself as a discipline, there was an overreliance on Barthesian semiotics, Althusserian structuralism and Freudian/Lacanian psychoanalysis – all theorising a passive and universal spectator (Reinhard and Olson, 2016, p. 4). Jean-Louis Baudry's apparatus theory (1970/1975), a text-activated approach, further decentred the spectator in film studies, privileging cinematic structures over individual interpretations. Cultural historian Stuart

Hall developed the encoding/decoding model and transcoding strategy, which allows the spectator to be able to reappropriate the meaning of a text. Some film scholars adopted Hall's theories to create a reader-activated approach to analysis, an analytic approach that features an active spectator who will accept, negotiate or resist dominant readings of the text. Privileging spectatorial responses to a text (over the text itself) returns agency to an audience, which is fundamental to understanding the queer connection to the horror genre. 'Seeing problems with the idealization of the spectator in both of these approaches', Janet Staiger offers a context-activated approach that argues: 'Meaning does not belong primarily to either the film text or the film spectator, but through the interaction of the two in some specific context of engagement' (Reinhard and Olson, 2016, p. 9). Staiger's context-activated reception theory creates space for the spectator's sociohistorical realities that are integral to interpretative strategies, which 'are derived in a material context' (Staiger, 1992, p. 58). Reception studies, as in Staiger's context-activated approach, emphasises the interaction between the film and the spectator and '[i]nterpretation, appropriation, sense-making and meaning-making all function as part of this interaction' (Reinhard and Olson, 2016, p. 9). Yet Staiger employs a historical 'found data' investigation of film spectators. This project, therefore, 'scavenges' together empirical research with a context-activated reception study of the queer horror film spectator, which constitutes an audience when gathered with other spectators.

To that end, this study inaugurates a new application of audience reception studies since there has been little prior empirical research completed on horror film audiences and, to date, there is not a significant study focused on queer horror film audiences. The film industry began engaging with audiences to better understand their tastes and habits to better market films, exemplified by the 1946 establishment of the Motion Picture Association of America's Department of Research (Handel, 1950, p. 4). Prior to this, the limited audience research that existed was focused on 'the educational aspects of motion pictures' (Handel, 1950, p. 3) and 'to address concerns about the susceptibility of vulnerable populations to mediated messages' (Reinhard and Olson, 2016, p. 3). Yet, as Bruce A. Austin points out, 'Leo Handel's pioneering efforts in the late 1940s and '50s to adopt more systematic approaches to the study of film audiences remained largely a one-man effort' (1989, p. 23). This remained so until Bruce A. Austin's study 'Portrait of a Cult Film Audience: *The Rocky Horror Picture Show*', published in 1981, which furthered the development of current audience research methodologies, including ones that are still employed, to better understand film audience preferences and reactions. In fact, Atkinson and Kennedy emphasise the importance of Austin's empirical audience work when they state that the 'audience research methodologies deployed here build on but significantly extend a trajectory that can trace its origins to this [Austin's] groundbreaking study' (2018, p. 5). To also build on and extend Austin's work, through my engagement of queer horror fans, I develop deeper, nuanced insights about the 'distance between what film theorists have thought that film was doing and what the film-going public believed about their experience' (Newton, 2019, p. 18).

This study is framed at the juncture of empirical audience studies and spectatorial reception studies, with the findings nevertheless adding to critical discourses in other disciplines, such as fan studies.[35] While this study uses the term 'fan', alongside terms such as spectator, this study is focused on how queer people 'receive' and 'interpret' the horror genre – both individually and as audiences; therefore, this work engages with audience reception studies over fan studies to understand the relationship between queer people and horror film. My thinking about queer engagement with the horror genre considers the conceptual and rhizomic overlaps between audience studies, reception theory and fan studies – as informed by the works of Camille Bacon-Smith (1992), Henry Jenkins (1992), John Fiske (1992), Matt Hills (2002), Cornel Sandvoss (2005), Mark Duffett (2013) and Francesca Coppa (2014). John Tulloch and Henry Jenkins, for example, distinguish between 'fans' who are 'active participants within fandom as a social, cultural and interpretive institution' and 'followers' who are 'audience members who regularly watch and enjoy media', such as horror films, 'but who claim no larger social identity on the basis of this consumption' (1995, p. 23). While this study did not analyse data on organised fandom or its concomitant culture, economy, products and activities, the study is part of a cultural galvanisation in which queers are finding an ever-increasing solidarity and social identity as queer horror fans.

This study, then, borrows from 'the first wave of fan studies' and should be understood 'as a form of activist research' (Gray, Sandvoss and Harrington, 2017, p. 3). This study has engaged in activist research to create the first comprehensive portrait of the queer horror spectator, with one aim to galvanise the community of horror-loving queers into a more connected network. Since this study privileges the data's consensus and queer solidarity, it bypasses engagement with fan studies' 'second wave', which 'highlighted the replication of social and cultural hierarchies within fan cultures and subcultures' (Gray, Sandvoss and Harrington, 2017, p. 5). This study engages with individualised fandom by forming a dataset based on multiple inputs, which the third wave of fan studies describes as 'the relationship between fans' selves and their fan objects' (Gray, Sandvoss and Harrington, 2017, p. 6). Since certain emotions and experiences are simply not quantifiable, qualitative data interviews are the best option for researchers '*to hear the meaning of what interviewees tell them*' (Rubin and Rubin, 2012, p. 6; italics in original). To find this meaning, I methodologically utilise an online survey and oral history interviews, both of which were completed by or created with individual queer horror fans.

The oral history interviews collectively constitute the Queer for Fear Oral History Collection, which functions not to uncover objective facts or truths, as those do not exist, but instead to reveal fifteen distinct subjective realities, experiences, emotions, thoughts, meanings and understandings. Archived transcripts are available to future researchers as a collection, in addition to this research being published, to make and mark a queer space in horror fandom. To assert *our* voices. To tell *our* stories. Together, the interviews help me better understand the *how* and the *why* of horror in the narrators' lives. As Horacio N. Roque Ramírez cleverly states, oral history is 'historiographic activism', which means that creating oral histories can insert otherwise undocumented voices or experiences into the historical record (2008, p. 182). The personal becomes political and the political becomes personal. A researcher's use of oral history methods can uncover the complexity of human emotions, perceptions and experiences, all of which show how meaning is always a projection of the present upon the past. Indeed, oral history is memory work, a memory method. Yet memories are reconstructions; memories are not static truths, but ever-shifting interpretations. In the construction and transmission of memory as a form of theoretical consideration, oral history is a creation, not a discovery. Oral history is a shared intimate act of creation, with both parties being simultaneously the researcher and the researched, in which, through the act of reciprocity, the interviewer and narrator together construct the document with two-fold biases and perspectives informing the route and the end result. Any forced methodological delineation decentres the contribution of the narrator and inadvertently creates a distinctive power dynamic that privileges the role of the researcher over a socially marginalised person's power in telling their own story. Oral history standing as an exchange between equals was fundamental to my process.

Since my entire project serves as the creation of a new queer space within horror studies, these collected oral histories further serve as the creation of a new queer space – a queer space created between the interview narrators, myself and any future queers who read the transcripts. Oral history actively works against the 'devastation of silencing' (Ramírez, 2008, p. 171). To actively counter the long history of queers being silenced or erased, I provide numerous full quotes from the oral history narrators and survey participants, as opposed to editing the transcripts down to shorter clauses or synthesised ideas. This method preserves the oral history narrators' subjectivity in order to reiterate that each narrator is an individual queer horror expert worthy of dedicated space in scholarship. As such, oral history work is political, personal *and* powerful. The knowledge that we collectively create through these interviews (each an intersection of perspective, location, time and intent) will serve to create a knowledge collective in and for the queer horror community. Preservation and access are foundational to proper oral history methodology, as well as historical equity; archiving the transcripts of this project's research interviews will ensure the posterity of important lives and knowledge. My own transcription process underscores the scholarship behind the merits of transcripts, as well as the bias present in all historical documents. Everything historical is created with a specific intention, motivation, mindset and audience – transcripts are no different. While I accurately represented my narrator and the interview in each transcript, in the process of creating a semi-verbatim transcript, I inherently altered the actual reality of a recorded interview. Meaning does not lie inherently with an interview; the process of examination and interpretation creates meaning. In other words, a transcript is an interpretation, a translation – not a duplication – of an interview.

The qualitative and quantitative data collected from horror-loving queers is used in aggregate to argue for the imagined community of queer horror spectators. That is to say, this study simultaneously investigates the opinions, habits and tastes of the individual queer spectator of horror while arguing for the social identity of a queer horror community, therefore, functioning as a bridge between understanding fandom as an 'individual engagement' and a 'social identity' (Coppa, 2014, p. 73). In order to cross that bridge, the theoretical foundation of this study remains grounded in audience reception studies, not the tenets of organised fandom, with empirical research, including the oral history interviews, as evidence for the claims. As Gray, Sandvoss and Harrington have proclaimed, an 'empirical shift' in research is vital to the third wave of fan studies (2007, p. 8), even if in horror studies this 'wave' has been more like a stream, since empirical research of the horror genre still remains scant and dated. Dhoest and Simons, in 2012, argue for LGBTQ+ research 'to back up its theoretical claims empirically' (p. 261), yet horror studies remains grounded in theoretical assumptions principally bypassing empirical studies. Their call highlights the need for this empirically grounded study, which breaks ground for queer spectators in horror studies discourse by demonstrating how and why queer horror fans forge a distinctive relationship to the horror genre.

In each forthcoming chapter, I present arguments with data that prove the distinctive relationship that queers have with the horror genre. This research project uses a mixed-method approach of collecting both quantitative and qualitative data and my survey design also employs a mixed-method approach. Borrowing principles from 'community-based participatory research', this study aims to empower research participants, or, in other words, 'to work "with" not "on"' the horror-loving queer community (Reisner and Hughto, 2019, p. 5). Chapter 2 presents the demographic information about the 4,107 survey participants. My survey yielded a large data set; therefore, I will introduce the overall aggregate data and highlight several salient sub-group distinctions from the data set, balancing larger patterns while highlighting distinctions. This will work to both underscore intersectional experiences and avoid essentialising the survey participants. The expositional nature of Chapter 2 functions to present the opinions, habits and tastes of the queer horror spectator and to establish the diversity of queerness in horror fans. Chapter 3 delves into two interconnected topics that further elucidate the distinctive relationship that queers have with horror: trauma and camp. The mixed-method data supports an understanding of the horror genre as a therapeutic experience for queer spectators, who find a connection to horror through their lived experiences of insidious queer trauma. The queer community forges a camp relationship to culture and its artefacts as a survival tactic from the constant experience of queer trauma. Thus, to survive the constant experience of queer trauma, the queer community forges a camp relationship to cultural texts. In Chapter 3, I analyse the queer camp-horror nexus, demonstrating incontrovertibly the importance of camp in the queer relationship to the horror genre.

A meaningful examination of queer horror spectatorship should not only document the quantitative and qualitative responses of queers about their consumption of horror film, but also analyse the queered reinterpretation/presentation of horror films through 'live cinema' (Atkinson and Kennedy, 2018) screenings that feature live drag performance prior to exhibiting a horror film. The addition of live cinema analysis when examining queer horror spectatorship is essential because reclamation and reinterpretation are core aspects of queerness, with the interpretative horror performances of queer reclamation illustrating one of the ways that queers distinctively engage with horror. Chapter 4, therefore, presents case studies on the live drag horror performances of Peaches Christ's Midnight Mass (San Francisco, California) and Carla Rossi's Queer Horror (Portland, Oregon), investigations which function to add drag performance/horror exhibition research to the emerging field of live cinema, and situates queer horror screenings as 'live exhibition experiences' that generate queered 'modes of audience engagement within instances of collective cinematic consumption' (Atkinson, 2014, p. 2). This study concludes with a summary analysis and indicates areas for further research, including the ways in which this study may be used to fill gaps in the critical canon of horror studies.

In addition to blurring the 'boundaries between the researcher and the researched' (Detamore, 2010, p. 177), this research ultimately amalgamates the theoretical, the practical and the personal. I am inspired by Robin Wood who 'believe[d] there will always be a close connection between critical theory, critical practice, and personal life' (1995, p. 13). My work, like my being, is a queer study beyond rigid boxes and norms, for 'queer studies has staked its claim by working within, against, across, and even beyond disciplinary boundaries, thereby blurring distinctions between the field and its methods' (Ghaziani and Brim, 2019, p. 4). The fabric of this project is made up of horror studies, queer theory, cultural studies, reception studies and empirical audience research, all stitched together with queered methods, all filtered through my *and* my queer research participants' understanding of and experiences with queerness and horror. 'If we stand by the argument that the knowledge resulting from research is a production rather than an observation', Detamore argues, 'then we do not have far to stretch to imagine the political in research' (2010, p. 178). This entire study is a political act of reclamation, as well as simply existing as queer – even in an age of increased assimilation. Miller argues that the death of the queer monster is due to cultural assimilation (2011) and Westengard discusses how assimilation is a form of cultural death (2019). The two theorists' ideas, taken together, should then be proven by data that shows queers have *decreasing* interest in horror. For, if queers were truly and meaningfully assimilated into mainstream culture, and therefore a distinctive queer culture did not exist, then a distinctive queer relationship to horror would not exist either. But instead, there is an ever-increasing interest in horror from a notable segment of the queer population.[36] In fact, while the sociopolitical forces of capitalism work to erode the radical queer into becoming an assimilated homonormative consumer market, conservative and religious institutions continue to take aim at stripping queers of human rights, an act that demonstrates how queers still remain in an uncanny liminal societal position. Exploring that liminal existence in *Gothic Queer Culture: Marginalized Communities and the Ghosts of Insidious Trauma*, Westengard examines 'how gothicism allows queer folks to live in an unsettled space that honors their traumas and that offers a vision of queer past, present, and future that resists neoliberal and neoconservative narratives of temporality and subjectivity' (2019, p. 20). This 'unsettled space' that queers occupy is the liminal in-between state of being between binarisms, between trauma and healing, invisible and visible, rejection and acceptance, nonlinear and linear. While queer representation and acceptance has increased, queer rights have largely come in the form of white cishomonormativity. Queers, and most especially our trans* and/or BIPOC family, remain the targets of familial, societal, political and legislative discrimination and violence. And significantly, this uncanny liminal existence reinforces, rather than weakens, the queer connection to horror. Moreover, there will be members of the queer community who straddle the line between radicalism and assimilation, a line that in and of itself represents this distinctive liminality. While there are those of us who continue to live, love and thrive in the liminal state, there will always be a community of horror-loving queers drawn to the radical queerness within horror.

A Note on Statistics

This study is a humanities research project that utilises transdisciplinary methodologies. I analysed the mixed-method data from my survey to establish and present a portrait of the queer spectator, including their emotions and experiences, and to confirm my hypothesis that queers have a unique relationship to horror film. To do so, I conducted empirical research through mixed-method data collection that I organised and analysed, which I now present using statistics. However, statistics is a mathematical theory, a language and framework – not an objective reality. Statistics privileges probability sampling and its concomitant mathematical tidiness. However, both human reality and research are not tidy, which demands boundary pushing in which researchers, particularly researchers working with marginalised communities, evolve existing and create new methodologies and methods 'to mitigate the violence of traditional methods' (Love, 2019, p. 35).

The realities of the queer community are prioritised here over the norms of cisheteropatriarchally created data analysis. For example, since current statistical theory does not incorporate or consider non-normative embodiment, statisticians need to confirm the value, accuracy and generalisability of non-probability sampling – especially since 'the majority of survey data collected online around the world today rely on nonprobability samples' (Cornesse et al., 2020, p. 6). Creating a non-probability sample, a sample in which some queer horror spectators had 'zero chance of being surveyed' (Laurie and Jensen, 2016, p. 97), for my data was both valid and the only prudent option to theorise to a large queer population – a non-mutually exclusive (more complex) community. Since I created a non-probability sample and the majority of my demographic data is not mutually exclusive, I judiciously employ various statistical tests to analyse, investigate, assert and underscore the opinions, habits and tastes of the queer horror spectator. I strongly encourage queer researchers to continue our practice of non-cisheteropatriarchal methodologies that push and queer the bounds of current normative methods for studies with marginalised communities. Furthermore, universities must re-evaluate the norms of humanities-based research that is conducted by and/or with marginalised communities. This boundary pushing and academic re-evaluation will further advance mixed-method research projects, projects that will continue to uncover and highlight marginal communities such as queer horror spectators.

I privilege the queer people – their stories and experiences – behind the data over the statistical analysis of the data itself because, 'following queer theory's aims to tear down and reimagine', I aim to 'decenter measurement and the way it has come to be defined in neoliberal and social scientific terms and focus instead on people and stories' (Robinson and Hunter, 2019, p. 166). Even still, this study utilises charts, graphs and/or tables to summarise and present the collected data. In the forthcoming chapters, I present analysis of both descriptive and inferential statistics. However, the reader need not be knowledgeable about statistics, statistical tests or Statistical Package for the Social Sciences (SPSS) to understand the arguments since I contextualise all data with clear, written descriptions and analysis. Descriptive statistics, including frequency charts and graphs, are used to summarise the data, while inferential statistics allows for generalised inferences from the data. My goal in the presentation of statistical tests in this research 'is to determine whether a consistent, predictable relationship exists and to describe the nature of the relationship' (Gravetter and Wallnau, 2011, p. 620), specifically the relationship that queers have with the horror genre. To prove my arguments, I present analysis from confidence intervals and Yule's Q, as well as frequencies, chi-square tests, correlations and t-tests using SPSS. While statistics is not a framework or language all readers will understand, I include this proof to show my arguments are not only theoretical, but also evidencable. I have included a statistics appendix for those who want to see the full detail of the tests and to better understand how the results were determined.

Notes

1. This study prefers and privileges the umbrella term 'queer' over 2SLGBTQIA+ (two-spirit, lesbian, gay, bisexual, transgender, queer, intersex, asexual, plus others) to represent the full spectrum of non-normative sexualities and genders, as will be discussed in this study, in part because the term queer is uniquely suited to the non-normative horror fan. As Alexander Doty positions, 'I am using the term "queer" to mark a flexible space for the expression of all aspects of non- (anti-, contra-) straight cultural production and reception' (1993, p. 3). To be explicit and leave no room for confusion, this study's survey participants and oral history narrators are myriad combinations of queer identities, including gay, lesbian, bisexual, asexual, polyamorous, cisgender, transgender, non-binary, genderqueer, agender and much more.

While many participants and narrators self-identify as queer, I am designating all 2SLGBTQIA+ horror spectators as queer, which will be explained later on to be an apt label for this group of horror fans.

2. The survey respondents are active participants in my research project. In fact, I employ the terms 'research participant' or 'survey participant' throughout this study to underscore their active engagement with this project and the fact that I share this project's success with all participants.
3. The Queer for Fear Oral History Collection narrators are: Gabe Castro, Harmony Colangelo, Lana Contreras, Jason Edward Davis, Mark Estes, Joe Fejeran, Joshua Grannell, Alex Hall, CJ Hodges, Anthony Hudson, Stacie Ponder, Kaitlyn Stodola, Kim Thompson, Michael Varrati and Christopher Velasco. I chose to interview these fifteen narrators in order to ensure that there would be enough varied experiences and voices to expose both patterns and differences in queer horror fandom. Selecting fifteen narrators also allowed me to intentionally represent and emphasise a diversity of voices since racism and transphobia far too often push the life experiences of BIPOC and/or trans* members of the queer community to the periphery of our already peripheral social experience. This study would not be the vibrant document it is without the oral history voices further expounding, supplementing and amplifying the survey data. All fifteen narrators in this study chose to be named and all were shown the sections of text in which they were quoted, and were given a chance to ask questions, make comments or request edits. My action to engage the narrators in this way works to keep the power in their hands and to actively work against 'muffl[ing] the voices of participants while authorising that of the researcher' (Bradley, quoted in Detamore, 2010, pp. 176–7).
4. Throughout this study, the phrase 'survey participant(s)' refers to the 4,107 queer horror spectators who completed the online questionnaire, whereas the phrases 'oral history narrator(s)' or 'narrator(s)' refer to the fifteen individuals with whom I conducted one-on-one recorded interviews. When referencing *all* queer people who love horror film based on statistical extrapolation and inference, the terms 'queer horror spectators', 'queer spectators of horror', 'horror-loving queers' or 'queer horror fans' are used. Queer people, to be absolutely clear, are not a homogeneous population; even with strong statistical evidence, the findings of this study do not uniformly apply to all queer spectators nor all queer spectators of horror.
5. To emphasise the collaborative nature of film-making, films in this study will be referenced by title and release date, but not include director name, which has been the norm.

6. BIPOC is an acronym umbrella term employed to represent the collective racialised experience of people of colour within sociopolitical systems that privilege the white experience and uphold white supremacy. When addressing BIPOC individuals' experiences, I will use their self-identified terms of racial and/or ethnic embodiment.
7. Most specifically, identity politics do not epitomise the economic determinants of that experience. Nor do identity politics engage directly with intersectionality, the theoretical model that explains how class, race, sex, gender, sexuality, ability, etc., simultaneously interconnect to create differing individual experiences of sociopolitical privilege and/or discrimination (Crenshaw, 1989).
8. The cisheteropatriarchy is the manifestation and institutionalization of cisgender heterosexual men designed to uphold their social dominance. The 'cisheteropatriarchy propagates the idea that biology naturally drives sex, gender, and sexuality, further perpetuating systematic and social scripts of patriarchy and biological determination' (Alim et al., 2020, p. 293). As white supremacist ideology and patriarchal domination are intrinsic to cisheteropatriarchy and cisheteronormativity, even if not repeatedly mentioned throughout this study, these constructed notions should be understood to be integral to the cisheteropatriarchal system.
9. Institutional research norms and practices functionally impede queer research by requiring adherence to white cisheteronormative practices. As Gust Yep explains, '[cis]heteronormative thinking is deeply ingrained, and strategically invisible, in our social institutions' (2003, p. 24). It is important to question institutional norms and call for organisational reconsiderations because to not do so normalises and upholds processes that advertently and inadvertently harm the marginalised members of society.
10. Importantly, intersectionality may complicate feelings and understandings about one's identity markers. For example, narrator Joe Fejeran touches on the homophobic legacy of colonialism for his CHamoru identity, while simultaneously remarking that his queer identity is rooted in a system of white supremacy: 'The one thing I'll say is that I feel that I connect more with my queer identity marker than I do my indigenous CHamoru identity marker. And that's been something that's been kind of this internal conflict in the last few years. It was also further complicated by my most recent trip to Guam where it's like, how can I reconcile this culture and identity that still has its roots in all of these other things, but at the same time, you know, how do I reconcile that with my queer identity and the community of queer folks. Then simultaneously with my queer identity – all of it is rooted in a Western

context, and in terms of media and cultural artifacts that are being consumed, a lot of it is from a very cis white perspective. Those are constantly things that I'm unpacking in terms of my own personal identity' (2020, p. 13).

11. The total population of both queer horror spectators and the LGBTQ+ community are unknowable since the data on the LGBTQ+ population varies, particularly because it is not safe for all queer people to publicly declare or report their identity. For example, queer population estimates in the United States fluctuate from 3.5 per cent to 12 per cent, depending on the reporting institution.
12. LGBTQ+ films do not comprise a genre or subgenre, but a category of film under different genres, such as horror, romantic comedy, drama, documentary, and so on.
13. The premise of this study is that queer spectators connect to horror because they recognise in the genre an intrinsic queerness. While women, BIPOC, people with disabilities and the economically disadvantaged may also connect to the horror genre because of or with the lens of their status as societal Others, their connections differ from the queer connection to horror. For example, a Black gay man and a Black heterosexual man share the fundamental experience of systemic oppressions as Black men in a white supremacist society; however, they recognise and connect with the horror genre in different ways because the Black gay man's perspectives and connections to horror are inseparable from his queerness, an intersectionality that a heterosexual man does not have. To this, narrator Mark Estes explains that the ability to connect with horror fans who were both Black *and* queer, sharing his intersectional perspective, was affirming and galvanising: 'I cannot believe that I found this group of people who love horror that's Black. And then later on, through them, I found the Black queer horror fans and that's when *everything* just came together for me' (2020, pp. 16–17).
14. The eight-digit codes used as citation credits throughout this study are the unique anonymous identifiers for the survey participants. I have included the citation codes to establish a sense of contributor individuality and so that researchers can note the participants who had multiple responses cited. Additionally, following the example of Barker et al., 'as a matter of courtesy' I have corrected misspelling and typos in the survey participants' written responses for readability and clarity (2016, x).
15. Narrator Kaitlyn Stodola asserts that 'the connection between queerness and horror is the sense of Other … In my experience that connects to being queer, as you're Other, you're not mainstream. You're this other thing that people are kind of afraid of – they don't really know what to do with' (2020, p. 5).

16. Intersectionality dictates that one's differing identity markers cannot be extracted from one another. For example, narrator Kim Thompson states that her 'womanhood and Blackness always come hand in hand as identity markers' (2020, p. 7). In other words, Thompson's experiences are always and inextricably as a Black woman.
17. Halberstam offers insight into how academia can foster innovation in knowledge production by embracing failure and frivolity: 'Being taken seriously means missing out on the chance to be frivolous, promiscuous, and irrelevant. The desire to be taken seriously is precisely what compels people to follow the tried and true paths of knowledge production around which I would like to map a few detours. Indeed terms like *serious* and *rigorous* tend to be code words, in academia as well as other contexts, for disciplinary correctness; they signal a form of training and learning that confirms what is already known according to approved methods of knowing, but they do not allow for visionary insights or flights of fancy' (2011, p. 6; italics in the original).
18. I worked to retain my questionnaire's fully anonymised aggregated data at Manchester Metropolitan University (MMU), making it available to future researchers via e-space, MMU's research repository. Future use of the data is important because, since this study stands as an important yet single subjective usage of the data, there are many more stories to be told and understandings to be made from the collected data sets. Data preservation not only creates a useful level of research reliability and transparency, but also, since research objectivity does not exist, ensures that a single data set can receive myriad analytic narratives from myriad perspectives.
19. Likewise, I strongly recommend that researchers who work with marginalised communities proactively offer an honorarium to their one-on-one research participants as recognition for their emotional and intellectual labour. The honorarium I offered sought to challenge and change racist, misogynist and homophobic systemic norms, as well as to honour the time and to value the life experiences of my narrators.
20. To accentuate this academic lineage, Darren Elliott-Smith in *Queer Horror Film and Television: Sexuality and Masculinity at the Margins*, states: 'Scholars including Robin Wood, Carol J. Clover, Richard Dyer, Ellis Hanson, Judith Halberstam and Harry M. Benshoff have covered significant ground in their respective analyses of homosexuality in the history of the horror genre' (2016, p. 1).
21. The 1992 publication date of *Men, Women, and Chain Saws* places Clover's work in the same cultural time frame during which queer scholars were galvanising queer theory into an academic discipline. Thus, Clover's analysis of the

slasher film at that time would not have had the ability to build on or benefit from a large body of established queer theory, even though queer scholars working at the same time as Clover were infusing their horror analysis with queer thought (see, e.g., Zimmerman, Creed, Dyer, Berenstein, Case, Hanson, Weiss, Castle and Stryker). This theoretical difference underscores the entanglement of intellectual output and intersectional embodiment. Clover's lack of engagement with the queer spectator becomes pronounced, however, in the new preface of the 2015 updated edition, where Clover neglects to reckon with queer theoretical advancements since her original publication to examine how the queer spectator complicates her original analysis of the slasher film.

22. Clover explicitly states that her analytical interest lies predominantly 'in the male viewer's stake in horror spectatorship' (1992, p. 7) because, in part, within horror audiences 'the preponderance of young males appears constant' (p. 6) and in particular because the slasher's 'majority audience, perhaps even more than the audience for horror in general, was largely young and largely male' (p. 23).
23. While queer horror spectators across the gender spectrum love slasher films, outside the queer community, slasher films are likely watched predominantly by men (particularly in consideration of Brigid Cherry's findings that (heterosexual) women dislike slasher films, with only 25 per cent of her survey participants liking all or most slashers, p. 88). My survey data thus demonstrates a difference in slasher film enjoyment between queer and cisheterosexual horror spectators.
24. The global LGBTQ+ population continues to face societal repression and criminalisation, legislative discrimination and physical violence. In March 2022, the Human Rights Campaign (HRC) reported: 'Last year, a record 26 anti-LGBTQ+ bills were enacted into law across ten states. In 2022, at least 320 anti-LGBTQ+ bills are already pending in state legislatures, more than half of which specifically target transgender youth and ban them from being able to fully participate in everyday life' (Berg-Brousseau, 2022, n.p.). The International Lesbian, Gay, Bisexual, Trans and Intersex Association reports that '69 UN member States still criminalise consensual same-sex sexual acts between adults' (Paletta, 2020, n.p.). In countries with some LGBTQ+ protections, such as the United States, the HRC reports that the 'FBI's hate crime statistics from 2016 to 2019 – the most recent statistics available – show an increase from 1,076 to 1,195 hate crime incidents targeted on the basis of sexual orientation' (Blanchet, 2021, n.p.). On 15 March 2021, the Vatican decreed that same-sex unions cannot be blessed because God 'does not and cannot bless sin' (Holy See Press Office, n.p.).

25. Both sexual orientation and gender identity exist on a spectrum, a continuum with variance and flexibility far beyond the binarism of homosexuality and heterosexuality.
26. Psychoanalysis, especially as used to analyse horror, is focused primarily on sexuality and gender; however, these psychoanalytical models of sexuality and gender have always privileged cisgender male heterosexuality because that is Freud's normative model (thereby Othering women and queers).
27. Steven Shaviro, in *The Cinematic Body* writes: 'Today, the most crucial task for any theory of sexuality remains how to get away from Freud. We are tired of endless discussions of the phallus, the castration complex, and the problematics of sexual representation. Psychoanalytic discourse, even at its ostensibly most critical, does nothing but reinscribe a universal history of lack and oppression. We cannot really oppose the dominant male-heterosexual order when our only language is the code that defines and ratifies precisely that order' (1993, p. 66).
28. Further, empirical evidence is lacking in support of psychoanalytic approaches to horror.
29. Gothic is an affective and aesthetic mode that investigates fear and is, therefore, virtually synonymous with horror for the purposes of this study.
30. Both Gothic literature and horror film have a long history of being politically, allegorically and ideologically reactionary. Horror films, as with all cultural artefacts, can be progressive or reactionary, depending on ideological intentions (regardless of whether those intentions are conscious or subconscious). Progressive horror films are those films that challenge or subvert the normative status quo, whereas reactionary (or conservative) horror creates narratives that function to uphold the normative status quo. Early on, Robin Wood 'stressed the genre's progressive or radical elements, its potential for the subversion of bourgeois patriarchal norms, it is obvious enough that this potential is never free from ambiguity. The genre carries within itself the capability of reactionary inflection, and perhaps no horror film is entirely immune from its operations. It need not surprise us that there is a powerful reactionary tradition to be acknowledged – so powerful that it may at times appear the dominant one' (1984, pp. 191–2).
31. In fact, queer theory is haunted by Gothic horror tropes, as Westengard has argued in *Gothic Queer Culture*, demonstrating that gothicism is woven into the fabric of queer theory from the 1990s until today.
32. I employ the term trans* throughout this study as an inclusive definition and umbrella term that includes a range of non-conforming gender subjectivities. As Jack Halberstam explains, 'the asterisk modifies the meaning of transitivity

by refusing to situate transition in relation to a destination, a final form, a specific shape, or an established configuration of desire and identity. The asterisk holds off the certainty of diagnosis; it keeps at bay any sense of knowing in advance what the meaning of this or that gender variant form may be, and perhaps most importantly, it makes trans* people the authors of their own categorizations' (2018, p. 4).

33. Whereas only 10 per cent 'strongly disagree' or 'disagree' with this same statement; the remaining 28.6 per cent 'neither agree nor disagree' or 'don't know'.
34. This assertion can be made because statistical extrapolation of this study's data indicates that young queer women were not a part of R. H. Weiss's original study. Evidenced with 99 per cent confidence, 58.5 per cent to 65.5 per cent of all queer cisgender women spectators of horror report having been fans for as far back as they can remember. Combining this data with the following confidence intervals evidences that the majority of cisgender queer women were active fans of the horror genre as teenagers and, therefore, suggests that the data from the Weiss study does not include queer teenage women. This conclusion was calculated using the normal approximation of the binomial distribution; the 99 per cent confidence interval indicates that 53.2 per cent to 62.2 per cent of the total population of queer cisgender women spectators of horror would report that they were under twelve when they first started watching horror films. Similarly, the confidence interval also demonstrates with 99 per cent confidence that 87.3 per cent to 91.6 per cent of all queer cisgender women spectators of horror were seventeen and under when they first started watching horror films.
35. Future research has many fruitful avenues to engage and investigate the queer spectator of horror film across a range of topics that will cement queer horror fandom in fan studies. For example, what does it mean for queer people to be horror 'fans' within a fandom that is dominated by white cisgender heterosexual men? Or, what can we understand about fandom by investigating queer products and performances that express queer peoples' distinct relationship to horror and, thus, queer horror fandom?
36. For example, the ever-increasing number of explicitly queer horror podcasts illustrates the relevance of the horror genre to queer spectators. When Patrick K. Walsh started the podcast *ScreamQueenz: Where Horror Gets Gay* in 2010, no other podcasts existed that analysed and discussed horror films through a queer lens for a queer audience. While there have been and will continue to be horror podcasts that feature one or more queer hosts, explicitly queer horror podcasts have tellingly proliferated since 2017.

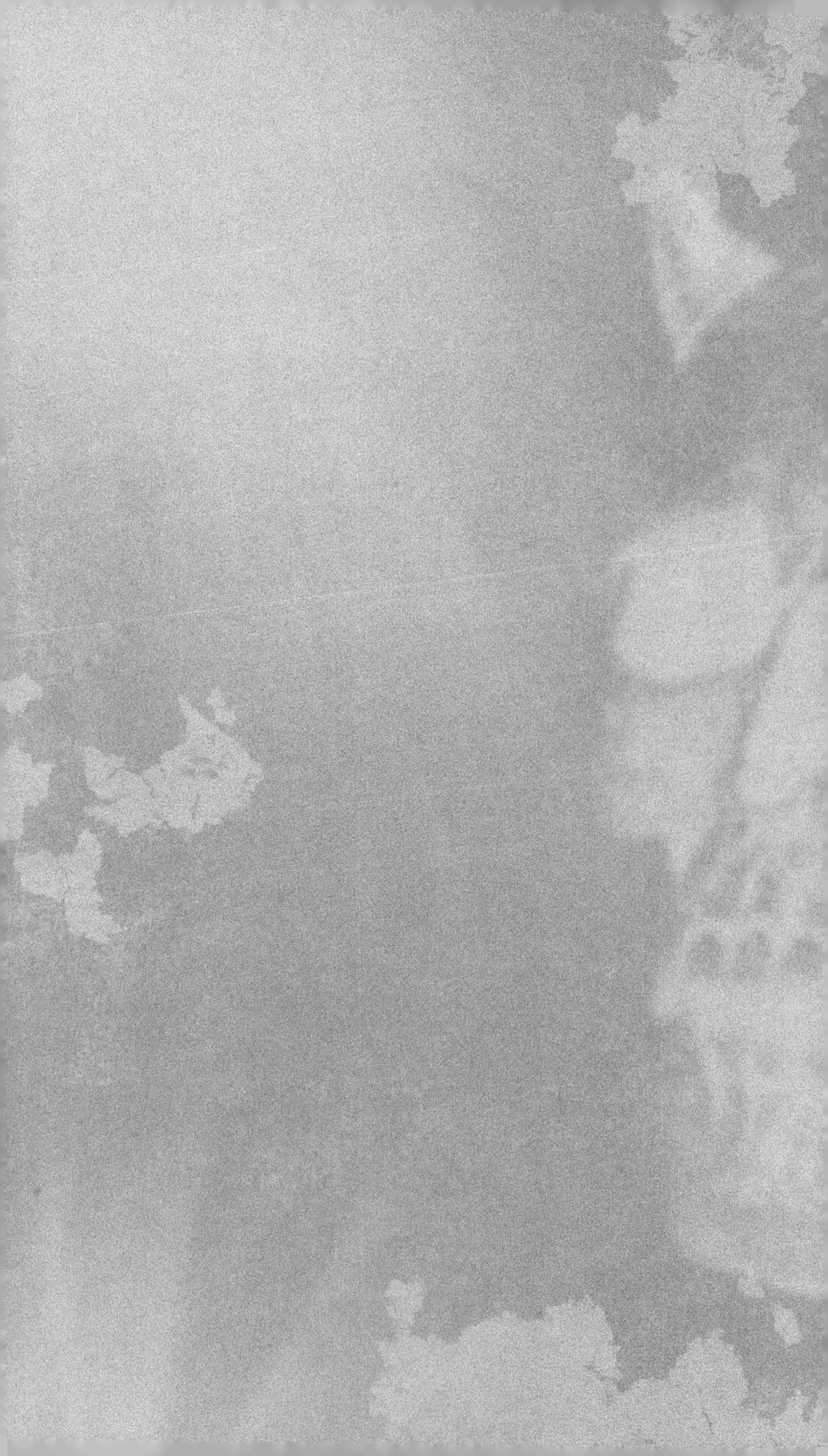

2

Portrait of a Queer Horror Fan

The Opinions, Habits and Tastes of the Queer Spectator

Queer people inherently relate to the otherness and subversion of horror.
(46974402)

There are parallels of queer survivorship with survival in horror films that cisheterosexual life experiences do not reflect on the axis of a/gender(s) or a/sexuality(ies).
(47167830)

I feel that a lot of horror is intrinsically queer as it relies on fear of the otherworldly and outsiders which can be a metaphor for the LGBTQ community.
(47081984)

Due to having an intrinsically different worldview and lived experience, the way I 'read' films is very different from hetero viewers.
(47079391)

THIS STUDY BOTH privileges queer identity over other identity markers and argues that the queer spectator of horror understands their queerness (one aspect of a multiplicitous identity) as the reason they form a distinctive relationship with the horror genre. This chapter will centre the expositional presentation and generalised understanding of queer fans of horror in aggregate; presenting and analysing this large data set in aggregate provides empirical evidence for meaningful assertions about the queer horror spectator that support or raise questions about a range of largely unsubstantiated claims that horror scholars have made for decades. This chapter, therefore, presents a large amount of aggregate data without complete in-depth analysis because its important purpose is to establish the first comprehensive empirical portrait of the queer spectator of horror film.[1] The chapters that follow, in turn, provide comprehensive explication of a selection of the data findings to more deeply consider the topics of queer trauma, camp and drag horror hosts. The overall demographics (age, race, gender identity, sexual orientation and education) of the survey participants are presented here, curtailing in-depth discussions of and distinctions in intersectionality. Fundamental to this study's argument that queer spectators distinctively connect with the horror genre is the understanding that this queer-horror connection is fostered in idiosyncratic ways and via myriad films. While the survey data demonstrates pronounced consensus in the overall opinions, habits and tastes of the queer spectator, the mixed-method data simultaneously reveals the diversity of and nuances in individual relationships with and interpretations of horror film, as reported by the research participants.

The process of data presentation is one of selection. Even though the principal aim of this study is to provide insights into the horror-loving queer population as a whole, the chapter will also present select statistically significant correlations and intersectional meanings extrapolated from the data in order to demonstrate how spectatorial subjectivity may alter reactions to the horror genre. To date, the limited number of empirical horror studies have yielded smaller data sets which, subsequently, has led to starkly cisheteronormative understandings of the horror audience. Because of this study's large sample size, I can detect differences in my participant population, horror's queer community, which allows for more reliable conclusions. Although this study privileges queerness and argues that one's queerness engenders a distinctive relationship with the horror genre, it does not completely ignore Browne and Nash's dictum that 'queer methodological approaches must be attentive to issues of intersectionality' (2010, p. 17). Just as queerness cannot be extricated from one's individual subjectivity, other identity markers cannot be extricated from one's subjective experiences as a queer person. A person's intersectional subjectivity directly relates to their sociopolitical access to safety and power, influencing nearly every facet of their life, since embodied subjectivity alters both how a person sees the world and how the world sees them. According to Janet Staiger, reception studies examines the relationship between 'actual spectators and films' (1992, p. 8). She explicitly states that 'each spectator is a complex and contradictory construction of such self-identities as gender, sexual preference, class, race, and ethnicity' (Staiger, 1992, p. 13). The thousands of diverse queer spectators of horror film that inform this study collectively demonstrate that one's queerness *is* the identity marker which becomes salient when analysing one's relationship to the horror genre. Because this research project is the foundational empirical study of queer horror spectators, priority has been given to presenting the aggregate data results centred on queerness. The survey's data can be extrapolated through calculations to approximate how the total population of queer horror spectators would have answered the survey questions, which is done by calculating confidence intervals for the population proportion. In other words, this data can indicate with 99 per cent confidence the opinions, habits and tastes of *all* queer spectators of horror, not just those who responded to the survey. Brigid Cherry found when extricating the female horror fan from obscurity that 'the male audience model [was] concealing an unrecognised female audience' (1999, p. 10). Likewise, the presumed cisheterosexual audience model has hitherto concealed the queer horror spectator. This study's empirical data emphatically evidences that queer spectators of horror film connect to the genre differently than cisheterosexual horror fans because the queer horror relationship is grounded in a non-normative embodiment, and proves that the connection queers have to horror transcends national borders, generations and intersectional subjectivities.

Queer Heterogeneity and Consensus

Queer spectators of horror film come from different countries, cultures, ages, races, ethnicities, genders, sexualities, educational levels and relationship statuses, yet the data substantiates impressive agreement in their opinions, habits and tastes as a queer community.[2] Harry Benshoff and Sean Griffin write about how a diverse group of individuals can become a connected and aligned community, can understand themselves as a queer community:

> Coming out meant becoming adept at reading queer subtexts, being able to bend straight culture (in film as well as the rest of the material world) into something new, and learning the often clandestine and coded practices of the era's queer subcultures. The sense of kinship created through such shared activity helped queer people begin to conceptualize themselves as both a community and a culture. (2006, p. 68)

In other words, queerness functions as a shared textual and subtextual language, a language not understood (certainly not fluently) by members from other communities to which queers belong. This queer language is developed outside the mainstream, often outside the childhood home, school and neighbourhood, outside physical borders and boundaries; this language often comes from pop culture encoding and references in media such as film.[3] Understanding this queer(ed) common language provides an analytic framework to develop and delineate the distinctive relationship that queer spectators have with the horror genre. Detailing the diversity of the demographic profile of the survey participants and narrators, while emphasising the overwhelming consensus in the data results, further elucidates queer spectators' distinctive love of horror. The demographic composition – age, race/ethnicity, gender identity and sexual orientation – of the survey participants and oral history narrators demonstrates a '*typological* representativeness', which results, with ample responses across all demographic categories, in being 'able to describe with confidence their patterned similarities and differences' (Barker, Mathijs and Trobia, 2008, p. 223; italics in the original). This study's survey participants, indeed, cross ages, races, ethnicities, gender identities, sexual orientations and nations. Since previous quantitative studies about the horror genre do not detail the racial and/or ethnic composition of their research participants, this study also then stands as the most racially and ethnically diverse empirical horror study to date. The survey participants live in the United States (n = 2,829);[4] the United Kingdom, Ireland, Canada, Australia or New Zealand (n = 897); or elsewhere in the world (n = 375),[5] thereby generating '*cross-country* and therefore *cross-cultural*' data (Barker, Egan, Jones and Mathijs, 2008, p. 7; italics in the original).[6] This cross-cultural data importantly evidences that the 4,107 differently embodied queer subjectivities collected demonstrate greater consensus than difference. The comprehensive mixed-method data results remain unwavering: the shared and distinctive relationship with the horror genre amongst queers crosses intersectional embodiment. The oral history narrators, whilst from varied intersectional backgrounds, deeply reflect this shared narrative – a through-line that speaks directly to the distinctive relationship that queers have with the horror genre. 'A common thread in much "new audience research" is a recognition that audience engagements are deeply interwoven with wider cultural memberships' (Barker, Mathijs and Trobia, 2008, p. 216). In this study, queerness is the cultural membership that foregrounds the participants' and narrators' distinctive relationship to horror. The following presentation of demographic data will evidence the heterogeneity of the queer horror spectator. Understanding who the queer spectator is demographically precedes the subsequent detailing of their opinions, habits and tastes of the horror genre.

Gender and Sexual Orientation Diversity of Queer Spectators

The multitude of gender identities[7] and sexual orientations represented by this substantial queer community, and the demonstrated ardent fandom of these queers, confirms that prior empirical research into horror audiences has both deliberately and inadvertently rendered the queer spectator invisible through cisheteronormative methodologies and methods. Until now, when scholars in horror studies have theoretically centred queerness, they have predominantly analysed the textual metaphor of queerness as monstrous and monstrosity as queer (see, e.g., Benshoff, Miller and Scahill). Moreover, the focus to date on queerness in horror or queer horror spectators privileges gay men (see, e.g., Scales and Elliott-Smith). A review of the gender identity of this survey's participants quickly ends the privileging of white cis gay men and establishes a comprehensive picture of the queer horror spectator, a portrait in which the queer demographic is comprised of cis women, trans women, cis men, trans men and transsexual, genderqueer, agender, non-binary people, as well as other gender identities written in by 120 participants (including gender-fluid, two spirit, demimale, transmasculine, bigender, questioning, butch, pangender, androgynous, femme, gender non-conforming and gender neutral). Given the survey's significant sample size, the nearly equal representation of cisgender women and men is quite remarkable, with 32.8 per cent (n = 1,341) of the survey participants identifying as cisgender women and 29.5 per cent (n = 1,207) of the survey participants identifying as cisgender men (see Figure 2.1).[8]

This balance becomes even more pronounced when including *all* women respondents (cis, trans and genderqueer women), since the participant percentage increases to 43.5 per cent, which is higher than the 42.3 per cent of men (including cis, trans and genderqueer men). This gender-balanced representation stands in direct opposition and as a significant refutation to previous assumptions about the horror spectator – both heterosexual and queer. Even with Berenstein's and Cherry's research evincing the female horror fan, the overall emphasis of previous empirical studies continued to reinforce presumed gender imbalances in and gendered consumptions of the genre.

This gendered reinforcement functioned, for one, to subsume the queer woman. For example, Stephen Follows states that the 'UK cinema audience for horror movies is 57% male and 43% female' (2017, p. 120)[9] and even Cherry's own preliminary horror audience survey reports a similar gender split based on eleven horror screenings, indicating a 68 per cent male (*n* = 446) and 32 per cent (*n* = 212) female audience makeup (1999, p. 234). Cherry suggests the reason for this binaristic gender divide when she states that 'social pressures, in addition to the fact that it is considered unfeminine for women to like horror films, make it likely that many women would not willingly admit to

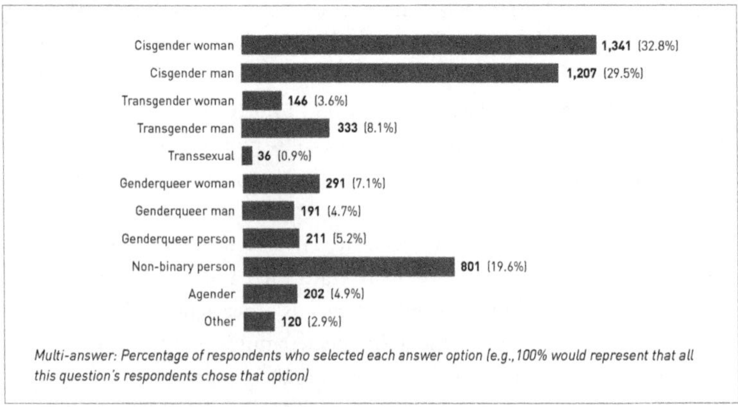

Figure 2.1. Bar graph of survey participants' gender identities. Note: this category was not mutually exclusive; therefore, participants could select more than one gender identity marker to align with their own identity.

a taste for horror' (2002, p. 44). However, this study's survey participant results demonstrate that queer cis, trans and genderqueer women are more than willing to stake their claim on horror. Furthermore, a review of the transcripts from this project's women narrators evidences that queer women seem to have no concerns that horror is considered an 'unfeminine' genre and are not self-conscious in these proclivities.[10] Strengthening this assertion about the queer horror spectator, the findings in Thomas Austin's audience study of *Bram Stoker's Dracula* (1992) rejected a 'simple and clear-cut gendered division' in horror audiences (2002, p. 137). This determination is further bolstered by Cherry's research findings on the female horror film audience (1999) and Richard Nowell's investigation into the North American film production and distribution companies, which understood that 'female youth [have] held the key to commercially viable horror' as far back as the 1970s (2011, p. 128). Daniel Humphrey, elaborating on the reporting of Christine Spines, unequivocally notes 'that women attend horror films more than men – at least in the theaters and at least on opening weekends' (2014, p. 53). Women who love horror have thus had their place cemented in horror studies, despite queer women undoubtedly being collapsed into the data about women horror spectators – until now. Women (including queer women) have always been a part of horror fandom and this study demonstrates that queers from myriad backgrounds and embodiments – not only white cis gay men – love the horror genre.

As established, then, queer horror spectators reflect a full and robust gender spectrum and, correspondingly, represent myriad sexual orientations. While survey participants most selected the questionnaire options bisexual (n = 1,427), gay (n = 1,290), queer (n = 1,252), pansexual (n = 854) and lesbian (n = 595),[11] 111 survey participants took the time to add their not-listed sexual orientation (thereby creating a more comprehensive understanding of nuanced or lesser-known sexual orientations), including: demisexual, biromantic, homoromantic, aceflux, teratophile, dyke, panromantic, demipolysexual, aromantic, greysexual, omnisexual, sadist and fictionsexual (see Figure 2.2). The wide spectrum of survey participants' sexual orientations underscores the complexity, fluidity and variety of queer subjectivity.

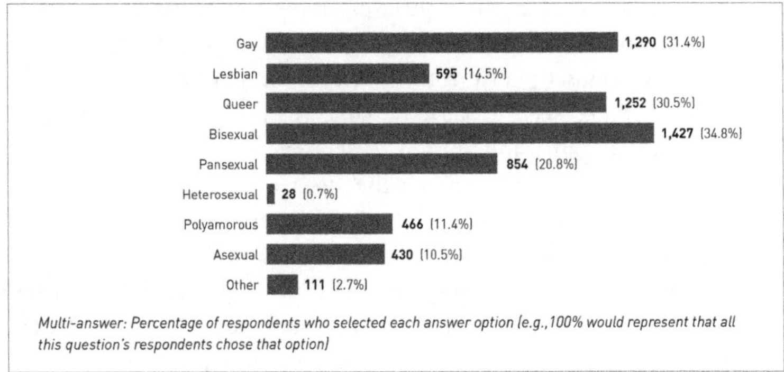

Figure 2.2. Bar graph of survey participants' sexual orientations. Note: this category was not mutually exclusive; therefore, participants could select more than one sexual orientation per their own identification.

Racial/Ethnic Identifications

Since this study stands as the most racially and ethnically diverse empirical horror study to date, detailing the race/ethnicity of the survey participants underscores the diversity of the queer horror fan population. The survey participants' racial and ethnic composition is as follows (see Figure 2.3):[12]

- 2.9 per cent American Indian or Alaska Native (*n* = 119);
- 3.4 per cent Asian or Asian American (*n* = 140);
- 3.1 per cent Black or African American (*n* = 126);
- 9.8 per cent Latinx (*n* = 403);
- 1 per cent Middle Eastern or North African (*n* = 42);
- 6.5 per cent multiracial (*n* = 266);
- 0.5 per cent Native Hawaiian or other Pacific Islander (*n* = 21); and/or
- 84.2 per cent white or Caucasian (*n* = 3,458).[13]

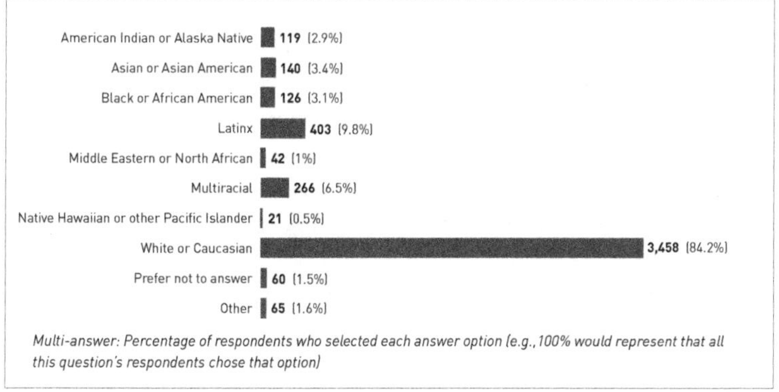

Figure 2.3. Bar graph of survey participants' racial and/or ethnic identities. Note: this category was not mutually exclusive; therefore, participants could select more than one race or ethnicity per their own racial and ethnic composition.

	United States	United Kingdom, Ireland, Canada, Australia or New Zealand	Elsewhere in the world	
American Indian or Alaska Native	101	17	0	118
Asian or Asian American	91	23	26	140
Black or African American	116	7	3	126
Latinx	329	13	60	402
Middle Eastern or North African	26	6	10	42
Multiracial	187	50	28	265
Native Hawaiian or other Pacific Islander	17	2	2	21
White or Caucasian	2,369	817	266	3,452

Figure 2.4. Chart that exhibits the number of survey participants from the United States; the United Kingdom, Ireland, Canada, Australia or New Zealand; or elsewhere in the world by racial and/or ethnic identities.

The demographic section of the survey opened with the following statement: 'Collecting demographic data for a diverse community can unintentionally leave some persons feeling unrepresented or unseen. With inclusivity as a goal, nearly every question provides an open entry box if the best answer for you has not been provided.' Multiple survey participants expanded the demographic data by writing in additional races/ethnicities such as: Ashkenazi/Jewish, Romani/Traveller, Aboriginal Australian and British Indian.[14] The survey participants selected:

- one race/ethnicity – 89.5 per cent;
- two races/ethnicities – 7 per cent;
- three races/ethnicities – 3.2 per cent; and
- more than three races/ethnicities – 0.3 per cent.

Educational Attainment and Age

Given the denigrated and 'low brow' status historically conferred on the horror genre,[15] the education levels achieved by horror fans merit observation because queer spectators disprove the fallacious assumptions commonly made about horror audiences being less educated (see Figure 2.5). Cherry documents that female horror fans 'appear to be well-educated or trained for a career. 54 per cent have university or college degrees, 10 per cent of these having post-graduate degree or diploma qualifications' (1999, p. 79). Correspondingly, queer horror fans are a highly educated population, with 59 per cent having obtained university/college degrees and 16.9 per cent of these being postgraduate degrees. While people under the age of thirty comprise the largest segment of the survey participants (n = 2,332), 43.2 per cent of the participants are thirty and older (n = 1,767) (see Figure 2.6).[16] This age skewing is likely informed by the survey sample-sourcing methods. In 'Sampling Lesbian, Gay, and Bisexual Populations', Ilan H. Meyer and Patrick A. Wilson explain that 'in the general population, a *digital divide* exists: Americans with Internet access are younger, have a higher socioeconomic status, and are less likely to be racial/ethnic minorities than those without Internet access' (2009, p. 29; italics in the original). Inarguably, the employment of an online survey and the use of Instagram as the main social media marketing platform will privilege responses from respondents who skew young, white and educated. Cherry's female horror fan and this study's queer horror fan both reach educational attainment at

➔ Frequencies

Statistics

Please indicate your highest level of education completed:

N	Valid	4104
	Missing	3

Please indicate your highest level of education completed:

		Frequency	Per cent	Valid per cent	Cumulative per cent
Valid	Some high school	89	2.2	2.2	2.2
	High school diploma or GED	469	11.4	11.4	13.6
	Some college or training	950	23.1	23.1	36.7
	Trade, technical or vocational training	141	3.4	3.4	40.2
	Associate's degree	276	6.7	6.7	46.9
	Bachelor's degree	1452	35.4	35.4	82.3
	Master's degree	539	13.1	13.1	95.4
	Doctorate and/or other professional degree	154	3.7	3.8	99.2
	Other	34	0.8	0.8	100.0
	Total	4104	99.9	100.0	
Missing	System	3	0.1		
Total		**4107**	**100.0**		

Figure 2.5. Frequency chart that indicates the highest level of education completed by survey participants.

levels beyond respective national averages, yet previous studies emphasise that horror fans come from less advantaged socio-economic groups. 'Using exit polls of UK cinema audiences', Stephen Follows and Bruce Nash state that, 'we can see that horror movies are disproportionately enjoyed by people on the lower end of the class spectrum when compared to all other genres' (2018, n.p.). The authors' unspoken implication is that horror is more often consumed by an undiscerning audience, which may say more about critical views of class than horror audiences. This study did not collect employment data; however, occupation is not the only vector of class position, which can be surmised by educational attainment. The majority of survey participants obtained college, undergraduate and/or postgraduate degrees across the United States (59.7 per cent) and the United Kingdom, Ireland, Canada, Australia or New Zealand (61.4 per cent). That rate of educational attainment for queer horror fans is particularly significant when compared to the total percentages of the US and UK populations who hold a bachelor's degree or higher, which are 36 per cent and 42 per cent, respectively (2020 US Census and 2017 Office for National Statistics). In direct contrast to the Follows report, which states that 78.6 per cent of the UK cinemagoing horror audience are 'Lower Middle Class', 'Skilled Working Class', 'Working Class' or 'Non-working' (2017, p. 123), this study's data on education levels further indicates that queer horror fans exist outside mainstream norms and expand the boundaries of previously studied cinemagoing horror audiences. In all, this study's demographic data

➔ Frequencies

Statistics

What is your current age?

N	Valid	4099
	Missing	8

What is your current age?

		Frequency	Per cent	Valid per cent	Cumulative per cent
Valid	18–23 years old	1006	24.5	24.5	24.5
	24–29 years old	1326	32.3	32.3	56.9
	30–35 years old	829	20.2	20.2	77.1
	36–41 years old	523	12.7	12.8	89.9
	42–47 years old	233	5.7	5.7	95.6
	48–53 years old	115	2.8	2.8	98.4
	54–59 years old	56	1.4	1.4	99.7
	60–65 years old	8	0.2	0.2	99.9
	66+ years old	3	0.1	0.1	100.0
	Other	34	0.8	0.8	100.0
	Total	4099	99.8	100.0	
Missing	System	8	0.2		
Total		**4107**	**100.0**		

Figure 2.6. Chart that shows the age of survey participants at the time of completing the survey.

evidences that the queer horror spectator exists across all genders, sexual orientations, races, ethnicities, educational backgrounds and ages. With the full demographic understanding of the queer horror spectator, the data then clearly reveals how – and allows us to understand why – queer identity finds an embodied and intellectualised commonality in the status of Other as represented in horror film.

The Othered Lens of Queerness

The queer horror spectator should be understood to be conscious and critical about how their queerness affects their consumption of cultural texts, as learned through statistical inference from this study's survey data. When asked if they, as members of the LGBTQ+ community, have a different reaction to horror films as compared with heterosexual viewers, the majority of survey participants report that they react differently to horror than heterosexuals. In fact, 57.1 per cent (n = 2,339), a majority of survey participants, think that their queerness alters how they react to the horror genre. The confidence interval indicates with 99 per cent confidence that 55.1 per cent to 59.1 per cent of *all* queer horror spectators would report that they have a different reaction to horror films as compared with heterosexual viewers.

Similarly, when survey participants were asked if they felt that being queer influences their taste in horror films, a 55.9 per cent (n = 2,290) majority report that their queerness alters their horror tastes. The 99 per cent confidence interval indicates that the actual percentage who would have answered that their queerness affects their tastes in horror films in the total horror-loving queer population runs from 53.9 per cent to 57.9 per cent. This further highlights that the majority of queer horror spectators report that their queerness is integral to their relationship with the horror genre. That belief is also found represented in early queer scholars, such as Vito Russo and Alexander Doty, who analysed film through the queer lens, deconstructing film texts to illustrate how 'lesbians, gay men, and other queers experience films differently than do straight viewers' (Benshoff and Griffin, 2006, p. 10). In response to being asked to explain why they think that they have a different reaction to horror films as compared with heterosexual viewers, one participant succinctly summed up the views of many when they wrote: 'Identity is a lens' (47742033). In other words, the majority of queer people understand their queer identity is a part of how they see and understand the world.

These two survey questions that captured data on how the participants think their queerness directly relates to the horror genre explicitly asked: 'As a member of the LGBTQ+ community, do you feel that you have a different reaction to horror films as compared with heterosexual viewers?' and 'Do you feel that being queer influences your taste in horror films?'. While there is comprehensive consensus among queers in the survey's data results, queer subjectivity (a queer person's gender, race/ethnicity, class, age, nationality and educational attainment), at times, indicates nuanced intersectional responses to horror, as underscored by examining the statistical results for a two-variable measure of association, the Yule's Q. For the majority of queer horror fans who report they have different reactions to horror film as compared with heterosexual viewers, the Yule's Q demonstrates no or negligible association when examining cis women compared with cis men (Yule's Q 0.02); US participants compared with non-US participants (Yule's Q 0.13); and white participants compared with BIPOC participants (Yule's Q 0.00). Whereas there is a very small association between participants under the age of forty-two compared to participants that are forty-two and older (Yule's Q 0.28), with those under forty-two more often stating that their queerness gives them a different reaction to horror. Moreover, cisgender participants compared to trans* participants demonstrate a moderate association (Yule's Q 0.39). Trans* participants more often report that their queerness gives them a different reaction to horror. Comparably, Yule's Qs examining whether participants think that their queerness influences their taste in horror demonstrate no or negligible association when examining cis women compared to cis men (Yule's Q 0.01); US participants compared to non-US participants (Yule's Q 0.08); and white participants compared to BIPOC participants (Yule's Q 0.04). There is a very small association between participants under forty-two compared to participants that are forty-two and older (Yule's Q 0.20) and participants with a university/college degree compared to participants without one (Yule's Q 0.19). This demonstrates that younger and degree-holding participants more often report that their queerness influences their taste in horror. Cisgender participants, when compared to trans* participants, demonstrate a moderate association (Yule's Q 0.31), indicating again that trans* participants more often report that their queerness influences their taste in horror.

The more educated the queer horror fan is, the more likely they are to report that their queerness affects their opinions, habits and tastes of the horror genre. The data reveals a small but highly statistically significant relationship between a queer person's highest level of education completed and them answering that their queerness creates a different reaction or taste in horror films ('different reaction' χ^2 (8) = 37.731, $p < 0.000$, Cramér's V = 0.10, n = 4,096 and queer 'taste' χ^2 (8) = 76.145, $p < 0.000$, Cramér's V = 0.14, n = 4,092). Moreover, the older the survey participant is, the less likely they are to report that their queerness affects their opinions, habits and tastes of the horror genre. A highly statistically significant but small relationship also exists between a queer person's age and answering that their queerness creates a different reaction or taste in horror films ('different reaction' χ^2 (6) = 45.696, $p < 0.000$, Cramér's V = 0.11, n = 4,080 and queer 'taste' χ^2 (6) = 43.118, $p < 0.000$, Cramér's V = 0.10, n = 4,077). Age and educational level having statistically significant relationships with a queer person's understanding of their queerness underscores how queer subjectivity always already exists in a sociopolitical context.

Nonetheless, this entire study analytically and purposefully privileges queerness over other identity markers, not because there is little to be learned from analysing the different intersectional embodiments of the queer community, but because one's queerness creates a different othering in the world, a different lens that warrants examination. As Audre Lorde states:

> Within the lesbian community I am Black, and within the Black community I am a lesbian. Any attack against Black people is a lesbian and gay issue, because I and thousands of other Black women are part of the lesbian community. Any attack against lesbians and gays is a Black issue, because thousands of lesbians and gay men are Black. There is no hierarchy of oppression. (1983, p. 9)

In this statement, Lorde concisely delineates how one's identity markers cannot be disentangled and detached. Just as there is no hierarchy of oppression, similarly, there is no hierarchy of identity. Queers embody their queerness in innumerable idiosyncratic ways – ways that are intrinsically *and* inherently tied to race, gender, ethnicity, class and ability. Queer otherness is salient alongside intersectionality and its salience is in part predicated on potential rejection from a queer person's other communities. For example, narrator Mark Estes discusses how being a Black gay man functions to isolate him from members of his Black community and being Black in white supremacist social structures exposes him to racist persecution: 'Being Black men, we're targeted. Being a Black gay man, you're targeted not only by the world, but by your brethren' (2020, p. 12). Similarly, narrator Lana Contreras explains her experience of this intersectionality:

> Simply the fear of being ostracized – the fear of being culturally Catholic and it [homosexuality] being this instilled sin … And it's not because of a fear of religion, it's fear of being shunned by my family. It's the fear of being shunned. The fact that I financially help my family and I think that they would not accept my money and they would be destitute and they would lose their home. Not pay their bills because they don't want to take fucking money from this dyke. That is the fear I have. (2020, p. 11)

Estes's and Contreras's experiences underscore how the queer lens can be formed outside of familial, racial and/or ethnic communities – how the queer lens is forged in one's otherness from all other social units. The following selection of responses from survey participants, who are various gender and sexual identity combinations (including cisgender, transgender, genderqueer, non-binary, gay, lesbian, bisexual and pansexual), accentuates this point:

> I often feel that the themes of 'otherness' and alienation (either from the monster side or the protagonist side) appeal to me in a different way than for a straight audience. (46894279)

> I think I'm more in tune to the idea of The Other in films and how we use othering to get to fears we can't name. (46811770)

> Queerness gives a unique perspective of what it means to be different. (46825875)

> I think that being far more of an 'other' than most heterosexual (white and cis) viewers means that I tend to have horror resonate in a deeper and more unique way, as it's akin to what I and other LGBTQ+ people experience. (47082671)

> I think the sense of isolation and fear on the part of the monster is more understood by an LGBT audience. (46914100)

> I think I 'read' horror films (and all art) with a different lens on it, often critiquing it where a heterosexual viewer would accept it or enjoying stories or characters that they would not appreciate or understand. (46764770)

> I think I find more truth in horror films than heterosexual viewers. I think heterosexual viewers sometimes see horror films as a thrilling fantasy whereas, in my experience as a queer person, I find their ruthless depictions of violence and sex and bodies as being reflective of my lived experiences. (47082733)

> Different experience of the world gives you a different lens on film. (47645409)

> Heterosexual people can't understand what it's like to be victimised or understand what it's like to love as an LGBTQ person. They don't know what it's like being on the journey of uncovering yourself. Those things have an effect on how people view the world and themselves and it changes how I relate to movies and understand characters. (47724006)

> I always think through a queer lens. (48157393)

> I feel that generally in life my sexuality has an impact on my reading of the world around me and particularly of films and literature. (47034871)

> Otherness is an essential part of my human experience, and so the Otherness of a monster's experience, for example, has different meaning for me than it would for someone who would be watching with the lens of heteronormative life experience. (48122378)

This othered lens expressed by many survey participants – a lens of queer identity and experience – is an anchor for the distinctive relationship that queers have with the horror genre. While 42.9 per cent of survey participants do not perceive that their queerness comparatively alters their reaction to horror films, this does not mean that their relationship to horror films is not actually altered or distinct. In other words, a person's queerness still shapes how they process and enjoy horror films, even if they might not understand their queerness to do so or be fully aware of their queerness as part of their understanding of self. It is imperative to emphasise that this question and the related question, about queerness influencing taste in horror films, are both investigating the queer lens and serve to document whether survey participants perceive or understand their queer lens, not whether their queer lens exists. With the notable number of survey participants who report that their queerness does not alter their reaction to or taste in horror films, 42.9 and 44.1 per cent, respectively, there are generational, gender, relationship and educational differences between the queer spectators who understand and report a queer lens and those who do not; queer spectators who are forty-eight and older, cisgender, in monogamous relationships and non-degree-holding are more likely to state that their queerness does not alter their reaction to or taste in horror films. These statistical findings suggest the need for further research on the effects that age, assimilative homonormativity and exposure to queer theory have on one's perception of their queer relationship to the horror genre (and the queer lens on media in general). Nevertheless, the mixed-method data of this study on queer horror spectators evidences a cohesive consensus, demonstrating that the majority of queer horror spectators recognise and report that their queerness alters their relationship to the horror genre. This study's data documents that the majority of queer spectators are aware of their distinct relationship to horror; even still, this data point is one of many that work together to evidence the *sui generis* relationship that queer spectators have with the horror genre. Even though *all* queers exist in opposition to the normative, a person's intersectionality entirely affects their individual subjectivity *and* their understanding or awareness of their subjectivity. As Andrew Gorman-Murray, Lynda Johnston and Gordon Waitt state: 'One challenge in queer academic scholarship is the difficulty in effectively communicating and achieving understanding across an increasingly wide range of sexual subjects, each with their own experiences, practices, relationships and subjectivities' (2010, p. 99). The 4,107 survey participants and fifteen oral history narrators represent the same number of individual queer subjectivities. Despite this, all survey questions that centre queerness and queer representation demonstrate a critical consensus. For instance, 76.8 per cent (n = 3,150) of survey participants report that the presence of a queer character affects their enjoyment of a horror film.[17] In fact, 2,989 survey participants elected to further explain in what ways the presence of a queer character affects their enjoyment of a horror film. These selected written responses centre reasons such as the sparsity of explicit queer characters in horror, the importance of *positive* queer representation, and the connection between queerness, the queer experience and the horror genre:

> If they're treated well (no tropes, no excess abuse, no bad coding, no bury your gays), I appreciate that. I would love love love love more queer presence in horror films. (47085220)

> If the character is heroic and lives, it makes me feel like I can survive horrible things and reminds me that I have. If the character is heroic and dies, it makes me feel mournful and fatalistic. If the character is maligned and lives, it makes me question the purpose of their character. If a character is maligned and dies, it makes me feel alienated and conflicted about celebrating their demise. (46828663)

> Just generally happy any time there's queer rep on film. Positive representation is great, and demonized/bad queers give me weird good complicated feelings. (46896188)

> Visibility is so important, it's why we need more queer narratives in horror as well as queer people making those stories. (47001060)

> LGBTQ viewers have an innately different perspective than the heterosexual viewer. We're still demonized in larger society, viewed by pop culture as something to be viewed, consumed, or exploited. We are the monster and the monsters are always for us if we claim them as our own. This perspective is entirely unique to the queer viewer. (47082922)

> I am interested in the representation of queer characters and themes in all Gothic fiction (inclusive of horror). If a queer character is featured, especially if they feature as more than a peripheral figure or a plot device, I will generally enjoy the film more. (47060348)

> To see representation of a queer character in horror connects me to horror, because I'm able to see people like me or people within my community on screen and in these films. It feels good. Even if the representation has often times been flawed or problematic, I'm still drawn to the film and can enjoy it. (47075790)

As a queer horror fan, I enjoy seeing queer representation in my favorite genre (including queer villains, whom I think are still very important). (47077323)

Queer identity is transgressive and transformative, and having an outlet and metaphor through fiction to explore that is healthy. Monster characters are a passion of mine, even when they're just played straight as evil monsters without any pathos or nuance. When they're sympathetic, sometimes it's hit and miss, sometimes it's great. Queer horror in that context for me often explores the horror of being the monster and wanting to just exist without having to hurt anyone, but still often wanting a sense of revenge or power over one's situation. (47112447)

We're faced with real horror daily, so I buy queers as heroes in extreme scenarios. (47140189)

Representation! I love seeing people outside of the cisgender heterosexual norm in horror. And hopefully some that aren't dying (as much! it is horror after all) because of the Bury Your Gays trope. (47075473)

Horror movies have always presented a space for allegorical dialogues about the Other, and provided that it's handled well I think we as queer people can find a lot to appreciate about working through our cultural struggles through the lens of horror media . . . We deserve to see ourselves as survivors. (47597139)

It's just nice to feel seen. Horror is maligned as the gutter of genre, but its place in the shadows means things can prosper there that couldn't elsewhere. So even if the queer representation in horror is 'bad,' like in SLEEPAWAY CAMP or SILENCE OF THE LAMBS, it's at least THERE, and I don't think it's worse than the navel-gazing, forlorn mirror shots of genitals that seem to dominate modern 'serious' trans films (by cis film-makers). At the very least in horror films, it gives me something to think about. (47708748)

Since most horror is queer coded anyway, I prefer horror with strong queer characters. (47747740)

> Horror provides a fantastic milieu in which to explore the queer gaze/queerness generally! As a genre, it relies on the manipulation, exploration, subversion of existing societal narratives (especially regarding gender and sex) – it goes hand-in-glove with queer explorations of those topics. (47754738)

> I think there is a sense of hyper vigilance or heightened sense of danger that many queer people experience as a result of living in heterocentric/heterosexist culture as well as a sense of 'otherness' and exclusion that gives me a stronger relationship to both victims and sympathetic villains that, say, an average heterosexual cis male viewer would. (47083609)

Numerous survey participants noted that they have never seen an explicitly queer character in a horror film and, unsurprisingly, almost all queer horror fans, 95.1 per cent (n = 3,898), agree that queers are under-represented in the horror genre. The 99 per cent confidence interval indicates that the actual percentage in the total queer population that would have answered that queers are under-represented in the horror genre ranges from 94.3 per cent to 96 per cent. 'How we are seen', Richard Dyer states, 'determines in part how we are treated; how we treat others is based on how we see them; such seeing comes from representation' (1993, p. 1). Queer horror spectators want to see themselves positively represented in horror film in meaningful ways since they so distinctively connect to the genre. Regardless of the desire for more explicit queer representation in horror film, generations of queers have created identification within its existing tropes and characters.

Monsters, Victims and the Final Girl

Collectively, the survey participant responses underscore the importance of narrative context and metaphorical meanings in the depiction of the 'monster', demonstrating an active engagement with horror film that is directly related to the queer embodied experience. In other words, queer spectators identify with horror film monsters when they feel it represents their own experience. As widely established and theorised, cisheteronormative society both victimises queers and renders them monstrous. Affirming this dual victimisation and monstrosity, Sam J. Miller states: 'For myself and many other LGBT viewers, the queer monster not only provides an opportunity to

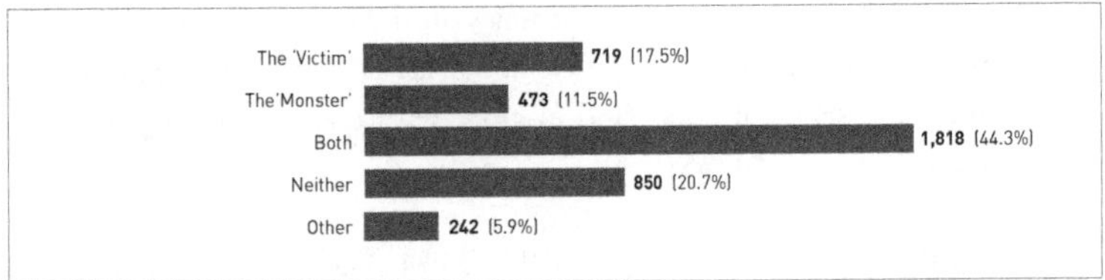

Figure 2.7. Bar graph that exhibits with whom survey participants identify in horror films.

identify with someone on-screen, it also allows us to vicariously live out our rage against a social order that oppresses us' (2011, p. 221). Survey results evidence that 73.3 per cent (n = 3,010) of survey participants are aware of this dual existence in society, as exemplified by the agreement that they tend to identify with the 'victim' (17.5 per cent), the 'monster' (11.5 per cent) or 'both' (44.3 per cent) in horror films (see Figure 2.7). The survey's open text box responses for this question illuminated queers' common identification with the 'female victim-hero' – the final girl (Clover, 1992, p. 4). Queer horror spectators' connection with the final girl trope significantly reveals how they specifically identify with the victimised survivor. This active yet fluid identification with the final girl is further reinforced by survey participants through responses such as: 'Mostly the Monster(s), and almost always the final girl, but never really the other victims' (47260208) and 'The survivor or the "final girl" ... distinct from "Victim"' (46927850). While Carol Clover concludes that the male spectator uses the final girl 'as a vehicle for his own sadomasochistic fantasies' (1992, p. 53), that assessment bypasses the queer male and, more importantly, the larger queer community's response to and use of the final girl as an identificatory victimised survivor. As a survey participant states, 'I identify with the final girl, who may be victim and monster but also neither' (47169996). Queers relate more to the act of survival than the passivity of victimisation, underscoring Linda Williams's observation that 'identification is neither fixed nor entirely passive' (1991, p. 8).

The queer spectator's affection for and association with the monster can be explained by Laura Westengard's consideration of 'queer dehumanization' (2019, p. 13) and Leila Taylor's suggestion that 'the process of dehumanization is a process of monster-making' (2019, p. 79), which signals the existence of the queer monster, a monster with whom queers can uniquely identify. Again, the process of queer people being dehumanised by society frames how not only the world sees queers, but also queers see the world.[18]

Overall, in horror films do you tend to identify with:

Overall, in horror films do you tend to identify with:	As a member of the LGBTQ+ community, do you feel that you have a different reaction to horror films as compared with heterosexual viewers?		No answer
	Yes	No	
The 'Victim'	49.37%	50.63%	0.00%
The 'Monster'	63.21%	36.36%	0.42%
Both	62.43%	37.29%	0.28%
Neither	45.06%	54.82%	0.12%
Other	67.77%	32.23%	0.00%
No answer	60.00%	40.00%	0.00%

Question	Response count
45	4099
12	4102

Figure 2.8. Chart that exhibits survey participants who report a different reaction to horror films (as compared with heterosexual viewers) and with whom they identify in horror films.

Unsurprisingly, then, a chi-square test of independence indicates a probability above 99 per cent that a relationship exists between queers who feel that they have a different reaction to horror films as compared with heterosexual viewers and whether they identify as both a monster and victim (χ^2 (4) = 108.794, $p < 0.00$). This same test also indicates that a relationship exists between queers who feel that being queer influences their taste in horror films and whether they identify as both a monster and victim (χ^2 (4) = 75.197, $p < 0.00$). Stated differently, queers who have a cognisant understanding that their queer subjectivity alters their perceptions and tastes are more likely to identify with both the monster *and* the victim in horror films (see Figure 2.8). The vacillation between identification with the victim and the monster is context-dependent on the film; it varies from one representation to another. Evidencing this point, survey participants state:

> This is very contingent on the film in question. But overall I identify with monsters in supernatural horror, but victims if the antagonist is human male. (46900710)

It really depends. If they are a monstrous Other (creature, etc.), I identify more with them. If it is a monstrous human (serial killer, etc.), I identify with the victim, unless the human is coded as a monster because they are from a marginalized identity group. (47076895)

It depends. I'm more likely to ID with the 'monster' if they're a compelling or sympathetic ghost/monster/alien than I am if they're a living human. I'm more likely to ID with the 'victim' if they're a compelling/sympathetic character. (47076579)

If 'monster' is human, then victim. If 'monster' is Other, then monster. (47079497)

It depends on the film. I tend to identify a lot with 'Final Girl' archetypes or the monster if they're somehow tragic or romantic. If they're shunned or somehow punished for simply existing and being what they are, then I'll definitely be drawn to them. (47079732)

It depends heavily on the characters themselves and how complex they are. Movies with character depth make it easier to identify with. I don't resonate with the monsters in terms of their brutal acts, but can resonate with being an outsider. (47150431)

It totally depends. Is the 'monster' coded as Other in a way that calls attention to the ways in which institutions like heteronormativity, white supremacy, capitalism etc. marks difference as monstrous (like in *True Blood*, *Frankenstein*, etc). If so, I feel sympathy and empathy with the monster. But if the monster is the embodiment of patriarchal violence (like in *I Spit on Your Grave* and *The Last House on the Left*), I do not identify with the monster at all. As for identifying with the 'victims,' that's tricky too! Who is represented? What choices are these folks making? (47249532)

It depends on which characters/figures in the film are presented. I can sympathise with the 'monster' if for example they're conflicted or outcast. Otherwise I tend to sympathise with the victims. (47756629)

GLAAD reports that queer-inclusive casting 'indicates progress, particularly for horror films which have historically portrayed LGBTQ characters as one-dimensional victims or villains, but which remain the most popular genre among LGBTQ moviegoers' (GLAAD Media Institute, 2020, p. 25). This overall sentiment is reductive, however, because categorising horror's queer characters as 'one-dimensional victims or villains' underestimates how some queers seek out or find in horror representations of their own socially-constructed 'monstrosity' and their resiliency to survive – and, in turn, reclaim them.

Women and Queers Represented in Horror

A review of two survey questions regarding female and queer characters illustrates how the data in this survey simultaneously exhibits overwhelming queer consensus yet displays nuanced intersectional differences. Of all survey participants, 75.2 per cent (n = 3,084) report that the presence of a strong female character affects their enjoyment of a horror film, which evidences an impressive consensus of queer horror fans.[19] When comparing the segmentation of white participants compared with BIPOC participants on this same question, race/ethnicity does not demonstrate an impact on the presence of a strong female character affecting a queer horror fan's enjoyment of a horror film; the survey data evidences through a Yule's Q of 0.02 that there is no association between these two variables. A gendered data breakdown, however, reveals that more women report that the presence of a strong female character affects their enjoyment of a horror film. For 85.4 per cent of women (cis, trans and genderqueer) and 68.4 per cent of men (cis, trans and genderqueer), the presence of a strong female character creates meaning for them. While the majority of all genders affirmatively report that the presence of a strong female character affects their enjoyment of a horror film, the Yule's Q of 0.50 demonstrates that there is a substantial association between these gender variables. Erin Harrington notes that 'women occupy a privileged place in horror film' (2018, p. 1), which largely stems from their significant representation in screen time; evidently, this representation connects with women. That 'privileged place' is emphasised by a survey participant who succinctly states that 'women are essential to horror. It doesn't exist without us' (47079311). The fact that horror is the only genre in which women are seen on screen more than men is, arguably, a concomitant reason why queer women love horror.

A Google report, 'The Women Missing from the Silver Screen and the Technology Used to Find Them', states that women are on screen 53 per cent of the time in horror, as compared with 45 per cent in romance, 36 per cent in sci-fi films, 30 per cent in biographical films and 29 per cent in action films (2017, n.p.). Representation matters to othered people; seeing ourselves represented in the world matters since the white cisheteropatriarchy predominantly privileges representing itself. The fact that women are not only seen and heard on screen more in horror than in any other genre, but also featured as strong characters, may be a key draw for queer women (irrespective of the characters' narrative outcomes).

Similarly, women and younger queer survey participants more often report that the presence of a queer character positively affects their enjoyment of a horror film, while the nationality, race/ethnicity or educational attainment of the survey participants does not demonstrate an impact on their enjoyment of a horror film due to the presence of a queer character. Of all survey participants, 76.8 per cent (n = 3,150) report that the presence of a queer character affects their enjoyment of a horror film, while moderate associations exist when comparing both women to men (Yule's Q 0.33) and participants under forty-two to participants who are forty-two and older (Yule's Q 0.39). There is no or negligible association when comparing responses about the presence of a queer character for US participants with non-US participants (Yule's Q 0.10); white participants compared with BIPOC participants (Yule's Q 0.01); and participants with a university/college degree compared with participants without one (Yule's Q 0.15). Since the horror genre features women on screen more than any other genre, I conclude that queer women want to see queer representation also, as queerness is another aspect of their multiplicitous identity. I also surmise that older participants are more accustomed to a lack of queer representation and do not base their identity or enjoyment on seeing queer characters, instead revelling in horror's ontological and subtextual queerness.

The majority of queer horror fans see and understand the world through a unique queer lens, distinctively relating and reacting to the horror genre as discussed earlier and evidenced by this study's mixed-method data. To reiterate, the presented data privileges reporting the queer horror community in aggregate over intersectional differences because of the data's extensive consensus and because my goal is to craft the first cohesive portrait of horror-loving queers. The following section presents statistically significant positive and negative correlations, as well as the non-correlative data from this study, to create a framework through which to demonstrate the broad and specific particularities of the queer horror spectator. The data evidences an overwhelming consensus, with the majority of queer spectators reporting horror genre opinions, habits and tastes that are widely shared within the community.

Fan Status of Queer Spectators

Queer spectators of the horror genre form a transnational, cross-generational and learned fandom. Evidencing this queer fandom in the horror genre through the mixed-method data presented here is critical because, until now, queer spectators have only been spoken for and about, not directly engaged to speak for themselves. The open-call internet distribution of a survey seeking to study 'how LGBTQ+ people view horror film' yielded participants who self-identify as queer horror fans and opt-in to complete the survey. The survey promotion asked, 'Are you Queer for Fear?', drawing in queer participants interested in establishing the first portrait of queer spectators and to evidence queer horror fandom. 95.7 per cent (n = 3,926) of the survey participants consider themselves horror film fans – although this was not a prerequisite – and therefore, 4.3 per cent (n = 177) of the 4,103 survey participants who answered this question do not consider themselves a fan of any type of horror film. Since the survey targeted horror-loving queers, this overwhelming fandom is hardly surprising; however, 'non-fans' participating does mean that the results presented throughout this study incorporate queers who may have a more

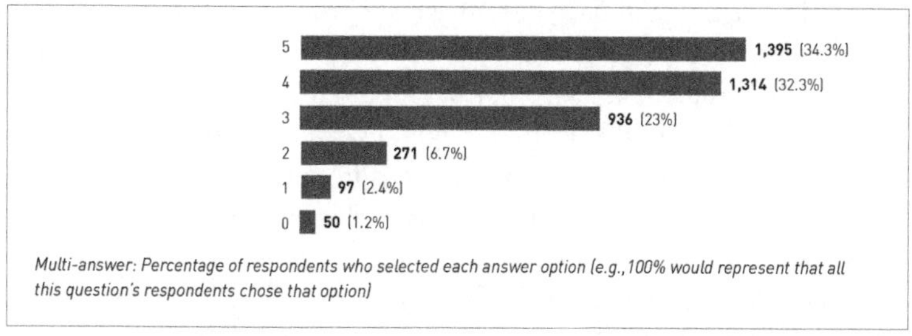

Figure 2.9. Bar graph that exhibits survey participants' reported level of horror fandom (0 = not a fan; 5 = massive fan).

complicated relationship to the genre than the more obvious designation of 'fan'. For example, the mixed-method data indicates that queer spectators have issues with the toxicity of cisheteropatriarchal horror fandom, which I speculate could be a reason that a small percentage of survey participants do not choose to identify as a fan. Narrator Gabe Castro offers a reason why queers might not feel comfortable within horror fandom. Castro states: 'It's acknowledging that the front-facing fandom isn't us. And we don't fit there. Even going into conventions that are horror related, we were like, "Ooh, we can't set up shop anywhere here. This is not for us. This isn't where we belong"' (2020, p. 20). This disjuncture in horror fandom could be one reason why only 18 per cent (n = 738) of the survey participants have attended a horror convention, such as Fantastic Fest, Fangoria's Weekend of Horrors or Crypticon. Of the survey participants who have attended, only 10.5 per cent (n = 77) consider horror conventions to be 'very queer friendly' spaces and 13.4 per cent (n = 98) consider them 'not at all queer friendly'. As narrator Christopher Velasco points out, horror fandom 'is very male. It's very white. It's very straight' (2020, p. 20). Similarly, narrator Lana Contreras 'do[es] not participate in organized fandom' because the 'realm unfortunately is predominantly white men' (2020, p. 16). These 'horror bros', as narrator Stacie Ponder identifies them, are the horror fans who 'wanted tits and blood and that's about it from their [horror] movies. They're the ones who are idolizing the killers in the film' (2020, p. 5). The 'horror bros' historically acting as the self-appointed gatekeepers of the horror genre is representative of the toxic masculinity that permeates numerous fandoms. In *Fake Geek Girls: Fandom, Gender, and the Convergence Culture Industry*, Suzanne Scott details: 'Spreadable misogyny is blatantly conceived and deployed as a tactic to win the space of fan culture, or at least definitively determine who is allowed to delimit and patrol its imagined borders by setting up gendered checkpoints' (2019, p. 85). Cisheterosexual men have established these 'checkpoints' to limit access to horror fandom for marginalised communities and to maintain the 'white, straight, cisgendered male conception of the fan' (Scott, 2019, p. 77). The learnings from this study further extend Scott's argument to include the targeted exclusion of non-normative genders and/or sexualities through misogynistic, homophobic and transphobic behaviours that are weaponised to uphold the cisheteropatriarchal horror fandom model. Narrator Joe Fejeran expresses the shared hope of many queer horror fans for there 'to be a queer exclusive horror convention. I'm just going to say that right now. There needs to be an exclusively queer horror convention' (2020, p. 28). Regardless of horror fandom's cis-heteropatriarchal toxicity, all the narrators and the overwhelming majority of the survey participants identify as horror fans. The survey data shows that the unambiguous horror-loving queer is an ardent horror fan (see Figure 2.9). When asked how much of a horror fan do they consider themselves to be on a scale of 0 (not a fan) to 5 (massive fan), 89.6 per cent (n = 3,645) designated their fandom in the top half (3–4–5) of the 0–5 scale, with 66.6 per cent (n = 2,709) selecting that they are either a massive fan (5) or the option under (4).

Childhood Introduction to Horror

Whether or not the participant self identifies as a fan, or the strength of their horror fandom, the data indicates that the majority of survey participants have a long relationship with the horror genre – 66.4 per cent (n = 2,599) of survey participants have thought of themselves as horror fans for as far back as they can remember (see Figure 2.10). Therefore, the majority of queers see their relationship to horror start in childhood, which is reinforced in the oral histories, as narrators discuss connecting with horror when they were young:

> I think my love of horror probably began properly with some of my aunties on my dad's side of the family showing me things that I probably wasn't really supposed to see when I was maybe eight or nine. My aunties showing me films like *Beetlejuice* and *The Addams Family* and things that you can watch as a kid. But the films were slowly

How long have you thought of yourself as a horror fan?

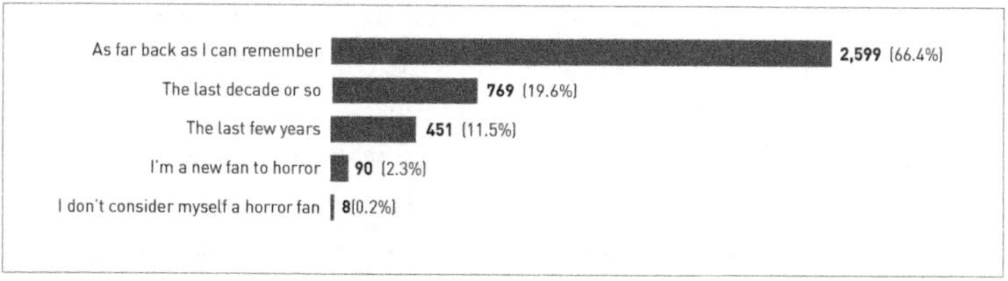

Figure 2.10. Bar graph that indicates how long survey participants have thought of themselves as horror fans.

getting more and more violent and horrific. The *Hellraiser* films. That sort of stuff that slightly older family members would sneak and let you watch and I remember being really really scared but very excited at the same time because you weren't supposed to be doing that. (Thompson, 2020, p. 2)

Ooh, my relationship to the horror genre first blossomed when I was . . . I would say three or four years old. I was obsessed with *Beetlejuice* (Hudson, 2020a, p. 2)

I think my relationship to horror is actually really funny because I think I was born into horror, in a way. My mom went into labor while watching *Cujo* in 1983 [laughs] around 10am or 9am . . . But then, growing up, I realized that I was just so fascinated by horror. (Velasco, 2020, p. 2)

I was always shown horror through my family – they're big horror fans themselves and are very much the type of people who don't really obey the rated R or understand that kids shouldn't see certain things. To them, you know, what doesn't kill you makes you stronger. (Castro, 2020, p. 2)

When I was really young *Scooby-Doo* developed my interest in monster movies and horror comedies. (Colangelo, 2020, p. 2)

Horror was always a part of my life. (Davis, 2020, p. 2)

I grew up with my two youngest aunts and my youngest uncle, and they were teenagers in the nineties. And we all lived together because we're undocumented and we're poor, and we're trying to make it in the United States. So we all lived in one apartment. I remember they were teenagers, and of course they want to watch a horror film, and they're babysitting me so that means that I'm watching it. And so I watched all the Chuckys. I watched *Children of the Corn*. I watched *Pumpkinhead* and watched Freddy. I watched it all and I watched it with them growing up. I mean, I couldn't sleep because I was fear stricken that *that* monster was going to come and get me. But that's how I started watching movies. (Contreras, 2020, p. 6)

> It started as a kid. It started with fear and gradually became an obsession. (Estes, 2020, p. 2)

> Honestly, I can't remember any defining incident – there's no memory that is specific as far as 'that's the moment' when I became interested in all things that were spooky or dark or macabre. I can only remember always liking that stuff, you know, for as far back as my memory goes. (Grannell, 2020a, p. 2)

> My relationship to the horror genre developed in childhood, I think as a lot of people's did. (Varrati, 2020, p. 2)

> It's been a huge part of my life for pretty much my entire life. My parents – my mother in particular – was a *huge* and still is a huge horror movie fan. (Ponder, 2020, p. 2)

> One of my first memories of seeing a movie – it wasn't even like a horror movie but one that was kind of scary that I loved – was my mom taking me to see that *The Brothers Grimm* movie with Heath Ledger. I just remember her taking me and I was really young, and I was scared but it was fun, and it was such a cool story and I thought to myself 'I like this,' 'I want to know more about this,' 'I want to know what else is going on'. (Stodola, 2020, p. 2)

As shown, the majority of queer horror spectators are engaged fans whose relationship with the genre started in childhood. Stated with 99 per cent confidence, 64.4 per cent to 68.3 per cent of *all* horror-loving queers have been horror fans for as far back as they can remember. This study's mixed-method data demonstrates that most queer horror spectators had a childhood relationship to horror and, as a significant counterpoint to the emphases of previous academic studies, the queer spectator does not lose interest in the genre as they age. Unsurprisingly, the survey results show that 59.2 per cent (n = 2,427) of all survey participants first started watching horror films under the age of twelve and that 91.4 per cent (n = 3,746) first started watching horror films by age of seventeen.[20] This data therefore bolsters extant empirical studies about the horror spectator that repeatedly reaffirm a young horror audience (even while privileging the cisheterosexual male subject), such as Tamborini and Stiff, who assert that the horror genre is '*enjoyed more by males and by younger viewers*'

(1987, p. 415; italics in the original). Tamborini and Stiff also reference Leo Handel's 1950 survey results to bolster their claim that horror audiences are young.[21] Vera Dika, while discussing a specific horror audience that was '55 per cent female', goes further to state that the 'audience for the stalker film, as is typical of the horror genre, is overwhelmingly young . . . frequented by adolescents between the ages of twelve and seventeen' (1987, p. 87). Similarly, William Paul writes that 'the predominant audience' for horror is 'young (roughly from adolescence to perhaps the late twenties)' (1994, p. 4). This survey's data supports these findings and goes further to show that the frequency with which participants watch horror films increased (55.3 per cent) or stayed the same (31 per cent) since they first started watching horror films, which either suggests that previous studies over generalised the youth of horror film audiences or, more interestingly and as I surmise, indicates that queer spectators have a more sustained relationship with the horror genre.

Horror as Interpersonal Connection

While this study argues that queer spectators have a distinctive relationship to the horror genre directly connected to their non-normative sexualities and/or genders, notwithstanding, horror serves as a connective bridge between queer people and people outside the queer community. Narrators Gabe Castro and Joe Fejeran affirm that while horror functions as a connective entry point with cisheterosexual people, the queer connection to the genre remains distinct. For Castro, horror offers 'an opportunity to be connected to a group of people and my family, but we were also enjoying [the films] differently' (2020, p. 7). Fejeran explains that horror is 'also a way for, again, as we mentioned that horror as heirloom, it was a way for queer people to connect with their cishet family members and to have that common connection. It's so funny, you know, we – Joshua and I – will go to conventions and we'll talk about loving a particular film that a heterosexual person will love. And we love it for completely different reasons, but we're able to use that connection' (2020, p. 19). The queer spectator's ability to connect with non-queer communities about horror does not diminish or alter the relationship between queerness and the genre, but instead indicates that queer spectators can code-switch in sharing their love of horror with others. Stated differently, queers discuss horror with other queers differently from how they speak to heterosexuals about horror. One explanation for this behaviour could be queer horror fans' passion for horror. Survey participant responses confirm that they are vocal about their love for the genre, with 96.3 per cent (n = 3,949) of them having close friends and 90.2 per cent (n = 3,690) of them having family of origin[22] members know that they are fans of horror films. Survey participants' love of the genre is also found to be common for their close social units, with 85.5 per cent (n = 3,503) of their close friends and/or partner(s) also being interested in horror.[23]

This human connection to horror is further highlighted by the 7.8 per cent of the survey participants who made the effort to write in answers not offered in the question's list of responses when asked about their introduction to horror (see Figure 2.11); the majority of those noted being introduced to the horror genre by parents, grandparents, siblings, aunts, uncles, spouses, babysitters and friends. While films are overwhelmingly the primary gateway to horror for 90.9 per cent (n = 3,733) of participants, many queer spectators are introduced to horror via a human connection. Similarly, Cherry's study ascertained that for female horror viewers '[t]here is a sense in which many feel that the taste for horror is inherited, not in a genetic sense, but in having parents who also liked horror' (1999, p. 210).

While some survey participants shared that their parents and grandparents introduced them to horror, the queer horror inheritance remains distinct (due to distinctly fractured or alienated relationships with first

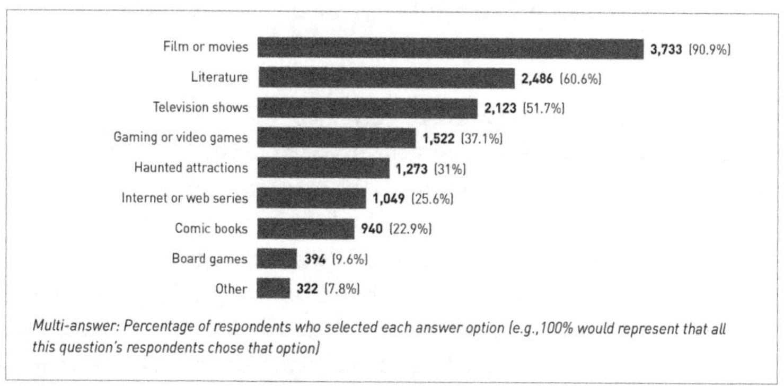

Figure 2.11. Bar graph that shows what started survey participants' interest in the horror genre.

family many queers experience); the majority of narrators discuss coming to the genre on their own, while several mention how their families of origin expressed concern about their taste for horror. The survey data confirms that nearly half, 47.4 per cent, of survey participants who come from families of origin with an opinion about their horror interests, report that their families either reacted with open discouragement or expressed reservations; whereas, 35.5 per cent received encouragement from their families of origin. For those and other queers, horror is inherited from their queer chosen family.[24] Narrator Joe Fejeran emphasises this point when he discusses 'horror as heirloom' and coming to his love of horror through his *Fright School* podcast partner and queer friend Joshua Napier – who inherited his love of horror from his mother (2020, p. 19). Fejeran shares: 'Joshua, in his infinite wisdom, decided to take it upon himself to show me different horror films. And we started to have these really in-depth conversations about horror and why horror is important and what it says about the times in which we're living and about people and all these things' (2020, p. 3). While Napier inherited horror from his family of origin and Fejeran from his chosen family, the survey data and the oral histories confirm that horror is a human connection regardless of how one was introduced to the genre.

Queer Spectators' Horror Genre Knowledge

Queer spectators are knowledgeable about horror films; however, they utilise this information as a point of connection rather than to reinforce differences or establish social hierarchies with others – 83.2 per cent (n = 3,397) of survey participants report that, overall, they consider themselves to have a level of knowledgeability about the genre. Specifically, 73.3 per cent (n = 2,483) of survey participants claim to be 'very knowledgeable' or 'knowledgeable' about horror film. The narratives gathered in the Queer for Fear Oral History Collection also underscore the dexterity with which queer horror fans seamlessly demonstrate their intertextual, extratextual and paratextual horror film knowledge. John Fiske, elaborating on the work of Pierre Bourdieu, notes that 'the accumulation of knowledge is fundamental to the accumulation of cultural capital' (1992, p. 42); however, this study's oral history narratives evidence different ways in which accumulated cultural capital functions for queer people. Their horror film knowledge is not only a mechanism for 'social prestige and self-esteem' (Fiske, 1992, p. 33), but also, distinctly and meaningfully, a source of human-focused connection and method of community-building with other queer horror fans – relationship forging that decentres the capitalistic emphasis of Fiske's theory. In fact, the mixed-method data considered together evidences that queer communities have their own economies of knowledge, with queer horror fandom as a germane part of that. However, a significant aspect of the queer spectator's accrual and use of cultural capital within queer circles is the emotional connection that cultural capital, such as horror knowledge, creates among queers and which holds no proper (or fiscal) function in the cisheterosexual world. Indeed, this study's oral histories exist in part because of an emotional connection between me and the narrators that is steeped in accumulated knowledge about the horror genre – a shared connection of queerness and a love of horror. Narrators and participants accentuate how queers connect with each other through horror:

> When someone who's queer and into horror comes up and we're like – 'we know' – whether I've ever met them in my life or not, there's just certain ways that we're going to talk about those movies. It's like, 'Gurl, you're going to love this and here's why.' It's just an instant connection and that double connection about the horror. There's just information you have about that person. And I think horror is closer to the queer community. A gay person that doesn't like horror, I'm like, 'Hold on!' [laughs] Like, not 'Can I see your papers?' but, you know, something's not quite right there. A gay horror person, I understand a little bit more, but a queer horror person, it's instant family. It's instant intimacy and you're like we're going to a different place. That's going to be already built in. It's already there. (Davis, 2020, p. 10)

> It's funny, I go to this convention in St. Louis called TransWorld – that's what it's called, of all things. It's not for the drag part of my life. It's the largest haunters convention in the world, and it's TransWorld [both laugh]. Isn't that hilarious? And most of the people there are these Midwestern haunters. It's still very much a straight white guy thing, and they have these giant haunted attractions and they roll in. It's the industry standard. But when you're walking around TransWorld and you see another queen, because you share these two things, immediately, there's an attraction like, [gasps] 'Oh, I need to be your friend.' And I love that, that there's still this world where I seek that out because it's not the norm. (Grannell, 2020d, p. 13)

> My love of horror has brought me together with other people. This is embarrassing, but I'm going to say it 'cause it's good for the research. Once I started to own my horror identity [chuckles], own that part of my identity, I put it in my online dating profiles. I just updated everything. It's like, 'I love horror movies!' And then I started to get more responses. I started to realize that as queer people there's that connection, that affinity, that we have for horror. (Fejeran, 2020, p. 19)

> I've found that by connecting with other queer horror fans online I can find people who share my feelings for the genre. (47082733)

> We can share the [horror film] experience in a way that you just can't with het people. (48902723)

These narrators underscore how queer horror fans are always already connected – a connection that relies on a shared queered love of horror despite any intersectional differences.

Queer Identities and Identifications as Queer

Since the majority of queer spectators of horror film understand their queerness to be a lens that alters their horror reactions and preferences, their explicitly queer interactions with the horror genre demonstrate nuanced differences in their opinions, as evidenced through a detailed evaluation of this subgroup through statistical analysis (presenting statistically significant positive and negative correlations in addition to the non-correlative survey data). The survey data reveals that queer spectators who have a conscious awareness that their queerness affects their tastes and provides them with a different lens have an even more distinctive queered relationship to the horror genre. Horror spectators whose queerness creates a different reaction to and taste in horror films are less inclined to enjoy experiencing jump scares, viewing explicit sexual violence and watching people get murdered, and, furthermore, do not experience increased enjoyment from increased gore in a film. When comparing those horror fans who report that their queerness creates a different reaction to horror films (n = 2,339) with the horror-loving queers who feel that being queer influences their taste in horror film (n = 2,290), the data demonstrates a large overlap, with a highly statistically significant relationship and a large effect size

(χ^2 (1) = 1133.022, $p < 0.000$, Cramér's V = 0.526, n = 4,088).[25] In fact, these two groups of horror fans are so aligned that they completely correlate in their agreement or disagreement with opinions about horror films. The survey presented twenty-four statements[26] to understand the horror-loving queer relationship to horror.[27] The results from forty-eight bivariate correlation tests, comparing how queerness affects queer horror fans' reactions and tastes, reveal matching positive or negative correlations for twenty (83.3 per cent) of the statement questions.[28]

Even though the Spearman's rho correlation test does not definitively state how the two examined variables positively or negatively affect one another, at times, the correlation can be ascertained despite the fact that correlations do not indicate directionality or causation. For example, a statistically significant negative correlation exists between perceptions of queerness altering reactions to or tastes in horror and opinions about jump scares. Jump scares affecting queerness are much less plausible than queerness affecting opinions of jump scares. While the 'startle effect or the "jump scare" is, quite easily, the most prevalent somatic effect encouraged and exploited by Horror' (Aldana Reyes, 2016, p. 151), only a slight majority, 51.4 per cent, of survey participants strongly agree or agree that they enjoy 'jump scares' or being startled while watching horror films, with 28.8 per cent strongly disagreeing or disagreeing with that statement. Horror affect – specifically the ubiquitous jump scare – 'is a lot more direct, corporeal and somatic than it is context-dependent' (Aldana Reyes, 2016, p. 18), meaning that bodily reactions may be analysed separately from sociopolitical and psychological contexts. The disentanglement of the affected body from its embodied contexts functions to strip away social, cultural, political and psychological meanings, which, in this case, translates into whether the affected body enjoys the physical reaction or not.[29] A love of the horror genre and having physical 'jump' reactions to startle scares in films does not predicate enjoyment of those 'corporeal and somatic' reactions. While 51.4 per cent of survey participants strongly agree or agree that they enjoy 'jump scares', the queer horror fans whose queerness affects their reactions to and tastes in horror enjoy jump scares less ('different reaction' $r_s = -.07$, $p < 0.000$ and queer 'taste' $r_s = -.07$, $p < 0.000$). Stated differently, queers who report that their queerness alters their reactions to or tastes in horror are less inclined to enjoy jump scares. Similarly, this same subset of queer horror fans had small effect negative correlations with the following statements:

- 'The gorier the horror film, the more I enjoy it' ('different reaction' $r_s = -0.04, p < 0.006$ and queer 'taste' $r_s = -0.05, p < 0.004$).[30]
- 'I like watching people being attacked or killed in horror films' ('different reaction' $r_s = -0.06, p < 0.000$ and queer 'taste' $r_s = -0.08, p < 0.000$).[31]
- 'I am comfortable viewing explicitly sexual violence, such as rape' ('different reaction' $r_s = -0.12, p < 0.000$ and queer 'taste' $r_s = -0.11, p < 0.000$).

This negative correlations data demonstrates that horror films do not function solely as vehicles for queer spectators to enjoy watching people being attacked or killed; the queer spectators who consciously report that their queerness alters their horror opinions and tastes are less inclined to love a horror film because of jump scares, gore or sexual violence. This data indicates that the 'obvious' aspects of the horror genre, overall, hold less appeal to horror's queer spectatorial majority who report a queer lens, which suggests that horror gives these queer spectators a more subtle and queer connection, such as coded or subtextual identification with the monster, the victim and/or the final girl.

The following positive correlations evidence that queer spectators who understand their queerness affects their reactions to and tastes in horror are more inclined to strongly agree with the majority of the following presented statement questions. Queer spectators whose queerness affects their reactions to and tastes in horror have small and medium, yet highly statistically significant positive correlations with the following statements:

- 'Horror films are cathartic' ('different reaction' $r_s = 0.17, p < 0.000$ and queer 'taste' $r_s = 0.16, p < 0.000$).
- 'Horror films help me face my fears' ('different reaction' $r_s = 0.13, p < 0.000$ and queer 'taste' $r_s = 0.12, p < 0.000$).
- 'Horror films help me work through trauma' ('different reaction' $r_s = 0.20, p < 0.000$ and queer 'taste' $r_s = 0.19, p < 0.000$).
- 'Horror films let me use my imagination' ('different reaction' $r_s = 0.07, p < 0.000$ and queer 'taste' $r_s = 0.06, p < 0.000$).
- 'Horror films make me laugh' ('different reaction' $r_s = 0.11, p < 0.000$ and queer 'taste' $r_s = 0.09, p < 0.000$).
- 'Horror films are more frightening than they used to be' ('different reaction' $r_s = 0.52, p < 0.001$ and queer 'taste' $r_s = 0.06, p < 0.000$).

- '21st-century horror films are too violent and gory' ('different reaction' $r_s = 0.07$, $p < 0.000$ and queer 'taste' $r_s = 0.06$, $p < 0.000$).
- 'I like horror films with a queer protagonist or character' ('different reaction' $r_s = 0.26$, $p < 0.000$ and queer 'taste' $r_s = 0.27$, $p < 0.000$).
- 'I most enjoy watching horror films with queer audiences' ('different reaction' $r_s = 0.34$, $p < 0.000$ and queer 'taste' $r_s = 0.35$, $p < 0.000$).
- 'I enjoy "camp-y" horror films' ('different reaction' $r_s = 0.16$, $p < 0.000$ and queer 'taste' $r_s = 0.17$, $p < 0.000$).
- 'There is too much heterosexual sex in horror films' ('different reaction' $r_s = 0.18$, $p < 0.000$ and queer 'taste' $r_s = 0.14$, $p < 0.000$).
- 'I watch horror films as a form of escapism' ('different reaction' $r_s = 0.09$, $p < 0.000$ and queer 'taste' $r_s = 0.07$, $p < 0.000$).
- 'I often relate to "the monster" in horror films' ('different reaction' $r_s = 0.25$, $p < 0.000$ and queer 'taste' $r_s = 0.22$, $p < 0.000$).
- 'I watch horror films for the special/practical/visual effects and make-up' ('different reaction' $r_s = 0.07$, $p < 0.000$ and queer 'taste' $r_s = 0.08$, $p < 0.000$).
- 'I empathise with or relate to the heroine/hero/final girl' ('different reaction' $r_s = 0.14$, $p < 0.000$ and queer 'taste' $r_s = 0.16$, $p < 0.000$).
- 'I have to shut my eyes/hide my face during horror films' ('different reaction' $r_s = 0.04$, $p < 0.013$ and queer 'taste' $r_s = 0.06$, $p < 0.000$).

This data indicates that, for the majority of queer horror spectators, the horror genre functions as a form of escapism, a cathartic release valve and a trauma processor (a topic that will be further examined in Chapter 3); horror films help queer horror fans face and deal with their fears. Queers also have a preference for explicitly queer representation and interactions, both liking horror films with queer characters and enjoying watching horror films with queer audiences. Queer horror fans relate to the monster and empathise with the final girl. Moreover, they have a preference for campy horror and, accordingly, tend to laugh at horror films. Queer horror fans think there is too much heterosexual sex in horror and they love special effects. These statistical correlations suggest that spectators who have consciousness of their queer lens (which, as a reminder, is the majority of horror's queer spectators based on extrapolation from this survey's data) also have a different relationship to horror. These queer spectators are less inclined to enjoy horror simply for the sex, violence and gore, and are more inclined to queerly, intellectually and imaginatively relate to the genre for its therapeutic functions, camp aesthetic, intentional (and unintentional) humour and relatable depictions of monstrosity *and* survival.

Queer Horror Spectators Compared with Female Horror Fans

Understanding how and why queer spectators uniquely connect with horror through this extensive mixed-method data set is furthered when compared with existing data on female horror fans. The significant study on female horror fandom by Brigid Cherry, completed in 1999, provides a direct comparative to determine any statistical differences between queer and female horror fans in their horror opinions. Ultimately, this study's data patently demonstrates that queer horror fans are a distinct subgroup of horror fans compared with the mostly heterosexual participants of Cherry's study. The vast majority of the queer spectator's data differs significantly from Cherry's data on female horror fans in which 'the majority of the respondents are heterosexual' (1999, p. 149), buttressing the argument for a *sui generis* relationship that queers have with the horror genre. The queer relationship to horror manifests in enjoying being immersed in some of the affects that are designed to scare people because horror provides queer spectators with a way to assuage the pain from life's challenges. The vast majority of queer spectators, then, have an elemental connection to the genre by gaining relief from life's ennui through the suspense, tension and frights in horror films. In fact, survey participants strongly agree or agree with the following statements:

- 93 per cent (n = 3,794) report, 'I like horror films with lots of suspense and/or tension'.
- 89.6 per cent (n = 3,660) report, 'I enjoy being frightened by horror films'.
- 84.8 per cent (n = 3,461) report, 'Horror films relieve the tedium of my everyday life'.

- 53.9 per cent ($n = 2,196$) report, 'I prefer horror films in which "the monster" is hidden or unseen'.

In comparison, Cherry's surveyed female horror fans also enjoy suspense and frights but do not use horror to relieve the tedium of everyday life in the same proportion, and more interestingly, in the same way as horror-loving queers. 47.7 per cent of the female horror fans agree strongly or agree with the statement that horror films relieve the tedium of their everyday life, and 31.8 per cent disagree strongly or disagree, whereas only 3.8 per cent of queer participants in this study strongly disagree or disagree with the same statement. This differential between female and queer survey participants distinguishes how the overwhelming majority of queer horror fans uniquely find relief through horror. 94 per cent of the below statement questions received majority consensus opinions from *all* the survey participants, whereas the female horror fans of Cherry's study reached consensus on only half of the questions. In all, the responses from queer horror fans demonstrate a distinctive difference between queer and female horror fans (including questions without a majority consensus opinion):

- 94 per cent of queer participants strongly agree or agree that horror films let them use their imagination, with only 1 per cent strongly disagreeing or disagreeing with that statement (compared with 73.1 per cent of female horror fans agreeing strongly or agreeing and 12.1 per cent disagreeing strongly or disagreeing).
- 93 per cent of queer participants strongly agree or agree that they like horror films with a lot of suspense and/or tension, with only 1.4 per cent strongly disagreeing or disagreeing with that statement (compared with 91.7 per cent of female horror fans agreeing strongly or agreeing and 3.7 per cent disagreeing strongly or disagreeing).
- 89.6 per cent of queer participants strongly agree or agree that they enjoy being frightened by horror films, with only 2.7 per cent strongly disagreeing or disagreeing with that statement (compared with 73.1 per cent of female horror fans agreeing strongly or agreeing and 19.4 per cent disagreeing strongly or disagreeing).
- 87.5 per cent of queer participants strongly agree or agree that they like horror films with a queer protagonist or character,

with only 0.6 per cent strongly disagreeing or disagreeing with that statement (no comparative data).

- 84.8 per cent of queer participants strongly agree or agree that horror films relieve the tedium of everyday life, with only 3.8 per cent strongly disagreeing or disagreeing with that statement (compared with 47.7 per cent of female horror fans agreeing strongly or agreeing and 31.8 per cent disagreeing strongly or disagreeing).
- 82.9 per cent of queer participants strongly agree or agree that they watch horror films as a form of escapism, with only 5.9 per cent strongly disagreeing or disagreeing with that statement (compared with 54.2 per cent of female horror fans agreeing strongly or agreeing and 28.4 per cent disagreeing strongly or disagreeing).
- 80.4 per cent of queer participants strongly agree or agree that they enjoy 'camp-y' horror films, with only 6 per cent strongly disagreeing or disagreeing with that statement (no comparative data).
- 73.5 per cent of queer participants strongly agree or agree that horror films make them laugh, with only 8.1 per cent strongly disagreeing or disagreeing with that statement (compared with 40.8 per cent of female horror fans agreeing strongly or agreeing and 32.4 per cent disagreeing strongly or disagreeing).
- 69.3 per cent of queer participants strongly agree or agree that they watch horror films for the special/practical/visual effects and make-up, with only 11.4 per cent strongly disagreeing or disagreeing with that statement (compared with 29.4 per cent of female horror fans agreeing strongly or agreeing and 34.8 per cent disagreeing strongly or disagreeing).
- 67.9 per cent of queer participants strongly agree or agree that they empathise with or relate to the heroine/hero/final girl, with only 8.2 per cent strongly disagreeing or disagreeing with that statement (compared with 16.5 per cent of female horror fans agreeing strongly or agreeing and 46.7 per cent disagreeing strongly or disagreeing).[32]
- 61.4 per cent of queer participants strongly agree or agree that there is too much heterosexual sex in horror films, with only 10 per cent strongly disagreeing or disagreeing with that statement (no comparative data).

- 59 per cent of queer participants strongly agree or agree that horror films help them face their fears, with only 12.5 per cent strongly disagreeing or disagreeing with that statement (compared with 21.5 per cent of female horror fans agreeing strongly or agreeing and 45.8 per cent disagreeing strongly or disagreeing).
- 54 per cent of queer participants strongly agree or agree that they most enjoy watching horror films with queer audiences, with only 4.6 per cent strongly disagreeing or disagreeing with that statement (no comparative data).
- 53.9 per cent of queer participants strongly agree or agree that they prefer horror films in which 'the monster' is hidden or unseen, with only 11 per cent strongly disagreeing or disagreeing with that statement (compared with 27.7 per cent of female horror fans agreeing strongly or agreeing and 42.6 per cent disagreeing strongly or disagreeing).
- 25.8 per cent of queer participants strongly agree or agree that they have to shut their eyes/hide their face during horror films, with a majority 54.4 per cent strongly disagreeing or disagreeing with that statement (compared with 19.2 per cent of female horror fans agreeing strongly or agreeing and 67 per cent disagreeing strongly or disagreeing).
- 17.4 per cent of queer participants strongly agree or agree that they are comfortable viewing explicitly sexual violence, such as rape, with 64.6 per cent, a majority, strongly disagreeing or disagreeing with that statement (no comparative data).
- 45 per cent of queer participants strongly agree or agree that they often relate to 'the monster' in horror films, with 19.7 per cent strongly disagreeing or disagreeing with that statement (compared with 21.1 per cent of female horror fans agreeing strongly or agreeing and 55 per cent disagreeing strongly or disagreeing).[33]

These statistical comparisons between the queer horror spectator and female horror fans indicate that queers, overall, demonstrate a more therapeutic relationship with the genre, experiencing beneficial alleviations, character identifications and imaginative connections through horror. Even though cisgender heterosexual women face marginalisation, discrimination and oppression in a patriarchal system, the data does not indicate that those women turn to horror for therapeutic relief. This comparative data further underscores the primary argument of this study that queer spectators have a distinctive relationship with the horror genre specifically due to their queer embodiment.

Non-Cinematic Modes of Horror Consumption

The preponderance of queer horror fans engage with the horror genre beyond simply watching horror films. This following list of extras enjoyed by queer horror fans intimates that queer spectators seek to understand both textual and extratextual information about horror films. The majority of queer horror spectators enjoy horror film 'extras', including:

- 71.3 per cent (*n* = 2,838) enjoy 'deleted scenes'.
- 67.9 per cent (*n* = 2,701) enjoy '"making of . . ." documentaries'.
- 61.3 per cent (*n* = 2,440) enjoy 'outtakes/bloopers'.
- 58.5 per cent (*n* = 2,326) enjoy 'Easter eggs'.
- 56.2 per cent (*n* = 2,235) enjoy 'behind-the-scenes footage'.
- 56.0 per cent (*n* = 2,226) enjoy 'director's cuts'.
- 52.8 per cent (*n* = 2,102) enjoy 'special/visual/digital effects footage'.

This textual and extratextual engagement further bolsters claims about the queer spectator's horror knowledge, as discussed previously in this chapter.

Queer Spectators and International Horror

The queer spectator's love of horror extends to a love of horror film beyond a fan's home country, demonstrating that queer spectators form a transnational fandom interested in international horror texts, with 86 per cent (*n* = 3,521) of queer horror fans, the vast majority, watching horror films from different countries around the world (see Figure 2.12). The majority of survey participants watch horror films from Japan (81.5 per cent), the United States (78.2 per cent), the United Kingdom (74.2 per cent), Canada (57.1 per cent), South Korea (54.7 per cent), Australia

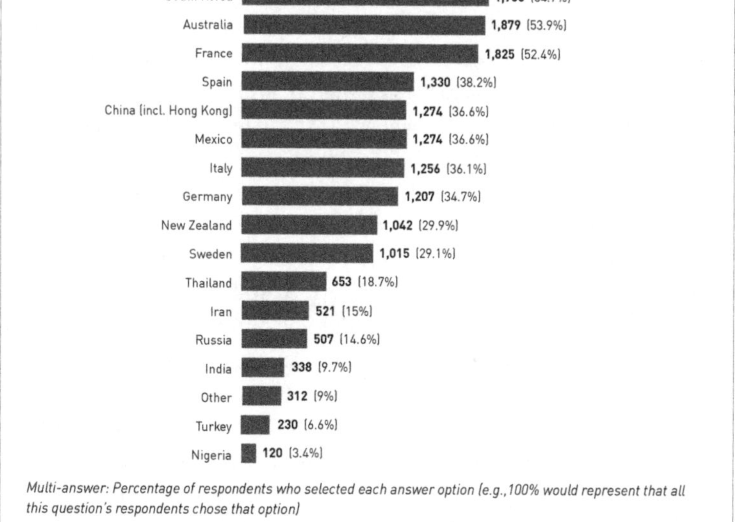

Figure 2.12. Bar graph that displays from which production countries survey participants report watching horror films.

(53.9 per cent) and France (52.4 per cent). Stephen Follows reports: 'By an overwhelming majority, the US produces more horror films than any other country in the world', and that the 'UK, Canada and Japan are unsurprisingly the next largest producers of horror' (2017, p. 62). Correspondingly, Japan (81.5 per cent), the United States (78.2 per cent), the United Kingdom (74.2 per cent) and Canada (57.1 per cent), the top four countries that produce horror films, are also the top countries from which queer horror fans watch horror films.[34] In sum, the data indicates that the queer spectator is internationalist in their horror-viewing habits, actively engaging with cultural manifestations of horror that may be different from their own.

Cinemagoing and Queer Spectators

This survey's data reveals that a significant portion of the queer population is among the most engaged cinemagoers, undoubtedly demonstrating that horror-loving queers are a fervent collective of cinephiles. The GLAAD Studio Responsibility Index report states that queers 'are a significant [cinemagoing] audience' (2020, p. 8), while the Motion Picture Association reports: 'Eleven percent of the U.S./Canada population are frequent moviegoers who attend the cinema once a month or more' (2020, p. 27). Survey results for this study, in fact, evidence that a remarkable 47.7 per cent of survey participants are 'frequent moviegoers' who go to the cinema once a month or more. Furthermore, this project's survey found that 28.7 per cent of survey participants watch horror films at the cinema or movie theatre a few times a month or more – nearly triple the 11 per cent of the general population who are frequent cinemagoers. As will be discussed in Chapter 4, queer spectators find sanctuary in both the filmic medium and the cinemagoing experience. Beyond horror films, survey participants enjoy many other genres, with 80.1 per cent watching thriller/suspense films, 76.3 per cent watching science-fiction films, 65.4 per cent watching fantasy films, 65.1 per cent watching comedy films and 63.2 per cent watching documentary films.[35] The predominance of survey participants also watch narrative (86.4 per cent) and documentary (79 per cent) films that are explicitly categorised as LGBTQ+. Inversely, only 2.9 per cent of survey participants watch sports films, 10.7 per cent watch war films, 13.9 per cent watch westerns, 23.1 per cent watch family films and 26.8 per cent watch romance films, rounding out the bottom five genres. Queer spectators are not only ardent horror spectators but also cinephiles who enjoy a wide range of film genres, barring the least watched that are arguably the most emblematic of patriarchal cisheteronormativity: sports, war, westerns, family and romance.

Horror Habits Beyond Film Spectatorship

Queer spectators of horror are regular cinemagoers, avid readers and social media users who actively engage in horror fandom, including enjoying horror in other media. This supports the fandom data reported earlier in this chapter that demonstrates queer horror fans are passionate about horror. Queer horror fans not only love film but are also socially engaged with the genre, as 77.8 per cent (n = 3,190) of survey participants follow horror accounts on social media.[36] Additionally, 65 per cent both actively ('read and comment' *n* = 742) and passively ('read only' *n* = 1,922) participate in fan forums, fan websites, online blogs and/or Facebook groups about horror. Significantly, all narrators interviewed are queer horror fans who explicitly *and* implicitly participate in horror fandom's cultural production as artists, podcasters, public programmers, performers, writers and/or content creators.[37] Creating a podcast, making art, writing blog posts and articles and curating a social media feed 'requires explicit action to participate in a community and consciously produce media texts and artefacts', while double-tapping or liking a photo or post 'exists below the threshold of explicit participation and goes beyond mere participation in a surrounding culture' (Schäfer, 2011, p. 44). These explicit and implicit forms of participation further underscore a distinctive engagement that queers have with the horror genre. The queer spectator's horror engagement, in fact, extends beyond a single medium, with 80.8 per cent (*n* = 3,284) of survey participants also watching and/or streaming horror genre television (including web television) programmes. As well, 69.5 per cent of these survey participants watch horror shows once a month or more, with 31.3 per cent watching them once a week or more. Moreover, queer horror spectators are horror bingers, as 80.5 per cent (*n* = 2,027) regularly binge new horror shows and/or new seasons of existing horror series.

The queer spectator's love for horror is not limited to moving images but extends to other subjects and art forms, including literature. A formidable 77.8 per cent of survey participants list reading as an activity they regularly enjoy; 75.7 per cent (*n* = 3,106) of those read horror and/or Gothic fiction, with 77.5 per cent (*n* = 3,148) specifying that horror is their top genre to read, followed by LGBTQ+ books (64.4 per cent) and graphic novels (60.8 per cent). Comparatively, Cherry found that for female horror fans reading is an 'extremely popular pastime' and reported that 47 per cent of female participants selected reading as a hobby/interest, with horror being the number one genre to read, followed by fantasy and science fiction (1999, p. 81). Another subject that queer spectators are passionate about is Halloween. Since 'Halloween is widely celebrated as a gay high holy holiday' (Skal, 2016, p. 124), unsurprisingly, 74.7 per cent (*n* = 2,950) of survey participants are interested in Halloween, Samhain and the Day of the Dead. Further, a majority of queer spectators are also interested in the following subjects:

- 73 per cent (*n* = 2,883) have an interest in real-life haunted places.

- 66.7 per cent (n = 2,635) have an interest in true crime and serial killers.
- 64.9 per cent (n = 2,564) have an interest in witchcraft.
- 63.1 per cent (n = 2,491) have an interest in entertainment haunted attractions/haunts.
- 52.3 per cent (n = 2,064) have an interest in tarot.
- 50.1 per cent (n = 1,977) have an interest in pagan religions.

Even though horror film is the genesis of the queer spectator's interest in the horror genre, the queer ontological connection to horror develops over time and finds more outlets in other media. In other words, the queer love of horror bleeds into other arts and interests. Collectively, this data evidences that queers connect to the 'horrific', 'haunted' and 'spooky' in myriad manifestations, with the majority of survey participants watching horror television, reading horror literature, experiencing haunted houses and places, celebrating Halloween, following horror on social media, being interested in witchcraft and hooking into true crime.

Violence, Gore and Tension

While queer spectators are not attracted to horror simply for the genre's 'obvious' elements such as jump scares and gore, they are, nevertheless, comfortable with the presence of many of these elements in the genre. The data evidences that the vast majority of queer spectators of horror watch films with tension, suspense, gore and graphic physical violence. Queer spectators are 'very comfortable' or 'comfortable' with horror film's common affects such as tension and/or suspense (94.3 per cent), gore (78.6 per cent) and graphic physical violence (76.7 per cent). Specifically, 74.8 per cent (n = 3,065) of survey participants across all demographics declared being 'very comfortable' with tension and/or suspense in horror films, with a further 19.5 per cent (n = 799) 'comfortable'.[38] Of survey participants across all demographics, 48.2 per cent (n = 1,978) report being 'very comfortable' with gore in horror films, and a further 30.4 per cent (n = 1,246) as 'comfortable',[39] while 36.4 per cent (n = 1,495) of survey participants across all demographics state they are 'very comfortable' with graphic physical violence in horror films, with a further 40.3 per cent (n = 1,655) selecting 'comfortable'.[40] Conversely, a significant percentage of queer spectators both do not like horror for and are not comfortable with the presence of sexual violence – 41.8 per cent (*n* = 1,714) of survey participants are 'not at all comfortable' with graphic sexual violence in horror films, and only 23.4 per cent are 'very comfortable' (*n* = 374) or 'comfortable' (*n* = 588) with graphic sexual violence.[41] I hypothesise that the element of sexual violence in horror film is not appealing or comfortable for queer spectators because of the prevalent and pervasive sexual or sexuality-related traumas that queer people experience in cisheteronormative society, although a consequential number of queer spectators of horror use numerous generic elements, including graphic sexual violence, to work through trauma, a topic that will be addressed in Chapter 3.[42]

Horror Subgenres

Queer spectators can be understood, per this survey's data, to not only be comfortable with a large number of horror's generic elements, but to also engage enthusiastically with a broad range of horror subgenres. This further evidences their fundamental passion for the genre as a whole, in

	Queer horror spectators	Female horror fans	Queer horror spectators	Female horror fans
	Love/like	**Like all/most**	**Hate/dislike**	**Dislike all/most**
Psychological	93.2% (*n* = 3,812)	81% (*n* = 85)	1.5% (*n* = 62)	2.9% (*n* = 3)
Supernatural/ occult/ghost	91.6% (*n* = 3,743)	85.7% (*n* = 90)	2.4% (*n* = 98)	2.9% (*n* = 3)
Witchcraft	88.9% (*n* = 3,626)	68.3% (*n* = 71)	1.5% (*n* = 62)	7.7% (*n* = 8)
Sci-fi horror	86.4% (*n* = 3,531)	74% (*n* = 77)	3.2% (*n* = 133)	5.8% (*n* = 6)
Monster	86% (*n* = 3,513)	55.8% (*n* = 58)	2.4% (*n* = 99)	13.5% (*n* = 14)
Vampire	78.8% (*n* = 3,220)	92.4% (*n* = 97)	5.4% (*n* = 220)	1% (*n* = 1)
Horror comedy or parody	76.3% (*n* = 3,122)	59.4% (*n* = 63)	9% (*n* = 368)	21.7% (*n* = 23)
Serial killer	75.8% (*n* = 3,098)	53.3% (*n* = 56)	8.4% (*n* = 341)	24.8% (*n* = 26)
Slasher	72.7% (*n* = 2,967)	25% (*n* = 25)	12.4% (*n* = 507)	54% (*n* = 54)
Zombie/ living dead	70.7% (*n* = 2,887)	54.4% (*n* = 56)	11.7% (*n* = 480)	18.4% (*n* = 19)

Figure 2.13. Chart that compares the top ten horror subgenres between this study's survey participants and Brigid Cherry's study of female horror fans.

contrast to findings from Cherry's study of female horror fans. Adam Scales notes about Cherry's (1999) findings that 'female audiences favour more subtle horror forms such as the vampire or occult/supernatural over the more gory splatter counterparts' (2015, p. 186). Scales further suggests that 'there is evidence to suggest that a substantial number of gay fans claim to consume . . . more "serious" or hard-core forms of horror privileged by straight fans' (2015, p. 186). For his analysis, Scales analysed gay online forum posts and comments, a netnographic method that can inadvertently privilege performative masculinity and thereby occlude the complete picture of the types of horror that queers prefer.[43]

This project's survey, however, has found that queer horror fans love films from all subgenres of horror (see Figure 2.13). Each survey participant was presented with options in order to select how much they like or dislike each of the twenty-two proffered horror categories/subgenres.[44] The following list accounts for the subgenres that the vast majority of queer spectators of horror love or like:

- psychological (93.2 per cent);
- supernatural/occult/ghost (91.6 per cent);
- witchcraft (88.9 per cent);
- sci-fi horror (86.4 per cent);
- monster (86 per cent);
- vampire (78.8 per cent);
- horror comedy or parody (76.3 per cent);
- serial killer (75.8 per cent);
- slasher (72.7 per cent);
- zombie/living dead (70.7 per cent);
- possession (69.3 per cent);
- werewolf (67.8 per cent);
- body horror (66 per cent);[45] and
- Universal horror (64.4 per cent).

As such, the majority of queer spectators love or like sixteen out of the twenty-two presented horror film subgenres, suggesting that the queer relationship to horror encompasses most horror subgenres. Only rape revenge films had more survey participants who hate or dislike the subgenre (45.6 per cent) than those who love or like it (22.5 per cent). Although a love for various horror subgenres is not exclusive to queer horror fans, the survey data indicates that queers experience a distinctly queer connection.

A brief analysis of the top three most beloved subgenres – psychological, supernatural/occult/ghost and witchcraft films – elucidates how queers may relate to the subgenres differently. For example, people with non-conforming sexualities and genders have a long history of being psychologically pathologised,[46] and coming to terms with one's queerness can be an internal psychological battle. Therefore, queer people find a connection to films that present psychological horrors as an outlet for the investigation of their traumas. When Darryl Jones points out that '[g]hosts are time out of joint' (2018, p. 80), he inadvertently highlights a queer temporality exhibited by supernatural and ghost films, a temporality that may resonate differently for queer film spectators who embody an existence outside the norm, including some rituals and institutions reinforced through religious traditions. As such, witchcraft is antecedent to institutional religion and, as Cynthia Barounis explains, 'has long been associated with queer sexual deviance and feminist rebellion' (2018, p. 232). Queers seemingly connect to these three beloved horror subgenres – psychological, supernatural/occult/ghost and witchcraft – in decisively queer ways through their non-normative consciousness, haunted sense of time and embodied resistance.

While Benshoff and Griffin determine that the 'vampire film has been especially meaningful to queer spectators' (2006, p. 76) and numerous scholars have analysed the vampire as queer (see, e.g., Case, Dyer, Zimmerman, Aldana Reyes and Sorcha Ní Fhlainn), queer spectators do not exhibit a strong preference for vampire films over other horror subgenres. Queer horror fans also have a stronger favourable opinion of most horror film categories/subgenres than the female horror participants in Cherry's study, with the exception of vampire films (Cherry's data shows that women like these films at a higher percentage than the queer spectator). Since vampire films were '[b]y far the most popular type of horror film' in Cherry's study, with 92.4 per cent of female horror fans liking all or most vampire films, the segmentation of the data from cis women, cis men, trans women, trans men, genderqueer women and genderqueer men who selected only a single gender identity was analysed to determine if women do indeed much prefer vampire films (1999, p. 88). This study's results show nominal differences, with 80.3 per cent of cis women (n = 1,077), 77.4 per cent of cis men (n = 934), 79.5 per cent of trans women (n = 116), 74.2 per cent of trans men (n = 247), 80.8 per cent of genderqueer women (n = 235) and 82.7 per cent of genderqueer men (n = 158) loving or liking vampire films. This data establishes that horror-loving queers, inclusive of queer women, are distinct from the mostly heterosexual female respondents of Cherry's study, with those female horror fans being more ardent lovers of vampire films. Moreover, the vast majority of queer horror fans, across the gender spectrum, love or like supernatural/occult/ghost films. Carol Clover speculates 'that occult films have a greater share of female viewers than other sorts of horror (there are no reliable statistics)' (1992, p. 65). The same gender breakdown, again, shows nominal gendered differences, with 92.3 per cent of cis women (n = 1,238), 92.2 per cent of cis men (n = 1,113), 82.9 per cent of trans women (n = 121), 85.6 per cent of trans men (n = 285), 90.4 per cent of genderqueer women (n = 263) and 90.1 per cent of genderqueer men (n = 172) loving or liking supernatural/occult/ghost films.[47] These statistics evidence that queer women indeed love or like supernatural/occult/ghost films, affirming Clover's speculation; however, this study's data overall demonstrates that *all* queers love or like supernatural/occult/ghost films.

Theoretical and empirical research has, until now, most often placed the emphasis on determining the maleness and youthfulness of the slasher audience; however, this study's survey data indicates that there is no correlation between age[48] and loving or liking slasher films ($p < 0.193$).[49] Historical documentation shows that women have long enjoyed slashers; indeed, Aljean Harmetz, Hollywood correspondent of *The New York Times*, reported in 1980 that 45 per cent of the audience for canon slashers *Halloween* and *Friday the 13th* were teenagers (aged twelve to seventeen) that 'breaks down as 45 percent male and 55 percent female' (C15). Yet previous scholarship focused on data that demonstrates (assumed cisheterosexual) women do not like slasher films. For example, in Cherry's study, 'the most disliked horror film type is the slasher film of which 54 per cent of the respondents who express a preference dislike all or most examples of the type' (1999, p. 88). However, this study's data on queer spectator's preferences for slasher film shows that 68.7 per cent of cis women (n = 921), 84.2 per cent of cis men (n = 1,016), 61 per cent of trans women (n = 89), 67.9 per cent of trans men (n = 226), 67.7 per cent of genderqueer women (n = 197) and 73.3 per cent of genderqueer men (n = 140) love or like slasher films. While cis men show a preference for slasher films, this project's survey data indicates that not only the large majority of cis, trans and genderqueer women love or like slashers, but also only 15.1 per cent of cis women, 19.2 per cent of trans women and 16.8 per cent of genderqueer women hate or dislike slashers, which further demonstrates a distinct difference between queer horror fans and the (assumed) cisheterosexual subjects of prior empirical research. The subgenre of witchcraft films reveals a nominal difference between the two cisgender identities, with 91.7 per cent of cis women (*n* = 1,230) and 89.6 per cent of cis men (*n* = 1,081) loving or liking witchcraft films. Regardless of gender binary or cisgender comparisons or dissensions, collectively the majority of queer horror spectators have a broad and collective love or like of most horror categories and subgenres.

The Favourite Horror Films of Queer Spectators

As is the case with the queer spectator's penchant for a wide range of horror subgenres, a review of queer spectators' favourite horror films reveals that, while there is some generalised consensus of beloved horror films, the queer relationship to the horror genre takes precedence over individual films, as survey participants report a great deal of variability in their favourite horror films (see Figure 2.14). Stated differently, queers distinctively and explicitly connect with the horror genre, yet that connection is fostered and maintained in innumerable ways, and is not based or centred on queer horror films. While the top twenty-five favourite films are a combination of horror canon and recent successes, the diverse list includes films from many eras across six decades, multiple subgenres and numerous production countries. This constitution of a 'favourites' list is typical, as Alice M. Mitchell, who completed a groundbreaking empirical audience study in the 1920s, explains: 'From the data gathered from the 10,052 children for the present study it seems apparent that the kind of movie a child likes best and the ones which stand out most vividly in his mind are of two classes: those which he recently has seen and those large, important films' (Mitchell, quoted in Fleming, 2016, p. 133). My data substantiates this determination, demonstrating a very similar human proclivity. Horror certainly has an established canon, with a collection of established and commonly beloved films. The survey participants' lists of twenty-five favourite horror films reflect a collected mix of those established and beloved canonical horror films, such as *Halloween* (1978) and *The Shining* (1980), alongside recent commercial or critical horror successes, such as *Get Out* (2017) and *The Babadook* (2014). This is replicated with the female horror fans who completed Cherry's survey; the favourite film list is a combination of horror canon, such as *Psycho* (1960) and *Night of the Living Dead* (1968), and then-recent productions, such as *Interview with the Vampire* (1994) and

Bram Stoker's Dracula (1992) (1999, p. 243). When asked to list their five favourite horror films, an average of 3,774 queer participants responded, making a final list of 18,870 films.[50] This list features nearly 1,500 different and diverse international horror films from every era, demonstrating that the complete list of queer spectators' favourite horror films is much more idiosyncratic than the top twenty-five favourite films indicate.

The large number of films listed, however, did not lead to needing much consensus to determine the top of the list. *Alien* (1979) obtained the number one favourite film slot for queer spectators because 670 survey participants listed *Alien* as a favourite film. This constitutes 17.8 per cent consensus on the favourite horror film; conversely, 82.2 per cent of survey participants did not choose *Alien* as their favourite horror film, further indicating that specific films matter less than the entire horror genre. To further evidence the argument that individual horror films do not stand out over the genre as a whole for queer spectators, I examined the data from five mutually exclusive[51] gender identities through a tabulation of the top five favourite horror film lists for cis women (n = 1,257), cis men (n = 1,165), trans women (n = 105), trans men (n = 207) and non-binary (n = 356) survey participants (see Figure 2.15). The number one favourite film slot for each of the five gender identity groupings was determined by a low minority of responses, with an average of only 22.3 per cent consensus needed to reach the number one favourite horror film for that gender identity.[52] These results further support the conclusion that queer spectators share a large consensus in their love for the horror genre, but not for specific films.

The range in era and subgenre for the top twenty-five favourite horror films for survey participants additionally indicates the holistic and far-reaching passion queer spectators have for the horror genre. The top twenty-five films are predominantly US modern[53] horror films that are not explicitly queer. The top favourite horror film list accurately reflects queer horror fans' favourite subgenres, representing psychological, supernatural/occult/ghost, sci-fi horror, slasher, witchcraft films and so on. The nominal variation in survey participants' favourite horror films further indicates that the queer connection to horror exists at the generic level.

Figure 2.14. Chart that displays survey participants' top twenty-five favourite horror films.

Rank	Film	Count
1	*Alien* (1979)	670
2	*Halloween* (1978)	604
3	*Scream* (1996)	484
4	*Hereditary* (2018)	465
5	*A Nightmare on Elm Street* (1984)	450
6	*Get Out* (2017)	413
7	*The Thing* (1982)	409
8	*The Exorcist* (1973)	357
9	*The Witch* (2015)	326
10	*The Shining* (1980)	311
11	*The Texas Chain Saw Massacre* (1974)	295
12	*Hellraiser* (1987)	292
13	*Suspiria* (1977)	291
14	*The Conjuring* (2013)	274
15	*It* (2017)	237
16	*The Silence of the Lambs* (1991)	235
17	*The Cabin in the Woods* (2011)	222
18	*Us* (2019)	221
19	*It Follows* (2014)	210
20	*The Babadook* (2014)	206
21	*The Evil Dead* (1981)	179
22	*Friday the 13th* (1980)	169
23	*Carrie* (1976)	162
24	*The Descent* (2005)	158
25	*Psycho* (1960)	156

Figure 2.15. Chart that presents survey participants' top ten favourite horror films, delineated by gender identity.

Cis women (n = 1,257)	**Cis men** (n = 1,165)
Alien	*Halloween*
Get Out	*Alien*
Hereditary	*Scream*
Scream	*A Nightmare on Elm Street*
Halloween	*The Exorcist*
A Nightmare on Elm Street	*Hereditary*
The Witch	*The Texas Chain Saw Massacre*
The Exorcist	*Suspiria*
The Shining	*The Thing*
The Thing	*Hellraiser*

Trans women (n = 105)	**Trans men** (n = 207)	**Non-binary** (n = 356)
Alien	*The Thing*	*Alien*
The Thing	*Hereditary*	*Get Out*
Get Out	*Alien*	*Halloween*
Hereditary	*Get Out*	*The Thing*
Hellraiser	*A Nightmare on Elm Street*	*Hereditary*
Suspiria	*Halloween*	*Scream*
Evil Dead II	*The Texas Chain Saw Massacre*	*Us*
The Witch	*Scream*	*The Witch*
Us	*Us*	*The Exorcist*
The Babadook (3-way tie)	*The Conjuring* (3-way tie)	*It*
It Follows (3-way tie)	*Hellraiser* (3-way tie)	
The Texas Chain Saw Massacre (3-way tie)	*Friday the 13th* (3-way tie)	

The fact that the top twenty-five films range across six decades speaks to the power of the horror canon and, as cultural critic Mark Fisher explains, demonstrates that 'the very distinction between past and present is breaking down. In 1981, the 1960s seemed much further away than they do today. Since then, cultural time has folded back on itself, and the impression of linear development has given way to a strange simultaneity' (2014,

p. 9).[54] This simultaneity is fostered by having unparalleled access to horror films from the past (and the present) through repertory theatres, streaming services, peer-to-peer sharing and distributors such as Arrow Films and Vinegar Syndrome. Queer horror fans embrace horror films from as far back as the 1920s with alacrity and facility, showing engagement with a range of eras as well as subgenres, and evidence that their passion for the horror genre is not solely connected to or held by specific horror films.[55]

Summarising the Queer Spectator of Horror Film

This chapter has presented the most significant data-led analysis of the opinions, habits and tastes of the queer horror spectator, providing the most comprehensive portrait of queer horror spectators to date. The mixed-method data additionally explicates how the queer horror fan's relationship to the horror genre is distinguished from previously documented data on horror audiences. The data demonstrates a diverse queer horror spectatorship and, in so doing, simultaneously challenges the focus of previous theoretical and empirical scholarship on white cis men and establishes an extensive picture of queer horror spectatorship. This study's survey participants (whose extensive data can be extrapolated to the larger queer horror spectator population) span ages, races, ethnicities, gender identities, sexual orientations and borders. It can be concluded, then, that queer spectators merit increased recognition and integration into horror studies. This study creates a permanent space for queer spectators in horror fandom and studies, much as Cherry forged a space for the female horror fan in academic discourse by composing their first empirical profile, convincingly establishing that 'women have always enjoyed horror and continue to do so' (1999, p. 20). As this study argues, queer horror fans, regardless of specific intersectional identities, share many more similarities than differences, not only deserving but warranting extrication from generalised demographic profiles of horror fans – both theoretical and empirical. This study's mixed-method data indicates that the opinions, habits and tastes of horror-loving queers do not map directly onto existing data. This means that queer horror fans exist outside of documented sources and, therefore, have a distinctive relationship with the genre. The queer horror fan is a knowledgeable *and* active spectator – a spectator who understands themself to have a queer lens that uniquely shapes their relationship to horror. Queer spectators of horror are a highly educated population who knowledgeably, reflectively, reflexively and insightfully engage with the horror genre. While Cherry affirms that 'the horror film audience has always been regarded as completely Other' (1999, p. 4), queer horror fans are further marginalised in horror fandom due to their queerness, as they are in society. Moreover, the majority of queer horror fans experience additional marginalisation due to gender identity and/or race.

Kim Newman acknowledges that '[f]ew areas of cinema depend so much on the loyalty and inside knowledge of their audience' as the horror genre (Newman, quoted in Cherry, 1999, p. 33), an argument that particularly applies to queer spectators. Specifically, queer fandom is built on a loyalty to and inside knowledge about horror films that decodes and addresses the genre's queerness. A survey participant underscores this when they write: 'I think the LGBT+ community regularly bonds more with villains due to their queer coding throughout cinema history' (47123425). Queerness itself is an embodied subjectivity steeped in both acute and insidious trauma, both historical and active. Horror films are anchored in expressions of physical and psychological trauma, experiences to which many queers directly relate; as a survey participant notes, 'the tropes of repression, desire, fear and trauma that are manifest within horror can be applied to LGBTIQ+ experiences' (47083771). The queer experience of 'surviving the trauma of living in the closet and being an out queer person casts a different light on [horror] films' (46973195), a light from which queers can turn trauma into a joyous rage expressed through camp sensibility. Camp is a queer insider language and lens that the vast majority of queer spectators of horror employ in their enjoyment of the genre. The camp connection to horror has rarely been examined even though, as narrator Michael Varrati notes, 'camp and horror walk hand-in-hand because they're both arts of heightened reality' (2020, p. 6).[56] The next chapter, therefore, provides an in-depth analytical examination of trauma and camp within horror spectatorship, anchored by the presentation of corresponding mixed-method data that explicates these uniquely queer experiences with and relationships to horror.

Notes

1. More than 6,000 aggregate reports, computed from many thousands of possible data permutations and combinations, from this survey are available for future research. Crucial to the ongoing discourse on the queer horror

spectator will be future in-depth analyses that examine the effect of gender identity, race, ethnicity, age, educational status, nationality, etc., on the queer relationship to the horror genre.

2. I made the active and political choice to allow participants to select as many races/ethnicities, sexual orientations and gender identities categories as they personally identify with – thereby queering the established methods (Ward, 2019, p. 262). In fact, my data set proves the need for all studies to open data collection to queer peoples' non-normative and/or not mutually exclusive lived experiences: 11 per cent of all survey participants embody and selected more than one race/ethnicity, 15 per cent of all survey participants embody and selected more than one gender and 38 per cent of all survey participants embody and selected more than one sexual orientation – these data points collectively indicate that an over-reliance on mutual exclusivity may prove harmful, unhelpful and dated to a significant portion of the queer community.
3. For example, popular queer performers, from Lady Gaga to Lil Nas X, have introduced new generations to camp performance, while queer films, such as *The Rocky Horror Picture Show* (1975), *Paris Is Burning* (1990), *Hedwig and the Angry Inch* (2001) and *Portrait of a Lady on Fire* (2019), continue to influence queer culture today.
4. Of the 2,829 survey participants from the United States, 2,783 (98.7 per cent) have lived in the US for the majority of their lives.
5. The survey asked, 'Do you currently live in the United States?'. If the participant selected 'No', they received a subsequent question that asked, 'Do you currently live in the United Kingdom, Ireland, Canada, Australia or New Zealand?'. If they selected 'No' there was no further follow-up question or open text box. Therefore, the country of residence is not known for 375 of the survey participants.
6. Instead of considering this research 'unconsciously Western in scope', this research is consciously a Western project, as my training and experience do not warrant a truly global perspective (Schoonover and Galt, 2016, p. 38). I want to emphasise the need for further research in this area, in particular because the differences in data from around the world seem to be rooted more in issues of access, hence exposure, to queer and horror events than differences in national identity. The tremendous participant response created an international survey of queer spectators of horror, demonstrating that horror is an affective genre with global appeal.
7. Historically (and sometimes presently), biological sex and identificatory gender are conflated and mistakingly presumed as one, leading previous (and current) academic studies, therefore, to subsume sex and gender. Previous horror

research that made conclusions based on the subsumed categories of 'males' and 'females' can be compared with the gender identity categories used currently in queer communities and, thus, in this study. This study does not seek to reconcile the previous conflation of sex and gender, but instead to acknowledge the needed disentanglement between sex and gender and to honour the gender expression and identity of all participants and narrators.

8. In comparison, Alexander Dhoest and Nele Simons in 'Questioning Queer Audiences: Exploring Diversity in Lesbian and Gay Men's Media Uses and Readings', declare that their 'sample was quite balanced in terms of gender (57 percent male, 43 percent female)' (2012, p. 266).
9. *The Horror Report* by data researcher Stephen Follows states that the 'principal research tool was a database of every horror feature film released in cinemas between 1st January 1996 and 31st December 2016' (2017, p. 203).
10. The women narrators did not speak of their love of horror in relation to constructed notions of gendered behaviours and expectations.
11. Of the 4,107 survey participants who reported their sexual orientation(s), only 0.007 (seven thousandths) per cent report that they are heterosexual. All twenty-eight of those who identify as heterosexual also report that they are transgender, further evidencing the queerness of all survey participants.
12. Since the survey allowed participants to multi-select on the race/ethnicity, gender identity and sexual orientation questions, the hard counts presented here represent the number of participants who selected that identity marker. For example, a survey participant may have selected 'Asian or Asian American', 'White or Caucasian' and 'Multiracial' – thereby appearing in the counts for all three.
13. For comparison, the Census Bureau's Population Estimates Program on 1 July 2019 reported the US 'Race and Hispanic Origin' as follows: American Indian and Alaska Native alone (1.3 per cent), Asian alone (5.9 per cent), Black or African American alone (13.4 per cent), Hispanic or Latino (18.5 per cent), two or more races (2.8 per cent), Native Hawaiian and other Pacific Islander alone (0.2 per cent) and white alone (76.3 per cent). The Office for National Statistics, the executive office of the UK Statistics Authority, reports in the 2011 census that 86 per cent of the UK population was white, 2.5 per cent was Indian and 2 per cent was Pakistani (see Figure 2.4).
14. Further responses could provide insights into countries/regions of residence or origin, such as: Filipino, Finnish, Slav, Armenian and Russian, Portuguese, Polish, Hungarian, Spanish, South African Indian (Indian, born in South Africa), Greek Turkish, Mediterranean/Sicilian, Métis, Afghan, Mauritian, Mayan, Argentinian and Greek-German.

15. Horror data researcher Stephen Follows analysed IMDB and Metascore ratings and determined that horror is the 'lowest regarded genre'. Follows's data analysis evidences that 'horror has been the worst reviewed genre amongst all movies with relative consistency' and 'that both critics and audiences view horror less favourably than any other genre' (2017, p. 113). Additionally, David Church's *Post-Horror: Art, Genre and Cultural Elevation* summary statement reads: 'Horror cinema has long been a popular but culturally denigrated genre' (2021, n.p.).
16. Of the survey participants, 89.8 per cent are under forty-two.
17. Using the normal approximation of the binomial distribution, the 99 per cent confidence interval indicates that the percentage in the total horror-loving queer population who feel that the presence of a queer character affects their enjoyment of a horror film ranges from 75.1 per cent to 78.5 per cent.
18. In 2019, GLAAD reported in 'A Survey of American Acceptance and Attitudes Toward LGBTQ Americans Conducted by The Harris Poll' about an 'erosion in LGBTQ acceptance', stating that there 'has been a decline in overall comfort and acceptance of LGBTQ people from respondents ages 18–34, with allies steadily declining among this audience since 2016' (n.p.).
19. Stated with 99 per cent confidence, 73.5 per cent to 76.9 per cent of all queer horror fans' enjoyment of a horror film would be affected by the presence of a strong female character.
20. Using the normal approximation of the binomial distribution, the 99 per cent confidence interval indicates that the actual percentage in the total horror-loving queer population who first started watching horror films aged seventeen and under ranges from 90.3 per cent to 92.5 per cent. The 99 per cent confidence interval indicates that the actual percentage in the total horror-loving queer population who first started watching horror films under twelve ranges from 57.2 per cent to 61.2 per cent.
21. Tamborini and Stiff's theoretical assessment is based on 155 survey respondents leaving a cinema in 'a large midwestern city' in autumn 1982 after seeing *Halloween II* (1987, p. 422).
22. Family of origin, also known as first family, refers to one's parent(s) and any potential sibling(s) with whom they were raised by and with, whether biological, adoptive or guardian.
23. Queers with a mostly LGBTQ+ friend group are those most likely to have a friend or partner also interested in horror, at 87.6 per cent.
24. '"Chosen family" is a term employed within queer and transgender (Q/T) communities to describe family groups constructed by choice rather than by biological or legal (bio-legal) ties' (Levin et al., 2020, p. 1).
25. Additionally, the Yule's Q of 0.83 indicates a very strong association between

the survey participants who answered 'yes' to 'As a member of the LGBTQ+ community, do you feel that you have a different reaction to horror films as compared with heterosexual viewers?' and to 'Do you feel that being queer influences your taste in horror films?'.

26. Thirteen of the twenty-four statements were borrowed, revised and repurposed from Cherry so as to have a direct comparative.
27. The Spearman rank-order correlations indicate that the same small to moderate correlations (whether positive or negative) also exist in the total population of horror-loving queers.
28. There are four statement questions that yielded no correlations: 'I like horror films with lots of suspense and/or tension' – 93 per cent (n = 3,794); 'I enjoy being frightened by horror films' – 89.6 per cent (n = 3,660); 'Horror films relieve the tedium of my everyday life' – 84.8 per cent (n = 3,461); and 'I prefer horror films in which "the monster" is hidden or unseen' – 53.9 per cent (n = 2,196).
29. For example, narrator Harmony Colangelo states: 'Jump scares are lazy. You'll be startled. You'll feel startled. But not scared. It's not a prolonged feeling. It's more of a visceral response' (2020, p. 34).
30. Of queer horror fans, 27.7 per cent strongly agree or agree that the gorier the horror film, the more they enjoy it, with 35.1 per cent strongly disagreeing or disagreeing with that statement.
31. Of queer horror fans, 43.7 per cent strongly agree or agree that they like watching people being attacked or killed in horror films, with 18.6 per cent strongly disagreeing or disagreeing with that statement.
32. Cherry wrote 'hero' and 'heroine' as two separate questions, so I calculated this by taking the average response from both questions – 15.2 per cent of female horror fans agree strongly or agree and 50.5 per cent disagree strongly or disagree with the statement 'I empathise with the hero'; 17.8 per cent of female horror fans agree strongly or agree and 42.9 per cent disagree strongly or disagree with the statement 'I empathise with the heroine' (1999, pp. 246–7).
33. Cherry's question stated: 'I empathise with the monster'.
34. While it may be surprising that the United States does not top this list, especially given the overall influence of US horror globally, a potential reason may be because the majority of the survey participants are from the United States and assumed that it would be understood that they watch US horror. Interestingly, while Japan is a top horror producer, Follows and Nash point out that the horror genre actually performs 'less well in Japan' than other genres (2016, n.p.).

35. Nielsen reports that the top five genres among LGBTQ audiences are horror, science fiction or fantasy, romance, drama and graphic novels/comics (2014, p. 4). Interestingly, while this study's results support Nielsen's findings that horror, science fiction and fantasy are in the top five genres, survey participants ranked romance in the bottom five, with only 26.8 per cent watching romance films. While this study did not capture data on the genre named as 'graphic novels/comics', the survey finds that 59.9 per cent of survey participants watch animation/anime films and 52.2 per cent watch superhero films.
36. The top three social networking services used by survey participants are Twitter (72.5 per cent), Instagram (68.8 per cent) and Facebook (58.8 per cent).
37. Future studies would be well served to capture data on the number of queer spectators who *explicitly* participate in horror fandom.
38. Of horror-loving queers, 4.7 per cent (n = 192) are 'somewhat comfortable' and just 1 per cent (n = 43) are 'not at all comfortable' with tension and/or suspense in horror films.
39. Of horror-loving queers, 17.4 per cent (n = 713) are 'somewhat comfortable' and 4 per cent (n = 166) are 'not at all comfortable' with gore in horror films.
40. Of horror-loving queers, 20.5 per cent (n = 843) are 'somewhat comfortable' and 2.7 per cent (n = 111) are 'not at all comfortable' with graphic physical violence in horror films.
41. Of horror-loving queers, 34.8 per cent (n = 1,428) are 'somewhat comfortable' with graphic sexual violence in horror films.
42. Narrator Velasco directly connects the therapeutic function of horror for him to a revenge film: 'There was another horror film that really helped me with my trauma – as it relates to my sexual abuse – and it was *I Spit on Your Grave*, a revenge film where I saw the female protagonist get her revenge after being brutally attacked. I instantly connected to her and wished I could have done the same to my attackers. But not actually killing them. Just getting back at them' (2020, p. 16).
43. To evidence a more complete understanding of the queer cisgender man's horror tastes, this study's data demonstrates, in fact, that queer cisgender men 'love' or 'like' the 'subtle' horror subgenres such as supernatural/occult/ghost (92.2 per cent), vampire (77.4 per cent) and witchcraft (89.6 per cent), as well as the more 'hard-core' subgenres such as slasher (84.2 per cent) and extreme horror (47.8 per cent).
44. Each survey participant was asked to select up to five of their most loved horror film subgenres resulting in a weakened consensus because they were limited to five subgenres, which further demonstrates that the overall horror genre matters more than individual subgenres. The most selected categories/

subgenres are psychological (58.2 per cent), supernatural/occult/ghost (52 per cent), sci-fi horror (36.6 per cent), slasher (35.1 per cent), witchcraft (28.9 per cent), horror comedy or parody (27.2 per cent), monster (26.5 per cent), body horror (26.2 per cent), serial killer (24.6 per cent), zombie/living dead (21.7 per cent). Only a single subgenre – rape revenge – received a majority consensus for most hated horror film subgenres at 61.1 per cent (n = 2,374).

45. The survey results show that transgender participants are more inclined to enjoy the body horror subgenre – 54.8 per cent of transgender women and 49.6 per cent of transgender men 'love' body horror, compared with 34.2 per cent of cisgender women and 34 per cent of cisgender men. One survey participant adds pertinent commentary to these data results: 'Being transgender, I think that a lot of body horror stuff resonates differently with me compared to cis people' (46935030). This data evidences an area of queer horror studies that transgender scholars could further, critically providing theoretical *and* embodied perspectives.
46. For example, in 1973, the American Psychiatric Association (APA) removed homosexuality as a 'psychiatric disorder' from the Diagnostic and Statistical Manual of Mental Disorders DSM-II, with it instead being downgraded to a 'Sexual Orientation Disturbance' and then, in 1980, to 'Ego Dystonic Homosexuality', until it was fully eradicated from the DSM in 1987. In 2013, the APA revised the diagnosis of 'gender identity disorder' to 'gender dysphoria' for DSM-5, the current manual.
47. Looking at the combined gender categories of women and men, *both* love or like supernatural/occult/ghost films exactly the same, at 88.9 per cent.
48. Since there were only eight survey participants who were between sixty and sixty-five years old and three who were over sixty-six, those age categories were removed from SPSS calculations both to meet the assumptions for utilising a chi-square and to not over-represent those two age categories based on only eleven survey participants.
49. Since the first slashers appeared decades ago, a longitudinal examination of slashers is now relevant and, unmistakably, the generation reared on slashers continue to connect with the subgenre.
50. Survey participants were given five separate open-text fields to list their favourite horror films, though not all were required to be filled in. Therefore, field one received 3,886 responses, field two received 3,869 responses, field three received 3,839 responses, field four received 3,710 responses and field five received 3,566 responses. This response rate averages out to 3,774 participants for the entire question.

51. For these calculations, I examined the cis women, cis men, trans women, trans men and non-binary participants who selected one gender identity.
52. The percentages that determined the number one favourite film across those five gender identities are as follows: 14.5 per cent consensus of cis women; 24.8 per cent consensus of cis men; 39 per cent consensus of trans women; 15.7 per cent consensus of trans men; and 17.4 per cent consensus of non-binary participants.
53. Reynold Humphries in *The American Horror Film: an Introduction* writes: 'One word can sum up the shift from classic to modern horror: *Psycho*' (2002, p. 85). The top twenty-five list features *Psycho* alongside other post-*Psycho* films.
54. Even though Fisher links this collapsed cultural simultaneity to the neoliberal (post-Fordist) refashioning of society – including time – to its own end, his perceptive observation holds resonance and application beyond a political context or a specifically Marxist reading of culture.
55. In part, the queer horror fan's interest in 1920s and 1930s horror may be attributed to the films by queer directors F. W. Murnau and James Whale.
56. This dearth of in-depth analysis on the connections between camp and the horror genre is particularly glaring considering that Jack Babuscio wrote in 1977: 'The horror *genre*, in particular, is susceptible to a camp interpretation' (p. 43; italics in the original).

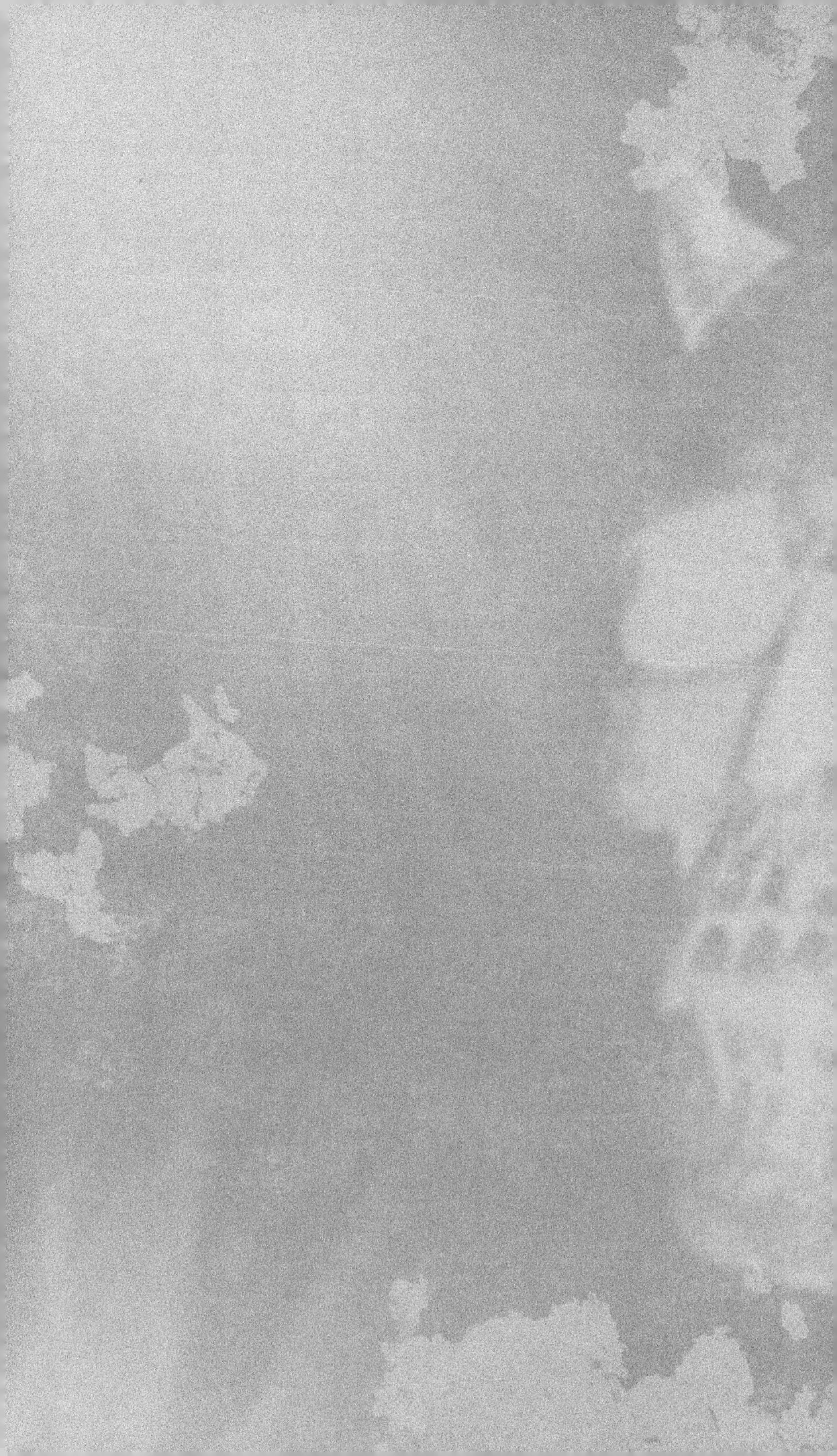

3

Trauma and Camp

Queer Connections to Horror

I'm able to bring the added perspective that oppression brings and therefore don't just take horror at face value. It's not always just entertainment, sometimes it's a way to escape real life trauma because you're able to be like while even though my rights are being hoisted away at least I'm not fighting undead werewolves from hell.
(47564845)

Horror is very inherently about trauma.
(47079311)

Camp is the element of horror that is exactly what I love about the genre and is probably what I consciously try to take from all of my favourite films. Camp is the thing that is making it really, really interesting to me because it's this fantastical – not trapped by any sort of boundary – loud, visual, and, hopefully quite garish celebration of art and creativity. Camp is a proudness in existing really loudly and boldly.
(Thompson, 2020, p. 20)

I think camp is queerness and horror is queerness. They're both tackling the same thing. They're both dismantling society. Camp is taking it and amplifying it and horror is taking it and throwing blood on it – but someone's laughing while throwing that bucket. It's all interwoven.
(Davis, 2020, p. 31)

I HAVE ANALYSED THE ontological and theoretical queer nature of the horror genre, providing a foundation to present the most complete understanding to date of the queer horror spectator's opinions, habits and tastes. This chapter explicates further the distinctive queer relationship to horror evidenced through the expansion and analysis of trauma and camp,[1] two different yet linked fundamental aspects to the queer connection to the genre. The intersections between trauma, camp, horror and queer studies have yet to be critically considered. This study's mixed-method data evidences that queer trauma and camp are deeply entwined in queers' relationship to their understanding and enjoyment of horror, which further establishes the queer spectator's *sui generis* relationship with the genre. This chapter, then, explicates horror's mediation of trauma for the queer spectator and queer spectators' employment of camp in their relationship to horror as a trauma processor, as well as expands the trauma cinema and camp theory canons to include the horror genre.

Queer Trauma, the Horror Genre and Traumatic Expressions

This chapter first investigates the yet considered convergence between the fields of trauma studies, horror studies and queer studies (including queer audiences). Scholars in trauma and trauma cinema studies have focused mainly on analysing historical and experimental films, while horror studies discourse has largely circumvented engaging empirical audience studies and considering the queer spectator when investigating trauma. The goal of this study is to analyse how queer trauma finds expression through the horror genre and to connect it to existing trauma theory. Two examples are the work of Adam Lowenstein, in *Shocking Representation: Historical Trauma, National Cinema, and the Modern Horror Film* (2005), and Linnie Blake, in *The Wounds of Nations: Horror Cinema, Historical Trauma and National Identity* (2008), who analyse horror in the context of (repressed) national traumas, with both effectively arguing that horror reflects back significant moments of political and social crisis. In addressing the cultural work of horror, Lowenstein and Blake connect the representational to the traumatic. In other words, horror allegorically and metaphorically reflects repressed societal concerns and anxieties. Lowenstein adopts a Benjaminian standpoint and Blake a culturalist and historicist framework to argue persuasively for the healing power of horror – the 'most traumatic and traumatised of film genres' (Blake, 2008, p. 1). Uniquely, this study builds on and extends that scholarship to recognise and analyse the therapeutic power of horror for the queer spectator, who forges an active connection to the horror genre. While this study centres the active and conscious connections made by queer spectators about the 'healing' elements of horror, I acknowledge that this understanding might not always be consciously the case. Significantly and undoubtedly, the therapeutic powers of horror may be sought by some spectators unconsciously. Some queer spectators might not be aware that there is a connection between their queer embodiment and their horror consumption, whereas others do not only watch horror for the explicit aim of horror's therapeutic function, even if this after-effect is plausible. This study does not propose that *all* queer spectators consciously consume horror as a form of therapy for healing purposes, nor does it suggest that horror's therapeutic powers are the singular reason for generic consumption. I argue, instead, that horror films can function therapeutically for queer spectators because the genre distinctively resonates with queer trauma – and that a substantial portion of horror-loving queers consciously engage with horror therapeutically.

I consider and analyse both the survey data and the oral history interviews to discuss why and how queer spectators connect with horror because of the trauma(s) experienced by queer people and displayed through the horror genre, ultimately underscoring the generic potentials of horror and demonstrating that queers use the genre therapeutically to alleviate trauma. Even though individuals experience and respond to trauma differently, this study's mixed-method data evidences queer people's shared therapeutic connection to horror, establishing that one's queerness creates a connection to the horror genre in which horror films function as one form of cathartic therapy. This study argues for and empirically demonstrates a distinctively queer cathartic emotional pressure release/relief from queer trauma, with the horror genre functioning as the valve. Therefore, this book presents a new dimension to previous theorisations of trauma, catharsis and the horror genre. Popularised by Aristotle and Freud, cathartic 'purges' or 'releases' have been topics of thought, theory and/or application for thousands of years. While this study engages catharsis theory, it actively disengages itself entirely from the ideological uses that the Freudian model puts forth, not least by Freud himself. This disengagement is due not only to the misogynistic and homophobic legacy of psychoanalytic practice, but also, and especially, the significant percentage of the survey participants who are *conscious* of the ways in which horror film engages their queer trauma (which is opposed to the Freudian catharsis model's basis on unconscious or the more generalised subconscious). This study's theoretical underpinnings understand catharsis as a subjective emotional processing of 'an individual's built-up negative feelings (e.g., anger, sadness) [that] can be processed effectively and safely through the use of purging activities (Jackson, 1994). Such activities might include any courses of action that actively engage with and then subsequently dispel these negative feelings' (Stark, 2021, p. 4). Thomas Scheff and Don Bushnell further clarify: 'Catharsis is a subjective experience manifested by certain external signals such as laughter and crying, and by subjective feelings of tension and of other emotions' (1984, p. 262). This study, then, examines a specifically queer catharsis: the processing of insidious queer trauma, which is consciously recognised by the queer spectators themselves, through the horror genre. Much like horror, queerness and trauma, I do not place strict parameters around the research participants' use of the term 'catharsis' or potential understanding of any catharsis theory. Queer spectators of horror seek catharsis in the genre in order to cope with the daily insidious trauma of the cisheteropatriarchy. Queers are cognisant of what traumatises us and horror enables an acting out and recognition of that trauma in a safe space with, perhaps, an alternative ending. As explained by a queer spectator: horror is 'a way for me to process the very real trauma and violence I have experienced for my [queer] identity' (47202774). Trauma is an interrelation between queerness and the horror genre since 'horror films, like queer people, often understand and convey the perspective of living with trauma' (46826850). My decision to evidence empirically the positive effects of horror for queer spectators is bolstered by Mathias Clasen affirming that the 'negative psychological effects of horror are much better documented in the research literature than are the positive effects' (2017, p. 61).[2] Despite trauma's 'resistance to narrativization, trauma demands to be spoken, and this leads to creative and sometimes unconscious attempts to communicate traumatic experience' (Westengard, 2019, p. 180). Following Laura Westengard, I argue for a *creative* queer spectatorship born from traumatic queer experiences, which actively finds outlets in the trauma narratives of the horror genre. Hence, this study bends and extends Westengard's theory that queer cultural production invokes and evokes the tropes of gothic horror to express trauma by applying it to the queer spectator's creative, cathartic and camp engagement with horror that is informed by insidious trauma.

In *Gothic Queer Culture: Marginalized Communities and the Ghosts of Insidious Trauma* (2019), Westengard argues: 'Trauma is integral to the connection between the queer and the gothic, and gothicism itself is a way of queering trauma' (p. 26). Having already explicated the affective and thematic connections between the Gothic and horror, here I apply Westengard's argument to horror film to argue that trauma is integral to the connection between queers and the horror genre. In fact, Westengard's theory underpins my argument that the queer connection to horror is partially informed by trauma. Westengard demonstrates how queers turn to gothicism to navigate and express trauma, determining that queer culture is inherently gothic. Whereas Westengard centres on literary analysis and queer cultural production, this study focuses on the queer connection with the horror genre as one form of traumatic expression. Moreover, Westengard points out that '[c]reative production is an inherent byproduct of trauma' (2019, p. 190), not only highlighting the queer trauma that is integral to both of our creative and academic cultural productions,[3] but also allowing for the creativity in the queer spectator's reception of horror films.[4] To understand the drive behind the queer spectator's creative engagement with the horror genre, it is important to explicate what 'queer trauma' means and how this study engages with this queer trauma.

Trauma can be individual, collective, cultural, national, historical, intergenerational or insidious; in fact, due to the pervasiveness of trauma, 'our entire global culture is sometimes characterized as traumatic or post-traumatic' (Davis and Meretoja, 2020, p. 1). While this study is specifically focused on the insidious societal traumas that harm queers, a focus on trauma that is specifically queer should not be understood as a process of universalising traumas across the queer spectrum. An individual's intersectionality shapes their own experiences of trauma, as trauma itself is prioritised based on hierarchies of race, gender, sexuality, class and ability as established and perpetuated by the white cisheteropatriarchy.[5] Marginalised people are further traumatised by the reality that '[b]eing recognized as traumatized is a privilege not equally available to all trauma victims' (Davis and Meretoja, 2020, p. 5). Moreover, essentialising trauma for a diverse spectrum of community members should be undertaken carefully because, as Jillian C. Rogers states, it is 'axiomatic that each person's trauma is different, and that how they experience, perform, and cope with trauma will vary based on myriad factors' (2021, p. 10). Queer trauma demands ongoing recognition and expression due to the continual development of queer subjectivity through the psychological and physical tolls of overt and insidious trauma. Fundamental both to understanding queers' trauma and to 'queering' trauma, as Kevin Nadal argues, 'is to ensure that trauma is conceptualized through queer lenses – meaning that people are not limited to simple or rigid definitions of trauma' (2020, p. 50). Previously defined or understood trauma theories may not fully explain or represent the queer experience because, historically, trauma and its therapies have been filtered through the cisheteronormative lens.

While trauma studies and theory is built on the foundation of psychoanalytic thought, this study is not concerned with the pathologisation of or institutionalised treatments for trauma, nor is it concerned with detailing the history of trauma theories such as Jean-Martin Charcot's 'traumatic hysteria' (1878), Pierre Janet's theory of 'dissociation' (1887) or Oppenheim's 'traumatic neuroses' (1889), nor trauma studies' extension into the humanities by scholars such as Felman (1992), Laub (1992) and Caruth (1996). Since bibliographic citations are ideologically driven, they function as a form of academic politics; therefore, as I have discussed, I intentionally diverge and disengage from direct engagement with Freud and the field of psychoanalysis due to the harm that psychoanalysis has inflicted on marginalised people for decades, particularly its pathologisation of homosexuality. This study, moreover, does not engage with the psychoanalytic lens in part because of the misogyny at the root of its origin. In fact, as Judith Herman critically states: 'Out of the ruins of the traumatic theory of hysteria, Freud created psychoanalysis. The dominant psychological theory of the next century was founded in the denial of women's reality' (1992, p. 14). Yet, it must be acknowledged that the queer spectator's horror-healing paradigm holds connection to Freudian and post-Freudian scholarship that deploys particular conceptions of the basic mechanisms of repression and catharsis, which are found in horror narratives through its themes, representation and affect. Psychoanalytic discourse as deployed in the humanities may then provide the critic with an engaging lexicon of terms that can be utilised to investigate queer subjectivity and its generic identifications. However, such use does not imply adherence to the homophobic and misogynistic ideology that, I maintain, underpins psychoanalysis itself. This empirical study is not based in a 'theoretical discussion of trauma's artistic representations' (Lowenstein, 2005, p. 4); therefore, this study privileges the understanding of trauma as 'socioculturally constituted' over the 'psychological considerations' that tend to dominate the field (Rogers, 2021, p. 9). My contention remains, accordingly, that queer spectators explicitly connect the representational traumas of the horror genre to the traumas of their embodied queer experience.

Cisheteronormative society traumatises queer individuals, leading to a queer trauma that is simultaneously personal, political, collective and historical. Queer existence is submerged in 'compulsory heterosexuality' (1980), as coined by Adrienne Rich, which is traumatic to queer individuals because non-normative 'individuals living in the heteronormative regime need to learn to conform, ignore, and banish their suffering to survive' (Yep, 2003, p. 19). While many members of the queer community endure acute traumas, all queers suffer from insidious trauma and, indeed, this trauma is a part of queer culture itself. This insidious trauma is identified and defined by Maria Root as one that is 'associated with the social status of an individual being devalued because a characteristic intrinsic to their identity is different from what is valued by those in power, for example, gender, color, sexual orientation, physical ability' (1992, p. 240). To exist simply as queer in a cisheteronormative world means daily encounters with dehumanisation, microaggressions, presumptions and prejudices. In other words, all marginalised individuals experience insidious trauma, with BIPOC and/or trans* members of the queer community experiencing not only compounding intersectional traumas but also hate crimes at significantly higher rates since 'LGBTQ people of color are consistently more likely to be targeted for anti-LGBTQ hate crimes' (Nadal, 2020, p. 46).[6] For queer people, again particularly BIPOC and/or trans* members of the community, the concomitant 'insidious trauma is constant and everywhere yet largely unacknowledged and invalidated, creating a cycle of insidious trauma in which the refusal to acknowledge experiences as traumatic serves as its own form of insidious trauma' (Westengard, 2019, p. 180). Having traumatic experiences, whether post-traumatic or ongoing, dismissed or not acknowledged is further trauma, perpetuating a trauma loop.

'Trauma is both event and condition' (Rutherford, 2013, p. 100) and 'insidious trauma's effects are cumulative' (Root, 1992, p. 240), with insidious trauma escaping attachment to a single event and being an ongoing condition. The cumulative effects of a shared queer trauma are apparent, given evidence such as the queer community being disproportionately affected by mental illness. Further, the 'stigma and shame' of being queer, 'as well as the many expressed and unexpressed hostilities encountered on a daily basis', all cause members of the queer community to experience higher levels of depression, anxiety, substance abuse and suicide; in fact, 'LGBT+ individuals are nearly three times more likely than straight, cisgender individuals to experience depression, anxiety, or substance abuse' (Alexander et al., 2021, p. 352). Other statistics further evidence the individual, familial and social cost of the strict enforcement of cisheteronormativity on queer people:

> The risk for suicide is also increased, with one study finding gay and lesbian individuals twice as likely to consider suicide, bisexual individuals at about three times the risk, and transgender individuals more than 13 times more likely to consider suicide than straight, cisgender individuals. (Alexander et al., 2021, p. 352)

The trauma that the cisheteronormative system causes in queer individuals results in increased mental health disorders and suicidality and in a collective, persistent traumatic state of existence for this non-normative community. Queer trauma may be unacknowledged or unknown by an individual for a long time or even indefinitely. For example, a queer person may be unaware that they have internalised homophobia, which is both a manifestation and a perpetuation of queer trauma.

Each queer individual experiences, understands and reacts to insidious trauma in their own singular way, yet this research recognises a sharedness in the queer traumatic experience and connects it to a common expression – an active queer spectatorship of horror film. This notion of active spectatorship as a part of queer trauma is found in Susannah Radstone's postulation that trauma theory has the 'capacity to consolidate work on displacing models of passive spectatorship' (de Bruyn, 2014, p. 7). Radstone states: 'Trauma could revise theories of spectatorship by considering the relations between fantasy, memory, temporality and the subject' (2001, p. 191). Accordingly, analysing the connection between queer trauma and the horror genre reveals an active queer spectatorship.

This study's data indicates that the queer spectatorship of horror is 'a way to work out traumas', providing spectators 'with forms of (sometimes ambivalent or problematic) pleasure' (Sher, 2015, p. 10). Since the language of the unconscious, repression, catharsis and trauma evoke Freud's work, I follow Ben Sher, who examines the link between cinephilia and trauma survivors of domestic abuse. Sher summarises Freud's theory 'that people can use spectatorship and performance of plays as means of working through trauma, [suggesting] that aspects of trauma can be represented, and that people can have profound engagements with representation' (2015, p. 10). This study's focus is intentionally set on an active queer spectatorial engagement with the horror genre in order to facilitate processing, surviving and/or overcoming the trauma of being queer in a cisheteronormative society. Indeed, queer identity exists in relation to the insidious and compounding trauma of living in a 'straight' world. The queer spectator's connection to horror is not simply grounded in a past historical trauma but, instead, an active and ongoing insidious trauma. Queer trauma is simultaneously historical and ongoing. Narrator Gabe Castro details ways in which horror representationally offers opportunities to work through queer-embodied trauma:

> In horror, we get to live out some of those traumatic experiences and confront them – and whether or not we end up with the protagonists at the end prevailing, we can feel a sense of fear and hope, too. It's also cathartic to see failure on screen as well. Just seeing someone coping and just dealing with how it is. (2020, p. 8)

Regardless of an individual film's narrative outcome, then, the horror genre serves as a method for queer spectators to connect with and/or confront – aesthetically, allegorically and affectively – trauma on the screen, even if they are not consciously aware of these processes.

Queers actively engage with the horror genre by searching for, recognising in, and connecting to the generic trauma. The notion of cultural texts serving as a mechanism for healing and transformation has long been considered. Discussing late eighteenth-century Gothic fiction, William Veeder explains that 'societies inflict terrible wounds upon themselves *and at the same time* develop mechanisms that can help heal these wounds' (1998, p. 21; italics in the original). Extending Veeder's argument, temporally and textually, my study's empirical data indicates that, for the queer spectator, the horror genre serves the therapeutic 'psychosocial function of nurture, of healing and transforming' (1998, p. 21). For example, one survey participant shares that they 'often seek out movies that have a particular psychological and "real" aspect in how it deals will mental illness and trauma such as depression, abuse from family, because even if these are not meant to be allusions to LGBT themes by the film's creators they are still aspects that many LGBT people can relate to' (47124820). Given the queer connection to the horror genre and horror's transgressive queerness, focus on the queer spectator is both warranted and necessary to illuminate a wider understanding of the function of trauma in horror.

Since the horror genre is predicated on engaging with and representing trauma both representationally and allegorically, the queer spectator forges an active therapeutic connection to horror because they recognise in the genre an intrinsic queerness and a reflection of their own queer trauma. I will now demonstrate how this study expands both trauma studies and trauma cinema to resolutely include queer spectatorship's trauma experience and trauma's expression through the horror genre. General trauma theory and queer trauma were explicated prior in order to provide a baseline to understand the specific field of trauma cinema, which, as defined by Janet Walker, is 'a group of films that deal with a world-shattering event or events, whether public or personal' (2005, p. 19). This definition is further cemented when considering the root of the word 'trauma', the etymology of which, according to the Oxford English Dictionary, is the Greek word, *τραῦμα*, for 'wound'. As such, the horror genre resolutely fits within the trauma cinema field, replete as it is with shattering traumas, from deaths and dismemberments to stalkings and survivals, and riddled with physical, psychological and/or psychic wounds. Given trauma's abject etymological nature, unsurprisingly, trauma manifests in human lives by 'haunting' (Luckhurst) and 'possessing' (Caruth) people, both of which are resolutely horror genre tropes. In fact, trauma is one of the 'recurring themes' that 'horror films seem to be built on' (Dumas, 2014, p. 21). This study is not focused on specific instances of representational or allegorical trauma in horror, nor is it concerned with investigating the particular cultural work of horror, as most scholarship has been until now. Instead, I am concerned with how queer spectators engage with cultural texts, specifically horror films, to temporarily alleviate their traumas.

As noted, trauma studies has yet to investigate meaningfully the horror genre, while horror academics have primarily deployed trauma studies as a means of reading history and nation. This study, then, queers this branch of horror studies by furthering the discourse framed at the juncture of trauma theory and horror studies built on the works of Lowenstein and Blake. Lowenstein is less concerned with horror as a category and more interested in identifying a film's 'allegorical moment' by asking 'does this film access discourses of horror to confront the representation of historical trauma tied to the film's national and cultural context' (2005, p. 9). Blake theoretically analyses national identity discourses that seek to silence sites of national trauma before the nation has healed, ultimately arguing that horror exposes ideology and enables a meaningful form of healing. In these analyses, the horror genre not only 'registers most brutally the legacies of historical trauma' (Lowenstein, 2005, p. 10) but also is 'generically driven by the abject and the uncanny' (Blake, 2008, p. 3). Further, Blake astutely recognises 'the abject and the uncanny as core signifiers of traumatic historical events' (2008, p. 3). To this end, queer spectators unsurprisingly find an embodied connection through the irrefutable queerness of the abject and the uncanny, which are sociocultural expressions shared by both the horror genre and trauma studies. For example, queer spectators explicitly connect their queer trauma(s) to the representational trauma(s) in horror films, with survey participants electing to add comments explaining as much: 'Straight people don't usually have to worry about the deaths, torments, or traumas enacted upon characters in the movie being direct reflections of actual things they face in their daily lives' (47720838); 'I feel like LGBTQ+ audiences accept horror more easily because we relate to them more. Whether we feel like outcasts and can relate with specific characters, or we experience trauma that is similar to feelings brought up in the films' (47713806); and 'I love movies about trauma survivors grappling with a dangerous world, which to me is the queer experience' (46826850). The circularity between horror, trauma and queer alterity is precisely why queer spectators find a therapeutic relief through this particular film genre, finding 'unique queer interpretations of the trauma that's often shown in horror' (47123425).

Lowenstein and Blake, through examination of international films, establish horror's therapeutic effect and argue that horror provides an outlet to collective healing when national trauma is prematurely shut down by ideologies of national identity. Their focus on the collectivity of national identity to examine identity politics is extended by this research, which adds the queer spectator to the list of identified recipients of horror's therapeutic benefits. I find particularly pertinent Blake's attestation that 'the power of horror may be to effect a certain productive re-engagement with the traumas' (2008, p. 187). Horror's therapeutic value to queer spectators exists not because all horror representationally and explicitly exhibits queerness, but because the genre ontologically, subtextually and allegorically engages with and connects to queer alterity. A survey participant explicitly identifies horror's specific connection with queer trauma: 'Based on the fact that almost all of my most fervent horror fan friends are queer and that the genre resonates with them because of this, I think there is a level of feeling so "seen" by the inherent trauma of horror that we also experience that is missed by heterosexual viewers' (47079311). In other words, this queer connection to horror is not anchored to any specific filmic representation because the horror genre, narratively and allegorically, as with all art forms, is open to individual interpretations (Ballon and

Leszcz, 2007, p. 228). Instead, the entire genre itself engenders a cathartic queer connection, as described by a survey participant:

> As queer viewers, I believe we identify more intimately with both victim and monster. In our lives we are so frequently victims, we have to be constantly vigilant, and a victim character who overcomes their monsters is intense and empowering. But we're also characterised as monsters, and we feel their anger and loneliness too. Set against a cast of our oppressors, their slaughtering can be cathartic and gleeful too. (47166187)

Indeed, queers feel seen by horror because they recognise a kinship between the trauma shown in horror films and their embodied queer traumas, as both societal victim and monster.

Being seen by horror functions as a form of therapy for queer spectators. Even though horror studies discourse about trauma to date has largely ignored the therapeutic function of horror for the queer spectator, horror's therapeutic capacity was established as far back as 1958 when Dr Martin Grotjahn of the University of Southern California hypothesised that horror films are 'self-administered psychiatric therapy for America's adolescents' (*Time*, 1958, p. 96). The therapeutic role of film for spectators was evidenced further in *Shocking Entertainment: Viewer Response to Violent Movies*, in which Annette Hill empirically investigates why people watch violent films. Hill demonstrates (not specifically analysing or recognising the queer spectator) that some spectators 'chose to see violent movies as a form of "immediate catharsis"', an act that culminates with them 'view[ing] violent films as a form of therapy' (1997, p. 23). As Isabel Pinedo asserts, the horror genre 'allow[s] us to exercise, rather than exorcise, emotions of tremendous importance that were otherwise denied legitimate expression' (1997, p. 2). This study confirms Pinedo and further establishes that horror serves a therapeutic function and role for the full spectrum of queer spectators, thus also extending Adam Scales's view of 'the therapeutic function of horror, as it aided young gay horror fans in coming to terms with their identity' (2015, p. 143). Whereas Scales argues that horror fandom 'serves as a form of therapy' (2015, p. 163) based on analysis of online blogs and discussion threads specifically for spectators who are 'self-identifying gay male fans of horror' (2015, p. 2), this study broadens the scope to include all non-normative sexualities and genders, and shifts the focus from the therapeutic benefits of horror fandom to the therapeutic connection queer spectators have with the horror film genre. As a survey participant concisely writes, 'I think a lot of LGBTQ endure trauma in early life and this perhaps draws them to darker cinematic material' (48757290). One of the reasons horror films help queers process trauma is because horror presents traumas that have narrative closure – an ending to the story – from which the spectator can find satisfaction. Or, at the very least, horror films offer othered queer spectators a different satisfaction, a perspective that their own situation may not be as severe as the traumas being faced on screen. Scales details this occurring in his own queer experience:

> In my later teenage years, as the realisation of my gay identity came to the fore, I took solace in watching these movies, of people being threatened and mutilated – knowing that whatever uncertain trajectory my sexual identity would take, nothing would be as bad as what was happening to the vulnerable characters on-screen. Somehow, watching horror seemed to promise a future utopia, giving me hope that everything would be okay. (2015, p. 49)

Scales sought 'solace' in horror films to assuage the trauma of coming into queer subjectivity specifically because the genre is anchored in the performance of trauma. In fact, 'cinema *performs* trauma' (de Bruyn, 2014, p. 15; italics in the original). E. Ann Kaplan details: 'Forms such as cinema may be especially appropriate to figuring the visual, aural and non-linear fragmented phenomena of trauma' (2001, pp. 204–5). Kaplan is suggesting that the medium of film itself is ontologically conducive to traumatic expression through the techniques of its making, including camerawork, sound design and editing. As such, horror films further this connection in particular by being centred on traumatic expression representationally, narratively and creatively. The horror genre functions to 'provid[e] a visceral and frequently non-linguistic lexicon in which the experience of cultural dislocation may be phrased', in which traumatic subjectivity (in Blake's case, nations; in this one, queers) can recognise, conceptualise and overcome 'traumatic dislocations' (Blake, 2008, pp. 189–90). The queer spectator connects with the horror genre by actively forging a therapeutic connection that includes the ontological, phenomenological, representational and allegorical; this process ultimately culminates with queers 'feel[ing] safe in horror films' (46809197). This feeling of safety amidst an unsafe world is considered by trauma cinema theorist Janet Walker, who examines traumatic representations in narrative and documentary films and argues for 'the ability of certain films and videos to externalize, publicize, and historicize traumatic material that would otherwise remain at the level of internal, individual psychology' (2005, p. xix). Walker's theorisation that particular films can convey trauma is pertinent to the queer spectator in explaining how horror externalises queer trauma, thereby forming a 'self-administered' therapeutic conduit for the queer spectator.

Evidencing Queer Trauma, Affect and Catharsis

This study has established the queer spectator's ontological connection to the medium of film and, in particular, the horror genre, then explicated how queer subjectivity is marked by insidious trauma, as well as the ways in which critics of horror film have deployed theorisations of trauma in their work. I now turn to presenting empirical evidence and providing analysis of the mixed-method data that establishes the queer spectator's direct, active and therapeutic engagement with the horror genre to alleviate queer trauma. To date, the preoccupation in horror studies discourse with the representational and allegorical facets of queer horror spectatorship has bypassed the significant affective, cathartic and ontological queer connections to the genre. In fact, this connection is entirely conscious and direct for many, as this investigation evidences, which stands in contradistinction to Charles Derry's suggestion that 'horror films speak to our subconscious and – as do our dreams – deal with issues that are often painful for us to deal with consciously and directly' (1987, p. 162). This study's mixed-method data evidences that queer spectators have an acute awareness of their queerness and its concomitant trauma and *knowingly* forge a distinctive relationship to horror. A survey participant, for one, explicitly elucidates the interrelated connection between queer identity, trauma and horror: 'My queerness is related to my trauma and I feel that horror movies are a way for me to experience my comfort zone in fear, but in a safer way' (47126140). Moreover, while this study centres the constant insidious trauma to which queers are subjected by the imposition and enforcement of 'normal' sexuality, gender and relationship models by our cisheterosexual society, as narrator Alex Hall points out, queers also suffer from 'the trauma of coming to one's queerness' in the first place (2020, p. 16). Queers share the experience of coming to terms with their own understanding of their non-normative sexuality and/or gender, even

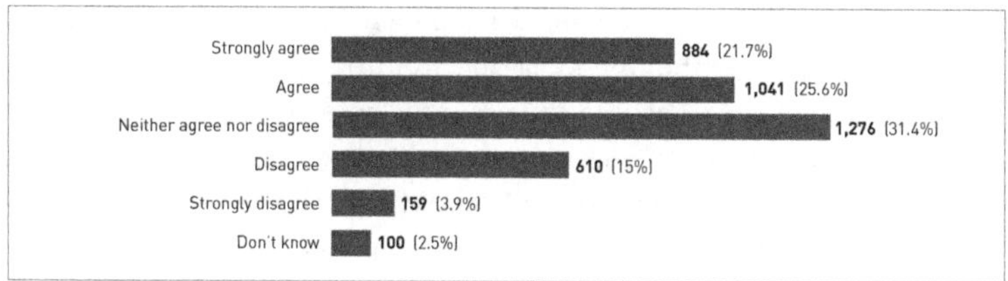

Figure 3.1. Bar graph that indicates survey participants' level of agreement or disagreement for the following statement: 'Horror films help me work through trauma'.

before confronting the hostile world and the trauma of 'social marginalisation or persecution' (Blake, 2008, p. 1). While the horror genre offers numerous therapeutic aspects to cisheteronormative spectators, the therapeutic benefits of horror for the queer spectator are intrinsically connected to their queerness, indicating not simply a correlation but a causation.[7]

Queer horror fans of all ages recognise the therapeutic benefits of horror, as evidenced by my survey data, which indicates that there is no statistically significant correlation between queer spectators' age and an awareness that horror films help them work through trauma. Likewise, no statistically significant correlation exists between queer spectators' highest level of education completed and an awareness that horror films help them work through trauma. 47.3 per cent of queer horror fans strongly agree or agree that horror films help them work through trauma; while that is not a majority consensus, only 18.9 per cent strongly disagree or disagree with that statement (see Figure 3.1). Therefore, it can be stated with 99 per cent confidence that horror films help 45.3 per cent to 49.3 per cent of all horror-loving queers work through trauma. Of the survey participants, 31.4 per cent neither agree nor disagree with the statement, and 2.5 per cent don't know. With a notable but minority percentage of survey participants selecting the neutral or unknowing opinions, and with 18.9 per cent of survey participants strongly disagreeing or disagreeing with the trauma statement, I posit that the data about horror aiding queers in processing trauma falls just short of a majority consensus because the therapeutic engagements with the horror genre might not be immediately understood or known to all queer spectators. The noteworthy neutral response to the trauma question accentuates the silence that surrounds queerness and queer trauma, further perpetuating the queer trauma loop. As previously noted, queer trauma in numerous forms, from social isolation to internalised homophobia and from being closeted to receiving microaggressions, may be unacknowledged, unidentified or unknown to each queer person. A segment of queer individuals may be unaware of or yet to understand all the ways in which they process their queer trauma. My assertion of horror as a queer trauma processor is further evidenced by the fact that the vast majority of narrators detailed their relationship between horror and trauma. Some spoke of the connection being affective, and others noted that horror films offer escapism from the trauma of being queer.[8] This variation becomes a salient point; horror does, indeed, function therapeutically for queer spectators but each queer person formulates that therapeutic salve to soothe their wounds. One example of the fluidity with which horror can confront trauma and offer therapy was provided by narrator Hall:

> Horror is very visceral and it's a physical experience – the way that you experience horror is very physical. As I was saying about horror allowing you to be more present in your body, it's a safe medium to process complicated feelings that you wouldn't be able to in your daily reality, but you could confront them through experiencing other people's experiences on screen. Whether or not it's super relatable, in a way, it can still lead to some sort of therapeutic exchange. Just being conscious of how your body is reacting to instances of witnessing trauma on screen, being conscious of your heartbeat and your breathing, and stuff like that. But also just bearing witness to the way queerness is treated on screen can be kind of a way to reclaim a fear of death or to reclaim death – like the legacy of queer characters that have died on screen, the celluloid gravesite of all these characters that didn't make it.[9] Or the desires that didn't make it – the desires that just were never told on screen, or had the potential to go there, and then didn't fully come to fruition. I feel a collective mourning through queers experiencing horror in that way. (2020, pp. 17–18)

Hall explicitly connects the therapeutic functions of horror to psychophysiological affect,[10] describing how the horror genre creates emotional/mental and physiological responses, such as fear and increased heart rate or sweating, in the queer spectator. Hall reflects that bearing witness to the traumas shown in horror films offers the queer spectator therapeutic reactions. These therapeutic psychophysiological reactions affirm the argument put forth by Xavier Aldana Reyes, in *Horror Film and Affect: Towards a Corporeal Model of Viewership*: 'Horror creates a correlation between the filmic and viewing bodies' (2016, p. 150). Hall further states that 'horror definitely has the ability to process trauma because it is such a visceral, physical genre' (2020, p. 18). Hall's words reveal a double meaning and benefit, because the action within a horror film is visceral and physical, *and* the genre itself provides the spectator with a potential visceral and physical response – in short, a psychophysiological affective experience. Narrator Hall connects the catharsis that comes from a psychophysiological affective experience, found through watching horror films, with the trauma of queer disassociation and invisibility:

> Horror is such a visceral, bodily experience. Just feeling very grounded in your body, experiencing fear in that way, is a good check-in to be present, I think. Especially, in the sense of the queer body and in the way that we dissociate a lot or feel invisible a lot, and being able to come back into the body while watching horror – experiencing and processing those feelings also feels … it's a very therapeutic feeling. (2020, p. 4)

Queer spectators like Hall reflect engagement with and rationale for further investigations into affect, as Aldana Reyes recommends, to 'help us dig deeper into the human need for fictional and mediated forms of distress, whether strictly corporeal or emotional' (2016, pp. 196–7). The experience had by viewing a horror film is simultaneously mental and physical, narratives from which the queer horror spectator seeks (and finds) a therapeutic relief. Aldana Reyes (along with other scholars such as Clasen) convincingly argues for horror studies discourse to investigate further emotional and physiological responses to the genre, as is empirically accomplished in this study. Horror films offer queer spectators, for one, the opportunity to develop and refine 'crucial coping skills' (Clasen, 2017, p. 147) and to increase 'psychological resilience' (Scrivner et al., 2021, p. 2) because the confrontation with fear and trauma in horror films 'always happens at a remove' (Aldana Reyes, 2016, p. 51). This study evidences that the therapeutic function of horror gives queer people the ability to confront and better cope with real-life traumas safely from a distance, as unambiguously explained by one survey participant:

I've felt hopeless with the world after homophobic experiences and

> no other movie or show will take away that bitter taste as much as a horror movie . . . in the controlled sense of being scared that you don't have when faced with real life danger. If anything, horror movies really teach you how to control your fear and how to react more clearheaded to danger. (46974221)

Further evidencing this felt reality of queer spectators is the empirical study completed during the COVID-19 pandemic, which hypothesises: 'Experiencing negative emotions in a safe setting, such as during a horror film, might help individuals hone strategies for dealing with fear and more calmly deal with fear-eliciting situations in real life' (Scrivner et al., 2021, p. 5).

The psychological and physiological effects achieved by horror films have also been established by previous scholars to occur in fairy tales. Fairy tales allow the reader to 'confront their fears through ritualized exposure in a protected environment' (Tamborini and Weaver, 1996, p. 5) while 'help[ing] them manage the fears and anxieties they encounter in everyday life' (Ballon and Leszcz, 2007, p. 215). Given the affective psychophysiological benefits of fairy tales, unsurprisingly, a significant number of them have been adapted into horror films. As a whole, the horror genre offers spectators the experience of controlled fear and trauma – quite simply, a sense of control they may not be able to have in their daily existence as a part of a vulnerable population. As a survey participant heedfully comments: 'Horror is a genre of vulnerability, both for characters and the audiences' (47708748). A marginalised subjectivity leaves a person vulnerable (in feeling or reality), with a lack of power and the threat of harm; horror can function as one coping mechanism by facilitating the experience of catharsis, a release from strong emotions. Narrator Michael Varrati describes the cathartic release received from watching horror films as such:

> Here is a terrible situation that has been encapsulated in 90 minutes, and when those 90 minutes are over, you get a resolution and you get to breathe, you get some release. It may not always end well for the characters, but you know where it ends. Whereas real-life trauma is something you carry with you forever in some way. And so I think that it's the micro ability to take your real world fears and invest them into something small – into a story, into a movie – and for that period of time, 90 minutes, two hours, whatever, you get to kind of check out of your life and check into somebody else's issue. And

> see it play out, and have the chance to just breathe and have release. (2020, pp. 5–6)

My study's mixed-method data offers empirical evidence to the importance of affect in the queer relationship to horror since the horror genre 'is a filmic experience premised on the affective and emotional states it prompts in its audience' (Aldana Reyes, 2016, p. 153). As a survey participant writes:

> Horror deals with the body – its fluids, its desires, its angles. My relationship to my body has been one filled with denial and dysmorphia and abuse, trauma and self-flagellation (former Catholic, former closeted queer), and now that I'm out and watching these films, I can't help but see my own reality reflected there in helpful and severely true ways. (46816302)

In analysing the relationship between domestic (home-based) trauma survivors and cinephilia, Sher demonstrates that 'trauma survivors often find their affective truths, and understand their traumatic experiences, through engagement and identification with sexually violent films, genre films, and low brow films' (2015, p. 48).[11] This study extends Sher's findings to include all forms of trauma whilst simultaneously focusing on queer spectators of horror. The queer therapeutic function of horror, a genre often denigrated for its sexual violence and low-brow status, is evidenced by a survey participant who writes: 'In a world that hates me for who I am, it's sometimes therapeutic to watch a film about murder and mayhem, almost like a release' (46895196). Horror films offer queer spectators a therapeutic cathartic release, a psychophysiological affective experience related to traumas directly entwined with queer identity.

My mixed-method data evidences that the vast majority of queer horror spectators find a catharsis through the horror genre.[12] Indeed, 82.4 per cent of queer horror fans strongly agree or agree that horror films are cathartic, with only 2.9 per cent strongly disagreeing or disagreeing with that statement (see Figure 3.2). Therefore, it can be stated with 99 per cent confidence that 80.9 per cent to 84 per cent of *all* horror-loving queers find horror films to be cathartic. This provides the emphatic empirical evidence that supports the theories of horror's effective and affective catharsis, contrary to various scholars' doubts. For one, Darryl Jones's 'difficulty accepting' the hypothesis that horror films are cathartic is plainly stated:

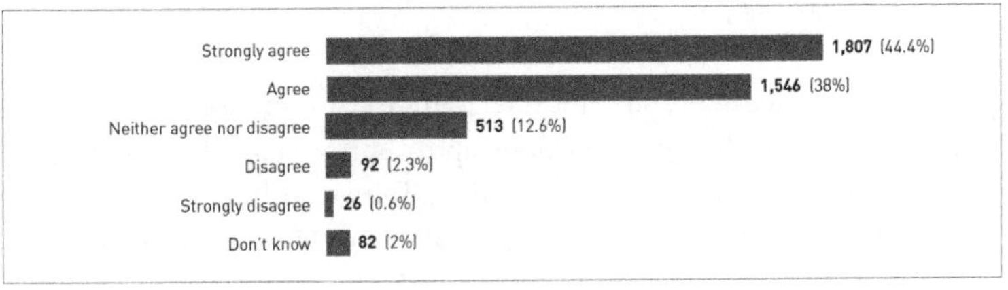

Figure 3.2. Bar graph that indicates survey participants' level of agreement or disagreement for the following statement: 'Horror films are cathartic'.

'It seems to me to be a classic example of an intellectual's gambit, a theory offered without recourse to any evidence' (2018, p. 5). Similarly, Zillmann and Weaver question the over-reliance of the 'catharsis doctrine', remarking that this 'doctrine has failed to attract empirical support of any kind (Geen and Quanty, 1977), but is used nonetheless to suggest that the consumption of horror is beneficial by relieving deep-rooted anxieties, and that the experience of relief makes for the genre's attractiveness' (1996, p. 88). Numerous scholars have theorised the cathartic benefits of the horror genre and, as shown, various scholars have questioned those theoretical assertions. However, this study's mixed-method data empirically evidences a cathartic experience and indicates that the specifically queer trauma experienced by queers produces a critical relationship for queer spectators between horror films and their cathartic function.

The reasons why 'horror films can feel cathartic' (47116502) are myriad. For some queer spectators, 'it's cathartic to watch and experience fictional larger than life traumas being played out that I can relate my own to' (47079421); for others 'seeing queer people be monsters/evil can be oddly cathartic' (46896188). The queer spectator's therapeutically cathartic relationship to the horror genre is a connection that is directly linked to their queer embodiment. In other words, queers connect the trauma(s) of their queer experience, existing within the cisheteronormative world, to the trauma(s) on the screen in horror films. Numerous survey participants explain this relationship between queer trauma and the therapeutic catharsis that horror provides: 'I think it can be scary growing up queer so there's a deeper catharsis when you watch horror movies and you see characters going through the horror and hopefully making it to the end of the film' (46979755); 'I think as an LGBT viewer I view horror more for catharsis and empathetic release than heterosexual viewers whose lives often don't allow for empathy with the high stress hypervigilance of horror films' (47757805); 'Having felt like an outsider and unsafe at times, I think I get a huge catharsis from getting to purge those feelings regularly' (47082203). These survey participant responses, alongside numerous others, not only explicitly connect queer spectatorship of horror films to queerness and queer trauma, but also clearly evidence the catharsis experienced from viewing horror films.

This study's survey data demonstrates that survey participants for whom horror films help work through trauma also exhibit an increased awareness that their queerness affects their relationship to horror. An independent-samples t-test was conducted to compare survey participants' responses to the question about the therapeutic function of the horror genre; the t-test compared the statistical means between participants who report that they have a different reaction to horror films (as compared with heterosexual viewers) and those who do not. A statistically significant difference exists in the therapeutic function of horror for participants who report that they have a different reaction to horror films versus those who do not ($p < 0.000$). The results indicate that survey participants who report more strongly receiving therapeutic benefits from horror are more likely to be those who report that they have a different reaction to horror films as compared with heterosexual viewers.[13] In addition, a statistically significant difference exists for horror films helping spectators work through trauma between participants who feel that being queer influences their taste in horror films and those who do not ($p < 0.000$). The results indicate that survey participants who more strongly receive therapeutic benefits from horror are more likely to be those who report that being queer influences their taste in horror films.[14] Having examined the therapeutic effects of horror for the queer spectator, I conclude that those survey participants who are cognisant that their queerness affects their reactions to and preferences in horror are also those more likely to be attuned to understanding their trauma as specifically caused by being queer in a hostile society, since living outside of normative structures can be a perilous state.

Two horror subgenres, slashers and body horror, positively correlated in my study's data with the therapeutic effects of horror, further evidence that the queer spectator's relationship to horror is explicitly connected to trauma. Spearman's rho correlation calculations, comparing those for whom horror films help work through trauma with preferences for each horror subgenre, yielded numerous highly statistically significant positive correlations, revealing the two subgenres with the highest effect sizes as body horror ($r_s = 0.20, p < 0.000$) and slasher ($r_s = 0.19, p < 0.000$).[15] As evidenced earlier, slashers are in the top ten of most loved and/or liked subgenres for queer spectators. While slasher films are discussed in copious academic discourse, far too little centres the significance of trauma, with the traumatic dimensions of the slasher film having been particularly neglected by critics given that slasher movies are ultimately about trauma.[16] The slasher film is predicated on the 'survival suspense' of the final girl, to whom queer spectators significantly connect and with whom they identify, as previously established and evidenced. Significantly, that filmic 'survival suspense is largely emotional and premised on the well-being of the character(s)' (Aldana Reyes, 2016, p. 119). For queer spectators, the final girl represents the ultimate model of triumphant survival against an overwhelming and threatening reality, as noted by a survey participant: 'Watching final girls triumph over killers and emerge victorious, or become monstrous themselves is so satisfying and affirming' (47079311). Queer trauma finds a cathartic release through the final girl's survival, creating a kinship and fondness for the final girl as representation for overcoming trauma, as explicitly commented by survey participants: 'I tend to relate to a final girl due to overcoming personal trauma in my own life' (46936127); the 'final girl trope is so important to me. I've always identified with her, with how she overcomes her fear and trauma and becomes stronger' (47082733). While Carol Clover argues for male spectators' catharsis through identification with the final girl, this study's data demonstrates that the final girl is a distinctly queer model of trauma survival.

Queers relate to the final girl and experience catharsis from the survival suspense of the final girl trope, whereas queer spectators' affinity for the body horror subgenre is centred on body betrayal. Body horror displays non-normative transgressions that render the body into 'an object over which the subject has no control' (Humphries, 2002, p. 169). Although the subgenre of body horror does not have a commonly accepted or clearly delineated definition, films categorised as such portray experiences of corporeal representations and transformations that are aberrant and/or grotesque.[17] The queer spectator, most specifically transgender members of the community,[18] find a therapeutic cathartic release from body horror films because they 'radically figured, disfigured, and refigured the human body, focusing on it relentlessly as a site of pain, and anxiety and disgust, but also of transformation and transcendence' (Jones, 2018, p. 94). Indeed, trans* survey participants express and explain a particular connection to the representations of transformed and transcended bodily norms as presented in body horror films, writing: 'Body horror grosses out many but is cathartic for me as a trans person, seeing others transcend the limits of their body via effects' (47078232); 'I'm trans, so I also think I have a different perspective on body horror than a cisgender person might, and often find themes of transformation in horror to be exciting and cathartic' (47082799). Body horror offers trans* community members ways to relate to and have an outlet for their 'dysmorphia' (47082888) and 'feelings of dysphoria' (47086892). A non-binary participant connects to horror because of 'the feeling that your body and the feelings you feel are still seen as abnormal, or monstrous, by many people who are not LGBTQ+' (47069306). This brief empirical investigation into the slasher and body horror subgenres demonstrates that the queer connection to horror is inseparable from queer embodiment, trauma and, as will be detailed, camp.

I have thus far examined the therapeutic effect of the horror genre for the queer spectator, relating queer identity with the trauma of living in the 'traumatizing processes and structures' of cisheteronormative society (Davis and Meretoja, 2020, p. 4). As discussed, queer trauma can take as many forms as there are individual queer subjectivities. For example, one survey participant shares that 'when the monster is a metaphor for abuse or grief I relate heavily to them because although I am transmasculine I was treated as a woman by the "monsters" in my own life' (47080740). Narrator Christopher Velasco recalls: 'Watching *A Nightmare on Elm Street 2: Freddy's Revenge*, really helped me deal with the trauma of being different. Though it wasn't a direct correlation to my life, I just knew this movie was about me' (2020, p. 16). The differences in how queer spectators understand and express their trauma matters less than the collective shared experience of cisheteronormativity traumatising queers. My study builds on and adds to earlier critical approaches of cinema therapy by specifically centring the horror genre's therapeutic potentials for the queer spectator.

Queer people have few communal gathering spaces, outside of the dwindling numbers of bars and clubs, but cinemas/movie theatres have become one, as will be discussed. The importance of movie theatres is argued by John Izod and Joanna Dovalis, in *Cinema as Therapy: Grief and Transformational Film*, who state: 'The movie theatre shares symbolic features with both the church and the therapy room: all are sacred spaces where people can encounter the archetypal and ease personal suffering, in the case of the cinema whether through laughter or tears, without inhibition or fear' (2015, p. 1). For the queer spectator, cinemas/movie theatres can function as safe, sacred spaces to watch films and ease their trauma; in particular, the queer spectator often experiences the medium through the combination of fear with laughter when watching a horror film in a darkened movie theatre. Often queer people experience this juxtaposition through camp because '[c]amp embraces and even flaunts a stigmatized identity in order to "neutralize the sting and make it laughable"' (Pellegrini, quoting Esther Newton, 2015, p. 179). Camp stems from queer trauma and survival, as a 'combination of dark humor, traumatic pain, and "resistance to vulnerability"' (Brickman, 2017, p. 28). Camp is known to be a queer sensibility, but its power for queers lies under the surface in its relationship with trauma; to this, theorist '[Ann] Cvetkovich recognizes the use of camp around trauma in queer culture' (Brickman, 2017, p. 28). Queers often filter traumatic pain through humour and laughter as a survival tactic. I argue, furthermore, that camp functions as a vulnerable resistance. By this I mean, camp's utility to resist and challenge cisheteronormativity is informed by queer vulnerability and trauma, evidenced through my study's qualitative responses, including this survey participant's direct connection of trauma and camp:

> I'm drawn to horror films that are stylized in such a way that focuses on either character or place in such a way that reflects what some may term 'camp,' or otherwise performative or affected sensibilities. The actual horror that I experience within such films is often a challenge to [the] ability of norms of family, love, or social relations to 'save' us from the legacy of trauma. (47573274)

A camp sensibility or aesthetic, such as exaggeration, can be deployed to communicate (and thus process) trauma, as noted by Nadin Mai in remarking on trauma theorist Janet Walker's '"quality of exaggeration" in style for an evocation of "trauma" which is employed in an attempt to adequately transmit the quality of the traumatic events' (2015, p. 61). Through the analysis and presentation of mixed-method data, this research has evidenced that horror offers queers a cathartic relief from their specific queer trauma. Not only that, queer spectators also realise a further dimension of trauma processing through the joyous, affective elements of camp. Camp, therefore, as a powerful expression of queer trauma, can be seen as a further, joyous, means of processing queer trauma in horror cinema.

To understand the dynamic between the queer spectator, horror film and camp, the difficult-to-define and intangible sensibility that is camp must be examined first.

The Camp Relationship to Horror

While Andrew Ross states that 'universal definitions of camp are rarely useful' (2014, p. 146), I grasp here a definition that provides an understanding of camp's role as a relationship queers have with horror through its function as a sensibility, as 'a system of meaning and a method of perception' (Taylor, 2012, p. 69). 'Camp' is a noun, an adjective and a verb. Camp is irreducible (Cleto, 1999, p. 29) and undefinable (Ludlam, 1992, p. 227), transgressive (Brickman, 2016, p. 383) and subversive (Babuscio, 1977, p. 42). Camp is a queer concept, lens, mode, code, sensibility, aesthetic, style, tool, critique, performance, essence, feeling, strategy, function, practice, product, reception, effect, taste and language.[19] Unlike Susan Sontag who, in her influential essay 'Notes on "Camp"', marks camp as 'wholly aesthetic' (1964, p. 49), this research defines camp as a queer sensibility that goes beyond the artistic surface. While defining camp may be a 'self-defeating' project (Core, 1984, p. 5), that effort is worthwhile because camp functions as an essential relational tool of queer non-normativity. As Michael Bronski writes, 'camp changes the real, hostile world into a new one which is controllable and safe' (1984, p. 42). Stated differently, queers use camp reimaginings to relate to other people and cultures (and cultural products), creating feelings of safety and connection. This study builds on the work of Cynthia Barounis, who 'is less interested in what camp *looks* like than in what camp *feels* like' (2018, p. 217; italics in the original). Since queer people feel they have 'a special appreciation for camp' (47150431), camp feels like a way of relating to normative society. As example, narrator Joshua Grannell has 'adopted and accepted this idea of camp that is queerness . . . I think you can take the word camp and really define it as an insider's queer perspective on what is wonderful and outrageous' (2020d, p. 11). Camp is active, involving the agency of the reader in a mode of cultural engagement and 'has the power to transform experience' (Sontag, 1964, p. 43).

Camp has previously been called apolitical (Sontag, 1964), the domain of the gay male (Dyer, 2002) and 'a distanced and distanciating reception practice' (Benshoff, 2008, p. 150). However, my study's mixed-method data demonstrates that camp is, in fact, entirely political, inclusively queer, deeply intimate and fully embodied. Since queer people use camp to relate to normative society, camp is an intimate and embodied politic. As Jack Babuscio, one of camp's early theorists, writes: 'Camp is never a thing or person *per se*, but, rather, a relationship' (1977, 40–1; italics in the original). While Babuscio remained focused on the gay camp relationship to 'activities, individuals, situations' (1977, p. 41), a relationship is still the most appropriate way to describe the queer connection to camp because relationships exist in many forms, none looking exactly the same.[20] One commonality to these distinct relationships, however, is the existence of genuine love, as Christopher Isherwood indicates: 'You can't camp about something you don't take seriously. You're not making fun of it; you're making fun out of it. You're expressing what's basically serious to you in terms of fun and artifice and elegance' (1999, p. 51). If camp is a queer way of relating to the world, it serves to examine this common camp relationship that queer people share. In this case, queer spectators' love of horror film is grounded in a serious connection to the genre facilitated by a camp relationship. In other words, queer spectators have a 'camp relationship' to horror.

Camp is, most significantly to this study, a relationship between a queer spectator and the horror film. In fact, 80.4 per cent of the survey participants report enjoying the confluence of camp and horror. Camp is an important relationship to horror in queer spectatorship because queers 'camp' what they see in this film genre, recognising in horror facets also fundamental to camp: over-the-top excess, flamboyant extravagance, exaggerated abjection, artifice, extremity and trauma. The queer spectator of horror directly connects horror aestheticism to camp, which is a politicised queer expression. This camp relationship to horror for queer spectators runs counter to prevalent attitudes about the horror genre being conservative, regressive, misogynistic, racist and/or homophobic. While Susan Sontag said that to talk about camp is to betray it (1964, p. 42), queers find a power through defining our meaning of camp based on our lived, and often silenced, queer experience. Queers are drawn to and connect with horror to process and alleviate the pain of societal marginalisation and demonisation in part because the horror genre is imbued with key camp attributes, such as 'the spirit of extravagance' (Sontag, 1964, p. 47) and the '[l]ove of the unnatural: of artifice and exaggeration' (Sontag, 1964, p. 42). This connection is particularly powerful since, as explained, both horror and camp are potent expressions of queer trauma. Olivia Oliver-Hopkins notes: 'Despite considerable crossover, relatively little theoretical work has been completed on the relationship between the horror genre and notions of camp' (2017, p. 151). This study, therefore, expands the current discourse on the intersections of camp and horror and does so through an explicitly queer lens.

Since queer horror spectators explicitly connect camp and horror each to their queerness, having a camp relationship to horror is a decidedly queer manifestation. As evidenced by this study's mixed-method data, queer spectators actively engage with camp and report that camp serves as a relationship to horror. My data demonstrates, in fact, that the camp connection to horror *feels* decidedly queer and entirely essential to queer horror spectators. As several survey participants state: 'There is a strong camp element to horror that queers seem to naturally understand' (47616489); and 'queer people have an innate understanding of the camp undertones that horror is based on' (47706009). This study positions camp as a relationship that queers have with a cultural production, the horror genre, as a personal and political relationship for processing individual trauma and community bonding through laughter.

The queer spectator's embodied connection to horror is genuine, in part due to the camp relationship; it is not a distanced and ironic reaction to hegemonic cultural production (see, e.g., Sontag, Babuscio, Benshoff, Brickman and Levitt). The queer spectator's camp relationship to horror uses camp as a political tool of disidentificatory practice.[21] Disidentification is a political act of survival in which minorities (re)negotiate dominant culture and its products through transformation to fit their own purposes and needs. This concept advanced by queer theorist José Esteban Muñoz examines queer BIPOC disidentificatory practices. As Muñoz states:

> Disidentification is about recycling and rethinking encoded meaning. The process of disidentification scrambles and reconstructs the encoded message of a cultural text in a fashion that both exposes the encoded message's universalizing and exclusionary machinations and recircuits its workings to account for, include, and empower minority identities and identifications. (1999, p. 31)

While written to explain BIPOC queer practices, the concept of disidentification can be applied to understand the political nature of queer horror spectatorship both because a significant percentage of the survey participants are BIPOC and all the participants are queer, thereby embodying a shared intersectionality that subsists outside dominant culture. Muñoz's concept of disidentification highlights, therefore, how queer horror spectatorship operates both 'within and outside' dominant horror spectatorship (1999, p. 5). Queer horror fans enjoy many of the same films as cisheteronormative horror spectators; however, queer spectators employ camp, a distinctively queer manner and method of relating to the world, as a relationship with horror, a genre always already connected to their queer embodiment.

While the definition of camp has eluded consensus and concrete determination, camp has been continually connected to queer identity. Indeed, for many queers, camp is the key performative and interpretative aspect of queer identity. Muñoz argues that 'to perform queerness is to constantly disidentify, to constantly find oneself thriving on sites where meaning does not properly "line up"' (1999, p. 78). The camp relationship to horror lines up the intrinsic queerness of the genre with the embodied queerness of the spectator. Through their camp relationship with horror, queer horror spectators 'resist the oppressive and normalizing discourse of dominant ideology' (Muñoz, 1999, p. 97), identifying with the queerness of the horror genre, engendering queer empowerment and fostering queer community. Queer spectators' camp relationship to horror neither functions to assimilate nor resist mainstream horror; instead, it represents how queer horror spectators form a *sui generis* horror fandom of disidentification, representing the 'crucial practice of contesting social subordination through the project of worldmaking' (Muñoz, 1999, p. 200). Queer horror spectators, individually and collectively, construct queer space, a campy horrific world in which their community flourishes.

Building on the existing scholarship that establishes the camp-horror nexus, my mixed-method data evidences the importance of queerness to this concept. This study specifically explicates how queer spectators relate to the nexus of camp and horror. Jason Lagapa defines the 'camp-horror nexus' as a fusion of 'campy stylistics and Gothic motifs into a single aesthetic, one that invokes B-movie horror to achieve humorous, mannered and uncanny effects' (2010, p. 93). Oliver-Hopkins, advancing Jason Lagapa's camp-horror concept from the aesthetic to the political, argues through a class-based analysis that 'the self-love present in the camp-horror nexus enables these minority cultures to feel pride and joy in place of fear of judgment or shame' (2017, p. 158). In their formulation of this concept, both Oliver-Hopkins and Lagapa bypass specifically discussing the queer spectator's active role in the existence of the camp-horror nexus. Indeed, this study argues that the intersection of horror and camp is forged *through* the queer spectator, in the prideful and joyous manner Oliver-Hopkins outlines and as part of a relationship – a relationship to horror that is constantly and actively mediated by queerness embodied by living queer spectators. The diverse spectrum of queer spectators directly informs the fluidity and dynamism of camp-horror expressions. In other words, there are as many expressions of the camp-horror nexus as there are queer embodiments because it is a relationship informed by each individual's sensibility.

The queer connection to horror is forged in both how queer people read horror (finding unintentional camp in the genre) and how they appreciate the explicit camp attributes of horror. Specifically, I argue that the *queered* camp-horror nexus can be defined by three primary queer relationship instigators and shared attributes between camp and horror: camp and horror's shared aesthetics and themes, transgressive natures and coded queerness. Horror and camp share core attributes that resonate with queer spectators. When discussing film genres, including horror, that hold particular appeal to queer audiences, Benshoff and Griffin allude to reasons connected to camp attributes, such as heightened aesthetics, writing: 'Other genres [are] popular with queer audiences precisely because of their elaborate, fantastic styles. Musicals, horror films, and cartoons all flaunt their lack of realism and their disdain for the "normal"' (2006, p. 71). This study's mixed-method data not only substantiates Benshoff and Griffin's claim, but also further refines the queer spectatorial connections with the camp-horror nexus. Specifically, the horror genre shares attributes with camp through its aesthetics and themes: over-the-top excess (gore and violence), emotional theatricality (expressions of fear and survival such as screaming, yelling and crying) and personified extravagance (delicious villains and hordes of monsters). For example, survey participants affirm the queer 'love of excess, extremes, hyperbole' (47165704) and that queers 'have a soft spot for camp and extravagance in horror' (46975767). These attributes pertain not only to horror films that are deliberately campy, but also – and more significantly – the horror genre's aesthetics. These horror genre aesthetics (whether found overall in the genre or specifically in campy horror films) include 'exaggerated depictions of the grotesque, preposterous death and dismemberments, detached humor, and conscious deployment of generic tropes' (Kelly, 2016, p. 93). Survey participants repeatedly demonstrate an appreciation both that 'camp can reflect the heightened reality of horror' (47034234) and that they have a connection with horror characters: 'I can read myself into characters that straight people can't or won't, I can map my experiences onto horror more easily' (47100974).[22] Whether the camp that queers experience in horror is deliberate in a film's production or through an individual's own queer reception of a film, camp enhances the queer connection to the genre, since queer horror fans take 'a pleasure in campness and a sort of willful excess' (47108216) and 'tend to have a good understanding of the genre's tropes and tendency toward excess, which they celebrate' (47081807). Camp, in fact, opens the queer spectator to the horror genre, as one survey participant affirms: 'My camp aesthetic taste allows me to be more open to the breadth of the genre' (46854175).

Through his examination of horror, Gregory Waller further shows how 'horror has proven to be a genre that accommodates and encourages a heightened sense of stylization in editing, camera movement, and mise-en-scène' (1987, p. 149). These 'excessive' aesthetics of horror (Cherry, 2009, p. 80) are a key connection point for queer spectators, with some queer horror fans discussing horror aesthetics in a manner that underscores the camp presence in the genre: 'Horror is deliciously aesthetic; it layers meaning onto image and moment in a way that seems to align with and highlight queer sensibility' (47182398). Another survey participant notes their reaction and relation to 'camp and over the top grotesque' (47238133) in horror. And another survey participant explains: 'The horror films I love tend to have characters and aesthetics that, in a somewhat hard to articulate way, I associate with queerness. It's not necessarily because they involve queer characters – they usually don't' (46826850). These quotes illustrate the awareness survey participants have of their specifically queer connection to horror being rooted in camp, directly linking to the camp aesthetic featured in horror: 'I think that queer people have a unique appreciation for the theatricality and aesthetic spectacle of horror films' (46826850) and queers '"get" camp a bit more and can appreciate the over the top nature of horror differently' (47109055). For horror-loving queers, the unique lens that allows them to find camp in horror is also that which facilitates repudiating normality and transgressing the cisheteropatriarchy's norms.

The sexual and gender transgressions of non-normative queer existence directly relate to the transgressiveness of both horror and camp. Harry Benshoff argues that 'camp was even used to destabilize and question the nature of cinema and reality itself' (2008, p. 170), alluding to a cinematic and ontological transgression facilitated by camp. Specifically, queerness, horror and camp all share a transgression of the normative, as transgression depends on the enforcement of norms to transgress. The horror genre continuously responds to individual as well as societal fears, anxieties and taboos while pushing the bounds of explicitness. Cynthia Hendershot states that the 'horror film is a genre that operates within a framework of taboo and transgression' (2001, p. 25). Since queerness itself is seen to transgress normative existence (which is centred on heterosexual, monogamous pairings for the primary purpose of reproduction), queer horror fans relate to the function of horror to transgress the safety and predictability of that normative society. In fact, the queer relationship to both horror and camp is partially formed through the embodied connection to transgression. Barbara Jane Brickman asserts that queers may find 'transgressive pleasures in camp readings' (2016, p. 383), which this study's data supports. In fact, queers take active agency in transforming horror through their camp relationship, forging an *explicitly* queer connection (as opposed to the implicit queer connection to horror – a genre that queers understand to be intrinsically queer). A survey participant encapsulates this queer connection to horror and camp: 'Queer folks seem to have an enhanced unconscious awareness of the uncanny, camp, and acts of transgressions' (47181591). The societal transgression embodied by queer people finds expression in the camp-horror nexus. Indeed, queer horror fans 'love anything campy and subversive . . . that codes as queer' (47026811).

Queer spectators also explicitly, or knowingly, connect the coded queerness within the horror genre with camp. The horror genre has coded the monster as queer, an othered character and representation of the queer experience in cisheteronormative society. The monster is often queer-coded in horror and 'queer desire is also coded as horror' (46914100). Queer-coded (and even overtly queer) characters and performances, particularly but not exclusively campy ones, have helped to define and differentiate the horror genre, from Dr Pretorius (*The Bride of Frankenstein*) to Dr Frank-N-Furter (*The Rocky Horror Picture Show*), from Renfield (*Dracula*) to Freddy Krueger (*A Nightmare on Elm Street* franchise). Camp, independent from and certainly within horror, has historically functioned as queer code. As Dolores McElroy argues, this is because camp was 'a way to be identified as gay by other gays, yet dodge explicit identification by straights (heterosexuals), who were often unable to read the ambiguities of the code. In other words, camp provided both advertisement and cover' (2017, p. 295). Historically, queerness needed to be coded in relationship with cultural production or cultural reception for queer people's safety and, indeed, survival – a relationship that is both a means of connection between queer people and a mode of queer survival within the normative mainstream. This manifests in queer subtextual/implicit production and reception within the camp-horror nexus. To this, a survey participant knowingly and rhetorically asks: 'Isn't everything in horror queer coded anyway? I think that's a lot of what draws me to it' (47114181). Since 'camp has evolved from a primarily private code of secret communication' (Horn, 2017, p. 16) to a shared and political relationship as part of the queer community's engagement with cisheteronormative society and its cultural production, camp often remains coded and subtextual (but no less potent). A survey participant underscores the queer connection in horror to the transgression, aesthetics and subtext in camp: 'We understand horror films as essential aesthetic modalities for our darker fears and behaviors. This goes hand in hand with the powerful queer cultivation of queer aesthetics, in which to encode, operate, and celebrate our reviled existence' (47114181). Indeed, queer horror fans are acutely aware that camp is an integral aspect of their relationship to horror, as a survey participant details: 'I think we're more likely to decode the subtext of a film and appreciate what is under the surface (ex. *Elm St 2*) or appreciate campier things for what they are (ex. also *Elm St 2*)' (47196839).[23] As another survey participant states: 'There is a lot of coded queer semiotics in horror movies that make some moments, images, and themes maybe more resonant for queer audiences' (47182398). Queer spectators recognise and read queer coding in horror film, a queer act that historically has been fulfilled also through camp, which was used covertly to see and be seen within the queer community. The queer use of camp in relation to society and cultural productions such as horror films supports numerous survey participants' conviction that 'cis-hets aren't as accepting of camp in horror movies' (47082931). The attributes shared between the horror genre and camp, including aesthetics, transgression and queer coding, both bolster the camp relationship between queers and the horror genre *and* cement the queer camp-horror nexus in the critical fields of camp, horror and queer studies.

Evidentiary Data on Queerness, Camp and Horror

This study demonstrates with data that the vast majority of queer horror fans connect camp with their enjoyment of horror films, enjoying both deliberately camp horror films and horror films decoded as camp by the queer gaze. Specifically, the mixed-method data evidences that queer spectators have a camp relationship with horror and recognise the queer camp-horror nexus.[24] This study's data stands in sharp contrast to Alexander Dhoest and Nele Simons's findings that 'the gay sensibility and camp as reading strategies' have 'largely disappeared' due to increased mainstream visibility and assimilation (2012, p. 274). The data, in fact, serves to establish camp as a critical facet in queer spectators' relationship with horror film. As noted by Brigid Cherry, empirical audience research can evidence the 'variation in the way different groups interpret or respond to different kinds of cinematic horror' (2009, p. 155). My mixed-method data, both the survey's single explicit question about camp in horror and the hundreds of related comments survey participants elected to write, reveals the importance of camp in the queer spectator's relationship to horror.[25] My data emphatically demonstrates, in fact, that the overwhelming majority of survey participants, and thus horror-loving queers in the world according to statistical extrapolation, report a camp relationship to horror regardless of sexual orientation, gender, age or nationality.[26] As already noted, it can be stated with 99 per cent confidence that 78.7 per cent to 81.9 per cent of *all* horror-loving queers enjoy 'camp-y' horror films (see Figure 3.3). As a survey participant observes: 'As a queer person, I think I enjoy camp so much more than a cishet person. And enjoying and understanding camp usually means that I'll like more horror movies than other viewers' (48126762). My data further affirms Elly-Jean Nielsen's call for 'a radical reconceptualization of camp as a queer counter-praxis, one that is inclusive' of all queer people (2016, p. 123).

This study employs qualitative and quantitative data from a survey of queer horror spectators to situate 'camp within a queer rather than

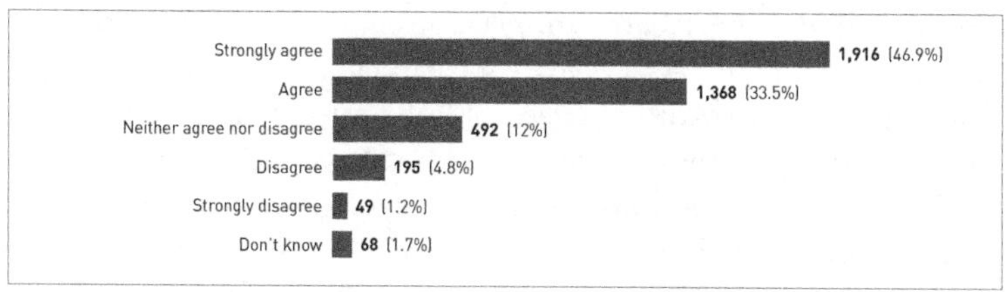

Figure 3.3. Bar graph that indicates survey participants' level of agreement or disagreement for the following statement: 'I enjoy "camp-y" horror films'.

exclusively gay male discourse' (Taylor, 2012, p. 67). In all, the survey data dispels the notion that camp is the provenance of the gay cisgender man, instead affirming camp is a decidedly queer relationship created through the wholly queer experience. Even though, as Andrew Ross states, 'camp works to destabilize, reshape, and transform the existing balance of accepted sexual roles and sexual identities' (2008, p. 62), numerous scholars theorise camp primarily in relation to gay cis men (see, e.g., Sontag, Ross, Dyer and Humphrey). Richard Dyer goes as far as to argue that camp:

> is just about the only style, language and culture that is distinctively and unambiguously gay male. One of our greatest problems is that we are cut adrift for most of the time in a world drenched in straightness. All the images and words of the society express and confirm the rightness of heterosexuality. Camp is one thing that expresses and confirms being a gay man. (2002, p. 49)

Camp theory's focus on gay cisgender men is somewhat unsurprising given the historical bias to white gay cisgender men in queer theory, which has, along with mainstream media, centred white gay cisgender men. As Melissa M. Wilcox details: 'Early queer theorists were typically cisgender white men whose writing focused on other cisgender white men' (2021, p. 23). This bias within the queer community has been further perpetuated by 'mainstream media's sanitized vision of sexual minorities: cisgender gay white men' (Chamberlain, 2020, p. xvi). However, my evidence directly disputes that patriarchal dominion on camp, as my survey participants identifying as gay, lesbian and/or queer all enjoy camp in nearly equal measure – and gay participants are not even those with the strongest reported connection to camp. 52 per cent (n = 651) of the survey participants who identify as 'queer' strongly agree with the statement that they enjoy 'camp-y' horror films, whereas 4.6 per cent (n = 57) strongly disagree or disagree with the same statement. Of the participants who identify as 'lesbian', 48.7 per cent (n = 290) strongly agree with the same statement, with 4 per cent (n = 24) strongly disagreeing or disagreeing. Of those participants who identify as 'gay', 48.5 per cent (n = 626) strongly agree with the same statement, whereas 6.1 per cent (n = 78) strongly disagree or disagree.[27] Similarly, people of all gender identification categories enjoy camp, with genderqueer people demonstrating a slightly stronger affinity towards camp than those who are cisgender.[28] The following statistics represent the survey participants who 'strongly agree' with the statement that they enjoy 'camp-y' horror films:

- 56.5 per cent (n = 108) of those who identify as 'genderqueer man'.
- 50.7 per cent (n = 107) of those who identify as 'genderqueer person'.
- 49.2 per cent (n = 394) of those who identify as 'non-binary person'.
- 47.5 per cent (n = 96) of those who identify as 'agender'.
- 46.8 per cent (n = 627) of those who identify as 'cisgender woman'.
- 46.4 per cent (n = 560) of those who identify as 'cisgender man'.

This data, all together, demonstrates that the wide spectrum of queer horror fans has a relationship with camp, affirming that camp belongs to all those who embody non-normative sexualities and/or genders. A survey participant succinctly summarises that camp is 'an important aesthetic and sensibility within queer culture' (46982544). Underscoring the long *queer* history of camp, Sue-Ellen Case shares that she learned camp from both lesbians and gay men: 'a multitude of other experiences and discourses continued to enhance my queer thinking. Most prominent among them was the subcultural discourse of camp which I learned primarily from old dykes and gay male friends I knew in San Francisco, when I lived in the ghetto of bars' (1991, p. 1). This example from Case evidences inclusive queer theory from critics such as Andrea Weiss, who emphasises that 'camp is a tradition which belongs to women as well as men' (1992, p. 4). Camp theory's focus on gay cisgender men upholds binaristic gendered fixations and perpetuates lesbian erasure, and obscures the entire queer community's shared relationship to camp.

Queer horror fans of all ages have a relationship with camp, as evidenced by my survey data, which indicates that there is no statistically significant correlation between age and preference for camp in horror films.[29] The fact that all generations of queer horror fans enjoy camp in horror films indicates that, as Harry Benshoff and Sean Griffin argue in *Queer Images: A History of Gay and Lesbian Film in America*, 'queer horror fans often enjoy the genre as camp' (2006, p. 77). This critical statement is further evidenced by the survey participants who write that 'camp belongs with horror' (47122384) since they 'go together' (47120553), 'are synonymous' (47182539), 'go hand in hand' (47125731 and 47121475) and 'share a family in spectacle' (47122384). My survey data demonstrates that queers of all ages have a camp relationship to horror, which indicates that camp is deliberately disseminated and acquired, making it an explicitly political queer relationship to cisheteronormative hegemonic culture. Camp is shared by being taught, learned, exhibited and absorbed within the queer community across generations in '"[t]wo of camp's most important channels of dissemination"' which are '"movie houses and gay bars"' (Benshoff and Griffin, 2006, p. 69).[30] While historically camp has been deliberately disseminated, those methods have remained covert and intangible, just as with queerness itself, which 'is often transmitted covertly' (Muñoz, 1996, p. 6). While indirectly shared, camp is an important aspect of the queer relationship to cisheteronormative society and its cultural products, including the horror genre, with queers of all ages finding agency and connection through a camp relationship to horror.

My survey data simultaneously highlights the relevance of camp across generations in queer culture and demonstrates its function as a relational tool for queers to joyously renegotiate and critique cisheteronormativity. Narrator Anthony Hudson posits that queers are 'in an ideal position to interface with camp and to use camp and to speak through camp because, existing as queer people, we see the faultiness of structures, we see the limitations and we see the artificiality for what it is' (2020d, p. 13). A camp relationship not only to cultural artefacts but also with sociopolitical and institutional structures plays a significant role in queers' formation of identity in opposition to hegemonic normativity. While numerous scholars have discussed camp as a queer mode of cultural critique, my mixed-method data demonstrates a more nuanced queer relationship to camp. Camp is a survival strategy for queer people, a very specific relationship and way of negotiating a relationship with the world. Narrator Varrati expands upon this notion, illustrating the 'queer uses of camp as tool of political protest' (Barounis, 2018, p. 220) that works to joyously critique cisheteropatriarchy:

> Camp is performative and camp is taking the piss out of society. Camp is Other. Camp is an otherness that holds a mirror up to the world at large and says, 'Look how you are. Look how you're acting. Isn't it kind of outrageous?' Who understands otherness better than queer people, because we've been othered *our whole lives*. So I think that we embrace camp because we understand the things that we

> were told growing up were so serious and so important – this is the word of law and this is how it is and how it shall always be – are kind of bullshit. Because all you have to do is take one step back to realize, 'Oh, this is really dumb.' And you're using this dumbness to subjugate and marginalize and push people down. So camp becomes both an element of fun and absurdity, but also a weapon to criticize all of those structures that have held us down. (2020, p. 6)

This and other responses from queer horror fans indicates that camp is neither, as Benshoff claims, a 'distanced and distanciating reception practice' nor 'a refusal to take seriously the serious forms and artifacts of dominant culture' (2008, p. 150). Instead, the camp relationship to horror for queer spectators is one that is joyously intimate and serious. A survey participant illustrates this camp relationship to horror, writing that 'because I carry the sexual trauma of homophobia I think I gravitate towards campier movies, slashers, and older horror movies because of their over the top sensibility that to me adds to it rather than takes away from its power' (47109055). Queers fostering this camp relationship to horror find a queer truth within this cultural production from a cisheterosexual society. Thus, this study amends Philip Core's oft-quoted axiom that 'camp is a lie that tells the truth' (1984, p. 9) because my mixed-method data indicates that camp is the way that queers find a truth in the lie. Queer people locate an empowering truth for their existence within the lie that cisheterodominant society tells us (including that horror film belongs to the young, heterosexual cisgender male). As one survey participant explicitly notes in connecting camp to the queer embodiment: 'I can embrace the weird and campy and outrageousness in horror movies more than my straight friends because these speak to my experience being gay' (46974343). Another affirms that 'camp and excess definitely resonate with a queer subjectivity' (46951892). Since mainstream cultural production overwhelmingly reflects cisheteronormativity, cisheterosexual people do not have a survival imperative to create a relationship beyond the surface presented. Narrator Jason Edward Davis discusses how cisheterosexual cultural dominance prevents a heterosexual relationship to camp due to the comfort found in this normative status. Davis states:

> I think camp is just something that's inherently queer because it is about that layer in front of the layer. There's this sincere thing and there's the image, and then you are trying to tell the difference. When

> straight people respond to camp, they just get the joke because they assume it was meant for them. They're like this isn't any deeper than the funny that's happening because my life is the default. They're not thinking about their existence and how that relates – but *all* queer people have that as a default. (2020, p. 32)

This also reflects how the coded, or subtextual, aspect of camp specifically resonates with queerness. Survey participants affirm this queer camp relationship through written comments, such as, 'Maybe straight people just have no concept of subtext' (47043096); and 'Very few straights get camp, but most gays do' (47124005).

This understanding by queer people that camp is a *queer* sensibility is affirmed by my survey data, which demonstrates that survey participants who have a camp relationship to horror also exhibit an increased awareness that their queerness affects their relationship to horror. An independent-sample t-test was conducted on survey participants' enjoyment of camp in the horror genre to compare participants who report that they have a different reaction to horror films (as compared with heterosexual viewers) to those who do not. A statistically significant difference exists in the enjoyment of camp in the horror genre between participants who report that they have a different reaction to horror films and those who do not ($p < 0.000$). The results indicate that participants who more strongly enjoy camp are more likely to be those who report that they have a different reaction to horror films as compared with heterosexual viewers.[31] Additionally, there is a statistically significant difference in the enjoyment of camp in the horror genre between participants who feel that being queer influences their taste in horror films and those who do not ($p < 0.000$). These results demonstrate that participants who more strongly enjoy camp are more likely to report that being queer influences their taste in horror films.[32] All combined, this data indicates that a horror spectator's queerness affects their relationship to camp and that knowingly possessing a camp relationship affects their relationship to horror.

The vast majority of queer horror fans have a camp relationship to horror, with statistically significant test results also demonstrating that these horror-loving queers are more engaged in horror fandom. Queer horror fans who have a camp relationship to horror consider themselves more knowledgeable about the horror genre, are more likely to collect horror films and are more likely to purchase horror memorabilia and/or collectibles. The survey results indicate that participants who more strongly enjoy camp are more likely to be those who consider themselves knowledgeable about horror film due to the statistically significant difference in the score of enjoyment of camp in the horror genre between participants who consider themselves knowledgeable about horror film and those who do not ($p < 0.000$).[33] The survey results indicate that participants who more strongly enjoy camp are more likely to be those who collect horror films, due to the statistically significant difference in the score of enjoyment of camp in the horror genre between participants who collect horror films in any format (e.g., Blu-ray, DVD, LaserDisc, VHS or any digital form) and those who do not ($p < 0.000$). Further results demonstrate that participants who more strongly enjoy camp are more likely to be those who purchase horror memorabilia and/or collectibles. There is a statistically significant difference in the score of enjoyment of camp in the horror genre between participants who purchase horror memorabilia and/or collectibles and those who do not ($p < 0.000$).[34] Queer horror fans actively forge a camp relationship to the horror genre, with the data also indicating these same horror-loving queers are more actively engaged with horror fandom, such as obtaining horror knowledge and collecting horror films and memorabilia.

Queer horror fans who possess a camp relationship to horror also have small and medium, yet highly statistically significant, positive correlations with the following statements: 'Horror films make me laugh' ($r_s = 0.32$, $p < 0.000$); 'I watch horror films for the special/practical/visual effects and make-up' ($r_s = 0.22$, $p < 0.000$); and 'I most enjoy watching horror films with queer audiences' ($r_s = 0.27$, $p < 0.000$). The data that horror-loving queers laugh at horror films provides statistical evidence for the connection between laughter and horror (see Figure 3.4). The data also indicates that queer spectators with a camp relationship to horror films watch to experience the heightened and exaggerated artifice of special/practical/visual effects and make-up in horror's extreme maimings and murders, which evidences David Bergman's statement that camp 'favors "exaggeration," "artifice," and "extremity"' (1993, p. 5). Narrator Kim Thompson confirms this, stating:

> My horror of choice isn't often something that is documentary style or based on something that I feel could really happen, or very drawn-out torture or human trauma. I don't really enjoy things that are too parallel to what I might read in the news or things that are linked to stuff that I see already in society that I think is awful. I'm not really

> drawn to things where a woman is being tortured and abused. I can open a newspaper for that. It's not just all horror that I necessarily find comforting and an escape. It tends to be supernatural stuff or things with great practical effects or things that are theatrical and camp and dramatic and visually nice to look at with an element of silly horror gore on the side. (2020, p. 19)

These aesthetic pleasures of horror films are enhanced for queer spectators with a camp relationship to horror when viewed among a queer audience, as evidenced by the data showing queer horror fans with a camp relationship to horror most enjoy watching horror films with queer audiences. Queer horror fans who have a camp relationship to horror also have small and medium, yet highly statistically significant, positive correlations with three horror subgenres: horror comedy or parody ($r_s = 0.31, p < 0.000$); monster movies ($r_s = 0.20, p < 0.000$); and slashers ($r_s = 0.22, p < 0.000$).[35] These results indicate that participants who more strongly enjoy camp are more likely to be those who love or like horror comedies, monster movies and slashers.[36] The horror comedy subgenre has a direct and explicit connection to laughter as a part of the camp relationship to horror, whereas monster movies and slashers both connect to queer spectators through the camp relationship's manifestation in the coded Other, as well as camp exaggeration and extremity found in horror special effects.[37] For queer horror spectators, horror's heightened narratives and aesthetic excesses are cathartic. As a survey participant shares: 'I tend to go for the more "unreal" things like slashers or monsters where usually the survival of someone is guaranteed, which isn't always the case with real life' (47079406). Queer

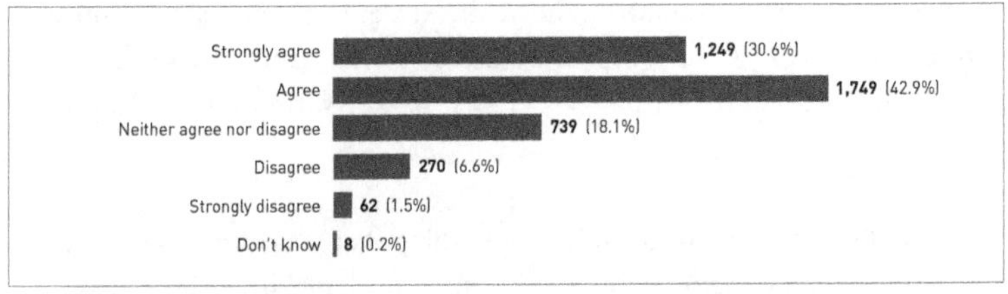

Figure 3.4. Bar graph that indicates survey participants' level of agreement or disagreement for the following statement: 'Horror films make me laugh'.

spectators actively transform horror's myriad manifestations of violence – whether psychological, physical or, indeed, supernatural or spiritual – and horror's presentations of monstrosity, victimisation and survival (e.g., the final girl trope) through a camp relationship. This camp-horror nexus connects with queer embodiment, facilitating queers across the spectrum to find comfort, experience empowerment, claim representation and foster healing.

Camp Laughter as a Trauma Processor

This research is specifically concerned with queer camp, as the qualitative and quantitative research data evidences that camp has a place in the queer spectator's relationship to horror representationally and figuratively. Esther Newton recognises camp as 'a *system* of humor', a 'system of laughing at one's incongruous position instead of crying', in which 'humor does not cover up, it transforms' (1979, p. 109; italics in the original). Camp's transformative function alleviates the pain of queer societal incongruity by connecting and bonding queer community through finding humour in shared suffering. While the horror genre provides a cinematic space for queers to work through trauma, the camp relationship that queers have with horror films provides further 'catharsis and ease[s] the burden' for queers 'living in an oppressive society' (McElroy, 2017, p. 298). Queer horror spectators both receive and create a camp relationship to horror through the heightened reality of the genre and in the over-the-top characters in the films.[38] Even with the advancement of queer rights since the 1970s, queer populations, particularly BIPOC and/or trans*, continue to experience personal, professional and political discrimination and violence. Queer people carry collective and individual traumas due to these pervasive and wounding societal threats. This is critical to reiterate because queer trauma finds expression through the camp relationship queer spectators have with the horror genre. The reason camp remains 'political' is because it is 'a means of communication and survival' that 'exaggerates and therefore diffuses real threats' (Bronski, 1984, pp. 42–3). As a survey participant writes 'there's something horrific and traumatic about many of our [queer] experiences and therefore I think horror tells them in a way we can appreciate artistically' (47109055). Even though Sontag capitulates that camp may concern 'grave matters' (1964, p. 42), her insistence of camp's apoliticality bypasses its ability to excavate the politics of queer joy *and* rage, healing *and* trauma.[39] As narrator Joe Fejeran asserts in explaining camp's complex nuances: 'Camp is not necessarily about drawing true to reality. It's about drawing the caricature and emphasizing those elements. And it's even more effective when you're dealing with serious subjects' (2020, p. 36).

While there has been much focus on the joyful side of camp,[40] my qualitative data indicates that camp has a more complex and nuanced relationship with cultural artefacts. Thousands of written survey responses, coupled with the oral histories, demonstrate that queer celebration and trauma are inextricably entwined in queer spectators' encounters with, understanding of and appreciation of horror films. In fact, the queer spectator's camp relationship with horror demonstrates Jodie Taylor's observation that 'camp is employed as a sign of a repressed alterity, which is transformed through parody, theatricality and carnivalesque spectacle into an empowering queer critique of dominant morality and social exclusion' (2012, p. 77).[41] The camp relationship to horror is directly established through queer alterity; queers use camp to reinterpret normativity to fit their non-normative reality as an Other, a status the majority of queer horror fans are acutely aware of possessing, as the mixed-method data previously presented evidences.[42] As a participant writes: 'I think we respond to the camp of the genre in ways heterosexuals do not. I also think we relate to the underdog fighting back from the hero perspective while on the flip side we relate to the monster, rejected from society but born anew and ready to subvert the order of things' (46854175). Horror-loving queers use camp to transform horror, knowing that 'camp has always, to some extent, urged us to take trauma and its aftermath seriously' (Barounis, 2018, p. 217). Being queer in a cisheteronormative society creates insidious trauma, which can be expressed and healed for queers through a shared and bonding use of camp. Narrator Fejeran emphasises the bond that he feels with other queers through his camp relationship: 'For me, camp and queerness have always been my way to relate to others' (2020, p. 38). Part of camp's power comes from queers' ability to turn a shared tragedy and pain into laughter. Camp's heightened emotionality and exaggeration renders trauma less painful for spectators because it rejects the norms of appropriate behaviour in response to tragedy and trauma. In Halperin's words:

> Camp undoes the solemnity with which heterosexual society regards tragedy, but camp doesn't evade the reality of the suffering that gives rise to tragedy. If anything, camp is a tribute to its intensity. Camp

> returns to the scene of trauma and replays that trauma on a ludicrously amplified scale – so as to drain it of its pain and, in so doing, to transform it. (2012, p. 200)

Horror can help heal queer trauma through its many methods of transformation, one of which is laughter – an essential way that queers process trauma through their camp relationship to horror.

Laughter is an exterior expression of humour, which 'constitutes the strategy of camp: a means of dealing with a hostile environment and, in the process, of defining a positive identity' (Babuscio, 1977, p. 47). The queer camp relationship to horror actively creates a specific levity that expresses itself in outward laughter in reaction to horrific scenarios. This simultaneously distinguishes queer horror spectatorship and empowers queer identity and community, particularly experienced when gathered together in movie theatres and laughing, an act which is at once bonding/inclusive *and* exclusionary. Julian Hanich explains that laughter 'sometimes has an *exclusionary* function: "Look, this – and precisely this – is funny for us, but *not for others*!"' (2014b, p. 51; italics in the original). In other words, queer people are both bonded together over their communal laughter and separated from others by it. The queer camp relationship to horror creates a shared non-normative bond of laughter for queer audiences that is often unavailable in cisheteronormative audiences. Queer horror fans provide examples of this phenomenon in describing watching horror films such as *What Ever Happened to Baby Jane?* (1962) or *Strait-Jacket* (1964)[43] with queer audiences (as opposed to cisheteronormative audiences). 'We [queers] also recognise the camp factor in movies more readily – *What Ever Happened to Baby Jane* is a comedy and a horror in equal measure, for example' (46867851). 'Straight people seem to love blood and gore for the violence, not the spectacle/pageantry. For that reason, they also don't seem to like classics like *Baby Jane*' (47100776). The difference in experience also manifests in viewing a horror film and sharing communal laughter (within a queer audience) versus viewing a horror film and being the only one to laugh (among a normative audience). The laughter is an important part of the camp relationship to horror because queers find a cathartic release through both laughter and screaming, as a survey participant elucidates: 'The best horror for me is the stuff that makes you scream but also laugh. There is a release to it I enjoy' (47291353). A camp relationship to horror liberates and releases through the catharsis that comes from screaming and laughing at horror. To this end, '[Esther] Newton's idea about camp's cathartic relationship to being queer in a world hostile to one's queerness' (McElroy, 2017, p. 299) directly links camp to both laughter and pain. Newton, an anthropologist, details camp as a queer tool that can function to alleviate the pain of being a queer Other in a cisheteronormative world: 'Only by fully embracing the stigma [of queerness] itself can one neutralize the sting and make it laughable. Not all references to the stigma are campy, however. Only if it is pointed out as a joke is it camp, although there is no requirement that the jokes be gentle or friendly' (1979, p. 111). As Newton indicates, camp exists in many forms, laced with a sharpness and pain, of which horror reflects one type. The queer spectator's camp relationship to horror creates queer inclusion through laughter, an intelligent and meaningful celebration, thereby both processing and excluding cisheteronormativity.[44] As one survey participant reflects:

> I participate in queer readings of texts along the lines outlined by Alexander Doty, or along the lines of a camp reading as discussed by Barbara Klinger. So, I recognise those themes or performative elements of the film that can be read as queer because of my own political investments and personal experiences that may not occur during a viewing of the film by a heterosexual viewer. (47725637)

While camp belongs to subjective individual perspectives, camp serves the queer community through both inclusionary and exclusionary functions in their relationship to horror. Through this camp relationship to horror, queers create a sense of belonging and healing through shared laughter.

This study evidences the intersection of queerness and horror, in part through queers' camp relationship to horror, which also creates a space in the academic discourse for camp's legitimacy as a queer relational tool with the horror genre. This powerful reclamation of space functions, as with Nielsen's work, to 'unghost' lesbian camp (2016, p. 131). Nielsen renders visible lesbian camp, while simultaneously calling on future researchers to 'sample a variety of gender and sexual identities to uncover which queer personalities are drawn to camp' (2016, p. 131). This study heeds Nielsen's call and demonstrates that the diverse spectrum of horror-loving queers' relationship to the horror genre is inseparable from their relationship to camp. For the queer spectator, a camp relationship to horror exists irrespective of the quality of a film, whether a horror film is 'good', 'bad', 'good bad' or, indeed, 'bad good'. Numerous scholars write about the intentional or unintentional camp of bad films (see, e.g., Ross and Benshoff), constructing a false dichotomy between filmic failure and camp success. However, a film being a failure is not a primary factor in queer spectators' camp relationship to horror. For some survey participants, their 'queer (and camp) sensibility influences [their] selection and enjoyment of horror films' (47101199). For others, they note their queerness as the reason that they 'appreciate camp, body horror, and politics in horror differently' (47808132). Regardless, the queer spectator's camp relationship to horror is not simply relegated to failed films or humorous subgenres. The shared attributes between the horror genre and camp, which queer spectators recognise and relate to, help horror-loving queers process trauma and connect within queer horror communities.

Even though the queer relationship to camp is subjective and individual, it becomes shared and known when queers express it, as in the camp-horror nexus. As Oliver-Hopkins astutely determines in analysing camp representation in the film *House of 1000 Corpses*, 'the camp-horror nexus suggest[s] the ideological work that needs to be done both covertly and overtly for a more equitable society to emerge from the relentless and aggressively homogenous dominant culture of twenty-first-century America' (2017, pp. 165–6). Whereas Oliver-Hopkins uses the 'white trash stereotype' to critique 'hegemonic notions of socially acceptable and unacceptable behavior' (2017, p. 165), this study similarly situates the queer camp-horror nexus as counter-hegemonic. The camp relationship to horror established by queer horror spectators functions simultaneously as a form of queer community inclusion and a 'queer critique of heteronormativity' (Benshoff, 2008, p. 170). Camp, understood as an act of resistance to overcome queer marginalisation and trauma, proves its continued value as a 'tactic that can be used to deconstruct the heterosexual presumptions of dominant culture' (Benshoff and Griffin, 2006, p. 70). Camp has a place in not only textual, intertextual, extratextual and paratextual readings by queer spectators, but also the drag artistry of performers such as Peaches Christ and Carla Rossi, as I will present and analyse next. As a survey participant elucidates: 'Horror frequently crosses over into camp and I feel that the experience of watching a horror movie in a drag performance setting allows that aspect of horror to shine' (47787515). For queer horror fans, the potential of camp is its use as a powerful aesthetic, political and performative relational tool for us to thrive, not simply survive, as non-normative people.

Notes

1. As with the definition of horror itself, this study does not mediate varied definitions and individual understandings of camp because of the idiosyncratic nature of camp relationships to cultural productions. Specifically, this study does not explicate camp distinctions in different horror films, even though individual queer spectators may distinguish between parody horror such as *The Rocky Horror Picture Show* (1975), contemporary queer camp horror such as *The Gay Bed and Breakfast of Terror* (2007) or *The Perfection* (2018), and traditional horror, especially the type that may be 'campily' consumed now due to historic distance, such as Bela Lugosi's and Dwight Frye's performances in *Dracula* (1931).
2. Even though, as noted, this study prioritises horror's positive effects for queer spectators, the mixed-method data indisputably establishes that blatant homophobia, transphobia, misogyny and/or racism in horror films is traumatic for some queer spectators, prompting them to have selective engagement with the genre and to eschew those types of films. Moreover, this study intentionally disengages with any case studies that document the connection between horror spectatorship and cinematic neurosis or psychosis.
3. Trauma is idiosyncratic and manifests innumerable creative production outputs; in my case, this study is a byproduct of my embodied queer trauma. This study exists because I sought to understand how my life-long connection with horror is entwined with the traumas caused to me from living in a homophobic, binaristic and misogynistic society. This study and document exist in their current forms in part due to a shared global trauma, having been partially conducted and entirely written during the globally traumatic COVID-19 pandemic – a pandemic that has disproportionately harmed and further traumatised the queer community, most especially the BIPOC and/or trans* members of the community.
4. Similarly, Rommi Smith and Jenni Molloy discuss 'the idea that creativity is one of many strategic responses to trauma' (2019, p. 209).
5. Future investigations in this field should specifically continue to examine empirically how women, BIPOC, disabled and/or economically disadvantaged people use horror to heal from the traumas of misogyny, white supremacy, ableism and capitalism/classism.
6. BIPOC and/or trans* members of the queer community experience traumatic violence at higher rates than white and/or cisgender queer people. 'People of color comprised 71 percent of all LGBTQ victims, and transgender or gender-nonconforming people comprised 52 percent of all LGBTQ victims.

As in the previous five years, the most common victim of an LGBTQ hate-motivated crime was a transgender woman of color' (Mooney, Clever and Van Willigen, 2021, p. 432).

7. Horror, as a cultural text, provides positive benefits to people other than the queer spectator. While the aim of this chapter is to analyse the specific relationship between queer trauma and the therapeutic function of horror, it must be noted that non-queer spectators may also find psychological benefits from the cathartic release that horror enables. For example, during the COVID-19 pandemic, a research team conducted an empirical study (n = 310) that concludes that horror fans (and the morbidly curious) are exhibiting greater psychological resilience through the pandemic (see Scrivner et al., 2021). However, it should be noted, in order to (re)emphasise how current quantitative methods of measurement and statistical analysis deny queer subjectivities, the research team explicitly excluded participants 'who answered something other than male or female' on their study's demographic question (Scrivner et al., 2021, p. 2).
8. For example, Narrator Harmony Colangelo connects her queerness and love of horror to escaping a transphobic world: 'I look at horror as a form of escapism – or at the very least in how it relates to my queerness – there's a power fantasy to some extent. Where certain trans films like *Dr. Jekyll and Sister Hyde* or *Sleepaway Camp* – the ever controversial *Sleepaway Camp* that I am a staunch defender of and Angela's currently on my back with a no TERF [trans-exclusionary radical feminist] sign [both laugh]. So I use horror as a way of escaping the ugly shit of the world and putting it in a more succinct and easy-to-understand way' (2020, p. 21).
9. Here, Hall references Vito Russo's 'Necrology', which details film's queer characters who have met premature deaths through suicide, murder and execution (1987, p. 347).
10. A psychophysiological affect is one that causes combined mental and bodily processes to occur in reaction to an event or stimulus, all of which produces an emotion.
11. Sher further notes that these 'sexually violent films, genre films, and low brow films' are precisely 'the very types of films that those who believe in a connection between film spectatorship and crime describe as dangerous and deserving of censorship' (2015, p. 48).
12. The survey participants provided their opinions about trauma and catharsis in the following two Likert scale statements: 'Horror films help me work through trauma' and 'Horror films are cathartic'. Even though a connection exists between trauma and catharsis, I designed the survey to collect data on

trauma and catharsis separately because trauma is an emotional response and catharsis is an emotional release.

13. A statistically significant difference exists in the mathematical means between survey participants who report they have a different reaction to horror films than heterosexual viewers ($M = 2.33$, $SD = 1.094$) and those who do not ($M = 2.78$, $SD = 1.091$) compared with responses to the statement 'Horror films help me work through trauma'; $t\,(3963) = -12.8$, $p < 0.000$, $d = 0.41$.
14. A statistically significant difference exists in the mathematical means between survey participants who report that being queer influences their taste in horror films ($M = 2.35$, $SD = 1.076$) and those who do not ($M = 2.76$, $SD = 1.119$) compared with responses to the statement 'Horror films help me work through trauma'; $t\,(3958) = -11.7$, $p < 0.000$, $d = 0.37$.
15. The other two of the top four are Rape Revenge ($r_s = 0.18$, $p < 0.000$) and Extreme Horror ($r_s = 0.18$, $p < 0.000$), rounding out the top four subgenres with highly statistically significant positive correlations and the largest effect sizes for queer spectators who report horror helps them work through trauma.
16. Sher bolsters this claim by remarking that '*Scream* draws attention to the fact that many horror movies, especially slasher movies, are about domestic trauma' (2015, p. 113).
17. In 2020, horror theorist Xavier Aldana Reyes put forth the following definition of body horror: 'The term "body horror" is used to describe a type of fiction or cinema where corporeality constitutes the main site of fear, anxiety and sometimes even disgust for the characters and, by extension, the intended readers/viewers' (2020b, p. 393).
18. The breakdown for cisgender and transgender survey participants (women and men combined) who 'love' and 'like' the body horror subgenre is as follows: 74.5 per cent of transgender ($n = 379$) horror spectators love or like body horror compared with 64.2 per cent of cisgender ($n = 1{,}627$).
19. Camp means many different things to many different queer people, as illustrated by narrator Alex Hall when she declares camp to be a lifestyle: 'I love camp. For me personally, it goes beyond aesthetics. It feels like a language and then also a lifestyle, but just encompassing more. There's queer joyfulness to camp that allows for pleasure to be experienced in a way that films that adhere to certain sensibilities probably wouldn't' (2020, p. 21).
20. Lauren Levitt underscores camp's subjectivity, writing: 'There is much disagreement as to the nature of camp. One of the few things that most scholars agree on is that camp is subjective' (2017, p. 172).
21. 'It goes without saying that camp has a crucial resonance in queer discursive histories and cultural practices', Daphne Brooks affirms, and 'may, in fact,

be the fulcrum of queer identity politics' (2006, p. 274). While outside the scope of this study, I recognise Black and class-based straight camp scholarship, indicating a relationship to camp for 'parallel marginalities based on race and class' (Brooks, 2006, p. 274). Arguing for the visibility of Black camp, Brooks states: 'Queer camp and the camp of cakewalking are not a conflated form of identity production; rather each works in the service of dismantling a dominant ontological paradigm' (2006, p. 274).

22. For example, as Adam Scales points out, 'Freddy serves as a gay/camp icon' (2015, p. 121).
23. Queer horror fans also report a love for 'campier characters in films, like Freddy, Pinhead, or Hannibal Lecter' (47112178).
24. The relevance and abundance of the queer camp relationship to horror became known as a result of the survey and its corresponding statistical conclusions. My arguments about the queer camp-horror nexus have been bolstered by the qualitative data gathered in the written survey responses and the oral history interviews. Future studies should empirically examine the queer camp relationship to horror in greater detail.
25. Hundreds of survey participants electively wrote comments that evidence they have a camp relationship to horror in response to questions about how their reactions to and taste in horror are altered by their queerness.
26. My survey data demonstrates notable differences in camp reception due to national differences, which further supports the need for future research beyond an American-centric study. The 'relationship of queer American culture and its love of "camp aesthetics" to the horror genre', Daniel Humphrey observes, 'has not been fully explored' (2014, p. 42). While the majority of all queer horror fans enjoy camp in horror, 82.5 per cent of participants from the United States, 78.3 per cent from the United Kingdom, Ireland, Canada, Australia or New Zealand, and 65.6 per cent from elsewhere in the world enjoy camp in horror. Of the participants from places other than the United States, the United Kingdom, Ireland, Canada, Australia or New Zealand, 6.7 per cent have the highest rate of not knowing whether or not they enjoy campy horror films (compare with 1.2 per cent of US participants and 1.1 per cent of UK, Ireland, Canada, Australia or New Zealand participants). This data further encourages empirical examination into international queer culture and its relationship with camp. Regardless of any differences, the data demonstrates an undeniable international queer connection to camp and horror.
27. The demographic sexual orientation data for the survey participants who 'strongly agree' or 'agree' with the statement that they enjoy 'camp-y' horror

films are as follows: 84.4 per cent (n = 1,056) of those who identify as queer; 82.3 per cent (n = 1,062) of those who identify as gay; 81.2 per cent (n = 483) of those who identify as lesbian; 79.1 per cent (n = 1,129) of those who identify as bisexual; 78.1 per cent (n = 667) of those who identify as pansexual; 78.1 per cent (n = 364) of those who identify as polyamorous; 75 per cent (n = 21) of those who identify as heterosexual; and 74.9 per cent (n = 322) of those who identify as asexual.

28. The demographic gender identity data for the survey participants who 'strongly agree' or 'agree' with the statement that they enjoy 'camp-y' horror films is as follows: 87.4 per cent of genderqueer men (n = 167); 83.4 per cent of cisgender men (n = 1,006); 81 per cent of genderqueer people (n = 171); 80 per cent of non-binary people (n = 641); 79.7 per cent of agender people (n = 161); 78.6 per cent of cisgender women (n = 1,054); 78 per cent of genderqueer women (n = 227); 77.8 per cent of transsexual people (n = 28); 76 per cent of transgender women (n = 111); and 73.9 per cent of transgender men (n = 246).
29. There is also no statistically significant correlation between the highest level of education completed and preference for camp in horror films.
30. The drag scene, from ballrooms and clubs to film and television, continues to be a significant community dispersal of camp. For example, *RuPaul's Drag Race* and the global *Drag Race* franchises, since 2009, have introduced millions of young queers to camp culture and language.
31. A statistically significant difference exists in the mathematical means between survey participants who report they have a different reaction to horror films than heterosexual viewers (M = 1.66, SD = 0.871) and those who do not (M = 1.94, SD = 0.970) compared with responses to the statement 'I enjoy "camp-y" horror films'; t (3426) = -9.436, $p < 0.000$, d = 0.30.
32. An independent-samples t-test was conducted to compare participants' enjoyment of camp in the horror genre between participants who report that being queer influences their taste in horror films and those who do not. A statistically significant difference exists in the mathematical means between survey participants who report that being queer influences their taste in horror films (M = 1.66, SD = 0.871) and those who do not (M = 1.65, SD = 0.870) compared with responses to the statement 'I enjoy "camp-y" horror films'; t (3556) = -10.156, $p < 0.000$, d = 0.33.
33. An independent-samples t-test is conducted to compare participants' enjoyment of camp in the horror genre between participants who consider themselves knowledgeable about the horror genre and those who do not. A statistically significant difference exists in the mathematical means between

survey participants who consider themselves knowledgeable about horror film (M = 1.74, SD = 0.904) and those who do not (M = 1.98, SD = 1.001) compared with responses to the statement 'I enjoy "camp-y" horror films'; t (862) = -5.659, $p < 0.000$, d = 0.25.

34. An independent-samples t-test is conducted to compare participants' enjoyment of camp in the horror genre between participants who purchase horror memorabilia and/or collectibles and those who do not. A statistically significant difference exists in the mathematical means between survey participants who purchase horror memorabilia and/or collectibles (M = 1.68, SD = 0.857) and those who do not (M = 1.95, SD = 1.012) compared with responses to the statement 'I enjoy "camp-y" horror films'; t (4011) = -8.981, $p < 0.000$, d = 0.29.
35. There is no statistically significant relationship between queer horror fans who exhibit a camp relationship to horror and the following horror subgenres: extreme; found footage; cyber/internet; home invasion; and psychological. In other words, the data suggests that a camp relationship to horror is not an indicator of whether a queer spectator will like or dislike these five subgenres.
36. A statistically significant relationship with a small effect size exists between queer horror fans who exhibit a camp relationship to horror with the following horror subgenres: body horror ($r_s = 0.12$, $p < 0.000$); witchcraft ($r_s = 0.13$, $p < 0.000$); werewolf ($r_s = 0.15$, $p < 0.000$); zombie ($r_s = 0.10$, $p < 0.000$); vampire ($r_s = 0.14$, $p < 0.000$); Roger Corman/American International Pictures ($r_s = 0.17$, $p < 0.000$); Hammer Horror ($r_s = 0.17$, $p < 0.000$); Universal Horror ($r_s = 0.18$, $p < 0.000$); and Silent Horror ($r_s = 0.16$, $p < 0.000$). In other words, these results indicate that participants who more strongly enjoy camp are more likely to be those who love or like the aforementioned subgenres.
37. As a queer spectator writes, 'monster and slasher narratives can be cathartic for me as a queer viewer' (47103058), indicating a specifically queer connection to the subgenres.
38. Underscoring spectatorial agency in the camp relationship, Charles Ludlam posits: 'Camp is a way of looking at things, never what's looked at' (1992, p. 227). This study deploys and empirically affirms Ludlam's understanding of camp as an active queer lens.
39. While this research focus concentrates on the queer spectator's camp relationship to horror, expressed particularly through laughter, it does not fully investigate the root of all sources of a camp relationship to hegemonic culture, which may be motivated by rage (Ludlam, 1992, p. 254), melancholy (Taylor, 2019, p. 100) and/or joy (Crosby and Lynn, 2017, p. 60).

40. Even though camp's seriousness is often obscured by humour, camp may even exist without humour. For example, Cynthia Barounis writes about the camp in *The Witch: A New England Folktale* (2015) and Daniel Humphrey considers the camp possibilities of *The Exorcist* (1973). As Barounis argues 'camp humorlessness makes ample space for depression, despair, anxiety, self-pity, and rage' (2018, p. 222).
41. As well, Richard Niles emphasises that camp can 'be used as a means of communication and empowerment within gay and lesbian communities' (2004, p. 42).
42. Of the survey participants, 55.8 per cent relate to representations of the monstrous. Specifically, 11.5 per cent ($n = 473$) of survey participants identify with the 'monster' in horror films, while 44.3 per cent ($n = 1{,}818$) of the survey participants identify with both the 'monster' and the 'victim' in horror films.
43. *What Ever Happened to Baby Jane?* (1962), *Lady in a Cage* (1964), *Strait-Jacket* (1964) and *Fanatic / Die! Die! My Darling!* (1965) are horror films also categorised as Grande Dame Guignol films, which are films featuring old Hollywood stars, such as Bette Davis and Joan Crawford, no longer in their patriarchally marketable 'prime'. This subgenre is also called Psycho-biddy or, the even more misogynistic terms, 'hagsploitation' or 'hag horror'.
44. William Paul correctly comments on the 'exclusionary' nature of camp but misinterprets camp's function when he states that 'camp condescendingly celebrates the vacuousness of the art work' (1994, p. 71).

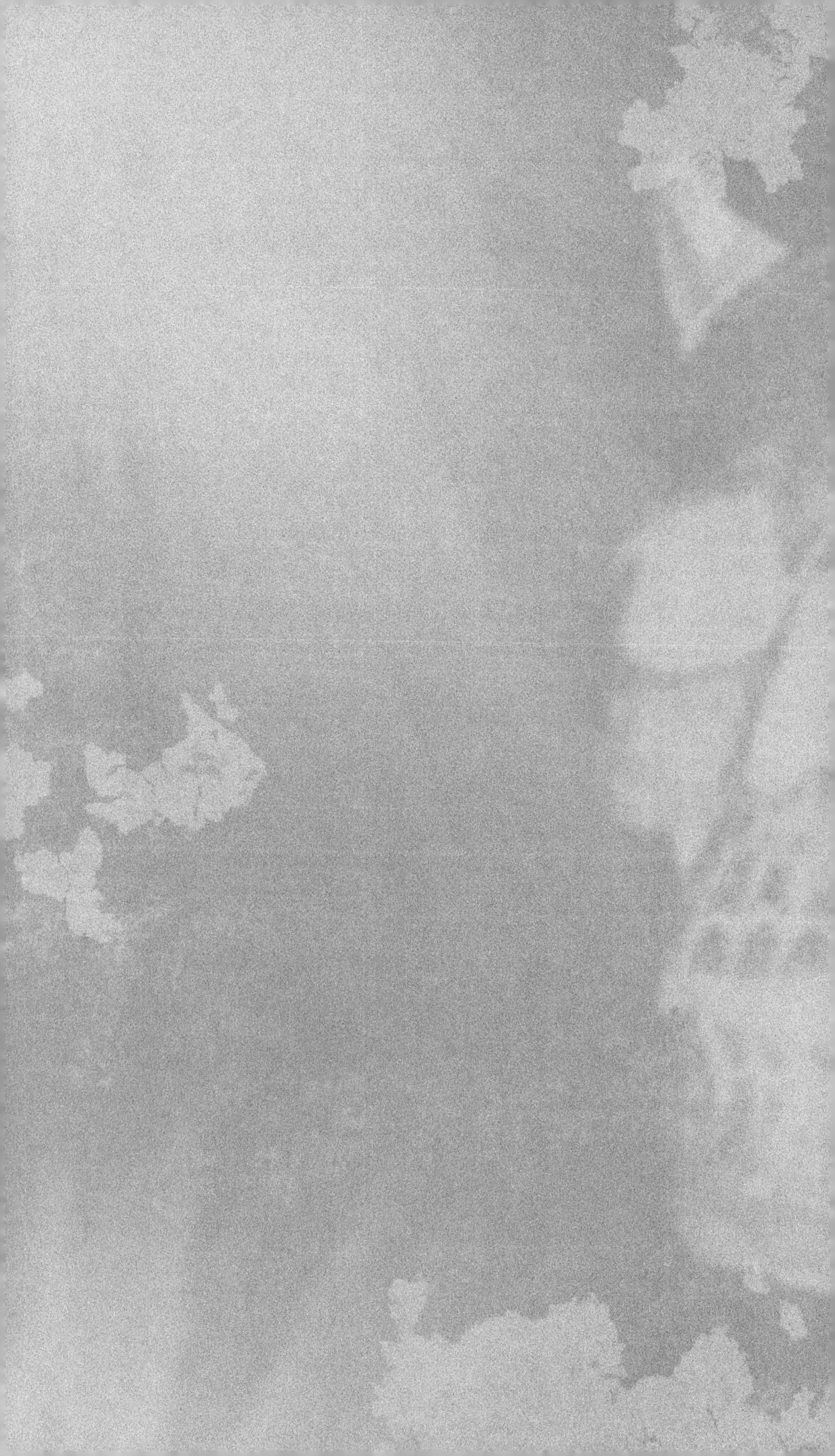

4

Drag Me to Hell

Queer Performance and Live Cinema

Horror and drag are both fringe entertainment and a match made in hell.
(47114640)

I think that queer people enjoy camp because it's a heightened reality. But it's heightened reality with the message that is poking fun at the things that we would not be able to normally say in 'straight conversation.' And I think that also speaks to why horror and drag are connected because, and again, it's the theatre of heightened reality – it's utilizing the art to say something and to say it in the most over-the-top strange or absurd or powerful way you can.
(Varrati, 2020, pp. 6–7)

I feel that a drag pre-show taps into the disruptive, queer nature of horror films, and lightens the mood so that the focus is on the campy fun of horror.
(47112178)

I've always picked up on the queer elements of horror, but as a lot of horror fans are straight cis men it can be alienating since I know we're not necessarily seeing the movie in the same way. Having a queen introduce the film lets me know I'm in a queer-friendly place and sets the film up for a non heteronormative viewing.
(48753875)

THE MIXED-METHOD DATA previously presented demonstrates not only that queer horror spectators share overall similarities in their opinions, habits and tastes, but also how the presented data exists in contrast to previous empirical audience studies on the horror spectator. I then elaborated on the queer relationship to the horror genre through trauma and camp. I now provide an extended illustration and interrogation of the camp relationship queer spectators have with horror by examining an entirely campy and decidedly queer engagement with horror: drag performers[1] who present horror films to queer audiences and perform a show before the screening. The interest here is on what the collective queer live cinema experience enables, not what it prevents. Invariably, people who do not identify as queer attend these live cinema events; however, this study is not concerned with their experiences, as this is a decidedly queer project that centres queerness over the cisheteronormative, which exists at the centre of society. This queer/queered examination leads to a critical academic connection of queer performance to live cinema studies. Analysing drag, a highly political and essentially queer performance art anchored in camp, including drag performers as horror hosts, has proven imperative in order to understand the phenomenological and theoretical foundations of queer live cinema events. An examination of Peaches Christ's Midnight Mass and Carla Rossi's Queer Horror (in San Francisco, California and Portland, Oregon respectively), including these queer events' historical precedents, reveals how event-led cinema firmly includes queer performance and drag horror host exhibition in the emerging field of live cinema, and further illustrates how '[c]inema makes queer spaces possible' – both on the screen[2] and in the auditorium (Schoonover and Galt, 2016, p. 3). These queer horror exhibition events should be understood as vital examples of live cinema.[3] This chapter, therefore, argues for the significance of queer interventions for live cinema studies.[4] Phenomenological theories of liveness, sharedness and laughter, as well as cult and failure theories, will be considered and should be understood as rhizomatically interlaced throughout subsequent topics of the carnivalesque, drag, horror hosts and queer events. This scavenged theoretical framework works with the mixed-method data of this study to define the qualities of and evidence the importance of queer live cinema events.

Establishing Queer Performance as Live Cinema

This work allows for an understanding of queer live cinema by demonstrating how and why key types of queer performance, including drag and horror host events, are categorically live cinema. Live cinema, distilled down to its simplest definition, is any exhibition that 'involves some form of simultaneous live action or addition to a cinema screening' (Atkinson and Kennedy, 2019, p. 339). For as long as there has been film exhibition, there has been a history of live accompaniment or 'liveness'; this exhibition history has been documented by scholars such as Barbara Klinger, Richard Maltby and Charles Musser. Sarah Atkinson and Helen W. Kennedy acknowledge that while live cinema studies is a new field, cinema exhibition, going back to exhibition in music halls and vaudeville venues, incorporated live elements, stating: 'Our examination of live cinema phenomena insists upon the recognition of these contemporary practices as having very clear antecedents in the early emergence of film and cinema' (2019, p. 336). Live cinema is an emergent field of study, with the collection *Live Cinema: Cultures, Economies, Aesthetics* (2018), edited by Atkinson and Kennedy, being the pivotal text that develops the theoretical foundation for this evolving discipline. Live cinema is commonly understood as 'a film screening utilising additional performance or interactivity inspired by the content of the film' ('Live Cinema in the UK', 2016, p. 4) or a screening 'that escapes beyond the boundaries of the auditorium' (Atkinson and Kennedy, 2016, p. 139), although the nascent field remains multifarious and ephemeral due to the range of interpretations and applications. I argue that Midnight Mass and Queer Horror are enhanced and participatory live cinema experiences that 'sit at the exciting intersection of a number of different art forms – film, music, theatre and performing arts' (Atkinson and Kennedy, 2018, p. 9). Both Midnight Mass and Queer Horror incorporate the exhibition of horror film, musical numbers and lip syncs, curated pre-show playlists, original theatrical horror parody skits and queer performance art, all of which creates an enhanced 'viewing experience [that] takes precedence over the film text itself' (Atkinson and Kennedy, 2018, p. 20). Simply stated, the audience is drawn in and attends not only for the film, but for the experience, as the live cinema viewing experience is 'more immersive' (46895404) than a film alone.

Midnight Mass and Queer Horror, as live cinema events, bring to the fore a specific queer culture of horror fandom that celebrates horror and connects queers through campy drag performances, 'solidifying the bonds between the Queer and the "queer" (meaning uncanny)' (47110480). This chapter focuses on Midnight Mass and Queer Horror as live cinema case studies because they each embody an enhanced film viewing experience in exemplary ways. Also, pertinently, these are two live cinema event series at which I have been a regular attendee and my direct experience is that of a community 'participant-observer' (Marchetti, 2008, p. 417), having attended Midnight Mass in the late 1990s through to the mid-2000s and Queer Horror ongoing since 2015. As well, Peaches Christ's Midnight Mass and Carla Rossi's Queer Horror are ideal queer live cinema events to examine, I argue, due to Peaches Christ (see Figure 4.1) being an internationally recognised drag legend[5] and Queer Horror being 'exclusively the only queer horror screening series in the United States' (Davis, 2020, p. 26). While Midnight Mass and Queer Horror function as ideal case studies, a multitude of other queer live cinema events have existed, such as Queer Fear in Toronto, Canada, Miss McGee's Creature Feature (an 'evening of glamour, gore and guffaws') in Tampa/St Petersburg, Florida and Make A Scene in Manchester, the United Kingdom.[6] Queer live cinema events that exhibit horror films to queer audiences create a particular type of energy, regardless of film, location or drag 'horror host' performer.

Since visible, named and known queer cultural productions such as these have existed only for a few decades (in part due to 'out' queer spaces only existing since the late 1960s), live cinema events that combine queer production with queer reception create a uniquely queer space for horror exhibition. As Anthony Hudson (drag persona Carla Rossi) explains, 'even if the het-ero-sexuals [said slowly and humorously inflected] or the straight audience shows up now to support [Queer Horror], it is under the understanding that this is a queer experience and this is a queer space' (2020c, p. 15). Queer artists who create a specifically queer culture with enhanced horror exhibition events for queer audiences embody John Fiske's theory of excorporation – 'the process by which the subordinate make their own culture out of the resources and commodities provided by the dominant system' (2003, p. 114). While all cultural production uses the material and means of the neoliberal capitalist cisheteropatriarchy, a rebellious subversion of capitalistic products permeates queer cultural production. This study, then, builds on Andrew Ross's concept that 'camp and cult appear to side with the exploited labourer in the struggle to gain control over the meaning of cultural products, and their outrageousness becomes a conscious attitude of revolt' (2008, p. 53). Inherent to both Midnight Mass and Queer Horror is a deliberate and enthusiastic subversion of

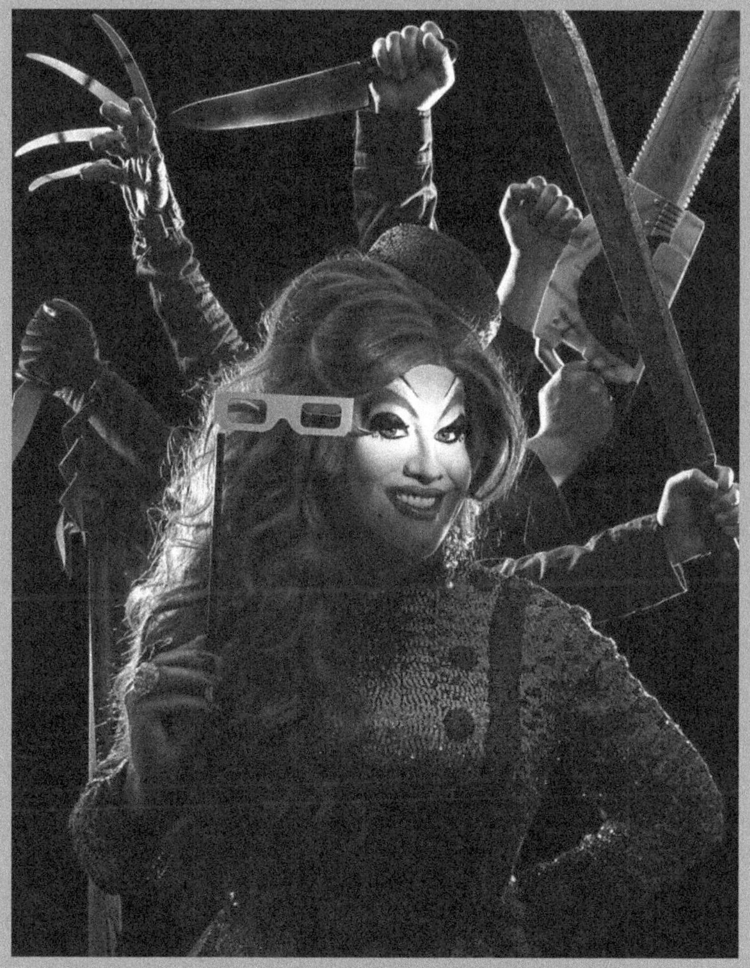

Figure 4.1. Portrait of Peaches Christ. Photo by David Ayllon. Image courtesy of Peaches Christ Productions.

mainstream attitudes about and understandings of horror film, as well as dominant culture and politics.

Based on an examination of Peaches Christ's and Carla Rossi's event series' temporary reclamation[7] of spaces for queer audiences, this study argues for and demonstrates the critical role of drag in *queered* horror film events. Midnight Mass and Queer Horror epitomise these queer live cinema events, which allows this work to incorporate a significant queer cultural production into live cinema studies. This assertion is further evidenced by queer performers who have been at the forefront of live cinema dating back to, at least, The Cockettes and *The Rocky Horror Picture Show* (1975), both of which will be historically situated in later sections. A concise historiographic examination of queered film exhibition additionally illustrates how queer drag performers have been at the forefront of live cinema and the experience economy (Pine and Gilmore, 1998). Queer exhibition thrived prior to academic terms such as 'live cinema' and 'the experience economy', illustrating the retroactive application of an academic term to a cultural art that has long existed and flourished under the groundbreaking work of a marginalised group. Importantly, my oral history interviews with Joshua Grannell/Peaches Christ and Anthony Hudson/Carla Rossi, alongside interviews with Queer Horror's resident artist Jason Edward Davis and two regular Queer Horror audience members, investigate and underscore that 'what [the] audience experiences in the moment of engagement is crucial to the exploration of the cultural significance of Live Cinema' (Atkinson and Kennedy, 2018, p. 13). The historic queer legacies of The Cockettes and *The Rocky Horror Picture Show* are important not only to the nascent field of live cinema studies, but also both Grannell and Hudson, as directly claimed by both performers. In other words, queer live cinema events of the past directly connect to queer live cinema events today and, furthermore, the live cinema events of today will influence the queer live cinema experiences of the future. About this future, Queer Horror regular and narrator Kaitlyn Stodola notes the need to create a queer horror space in their life since they have moved away from Portland, Oregon: 'I want to make my own Queer Horror. I wanna make my own space … Now that I've had that, I don't want to give it up. So I will fucking make it if I have to' (2020, pp. 26–7). Queer live cinema events such as Queer Horror have an impact, specifically a queer cultural significance, that creates a queer space with both individual and shared meanings. Within this context, this study positions that the horror host works of Joshua Grannell, as Peaches Christ, and Anthony Hudson, as

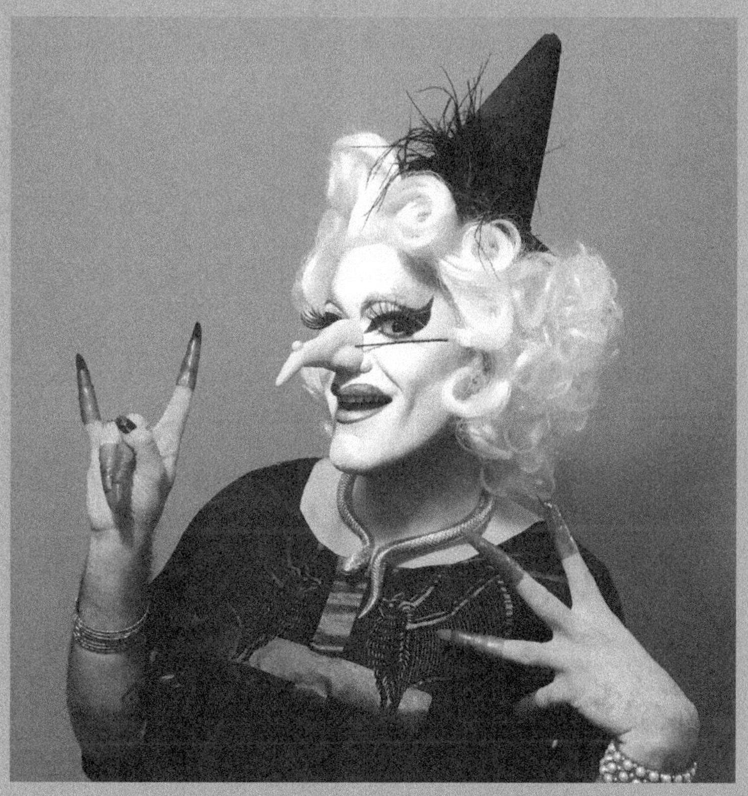

Figure 4.2. Portrait of Carla Rossi. Photo by Jason Edward Davis. Image courtesy of Anthony Hudson.

Carla Rossi (see Figure 4.2), constitute a distinctive queer interpretation of live cinema and contribution to live cinema studies, expanding what is defined and understood by it. Midnight Mass and Queer Horror as live cinema events, determined by key works in *Live Cinema*, also further the phenomenological understanding of queer performance by building on theories of liveness and sharedness, the carnivalesque and cult cinema.

The Phenomenology of Queer Live Cinema

The term 'liveness' is precisely what categorises particular exhibition experiences as live cinema. Philip Auslander establishes the significant characteristics of liveness on which this argument is built. A clear parameter for defining liveness is the '[p]hysical co-presence of performers and audience' (2008, p. 61), which is found in a wide range of performances, from theatres to streets. Furthermore, for an event to possess liveness, it must be presented and seen in the same moment, possessing '[t]emporal simultaneity of production and reception' (Auslander, 2008, p. 61). The physical co-presence and temporal simultaneity of liveness, then, create an 'experience in the moment' (Auslander, 2008, p. 61). Thus, liveness is predicated on those three characteristics to be contained in an impermanent, in-person performative interaction. Live cinema experiences are difficult to document in part because their very 'liveness' resists expression and live performance itself is 'a language that resists capture' (Hudson, 2020d, p. 10). Hudson further contends that a live cinema performance like theirs:

> is like witchcraft. It's the Sabbath. It's the magic circle. It's a place removed from time and space that only exists for us in that moment . . . But you'll remember it and that will impact you and that will impact how you access other experiences like that and the things you seek out . . . And I think that's what all theatre should be striving to do – to make something that is really special and removed from time. (2020d, p. 10)

Midnight Mass and Queer Horror are live cinema events crafted, respectively, by Grannell and Hudson; therefore, examining their audiences demonstrates how queer audiences affect the collective live cinema experience and adds to the 'limited attention devoted to the collective cinema experience' (Hanich, 2018, p. 70). In *The Audience Effect: On the Collective Cinema Experience* (2018), Julian Hanich centres the audience, not the film text, to theorise phenomenologically the collective cinema experience. Queer audiences are aware of live cinema's experiential sharedness, as evidenced by survey participants who note their enjoyment of the 'collective group experience' (47093051) while being at a queer horror screening with drag horror hosts and of the drag horror host who 'instantly makes for such a stronger connection and a sense of unity' (47755040). Hanich's phenomenological approach to audience studies puts the focus on cinema's collectivity and its effect on the subjectively lived experience of watching a film in a darkened theatre with others (2014a, p. 343). This study employs Hanich's approach specifically to examine the experience of being part of a queer audience when a drag performer introduces a horror film. Hanich's phenomenological approach bypasses textual analysis in order to examine the collective audience responses to both the screened film and other audience members. The phenomenological nature of events such as Queer Horror are evident to a host such as Hudson, who addresses the audience collectivity that engenders queer connection. In Hudson's words:

> While there is a grotesque side to that hive mentality, there is a really wonderful aspect, also, to it. At the other end of it is that we want to experience things collectively, and for the first time, we feel greater than ourselves – which we truly are because our bodies don't end with our skin, our bodies extend into our communities, and into our ideology, and our history, and our environment. We become more aware of that when we're in crowds, and when we're experiencing something that we all care about together, and then we feel closer to each other. And the act of experiencing that, at its core, is what Queer Horror is about. (2020d, p. 8)

Being queer in this cisheteronormative society can be an isolating experience for many; therefore, queer people seek to find a space that fosters a queer connection while simultaneously and collectively celebrating horror film.[8] In fact, Hanich argues that 'collectively watching a film with quiet attention should be regarded as a joint action' (2014a, p. 338). Sitting in a cinema with others to watch a film is a joint action, a shared activity. My study builds on Hanich's theory by expanding the nature of a joint action, as evidenced by Midnight Mass and Queer Horror, examples of collectively watching a film as a joint action, but with boisterous and participatory attention. These live cinema events are joint-action celebrations of queerness and horror in the movie theatre.

According to Richard Maltby, 'for most audiences for most of the history of cinema, their primary relationship with "the cinema" has not been with individual movies-as-artefacts or as texts, but with the social experience of cinema' (2006, p. 85). Midnight Mass and Queer Horror are social experiences for queer people drawn together by horror films. These live cinema events even inform new ways of understanding audiences. According to Hanich, 'quiet-attentive' and 'expressive-diverted' are the two categories of collective cinematic viewing. Quiet-attentive audiences jointly yet silently concentrate on the filmic object, whereas the expressive-diverted viewing experience exists when an audience divides attention between the film and awareness of the audience. Significantly, these inverse types of viewing can coexist, as quiet-attentive and expressive-diverted collective viewing 'can rapidly succeed each other and easily blend, fuse, morph into one another' (Hanich, 2018, p. 65). Furthermore, both serve as joint actions of pleasure which are specifically 'mediated by the film' (Hanich, 2018, p. 134). Even when a queer spectator is expressively absorbed into the film, my research participants' comments show that an attentive awareness of being a part of a queer audience collectively enjoying a horror film is phenomenologically part of queer horror fans' live cinema experience.

The queer situatedness of the screening and audience is fundamental to the experience. Hanich notes that the 'intimacy of the social connections may influence the collective experience', which depends on whether the other audience members are known or anonymous (2014a, p. 341). As such, viewing a film as part of an audience of known people will afford a distinct experience from viewing alone among strangers.[9] This study of Midnight Mass, Queer Horror, Queer Fear and other events by drag hosts presenting horror films to queer audiences offers a third audience category: a group that may be mostly anonymous but feels familiar through a shared cultural or social connection. Stated differently, the queer horror spectator finds, among an audience of predominantly anonymous people, a queer connection that makes those audience members feel known. Some of the survey participants explicitly address and describe this connection with comments such as: 'sense of community built on seeing something that touched my little queer heart surrounded by people who related to the film in similar ways' (47079751); 'we all understand each other' (47081172); 'instantly created community around horror films, and recontextualized the experience as Queer' (46893626); 'love the sense of community among the audience' (47645711). As such, this evidence demonstrates a celebratory awareness and appreciation of collectively experiencing horror as a member of an audience with like-minded queers.

Queer people uniquely experience each other at events such as Midnight Mass and Queer Horror, which is in opposition to collective viewing in which 'the audience predominantly experiences jointly without reflectively experiencing each other' (Hanich, 2014a, p. 339). Survey participants highlight how live cinema events that combine queerness and horror with a drag horror host function to create uniquely shared queer horror experiences: 'Drag queens at a horror show are able to unify the audience, validating our shared love of horror' (47119972); 'It was a fun time that helped to bring everyone in the audience into a shared experience, which was then reflected while watching the movie' (46829466); and 'I feel like Drag Queens add to the fun and fan culture of the horror film. Enriches the fun of the experience and gets the audience in the mood as a whole (they bring the audience together)' (47117167). Drag horror hosts not only heighten the queer connection to horror film, but also solidify the collective experience.

Part of the collective experience is found in the shared expression of emotion that unifies Midnight Mass and Queer Horror audiences, as confirmed by my survey data and explicated prior, which is laughter.[10] In researching the phenomenological responses of audiences, scholar Jessica Hughes points out that analysis should do more than 'simply identifying the emotions evoked by the films being examined to consider how these emotions connect us to the collective audience of which we are a part' (2016, p. 43). While laughter can be understood as an expression of a range of emotions, Walter Benjamin calls laughter 'the most international and the most revolutionary emotion of the masses' (1999, p. 224). Laughter can function as a tool of liberation from normative domination because it functions to delegitimise and deflate authority, removing the seriousness and severity of the dominator. Shared laughter is the expressive glue that holds together these temporary live cinema communities, already united in queerness and a love of horror, 'thus enabling a collective experience' (Hanich, 2014a, p. 358).[11] As evidenced, camp is an integral part of the queer spectatorial relationship to horror and laughter is an integral part of camp. This collective experience, moreover, both lives and perpetually changes with the audience (Hanich, 2018, p. 3). The tone of live cinema experiences is accordingly as dependent on the audience as the performance artists and the host. A survey participant states that the drag horror host 'created a feeling that the audience was more connected and on a journey together. They also created a space for laughter, something I enjoy while watching horror films' (47802670). This shared laughter is important to a queer shared experience because laughter 'draws you closer in a collective bond, strengthening the audience's we-connection' (Hughes, 2016, p. 51) – a connection forged through shared emotional expression. Narrator CJ Hodges highlights how it is distinctive and political for queer audiences to share laughter and collectively bond over horror: 'I think in a lot of ways horror can and has perpetuated stereotypes about queer people and POC people that are extremely damaging. But, at the same time, there's this other aspect of it that has allowed queer people to come together and laugh at this stuff and examine it and I think that's really important, too' (2020, p. 13). In phenomenologically investigating collective expressive reactions, Hanich discusses how the movie theatre's 'darkness "equalizes" and "democratizes" laughter', a democratisation that results in temporarily enshrouding individual identity markers and thereby creating 'laughing collectives [that] can momentarily dissolve social hierarchies and categories' (2018, p. 212). The laughing collectives of queer live cinema events, such as Midnight Mass and Queer Horror, are not predicated on temporarily masking identity markers but, instead, on heightening the collective queer connection through the cinematic joint action of laughing (and/or screaming).[12] Hudson shares that Queer Horror pre-shows are 'a way for me to hear laughter from a whole bunch of queers, and to all gather together and to not feel alone and immersed in the horror – the horror of everything that was happening in the American political system at that point' (2020c, p. 13). This fleeting queer freedom becomes a 'carnivalesque action' that 'frees the imagination to envision a different world' (Rich, 2013, p. 210), an imagining of new realities such as the dissolution of cisheteronormativity.

Queer live cinema events centred on horror films (as found at Midnight Mass and Queer Horror) embody Mikhail Bakhtin's carnivalesque mode through both the queer gaiety and the horror films themselves, all of which 'seek to create a *festive, communal* atmosphere in the theater' (Paul, 1994, p. 65; italics in the original). The carnivalesque model is an 'instrument of power available to the powerless' that functions as a mode of 'sociopolitical intervention' and 'political interference' (Rich, 2013, pp. 209–10). When queers, a marginalised community, gather to celebrate horror, a marginalised film genre, the celebration becomes inherently political – a politic of exuberant transgressive queer collectivity. This study takes as axiomatic the fact that queers gathering together is progressive and celebratory. If Bakhtin argues that the carnivalesque model enables the maintenance of the status quo after or outside of the carnival, I argue that queer gatherings, such as queer live cinema events, offer invaluable emotional and communal outlets that strengthen bonds within the queer community and stand in opposition to cisheteronormativity, both of which are necessary to counter hegemonic society and imagine new social structures and understandings. Halberstam explains that 'queer lives exploit some potential for a *difference in form* that lies dormant in queer collectivity not as an essential attribute of sexual otherness but as a possibility embedded in the break from heterosexual life narratives' (2011, p. 70; italics in the original). This means, simply, that the act of queers gathering together opens alternative potentialities to cisheteronormative existence. Yet the latent possibilities that these queer carnivals offer may not register with members of the normative majority. Narrator Stodola, a Queer Horror regular, recounts and reflects on the carnivalesque queer space not resonating with cisheterosexuals:

> I took one of my straight friends to see *The Sentinel*, the one with the cat birthday party. It was really funny and the preshow was hilarious and me and Cable were laughing the whole time. And then we watched the movie. Afterwards, Cable and I were talking about how good it was, and my friend just goes, 'I think I was too straight for this' [laughs]. I was like, 'Oh!' And he was like, yeah, 'I didn't like the movie. I didn't understand anything that was going on in the preshow. I just think I'm too straight for this'. (2020, p. 17)

Midnight Mass and Queer Horror are, fundamentally and consciously, live cinema experiences made by queer people for queer people. While the carnivalesque has been connected to horror and cult film fan practices by previous horror scholars such as Brigid Cherry (1999, p. 209) and John Lynskey (2020, p. 33), this intervention specifically considers and extends it to live cinema events at which drag performers are horror hosts for queer audiences. To Bakhtin, the 'carnival is more than a mere festivity; it is the oppositional culture of the oppressed, the symbolic, anticipatory overthrow of oppressive social structures' (Stam, 1989, p. 173). In other words, Midnight Mass and Queer Horror create a space for queers to temporarily invert the sociopolitical realities of mainstream culture through a simultaneous celebration of queerness and horror. Moreover, when Bakhtin argues that laughter 'lies at the core of a carnivalesque spirit', he offers the potential of a 'radical rethinking of the world' (Moser, 2008, p. 181). Inarguably, laughter permeates these queer live cinema events whereby the collective queer joy offers the audience release from the pressures of insidious trauma caused by pervasive cisheteronormativity. Midnight Mass existed and Queer Horror exists as lively reclamations of queer space in which both performers and audiences temporarily overturn the dominance of cisheteronormative society in an atmosphere of festive queer community. The inclusive and rebellious queer spaces forged and found at Midnight Mass and Queer Horror also bring together the queer performers on the stage, extending the impact beyond the audience. Grannell explains:

> The other thing that we did both at Trannyshack[13] and at Midnight Mass is that we continued a legacy of drag culture and drag performance that was inclusive of literally everybody. So if you wanted to play with us, you were invited to play and you could be heterosexual, homosexual, or bisexual. You could be a man, a woman, nonbinary, or trans. These things just didn't matter in this world. And there were no limits to it. You could be young, old, Black, white, whatever. It was all about coming together and putting on a fun show and sharing in something together. (2020c, pp. 11–12)

Similar to Grannell's Midnight Mass, Hudson's Queer Horror intentionally showcases an inclusive roster of performers. Hudson explains: 'We work with a lot of trans and nonbinary performers. I think they're used to looking at the world in complex ways and I think they're willing to undertake potentially complex things full force and with a lot of humor. And women, too. I love working with female-assigned people on the show because also there are so few avenues for them' (2020d, p. 5). Correspondingly, Jason Edward Davis, narrator and Queer Horror's resident artist, directly affirms the inclusive audience composition as 'a good dynamic of all genders and in-between. There's no majority. So it's people that don't necessarily have those spaces to interact that get to interact' (2020, p. 25). Queer curators and performers presenting queer performances to inclusive queer audiences is a counter-hegemonic political act simply by being drag art performance from the oppressed for the oppressed. '[C]arnival celebrated temporary liberation from the prevailing truth and from the established order; it marked the suspension of all hierarchical rank, privileges, norms, and prohibitions' (Bakhtin, 1984, p. 10). During this liminal liberation, Midnight Mass and Queer Horror engender 'carnivals of fan participation' for queer horror fans (Fiske, 1992, p. 41), which is rarely found.

Queers seldom experience and share queer space outside of bars, queer centres or annual parades; furthermore, these public queer spaces are already under threat of disappearing or closing for multiple reasons, despite existing for a short time or never existing for some areas or communities. Queer life and its concomitant spaces have been increasingly altered by cultural, sociopolitical and technological shifts ranging from marriage equity to social media apps. It would be injudicious to historically romanticise queer spaces since the queer community has often been spatially and temporally fragmented and limited, often due to systemic issues such as misogyny, racism and ableism. Yet the diminishing number of shared, public queer spaces further fragments and isolates the queer community. Narrator Davis details the importance of queer spaces and the impact for queers not to have them:

> When you're not exposed to any gay places or gay people (I didn't know any gay people – it was never a part of my life, it was very isolating), eventually that turns into self-loathing and you carry that with you for a very long time. I feel like I've been able to build a life that is surrounded with everything I need. But that's hard work and having to choose things: I choose queer. I choose queer spaces. I choose to make art that is not straight. (2020, p. 16)

Here, Davis, as a Queer Horror collaborator, directly speaks to the intentionality to create queer space and have a queer lens in his life, art and work. A survey participant's comment concurrently emphasises the importance of queer spaces and the lack thereof: 'As a young queer person [seeing a queered horror screening] was one of the first times that I'd seen outwardly queer people in a public space' (47074469). The queer spaces of Midnight Mass and Queer Horror are created in temporary commune between performers and audiences, all of whom are gathered around and absorbed in a shared love of horror films. This engagement for all in attendance is the active embodiment of the carnival, not a passive presentation. 'While carnival lasts, there is no other life outside it. During carnival time life is subject only to its laws, that is, the laws of its own freedom' (Bakhtin, 1984,

p. 7). The queer freedom of these live cinema events 'exist[s] as a challenge to the dominant culture' precisely because of the queer celebrational nature and, as Oliver-Hopkins suggests, reflect 'that minority cultures do not require a relationship with hegemonic society to feel complete, which could be seen as more radical still than an attempt to reframe the values of the dominant culture' (2017, p. 154). Through this, albeit temporary, carnivalesque reprieve, queer spectators have engaged in collective action that reaffirms the queer healing power of both camp and horror, even after they exit the movie theatre to an unchanged world.

Midnight Mass and Queer Horror create queer carnival spaces predicated on celebrating queers and the queer love of horror. Queer subjectivity is continuously discriminated against by cisheteronormativity because mainstream culture is not created for queers; therefore, fleeting moments of a queer majority can only exist in temporary communities. A survey participant discussing drag-hosted live cinema horror events emphasises the need for queer spaces caused by cisheterosexism, explaining that 'our communities are largely pushed out of cinema culture so it's great that there is a movement of bridging the gap and creating our own spaces' (47073933). Atkinson and Kennedy postulate that live cinema events allow for 'new forms of embodiment and new possibilities for community engagement and participation' (2018, p. 20). As such, numerous survey participants' comments about seeing a drag performer introduce a horror film underscore the importance of both queer space and 'bond[ing] the audience as a community' (46829309). Notably, within their temporary communities and as bonded by the drag host, queer audiences are able to collectively claim and connect with the Other in horror in part because queers possess 'the inherent understanding of horror as the worship and celebration of "otherness" and the idea of "cult" as community' (46974402). Indeed, Midnight Mass and Queer Horror are cult queer carnivalesque celebrations of both horror and cult films.

The Cult of Queer Live Cinema

This research defines queer live cinema events as cult events, thereby transforming both the films and audiences into cult – regardless of categorisation beyond the bounds of the live cinema event experience. This study adopts Ernest Mathijs and Xavier Mendik's broad definition of cult film, which they define as 'a film with an active and lively communal following'

(2008, p. 11). Queer spectators actively gathering together to form a lively queer audience demonstrates how queer live cinema events not only offer critical queer engagement with the horror genre but also contribute to our understanding of cult. A phenomenological approach to investigating the queer celebration of horror and cult cinema sees the subjectivist process 'as a mode of reception, a way of seeing films' (Mathijs and Mendik, 2008, p. 15). At queer live cinema events, both the audience and the films are received as cult, since, as Anne Jerslev asserts, 'the cult event transforms the film into a cult film and positions the spectators as a cult audience' (2008, p. 91). Queer live cinema events, such as Midnight Mass and Queer Horror, phenomenologically alter the reception of horror films, creating a cult around the queer audience's experience of horror. Following and expanding on Jerslev's declaration that '[c]ult film is fundamentally an event' (2008, p. 92), this study emphasises that the meaning of live cinema events is determined by not only the audience's shared reaction to the filmic text, but also the pre-show's contextualising liveness. Stated differently, Midnight Mass and Queer Horror are events that screen and celebrate horror and cult films to queer audiences, thereby also making the event and the audience itself cult. Furthermore, while not all cult films are horror, many horror films are 'counted as cult' (Mathijs and Mendik, 2008, p. 20). 'Cult films are not *made* (as, for example, a producer sets out to *make* a musical or Western) as much as they *happen* or *become*', as Bruce A. Austin points out – indeed, 'it is the audience that turns a film into a cult film' (1989, p. 83; italics in the original). A cult film is dependent on an event that is centred on participatory reception by an energised audience. Progressing Austin's point, if an audience 'makes' a cult film, a horror film is made cult by queer drag horror hosts, performers and audiences at live cinema events. Relatedly, Alexander Doty has argued, by expanding Barthesian semiotics, that a queer reader makes queer any text (1993). Hence, these hosts, performers and audiences being queer thereby render queer the live cinema events.

The overlap between cult audiences and films and the horror genre directly resonates with queers and the queer experience due to their common social element: being othered. As a survey participant states: 'Queers are outsiders, and so is horror and its fans. They're a perfect marriage' (47717803). Affirming this point, Jessica Hughes discusses how cult cinema possesses 'qualities marking it as "other"' (2016, p. 38) and cult cinema becomes cult as it is defined by the audience, which is also Other in the case of horror-loving queers. Queers, ontologically and phenomenologically, connect to the othered status of both cult and horror films. Barry K. Grant argues that 'in cult movies viewers laugh at the normal, tame the Other, but nowhere see themselves', surmising that 'this is why cult audiences tend to be composed of teenagers, disenfranchised youths who are caught between childhood and adulthood, who have little sense of belonging' (2008, p. 87). Furthering this notion, my mixed-method data indicates that queer audiences develop their identity as adults in part by embracing the Other in horror film and by finding joy in what is rejected by cisheteronormative society, in what can be made a cult film. Hudson emphasises this point: 'There's just something about that energy of creating a site where we can all get together and all watch a movie, and *all* see everything that that movie was never celebrated for, but that we celebrate it for, all come to a head in one space, in one night' (2020c, p. 15). When queers embrace and reclaim a film that was rejected by the mainstream, an emotional connection is forged. As Matt Hills explains: 'Cult fandom is a project of the self which is primarily and significantly emotional' (2008, p. 134). In fact, 'cult fans create cultural identities out of the *significance* which certain texts assume for them' (Hills, 2008, p. 134; italics in the original). A queer spectator's own identity then creates significance out of both cult and/or horror texts.[14]

Cult films become 'cult' as a result of active audience reassessment, engagement and, ultimately, reanimation of a mainstream filmic failure. Queers connect with a film's inability to resonate with its intended audience, distinctively understanding and embracing the film's failure to be understood and embraced, 'enjoy[ing] these stupid silly movies or movies that are dismissed as stupid and silly' (Hudson, 2020c, p. 13). The entire realm of cult cinema exists at an incongruous juncture of failure and engagement.[15] Those films that failed because of a decidedly campy perspective will directly connect with queer audiences and be 'reanimated' as successful representations of the queer experience.[16] The 'cult of Midnight Movies appealed primarily to feelings of awkwardness and alienation, to people who themselves felt "different" or anathematized – teens, gays, college kids' (Chute, 1983, p. 13). In other words, teens, young adults and queers comprise the audiences that turn a mainstream failure film into a cult success. Notably, this cult audience make-up carries a key distinction between its constituents: age-based demographics versus an identity demographic. While teens and college kids change their demographic over time by growing older, queer identity is neither temporary nor age dependent; instead, queerness exists as a constant identity outside of mainstream society. Young moviegoers likely age into becoming productive heteronormative adults, yet queers always remain othered; a queer person's very existence is anathema to cisheteronormative (re)productivity and success. Unsurprisingly, then, many queers feel a kinship with failure (a meta failure itself that entirely represents the queer experience), the kinship often transforming into proactive engagement with and affinity towards 'failed' films.

In *The Queer Art of Failure*, Halberstam envisages queer failure, stating: 'Failing is something queers do and have always done exceptionally well; for queers failure can be a style, to cite Quentin Crisp, or a way of life, to cite Foucault, and it can stand in contrast to the grim scenarios of success that depend upon "trying and trying again"' (2011, p. 3). Importantly, queer failure must not be mistaken for queer incompetence. Queer failure is the successful and purposeful rejection of the cisheteronormative paradigm, which always already fails the queer. The epitome of queer is to embrace and flaunt your failure to be normative. An example that perfectly illustrates this point is Peaches Christ's official sidekick, Martiny Downsize, 'the most flawed and tragic drag queen in all of San Francisco' (Cotter, 2017, p. 113). Martiny became a beloved part of the Midnight Mass pre-shows precisely because of her failings in drag ambition, wardrobe and performance. Martiny's failure to be a 'good' drag queen as Peaches Christ's flawed sidesick led Peaches to coin the expression 'flawed is the new fierce' and feature it on Midnight Mass merchandise. Wearing the failure of normative and even queer ideals as a badge of pride is an act of queer liberation and strength. Narrator Davis succinctly concludes why many queers identify with failure, stating that 'we're always pretending, we're always performing, and we're always failing' (2020, p. 32). A key part of self-acceptance for queer people is finding a way to the joyful and celebratory political dimension within the queer reclamation of failure. This reappropriation 'recognize[s] failure as a way of refusing to acquiesce to dominant logics of power and discipline and as a form of critique' (Halberstam, 2011, p. 88).

If queer failure functions to counter cisheteronormative hegemony, then queer reclamation of the horror genre or failed mainstream films functions to counter hegemonic cisheteronormative fandom. That purposeful perspective and intention of the drag horror host (or performance artist) can reach and be understood by the audience, as alluded to by narrator Stodola who describes the queer failure and temporality of the Queer Horror pre-shows as 'that mix between barely rehearsed chaos with very cutting commentary on things that are happening locally and on a grander political scale' (2020, p. 20). While the Midnight Mass and Queer

Horror pre-shows are led by skilled drag horror hosts who are intelligent, talented, quick-witted and incredibly knowledgeable about film and the horror genre, the pre-shows rely on and are made special by the untamed reciprocal queer energy from and between the performers and audiences. Instead of creating a seamless, 'perfect' facade, hosts such as Peaches Christ and Carla Rossi embrace spontaneity and fluidity in their pre-shows, since 'professionalism' and 'perfectionism' function as white cisheteronormative tools for limiting advancement and reward. The pre-shows of these live cinema events challenge normative notions of art and performance, creating a distinctively queer engagement with live cinema and, in turn, with the horror and cult films themselves.

The extensive historical overlap between horror and cult films can be traced to a horror musical and the most prominent cult film of all time: *The Rocky Horror Picture Show*, 'an outrageous tongue-in-cheek tribute to the cult spectrum of late night picture shows – a trashy brew of B movie, schlock sci-fi, and junky horror productions' (Ross, 2008, p. 59). The initial 1975 release of *Rocky Horror* was deemed a 'disaster' by 20th Century Fox and 'subsequently distributed poorly and promoted unenthusiastically' (Austin, 1989, p. 84). However, a young gay audience at the Waverly, a movie theatre in the heart of Greenwich Village,[17] resurrected *Rocky Horror* on April Fool's Day in 1976. By Halloween 1977, the cult phenomenon had taken hold through avenues that included increasingly ritualised audience participation (such as dancing, throwing objects and call backs), and quickly spread to other movie theatres and cities (see, Henkin and Piro).[18] Certainly, *Rocky Horror*, 'the best-known cult film' (Austin, 1989, p. 84), would not have received renewed life without the queer audience who saw themselves in the commercially and critically failed text.

Rocky Horror has had extensive cultural influence, including on horror hosts such as Peaches Christ and the live cinema events that celebrate horror cinema. *Rocky Horror* also impacted audiences and their collective engagement, specifically queer audience engagement. As John Lynskey explains, '*Rocky Horror* screenings began to develop as alternative, radical spaces that promoted participation, allowing for an open demonstration of queer identity in response to conditioned, mainstream cinema practices of passive cinema viewing' (2020, p. 32). *Rocky Horror* enabled queer audiences to collectively embody their fandom in ways previously unknown. Narrator Mark Estes shares that '*Rocky Horror* was the most recognizable way for queers to get together and just enjoy something on screen that celebrated us and our love for the macabre and the strange and unusual' (2020, p. 30). Midnight Mass and Queer Horror are live cinema events that feature not only film exhibition but also an 'embodied live experience' (Atkinson and Kennedy, 2018, p. ix) that reaches 'beyond [cinema's] typical boundaries' (Klinger, 2018, p. xvii). In fact, these queer live cinema events form a cult community built around the celebration of films from the fringe, as established by *Rocky Horror*. Moreover, as Mathijs and Mendik point out, 'what all cult film consumptions have in common is that they are "lived" experiences' (Mathijs and Mendik, 2008, p. 4). Mathijs and Mendik further observe, in discussing film festivals, that queer audiences 'play a unique role in the reading and reception of cult cinema' (2008, p. 376). Cult and horror film reading and reception that is led by drag hosts underscores a transgressive queerness that exists at the margins of society. As a survey participant writes, 'cult horror goes hand in hand with the camp art of drag' (46877531). Cult films and the horror genre exist outside the cinematic mainstream, yet in queer live cinema events they are embraced and extolled by drag artists and queer audiences. Cult cinema exists through the queer community's salvation of failed, misunderstood films and numerous mainstream commercial and/or critical film failures have found themselves reanimated through queer subversiveness, productivity and artistry.[19]

Examples of queer subversiveness, productivity and artistry exist across latter twentieth- and early twenty-first-century history, with a number providing a foundation for today's key representations of queer live cinema. While a complete examination of queer contributions to live cinema lie outside the parameters of this study, the history of San Francisco's The Cockettes and The Sick & Twisted Players serve as key examples of the queerly distinct and distinctively queer relationship to horror film. Since the horror genre historically has rendered the queer subtextual, queer performers and audiences have found and revealed their queer connection to horror film, setting the stage for generations of queer artists. The Cockettes and The Sick & Twisted Players are two such queer performance troupes that incorporated horror film, both informing the San Francisco drag culture and impacting on queer culture beyond their historic temporal and spatial bounds. The Cockettes were a San Francisco theatrical drag review, a group of performers including non-normative sexualities and genders,[20] that created performances and presented midnight movies at the Pagoda Palace from 1969 until 1971, reaching a level of international notoriety due to their raucous queer shows. In 1970, the troupe staged the Halloween Horror Spectacular, featuring The Cockettes 'on stage in *Les Ghouls* plus on the screen *Night of the Living Dead*' (Hauser, 2020, p. 230). The Halloween Horror Spectacular also included a midnight horror movie marathon screening of *Masque of the Red Death* (1964), *Bluebeard* (1944) and *The Cat and the Canary* (1927) (Hauser, 2020, p. 207). Peaches Christ had 'the benefit of being part of the legacy of The Cockettes', so there was never a need for Grannell to 'redefine a drag culture' that would be rooted in horror and inclusive of all genders and sexualities (2020d, p. 14).[21] Grannell, when pitching the idea of the now legendary film event series Midnight Mass, to Landmark Theatres in 1998, 'begged and pleaded and explained the history of The Cockettes as a reason to allow [him] to do this' (2020c, p. 3). The legacy of The Cockettes also directly impacted on Hudson, an Oregonian growing up in the 1990s, who explains: 'The Cockettes were really inspiring to the early Tampon Troupe [Hudson's early drag troupe]. We would watch The Cockettes and the Leigh Bowery documentaries on loop' (2020c, p. 17). The queer live cinema legacy begun by The Cockettes was carried and furthered three decades later by The Sick & Twisted Players, who, inspired by horror films, created live theatre events in San Francisco, starting in 1990. The Sick & Twisted Players were a queer theatre troupe that became an underground phenomenon by recreating horror film scenes at the floating cabaret Klubstitute. They then began performing full-length horror films, creating thirty-five productions that included *The Shining … The Musical*, *The Exorcist: A Dance Macabre* and a live stage production of *Carrie*. The troupe founder Tony Vaguely also 'pioneered the theatrical mash-up', writing live theatre events that combined horror films with other films and shows, such as *A Very Brady Friday the 13th*; *Texas Chainsaw 90210*; *Alien: Starring Josie and the Pussycats in Outer Space*; *A Facts of Life Prom Night*; and *The Fog: Starring Gilligan's Island* (Orloff, 2019, pp. 183–4). The Sick & Twisted Players also incorporated famous special guests, a precursor to Grannell's Idol Worship – in-person interviews with famous guests as part of the Midnight Mass live show.[22] In 1996, The Sick & Twisted Players held a live cinema event called the Linda Blair Affair, a queer Pride event for which the audience was encouraged to 'dress possessed' for entering *The Exorcist* look-alike contest. The performance included live 'interpretations' and 'selective spoofs' of actor Linda Blair's horror classics, such as *The Exorcist*, *The Exorcist II* and *Hell Night* (Van Iquity, 1996, p. 41). The Sick & Twisted Players' shows not only 'acted as agitprop for an enlightened gender sensibility' (Orloff, 2019, p. 186), but also further primed queer audiences in San Francisco and beyond for queer live horror cinema entertainment.

Drag as Queer Performance and Drag Performers as Horror Hosts

Drag has long existed as an art form at the margins of the queer community, even as *RuPaul's Drag Race* may have permanently changed the perception of the art of drag, bringing it mainstream exposure and new legions of cisheterosexual fans.[23] C. Winter Han states that, 'there is a long history of various gay organizations actively attempting to exclude drag queens from participating in gay pride events and gay social settings by arguing that drag queens fail to meet respectable community standards' (2015, p. 146). In the fight for human rights, many gay and lesbian organisations chose messaging and arguments that would convince heterosexuals that queer people are 'just like them', and, therefore, deserving of equal rights. Their goal was to normalise cisheterosexual perceptions of gay, lesbian and bisexual people. However, some trans* members of the community, gender non-conforming individuals and/or drag performers complicated this normalisation tactic due to their non-normative gender expression. 'Trans* bodies represent the art of becoming, the necessity of imagining, and the fleshly insistence of transitivity' (Halberstam, 2018, p.136); therefore, these individuals were marginalised within the gay and lesbian community and left out of those advances. Grannell reflects on the perception and treatment of drag performers within the community:

> I think within the gay community we [as queer drag artists] were still outsiders. Trannyshack and Midnight Mass flew in the face of 'sweater gays' and 'corporate gays' and the HRC [Human Rights Campaign]. They would hate to acknowledge this, but there was a big part of the gay rights movement – the marriage equality movement – that did not want us anywhere *near* them. In fact, they really wanted us to just be pushed to the side. And so I think what we were creating was essentially – as you said – a queer space that was inclusive of every freak, every weirdo, every deviant. (2020c, p. 11)

In fact, throughout the 1960s and 1970s, drag performers were 'a source of contestation among gay activists' (Hillman, 2011, pp. 154–6) because the 'extreme' non-normativity of drag queens was seen as an inhibitor to rights and acceptance. Even today, drag horror performers (sometimes referred to as 'horror queens' or 'scream queens') exist at the margin of the already marginalised art of drag (evidenced in part by the difference in mainstream popularity between *RuPaul's Drag Race* and *The Boulet Brothers' Dragula*).[24] Speaking directly to the 'horrific' nature of drag and, thus, the shared transgressiveness between drag and horror, Grannell explains:

> If you're looking at drag from the point of view of some white redneck who's been raised to believe that queerness is scary, then *all* drag has horror embedded in it. Whether you're a Liza Minnelli impersonator or Peaches Christ. Okay. So, taking that out of the equation, that *all* drag is transgressive – which it is – *any* drag could be scary depending on who's viewing it. But I would say that, in general, in the larger drag world, that horror has not been part of people's attraction to drag. However, I think because of queerness being such a big part of why some of us are attracted to horror *and* why some of us are attracted to drag, that there is this way that they've been merged for a bunch of us. (2020d, p. 12)

Describing drag performances can be difficult, as Richard Niles explains 'because of the unique collaboration between audience and performer and the elusive factors of "camp" and "gay sensibility"' (2004, p. 41). Nonetheless, survey participant and narrator responses indicate that drag performances enhance the significance of live cinema events. A drag performer introducing a horror film carries meaning beyond simply the representation of a campy queer performance art onstage. Drag and horror share that transgressive core; as another survey participant emphasises, 'drag is subversive and so is horror, I think they can go hand in hand' (47082634). Furthermore, drag horror hosts enhance the experience of horror exhibition, altering the reception experience of the horror film.[25] A survey participant discusses drag horror hosts bringing 'a campy, gay, smart take on horror films to a queer audience, which made me enjoy the films more' (46764770).

Drag is an art form that (re)interprets and (re)presents. In the groundbreaking ethnographic study *Mother Camp: Female Impersonators in America*, Esther Newton examines drag as the art form in which 'appearance is an illusion' (1979, p. 103). Newton's early elucidation of gender as a socially constructed performative act stands as an ideological influence on gender studies. This influence extends to the work of Judith Butler (1990), whose argument demonstrates 'drag *as a practice* divulges a series of discordant elements that ultimately undermine both the assumption of heterosexual coherence and the idea that heterosexuality is original' (Lloyd, 2007, p. 43; italics in the original). In other words, heterosexuality relies on the essentialist 'natural' construction of the gender binary; the gender dissonance of drag can function to disrupt, subvert and denaturalise heteronormativity by revealing '*all* gender as *parody*' (Lloyd, 2007, p. 44; italics in the original). Regardless of the performer's intention, drag 'camps' the socially constructed nature and performativity of gender. A drag performance's gender (dis)illusion fundamentally transgresses and politically resists binaristic gender construction.[26] When that drag commentary, artistry and performance introduces horror films to audiences composed of non-normative genders and sexualities, it serves as a bridge between embodied queer experiences and the filmic representation of the trauma they endure. This queer horror connection is evidenced by numerous survey participants:

> I love going to see horror films in a theater and having some sort of program introduce it, it's especially affirming when they are drag queens. I feel at home in my own monstrosity when this happens. And while I don't think all drag queens would consider themselves to be monsters, drag is a political framework that understands, embraces and affirms our 'otherness'. (46926354)

> I love drag queens (and kings) because they highlight the performative nature of gender and identity and their performance of camp engages with the idea of the horrific uncanny. (47076895)

> The theatrics of the drag show compliment the heightened energy of most horror. The queerness also compliments the often overlooked and disrespected genre. (47603598)

> I felt a shift in target audience. No longer was the target white, cis men, there was a sense of a larger queering of interpretation and acknowledgment of significance to a queer audience/community. (46919087)

> Drag as an art form sort of captures the same anti-establishment, weirdo, politically incorrect, rebel mentality that all the best horror films do. (46824603)

> She [the drag queen] always engages with the queer undertones presented in the film and works through the problematics but also the potential empowerment by reading horror as queer to work through the demonization of queer identities. (47593223)

Drag performers hold an important community role by being horror hosts for queer live cinema events. Understanding the history of horror hosts and the importance of the role of horror host being held by a queer drag artist is essential to properly situate queer live cinema events, as will be evidenced by forthcoming explanations of Midnight Mass and Queer Horror. The long history of horror hosts includes over-the-top personalities, the essence of camp, heightened by make-up and costuming, a drag aesthetic. Campy drag personas are integral to two of the most iconic horror hosts: Vampira, the earliest horror host, and Elvira, a horror icon who is indebted to Vampira and became 'the most famous horror host of all time' (Watson, 1991, p. 162). This drag element and the 'campy flair of Elvira and other movie hosts' (47117296) has a particular resonance for queer horror fans, taking on a pointedly queer and, therefore, political dimension. Horror, furthermore, is the only genre with a long history of being presented to audiences by theatrical hosts, commonly on the television screen.[27] The majority, 59.4 per cent (n = 2,437), of queer horror fans have watched, on television or streaming, a horror host (such as Elvira, Mistress of the Dark or Joe Bob Briggs) introduce a horror film. Horror hosts reached a cultural zenith in US culture during the 1980s with the international popularity of Elvira, Mistress of the Dark. To this point, a statistical test reveals a correlation between the age of survey participants and reporting having seen a horror host, with those raised during the pinnacle of televised horror hosts most likely to have seen one. The youngest participants (eighteen to twenty-three years old) were least likely to have seen a horror host, with 36 per cent having seen a horror host; whereas, 100 per cent of participants sixty to sixty-five years old have seen a horror host.[28] Furthermore, survey participants from the United States (66.8 per cent) are more likely to have seen a horror host compared with those from the United Kingdom, Ireland, Canada, Australia or New Zealand (46.7 per cent) or elsewhere in the world (33.6 per cent), indicating a cultural dimension to this viewership. Regardless of age or nationality, a large percentage of the entire horror-loving queer community has seen a horror host. As such, a queer live cinema event 'fosters cultural appreciation for camp horror queens, such as Elvira and

Peaches Christ' (46967128). Another participant extols, 'I enjoyed the camp of hosts like Vampira and Elvira growing up and the drag introductions both hearken back to that and add a queer(er) dimension which I enjoy' (47434988).

Televised horror hosts nurtured and grew generations of horror fans, whereas the drag horror hosts who helm live cinema events today nourish the queer community's connection to horror, setting the stage for critical queer horror audience engagement. Peaches Christ and Carla Rossi, along with other drag performers who introduce horror film to queer audiences, establish an embodied queer connection between horror fandom and horror film. A queer ceremonial leader, or campy carnivalesque guide, functions to reinforce the queer connection to horror. Performance artists such as Peaches Christ and Carla Rossi represent as more than drag performers to their audiences, manifesting as drag horror hosts. One participant reflects on watching Peaches Christ in a show, stating, 'I just LOVE horror hosts and was watching her as a horror host character like Elvira or Count Gore' (47099527). Even though some survey participants recognise that 'there's a lineage of inspiration between drag and horror' (47244225), this lineage is not manifested often through queer embodiment of the horror genre. This scarcity of representation is highlighted by a survey participant who notes that 'horror isn't often linked with queer performance so it's exciting to see it done' (47244225). The drag horror hosts themselves also identify their introduction to drag as stemming from horror, as Grannell notes when he explains that he 'was introduced to drag through Frank N. Furter and Divine, and, inherently, both those performers and performances are horror. They come from the world of horror . . . So, for me personally, drag has always included horror' (2020d, p. 12).[29] The historical legacy and cultural influence of horror hosts is evident in Grannell's creation of Peaches Christ.

Midnight Mass with your Hostess Peaches Christ

Grannell created his horror host identity, drag persona Peaches Christ, after he landed in San Francisco in 1996 and entered a queer and drag cultural landscape that largely was shaped by the International Imperial Court System, The Cockettes, The Sisters of Perpetual Indulgence, The Sick & Twisted Players and Trannyshack. Grannell's inspiration to move west came when he, as a Pennsylvania State University film student, was part of a committee with Michael Brenchley that brought John Waters to Penn State. Waters told Grannell about San Francisco's flourishing queer and underground film scenes; shortly after, Grannell (and Brenchley) decided to move to San Francisco. Grannell recollects:

> I barely heard about The Cockettes and John told us about how they used to do shows at movie theatres at midnight – 'cause this is before the documentary. And he told us about the Kuchar Brothers. So I looked up the Kuchar Brothers. And he told us about Canyon Cinema and how San Francisco was really a great place for underground filmmakers. And that's literally all I needed to hear. Like that was it. That was all I needed to hear. (2020b, pp. 13–14)

Soon after moving, Grannell, who 'wanted to be John Waters meets Wes Craven' (2020b, p. 17), was managing the Bridge Theatre, a local single-screen arthouse theatre, and created Peaches Christ – both of which culminated in his creation of Midnight Mass. Grannell explains the concept behind Midnight Mass: 'My idea was that I wanted to create an experience that wasn't necessarily either a drag show or a midnight movie screening but both combined. It was my love for Trannyshack and my love for midnight movies mashed up into one experience on Saturday nights at midnight at the Bridge Theatre' (2020c, p. 3).

Grannell synthesised the influences of The Cockettes and *Rocky Horror* into horror hosting and queer performance alongside sustained horror film exhibition,[30] creating Midnight Mass as a summer series from June 1998 until late 2009 at the Bridge Theatre, 3010 Geary Boulevard, San Francisco, California.[31] The Bridge, named after the Golden Gate Bridge (construction of which was completed in 1937), was a 360-seat single-screen movie theatre that opened in 1939.[32] Grannell, as a movie theatre manager in the 1990s, understood that the future of cinema would be event-led.[33] For more than ten years, Grannell's Midnight Mass provided a queer cinematic space, exhibiting horror films such as *The Bad Seed* (1956), *Homicidal* (1961), *Spider Baby* (1967), *Carrie* (1976), *The Evil Dead* (1981), *Sleepaway Camp* (1983) and *Dead Alive* (1992), all combined with immersive thirty-minute long drag productions staged before the start of the film.[34] Each Midnight Mass also included events such as drag 'mother/daughter' mud wrestling, 'Filthiest Person Alive' contests, werewolf-a-lympics, zombie beauty queen pageants and drag queen roller derby, the last requiring the audience to sign release forms due to its raucous nature. The preciousness of this movie theatre space being made temporarily and enthusiastically queer was further evidenced by the after-parties, in which the rowdiness and energy continued, even as the audience numbers dwindled, often until dawn. Midnight Mass was built around a midnight start time, well after the 'normal' movies finished and normative crowds were home. Midnight, a signifier of darkness and of the otherworldly possibilities that the dark brings, holds special resonance for queers since much of queer history has existed in the shadows of night, sequestered away from the normative productivity of the day. Film critic David Chute highlights that 'trotting off to a midnight screening defies conventional viewing habits' (1983, p. 13) and, as film scholar Jessica Hughes notes, 'suggests a welcoming of alternative behaviors' (2016, p. 49). Certainly, Midnight Mass was an anti-conventional boisterous amalgamation of queer, horror, cult, camp and drag. With Divine, Frank-N-Furter and Elvira as his 'spiritual drag mothers' (Grannell, 2020c, p. 12), Grannell's 'Midnight Mass made horror the campy spectacle it's meant to be!' (47124411). Even though the entire Midnight Mass experience was filtered through a horror lens, Grannell sometimes created a shorter all-horror Midnight Mass series in the autumn to build excitement for the 'high homo' horror holiday that is Halloween (2020c, p. 14). 'Horror, to this day, has always colored my midnight movie, cult movie career', Grannell explains, and Midnight Mass was created 'under the umbrella or through the lens of horror' (2020c, p. 9).[35] This queer horror utopia was furthered as a live cinema experience outside of the bounds of the auditorium of the Bridge Theatre with the Russian River Massacre. Peaches Christ, in partnership with Putanesca (José Guzmán Colón) and Vinsantos (Vinsantos DeFonte), conceived of and produced the Russian River Massacre, a queer horror weekend in Guerneville, California, the 'Gay Riviera', approximately 70 miles north of San Francisco. In a forest clearing, with a piece of spandex stretched between two trees as the screen, Peaches Christ hosted Midnight Mass under the stars with the horror films *The Texas Chain Saw Massacre* (1974) and *Sleepaway Camp* (1983). The extension of Midnight Mass into the woods demonstrates that queer space is not only transitory but unlocalised – queers can create queer spaces wherever they go.

With horror at its heart, Midnight Mass was the time and place for Grannell to create 'a space for the fringe folks to come together under one roof, which was inclusive of all drag performers' (Grannell, 2020c, p. 11). Midnight Mass[36] celebrated the fringe through its embrace of cult cinema, with horror being integral in the broad cult category. Grannell made that connection clear through his understanding and presentation of cult films that are not usually attributed to the horror genre but have many transgressive horror elements. For example, the films of John Waters include dismemberment, mayhem and murder, about which Grannell speaks directly: '*Female Trouble* is not necessarily something people would put in the horror genre, but I would argue that horror is a big part of *Female Trouble*. Divine having acid thrown on her face and a woman being locked in a birdcage and having her arm cut off and a child being beaten with a car aerial – yes, this is all played for comedy – but it's also horror' (2020c, p. 9). This knowledge about and life-long passion for horror informs Grannell's work as a writer, drag performer and host. The drag pre-shows were just as important as the films to the queer audience because Peaches Christ 'know[s] a great deal about the film' (47114605) and 'her showmanship and gravitas really charged up the audience and let us know it was okay to be loud, and release our tension' (48127872). Peaches Christ, as a drag horror host, crafted campy queer horror experiences that gave audiences full of horror-loving queers a cathartic queer home. Because 'camp is the voice of survival and continuity in a community that needs to be reminded that it possesses both' (Bergman, 1993, p. 107), the queer, campy drag connection made by the live drag performance to the presented horror film resonates deeply with and holds life-changing significance for audience members. A Peaches Christ production, whether Midnight Mass or feature-length drag parody plays, offers queers a space to find community, especially young queers. A survey participant who saw Peaches Christ and other drag performers in *The Silence of the Trans* emphasises this importance, noting that show as the 'first time I ever saw drag theater and horror all together. I was a high schooler and it rocked my world' (47123315). Queer attendees, then, attach an importance and significance to their queer horror host and performer, noting about Grannell that 'Peaches Christ is God' (47406435) and is an 'absolute legend' (47093264). Grannell built this influence over a decade through Midnight Mass as a live cinema event that created a queer space in San Francisco and fostered the queer love of horror.[37] For over a decade, Grannell's Midnight Mass altered the history of horror exhibition, informed by its queer liveness and sharedness, and created a queer live cinema experience that has carried meaning beyond the borders of San Francisco and the bounds of time.

Welcome to Queer Horror

Queer Horror, which, on its start in 2015 at the historic Hollywood Theatre (which opened in 1926 at 4122 NE Sandy Boulevard, Portland, Oregon), filled a space in the Portland culture scene and a need for the queer community. An influence for its creation came to Anthony Hudson, a generation younger than Grannell, in part from their knowledge of Midnight Mass, with Grannell as an influence. Hudson, when creating Queer Horror:

> very consciously pitched it as partially in tribute to Peaches Christ, who was doing something I'd always wanted to do. She was both of the things I'd always really been drawn to, which was horror hostess and drag queen. So that was a *huge* influence for me in starting Queer Horror. And then the preshow idea, too – I was thinking, 'Oh wait, we can perform before the movie and not just show these short films'. (2020c, p. 17)

Hudson's pre-show performances as Carla Rossi[38] are an amalgamation of queer culture, horror references, political commentary, pop culture and current cultural events references. As Queer Horror grew in popularity, Hudson created increasingly elaborate and sharply political pre-shows.[39] For example, the pre-show for *The Stepford Wives* (1975), titled 'The Portland Wives', opened with Krzysztof Komeda's musical composition 'Lullaby' from *Rosemary's Baby* (1968) and text projected on the movie screen that read: 'Yes, we know this is from a different Ira Levin adaptation'. A few beats later, the screen displayed the word 'nerds', an acknowledgement of the intertextual horror knowledge held by the audience, which was met with a burst of laughter. Hudson had simultaneously situated the Queer Horror pre-show within the history of the horror genre (both films are Ira Levin adaptations) and knowingly recognised the horror proficiency of the queer audience. The pre-show[40] continued with a loving, lacerating critique of Portland, Oregon as a 'liberal mecca' overrun with 'untreated white guilt' (Hudson, 'The Portland Wives', 15 March 2019). Hudson's plot adroitly and humorously comments on the gentrification of the Alberta Arts District, a historically Black neighbourhood that became an increasingly white arts District after the first wave of artist gentrifiers in which neither the Black nor artist communities can afford to live any longer. Hudson's pre-shows present this type of political commentary through a perspective that includes queerness, horror, queer failure and camp.

Hudson approaches the creation of Queer Horror with the understanding that both horror and camp are queer art forms (2020d, p. 13), writing the one-act pre-shows affected and inspired directly by the queer 'drag theatre of the eighties/the ACT UP era' (Hudson, 2020c, p. 17). A queer politic permeates Hudson's work, in which the Queer Horror event 'becomes a weirdly spiritual and political and important exercise for me' (Hudson, 2020c, p. 16). For Hudson, camp is an important queer political tool since 'camp can become a way to zero in on just how absurd a political structure is. It's by playing up the artifice so high that it exposes the artifice underlying everything at its core as we encounter it in the world' (2020d, pp. 12–13). Hudson's pre-show intentions are both received and appreciated by the Queer Horror audience, as noted by survey participants:

> What I like about it is how the drag queen (Carla Rossi) performs small skits that relate to key points in the film while also providing contemporary social commentary on the films. In addition to this, having a drag queen introduce a film makes me feel more comfortable and, in a way, affirms that I am in a queer-friendly environment where I can be as queer as I wish to be. (48160651)

> Carla Rossi is a genius. (47158068)

> I attend Queer Horror in PDX – I like it because Carla Rossi talks about the social/political impact of the film and its significance. (46932948)

Hudson's Queer Horror pre-show rosters feature an inclusive spectrum of local drag performers who are employed[41] to contribute engaging performances, which audience members enjoy. Narrator Hodges recounts enjoyment of:

> getting to see other drag queens show up and participate in [the pre-shows] and kind of get away from just lip-syncing and really doing more acting as a queen than lip-syncing as a queen. I think that's great. It also really queers the whole thing because you're like here's a drag queen acting out a scene from this kind of racist movie like *Candyman*. (2020, p. 20)[42]

Queer Horror, like Midnight Mass before it, creates a queer space for queer audiences to investigate and appreciate the horrors in society, politics and films safely together.

The bimonthly Queer Horror screening series is a collaboration between partners in life and sometimes in art, Anthony Hudson and Jason Edward Davis, Queer Horror's resident artist. Davis paints art 'based on the movie we were gonna watch' and sells it in the lobby at the shows (2020, p. 21). Hudson is the show writer, programmer and host as Portland's premier drag clown Carla Rossi. Carla Rossi is performed in whiteface, a deft and silent social criticism, which Hudson explains is in 'direct allusion to whiteness, clowning, and as a critical inversion of blackface' (Hudson, n.d.). Carla Rossi's embodiment and self proclamation as a drag clown (as opposed to the more common terms drag queen/king), holds particular resonance when regarded with the culturally significant 'special power of the clown' (Ludlam, 1992, p. 30).[43] Carla Rossi, as a queer form of performance art, is laced with Hudson's eviscerating political wit aimed directly at white supremacy and cisheteronormativity, as informed by Hudson's half-Native (enrolled Confederated Tribes of Grand Ronde, Siletz descendant) and half-German heritage, as well as Hudson's non-normative gender and sexuality. Carla Rossi wields the clown's special power of being able to 'say serious things in a way that [they] cannot be punished for' (Ludlam, 1992, p. 30). When the Queer Horror event series first started, the programming was focused on films that have a direct queer connection to horror, containing explicit (sub)textual queerness in the narrative or being a film by a queer director, writer and/or actor. As Queer Horror evolved, Davis explains, the understanding of what makes a horror film queer became more amorphous: 'We know it's queer when we know it . . . some films are queer just by queer people watching them' (2020, p. 21). Being a live cinema event, Queer Horror is more than solely a film screening or a drag performance, as narrator Stodola proclaims: 'Queer Horror is the Holy Trinity, honestly. It's a horror movie that I wanted to see, I wanted to see the drag show, and it was the idea of being around a bunch of queer people who wanted to see the same old horror movie as me' (2020, p. 19). The 'live' augmented amalgamation of queerness, horror, performance and drag creates an experience that only exists in that space, for that duration, for those attendees. The temporary queer community forged through the Queer Horror series has lasting value in queers' lives, as narrator Hodges emphasises: 'The big draw for me is that feeling of community' (2020, p. 20). Underscoring the importance of live cinema events creating queer spaces and forging a queer community, narrator Stodola comments:

> I haven't really had the experience of being around queer audiences since Queer Horror. It's harder in smaller communities and small areas where it's not as safe to be out. I definitely miss that. I miss being able to walk in and knowing that this is my spot. I know exactly what I'm about. I know what everyone else is about. I'm here. (2020, p. 26)

Stodola's comment confirms not only the importance but also the need for the temporary queer communities created at events such as Midnight Mass and Queer Horror. These queer communities create feelings of safety and solidarity, all in celebration of queerness, the art of drag and the horror genre.

When Live Cinema Becomes a Significant Queer Event

Both Grannell and Hudson write, create and perform their original pre-shows, at Midnight Mass and Queer horror respectively, to augment the experience of the screened horror film they programme specifically for a queer audience. As a survey participant writes: 'They always talk about whichever film through a queer context/lens and how meaningful/impactful these films have been to queer people, either individually or as a community, and how the films, when seen through a queer lens, portray our experiences with mainstream/straight society' (46826839). The drag performance that Grannell and Hudson use in their live cinema experiences strengthens the queer bond to horror through their creation of safe, connective and celebratory queer spaces. These live cinema experiences have the ability to shift the queer connection to horror, as narrator Hodges states: 'Going to Queer Horror has changed how I think about horror' (2020, p. 11). Moreover, their intentional 'combining [of] queer culture and horror' (47122859) makes both Midnight Mass and Queer Horror movie events that form temporal and temporary communities blending identity (queer) with genre (horror).[44] Being events for queer audiences that are 'festivalized by means of their rarity' and contain accompanying 'live content' (Dickson, 2018, p. 90), Midnight Mass and Queer Horror exist as ritualised experiential ephemera and are thus distinct as a new class of specialised temporality in live cinema studies. In fact, when queers gather together for an event that celebrates a shared love of the horror genre, they create a 'queer temporal mode governed by the ephemeral, the temporary, and the elusive' (Halberstam, 2011, p. 54). These transitory exhibition temporalities imbue 'the festival with a sense of "event" … that is bound up in the ontology of the festival' (Atkinson and Kennedy, 2018, p. 79). Similarly, because of Midnight Mass's and Queer Horror's rarity, liveness *and* queerness, these live cinema experiences are understood by audience members to be events that enhance 'interactivity and community' (47001519). Numerous survey participants noted that they enjoy seeing drag performers introduce horror films because it feels like an event:

> Welcome element of communal kitsch, nice to be at an event with queer visibility. (46895883)

> It made watching the movie feel like an actual event and not just here's a movie you could be watching at home. (46938033)

> The showmanship really made the viewing more of an event. It was much more exciting especially when the drag queen is as passionate about the film as the audience. (47165769)

> I enjoyed the sense of community and event that it built. (47718111)

> It becomes more of an event than just going with friends to see a movie. We dress up, kind of a combination of goth and camp. And it means the audience is likely going to be made up of majorly lgbtq people, which is a different environment. It's our space. Also, the jokes in the pre-show are often relevant in a way that feels cathartic. (48010204)

Grannell and Hudson, reciprocally with their audiences, transform Midnight Mass and Queer Horror into serialised queer live cinema events. The seriality of these queer live cinema events is significant because regularly repeated screenings establish known queer spaces and events for queer horror spectators, giving queers something to look forward to, something they know will bring them together around a shared passion and their shared non-normativity.

The queer audiences of Midnight Mass and Queer Horror reject cisheteronormativity and embrace their shared non-normativity. Queer horror audiences collectively participating in horror fandom 'allow[s] for sexual expression and nonconformity (as well as subversion and the rejection of heteronormativity), namely through the display of queer performance' (Lynskey, 2020, p. 31). As Hudson notes, the Queer Horror:

> audience is rowdy, but they're not disruptive and everyone is on the same wavelength. You can tactilely feel the flow of energy in the room – I sound so Sedona right now – but you can feel everyone experiencing the jolts, the pangs. All the queer coding comes out explicitly when you're in that crowd with that audience. We all dial in. (2020c, p. 15)

Through my own 'active participation in and observation of' both events (Atkinson and Kennedy, 2018, p. 19), I attest that the audience energy and art performances of these live cinema experiences are joyous, rowdy, campy, raunchy and inclusive queer expressions of horror fandom in the public sphere. My observations are supported by a survey participant who breaks down the dynamic simply: 'Audience interaction. Audience participation. Breaking the fourth wall. Audience reaction' (47567830). Another survey participant highlights how a queer live cinema event functions to create a shared journey for the queer audience:

> What's not to like! I enjoy the campy, macabre, over the top elements of horror more than the gore and violent elements, so it feels fun to be able to celebrate those elements in my own queer community instead of at home by myself … I am delighted and also, I guess, comforted, by some kind of campy psychopomp mediating between the world of reality and the underworld of scary fantasy. (47470912)

The shared queer joy and energy of simultaneously celebrating drag, camp and horror remains unchanged, whether evidenced by Midnight Mass (1998–2009), Queer Horror (2015–present), or other events by drag performers who present horror films to queer audiences. In fact, narrator Alex Hall describes this same specific energy at the Queer Fear series in Toronto:

> To explain Queer Fear to someone who's never been … it's the pairing of the two – drag and horror film – and the drag performance always has to do with the movie itself. I wish I could remember the performances better. It's curated by a gay man who stated that he was new to Toronto … He opens the film with some context of his reading of what the significance of the film is within the queer horror canon. They've done *The Birds*; obviously, *A Nightmare on Elm Street 2*, which I missed, but I snagged a poster from a billboard. So I have that commemorating a queer experience. It's a *very* energetic space. (2020, p. 19)

While I have never attended Queer Fear and Hall has never attended Midnight Mass or Queer Horror, our experiences with these live cinema events mirror one another. My experience as a Midnight Mass and Queer Horror participant over decades, combined with the oral history interviews and survey responses, indicates that all live cinema experiences with drag horror hosts are imbued with a particular queer energy, one that is at once joyfully defiant and exuberantly Other and that is generated from a marginalised community finding shared temporary release, in this case through horror, a marginalised genre.[45] Narrator Hodges, when discussing Queer Horror, states that 'being around a bunch of queer people when you're queer is totally addictive' (2020, p. 20), alluding to the queer energy that is at once unparalleled and uncommon for queers to experience in their daily lives. Similarly, narrator Kim Thompson discusses how watching horror films with queer audiences augments the experience:

> Being in a crowd with other queer people and just enjoying together this particular genre, which we have all somehow come to and are united in agreeing that this is this really magic moment of cinema history that we all, for some reason, really, really enjoy. It's just really a magic feeling to be in that space surrounded by your people enjoying this thing that you get so much joy from. It kind of magnifies the experience, really. (2020, p. 24)

Narrator Alex Hall further confirms that queer live cinema events hold:

> a different energy, obviously when you're in a public space with a bunch of queer people, queer strangers. And it's not just going to your regular queer film fest, too. It has a different energy. And maybe coming from people that are into horror or the fact that you're going to see a horror film – it's a particular kind of energy and queer energy. (2020, pp. 20–21)

This specific queer energy results from a drag horror host exhibiting a horror film to a queer audience, regardless of film, location or drag performer, as well as resulting from the act of queer horror fans coming together to simultaneously celebrate their queerness and their love of horror film. In fact, those two elements coexist because '[s]haring films is a way for people to share their lives, their identities and parts of their emotional fabric with others' (Levitt, 2018, p. 21). In darkened movie theatres, queers have found connections on the screen and with other audience members because 'cinema as an institution creates pockets of queer space, time, and experience' (Schoonover and Galt, 2016, pp. 266–7). Queer live cinema events such as Midnight Mass and Queer Horror can be understood as Foucauldian heterotopias that are localisable places existing 'outside of all places' (1986, p. 24). The temporary queer spaces created through these live cinema horror events become shared experiences that can only exist within the bounds of their place outside normative existence. 'Cinema persists in queer culture as a site of political ferment', Galt and Schoonover explain, while it 'also provides spaces in which to nourish more diffuse experiences of affinity, belonging, and intimacy' (2016, p. 20). Midnight Mass and Queer Horror as live cinema events accentuate the collective experiences of queer solidarity while they also create spaces for 'exploring and celebrating the intersection between queerness and horror' (48537827).

Evidencing Queer Live Cinema with Empirical Data

The establishment of the queer connection to 'queered' live cinema is first evidenced by the case studies of Midnight Mass and Queer Horror and will be further evidenced by my study's empirical data. To date, in live cinema studies, researcher observation has been privileged over direct audience engagement, or empirical data collection, with the result that 'even when the work provides an account of audience experiences, their voices are hardly present' (Vivar, 2018, p. 119). Methodological practices that evade direct engagement with audiences are neglecting a fundamental aspect of the live cinema experience, as live theatre requires an audience and that audience becomes a part of the performance itself. Atkinson and Kennedy wrote in 2017 that live cinema studies 'remains largely uncharted' and made a 'call to all researchers to take up the continued mapping and critical study of this ever-evolving field and its ecosystems of production and participation' (2018, p. 267). Therefore, this research and intervention into live cinema studies represents that direct engagement and incorporates voices from queer audiences and performers of queer live cinema events.[46] The following comment from a survey participant, writing about what they enjoy about taking part in a live (horror) cinema experience, underscores the importance of both a queer audience and a drag performance for queer horror fans: 'Sometimes the horror film fan world can feel very straight, but to me (and I'm sure many others) it's always felt very closely connected to queerness, and seeing a drag queen introduce the film felt like a confirmation that I was in a room where I felt understood and that it was a special occasion' (47336309). For the audience to feel that a film screening is a special occasion, the total live cinema experience – or 'the unifying aspect of live cinema events [which] seems to be their connection to and enhancement of a specified film' (Jones, 2018, p. 197) – is manifested, in this case through horror film curation, drag performances *and* the shared energy of a queer audience.

Queerness, drag and horror film exist at a confluence of reclamation and reanimation because queer people, drag performers and horror fans are all marginalised communities that exist at the periphery of normativity, individuals and groups who transgress the norms and boundaries of mainstream acceptance and 'respectability'. My survey data soundly demonstrates that the majority of queer horror fans both engage with drag performance and prefer to see horror films with queer audiences.[47] Of queer horror fans, 65.1 per cent (n = 2,666) have been to a drag show, while 1,105 (77.7 per cent) of the 1,430 who have not been to a drag show would like to go. This large majority engagement with drag illustrates, undeniably, that queer spectators of horror connect with the art of drag.[48] Further, 54 per cent (n = 2,819) of queer horror fans strongly agree or agree that they most enjoy watching horror films with queer audiences, with only 4.6 per cent strongly disagreeing or disagreeing with that statement. Moreover, as discussed previously, horror fans whose queerness creates a different reaction to and taste in horror films, indeed, have the queerest relationship to horror and are therefore more inclined to enjoy watching horror films with queer audiences. There are positive correlations with the following statement: 'I most enjoy watching horror films with queer audiences' ('different reaction' $r_s = 0.34, p < 0.000$ and queer 'taste' $r_s = 0.35, p < 0.000$), both with moderate effect. Considering that queer people are not often afforded the opportunity to watch horror films together, this data strongly demonstrates the queer community's need and desire for more occasions to gather to watch horror films. While live cinema events such as Midnight Mass and Queer Horror combine queers' desire to be within a queer audience to watch horror films with drag performance, the majority of the oral history narrators have, unfortunately, not seen a drag performer introduce a horror film, and only 15.7 per cent (n = 642) of the survey participants have been to a movie theatre to watch a drag queen introduce a horror film with a short drag pre-show.[49] An overwhelming majority of survey participants – 87.8 per cent (n = 3,019) – would like to see a drag queen introduce a horror film in a cinema or movie theatre, as would all of the oral history narrators who have not yet had that opportunity. Even though a significant segment of queer horror spectators have not been to a queer live cinema event hosted by a drag performer, the fact that the overwhelming majority of survey participants want to see a drag horror host suggests that the primary limiting factors are lack of access or being unaware of such events. The queer live cinema events mentioned in this study are located in urban areas (San Francisco, Portland, Toronto, Manchester and the Tampa Bay area), indicating that these events are localised in cities with significant queer communities. This study's mixed-method data patently indicates that queer horror fans would attend these events if other drag performers created these meaningful queer experiences.

The appeal for queer people to see a drag queen introduce a horror film, in part, stems from the temporary centring of queerness that comes from having a space be reclaimed by and for queers. George Chauncey states: 'There is no queer space; there are only spaces used by queers or put to queer use' (2014, p. 202). Queer performers presenting queered horror film to queer audiences is an act of queer reclamation in which a theatrical space is put to queer use. A survey participant speaks directly to this queer reclamation when they state: 'It felt like a reclamation of a hetero-bro genre, a "queering" and even celebration of otherness from a different perspective that facilitated a fresh approach to viewing with an audience very much attuned to my own life experience' (47799428). Narrator Lana Contreras further evidences the importance of claimed queer space when she states: 'I feel like a queer space is a safe space to be who you are, be acknowledged of who you are, and not fear that something might happen' (2020, p. 22). Similarly, narrator Hodges clarifies that events such as Queer Horror create:

> space where I don't have to think about my identity anymore because everyone around me is accepting and gets it …When you're in a space like that you can all celebrate the fact that you're fucking queer and, at the same time, stop giving it the negative space that it can sometimes take up in your mind. (2020, p. 20)

Narrators Kaitlyn Stodola and Mark Estes both further underscore the importance of having queer space and queer connection within it:

> Queer Horror was one of my first experiences going and being around other queer people, and seeing that they like the same movies as me, and a lot of them wear the same kind of clothes as me. I'm like they're all super nice and they're super fun and super sweet, even though we're seeing horror movies about people getting murdered [laughs], and it was such a huge thing. And we waited after the show and we went up and we talked to Anthony, and Anthony was so nice and just immediately was like, [in their best Carla voice] 'Oh, my babies welcome.' I wanted to cry because I was like, I have a place now. I can be here and I can interact with other people who are like me and like the same things as me. (Stodola, 2020, p. 16)

> I want to see a horror movie or a queer horror movie in a crowd with a bunch of queer people and just sit there and be with the family. I haven't yet got to see that, but it's on my bucket list. Like if they got to bring my ashes in there and just put me in the damn seat, that'll still be great. I feel like that's a rite of passage for any queer horror fans – to sit there and watch a movie with your peers. *Maybe Hello Mary Lou: Prom Night II.* Maybe *Sleepaway Camp.* Maybe, hell, something new that's coming out. It could be campy. It could be serious. Just something where I could sit there and look at the person next to me and be like we're here. We might be a different shade of people – we're different shades, different backgrounds – but we're *all* here on this screen. (Estes, 2020, p. 28)

Queer audiences remain fundamentally disenfranchised from cisheteronormative society. For this reason, they find a specific queer connection in the collective experience of watching horror films. A live cinema horror screening with a queer audience, or a 'participatory screening', 'acts as a space for the Other, one who may be subject to discrimination and marginalisation by heteronormative society, to express a certain queer identity and disengage this marginalisation through transgressive acts' (Lynskey, 2020, p. 34). As a survey participant affirms, queer people have 'a physical representation that all horror films are based in, the concept of being the "othered" or rejected by the mainstream' (46896918). This quote emphasises both an emotionality and an explicit awareness of queer as Other. Another survey participant corroborates this when they share that they like seeing a drag queen introduce a horror film in a movie theatre because of 'the sense of community and empowerment that comes from the shared experience of a lot of people on the outside of the social status quo being able to be in a big role or position. Also, there's a great, high energy created typically due to the theatrical nature of drag' (47082773). In fact, the majority of the 585 survey participant written responses (from those who had seen a drag queen introduce a horror film with a pre-show [n = 642]) emphasise the importance of queer audience interaction with, participation in and reaction to live cinema events with drag horror hosts such as Midnight Mass and Queer Horror.

While the emerging field of live cinema has yet to investigate explicitly queer events or audiences, Rosana Vivar has empirically examined the San Sebastian Horror and Fantasy Film Festival (Horror Week). Vivar's findings reveal the masculinised behaviours of Horror Week fans, which comparatively have a marked difference to queer horror audiences. Vivar observes that the Horror Week 'festivalgoers engage in boisterous acts of disapproval towards films and guests that are introduced during the screenings' (2018, p. 117). Vivar notes the comments 'Take your panties off!' and 'I just got a hard on!' as 'the most recurrent phrases dedicated to female guests that venture on to stage' (2018, p. 127). Conversely, the queer audiences of Midnight Mass and Queer Horror engage in boisterous acts of approval and, indeed, love, towards both films and guests. For example, Midnight Mass was centred on the 'worship' of cult and horror films.[50] As Grannell states: 'We are coming together to worship movies like *Faster, Pussycat! Kill! Kill!* at this fellowship called Midnight Mass. And Tura Satana is our idol. Varla is our idol and we're going to worship her' (2020c, p. 4).[51] The 'worshippers' at both Midnight Mass and Queer Horror are queer spectators from all genders and sexualities – both on the stage and in the audience to complete the holistically inclusive space. Vivar writes about 'the overwhelming presence of men in horror-themed events', citing examples from both Horror Week and research by Van Extergem (2004) (2018, p. 124). Vivar concludes that 'Horror Week is a good example of horror and fantasy film viewing contexts being sites that provide room for certain conservative facets of masculinity in the public sphere' (2018, p. 132), further contrasting the behaviours and tone of that audience compared with the queer audiences of Midnight Mass and Queer Horror. The tonal distinction between 'queer' and 'straight' live cinema events, particularly when considered with the empirical data that evidences the research participants' overwhelming desire to experience a queer live cinema event, underscores the individual, social, cultural and academic impact of queer spectators gathering and celebrating both their queerness and their shared love of horror at these events.

Film as the Cinematic Church of Queer Community and the Future of Queer Live Cinema

This chapter has used evidence from survey participants, oral history narrators and case studies on Grannell's Midnight Mass and Hudson's Queer Horror to argue that the queerness of the audiences and the drag performers is fundamental – that a movie theatre full of *queer* horror fans is vital – to these live cinema experiences. Hanich discusses collective film viewing as 'a theory and phenomenology of the influence other spectators have on our film experience and the influence we have on theirs' (2018, p. 4). However, queer horror fans primarily exist as imagined and temporary communities, rarely having the opportunity to gather physically in large numbers to celebrate anything, much less horror film. These live cinema events with drag horror hosts offer queers the opportunity to move from imagined to intentional communities. Ulrika Dahl observes that researching cultural events, as conducted here with Midnight Mass and Queer Horror, 'reveals that community is made and remade through the events that bring people together' (2010, p. 153).

Queer people find a stabilising commonality and inspiring energy when gathered together as an audience of horror films.[52] Nicholas Ray famously referred to film as 'the cathedral of the arts' (Scheibel, 2017, p. 110), an observation that directly reflects the film medium's ability to incorporate all other art forms. Film as an art form *and* a joint social action offers sanctuary to queers. Grannell highlights this point, stating: 'I do believe that for some of us, films were our salvation. They were the things that became our teachers, our guides to living. And so, in many ways, I do think my love for film and the film-going experience is equivalent to going to church' (2020c, p. 5). Cinema creates queer connections and meaning, as evidenced in this study, that go beyond what may be expected or evidenced otherwise. Survey participants and narrators referring to movie theatres as queer community 'church' is a significant designation of spiritual meaning and ritual worship. Hudson further evidences this idea of movie theatres/cinema being the place for a devotional experience for queers as they gather to celebrate something we love, horror: 'I think of Queer Horror as a church in a way. There is something holy that happens when you gather all of us together in a space' (2020c, p. 15). Hudson's philosophy is shared by Queer Horror attendees; as one survey participant states, 'Carla Rossi is the Hollywood's High Priestess. I go to that church' (46893342). Narrator Stodola also used this language of spiritual fellowship, noting that attending Queer Horror 'is definitely like church. It's a feeling of coming home almost' (2020, p. 18).

Given how organised religion, historically and presently, harms and ostracises queers, many queers must make and/or find their congregations elsewhere. Émile Durkheim, when discussing the sociology of religion, states that the 'very act of congregating is an exceptionally powerful stimulant. Once the individuals are gathered together, a sort of electricity is generated from their closeness and quickly launches them into an extraordinary height of exaltation' (quoted in Morrison, 2006, p. 240). For many queers, that joy is found in a movie theatre connecting with other queers over their shared love of horror, over an embrace of being Others together. Grannell, reflecting on the beginning of Midnight Mass, shares his experience of that connection taking shape around his events:

> My best memory is that people were really grateful to find their tribe and Midnight Mass, and Peaches, in a lot of ways, was a lighthouse or a beacon that attracted these people. Even in San Francisco, queer folks – men, women, trans folks – who loved horror, who loved this transgressive stuff, who loved trash or things that were dismissed as trash – we were the church that allowed them to gather. (2020c, p. 14)

As explained by Durkheim, this evidences how social gathering is essential for creating community bonds. Queers gathering in movie theatres to celebrate horror films creates temporally and spatially bound bonds within the queer community, functioning as liberating carnivalesque spaces in which queer people celebrate their shared non-normativity.

Live cinema events represent queer possibilities and collectivity in horror fandom, with the temporarily reclaimed spaces and sense of community being vital to queer community, even if the majority of fans have yet to have the opportunity to experience live cinema events such as Midnight Mass and Queer Horror due to limitations in access and exposure. This precious queer space and communing is threatened by the global pandemic that continues as I write this work.[53] Most movie theatres in the United States were closed for well over a year.[54] Current evidence indicates that cinemas have not fully recovered from the COVID-19 pandemic prolonged closures, certainly in the United States. The institutions that do survive will need more than film exhibition alone to draw cinema audiences back. Live cinema events will, indeed, prove valuable as well as meaningful to attract people away from their homes, with mobile devices and streaming platforms, and back into movie theatres. Live cinema events such as Midnight Mass and Queer Horror offer 'new forms of embodiment and new possibilities for community engagement and participation' (Atkinson and Kennedy, 2018, p. 20). The future of queer spaces remains in flux, as multiple factors have hastened the closure of dedicated queer spaces, such as bars and clubs. Post-pandemic trauma is likely to be significant within the queer community, taking longer for some to adjust to life after the COVID-19 pandemic and the MPXV outbreak, since many queer community members, primarily Generation X and older, remember and hold trauma due to the AIDS epidemic. These viruses have and will continue to exacerbate queer inequalities, which may lead to additional trauma, furthering what sociologist DaShanne Stokes identifies as existing due to 'politics and widespread discrimination', creating 'significant disparities in LGBT [queer] medical rights and health care outcomes' (2020, p. 81). Stokes further details how preexisting 'health care disparities amplified by the pandemic are set to magnify LGBT social and political inequality on a national scale. In addition, the pandemic has contracted space in public discourse and media coverage – which is needed to advance LGBT equality – creating new opportunities for exploitation to advance anti-LGBT political agendas' (2020, p. 81). Queer people, particularly BIPOC, trans* and/or disabled community members, remain at the marginalised peripheries of cisheteronormative societies medically, socially, politically and economically. With the ability for the marginalised queer community to gather in queer spaces or movie theatres to be permanently altered, the possibilities are reduced for queer horror fans collectively to experience horror films. As this work affirms, experiencing and celebrating horror together holds the utmost significance to queer spectators, queer performers and drag horror hosts. Queers who create horror spaces for our queer community recognise the need for a horror connection forged in queerness and camp that outwardly embraces the non-normative and queer failure. These temporary queer live cinema events are transformed into cult horror events of the carnivalesque by both the drag hosts and the queer audiences through their very liveness and sharedness. In particular, the case studies of Midnight Mass and Queer Horror demonstrate how queer horror events expand the 'embodied live experience' (Atkinson and Kennedy, 2018, p. ix) and make much-needed space for the queer spectators of horror in live cinema studies.

Notes

1. While a drag queen, a cis gay man 'impersonating' a woman, is the most common perception of a drag performer, the entire drag umbrella more extensively represents a wide range of performers, including 'drag kings (typically queer cisgender women and trans men who perform as men), bio femmes (sometimes called bio queens or faux queens, cisgender women who perform stereotypes of femininity onstage as a critical practice), bio males (also known as bio kings or faux kings, cisgender men who critically perform stereotypes of masculinity), genderfuck artists who challenge binary understandings of gender through androgyny or deliberate mashups of traditionally masculine and feminine characteristics, and other types of gender performance too many to name' (Horowitz, 2020, pp. 2–3).
2. When a film includes a queer story or character, the creators make a space in cisheteronormative society for a non-normative existence. Cinema, as both a cultural artefact and theatrical space, allows queers to see themselves in the narratives and characters within a film text that is projected onto a cinema screen.
3. An overwhelming 87.8 per cent of queer horror spectators would like to see a drag performer introduce a horror film, while less than 16 per cent of the survey participants have experienced such an event. Even though the COVID-19 pandemic complicated the proliferation of queer live cinema events (and therefore queer spectators' ability to experience in-person screenings presented by drag horror hosts), drag performers, including Bunny Galore, Mr Wesley Dykes and Adam All, entertained queer audiences by introducing horror films streaming online.
4. The very liveness and the uniqueness of the queer live cinema events analysed in this chapter imbues them with cultural value, at times considered to be subcultural capital. The subcultural capital discourse, developed across numerous scholars, analyses how particular fans earn a rarefied status based on their participation in or experience of select events that are deemed subculturally valuable, thereby conferring on the attendee an elevated social status. Sarah Thornton, the scholar who coined the term, explains that subcultural capital 'confers status on its owner in the eyes of the relevant beholder' (1995, p. 27) and that this capital is 'a currency which correlates with and legitimizes unequal statuses' (1995, p. 163). Subcultural capital, considered to be both embodied and objectified (Thornton, 1995, p. 27; Hills, 2010, p. 89), is a hierarchical concept that is imbued with capitalistic notions and discussed in capitalism's terms. An individual can claim, invest,

monetise, accumulate, negotiate, accrue, generate, trade on, perform, display and/or demonstrate subcultural capital; conversely, a person's subcultural capital may be considered to be eroded, diluted, unrecognised and/or diminished. The theoretical employment of subcultural capital, thus, segregates and ranks a fan community into sub-communities with stratified social statuses. This work purposely and pointedly does not employ the fracturing and hierarchical concept of subcultural capital to understand the queer horror spectator because, as discussed, this study prioritises data-based collective consensus and community cohesion over any individual (and subcultural) status or gains.

5. Peaches Christ is most often written about in the press as a legendary drag icon with a reach far beyond San Francisco, enjoying an ever-growing international reputation. Peaches Christ's role as a horror/cult film maven or aficionado is bolstered by appearances in documentary films about Divine, *Showgirls*, Jayne Mansfield and Tura Satana. Peaches Christ's creator Joshua Grannell is also a horror director, having written and directed numerous horror parody shorts starring Peaches Christ, including *Season of the Troll* (2001), *A Nightmare on Castro Street* (2002) and *Whatever Happened to Peaches Christ?* (2004). Grannell adapted his horror short film *Grindhouse* (2003) into his feature debut film *All About Evil* (2010). I was a part of Grannell's 'zero-budget' crew as director of photography for all the aforementioned short films.
6. Queer Fear, Miss McGee's Creature Feature and Make A Scene are also queer live cinema events that screen horror films with drag performers as the host. These three queer live cinema events are examples to demonstrate that queer live cinema events exist outside of both the West Coast and the United States.
7. I employ the term 'reclamation' in this chapter with an intended meaning beyond its dictionary definition: to claim something that was never yours in the first place. This shift in meaning is intentional because both the queer live cinema events under study are serialised events that regularly return to claim a queer space (temporarily), and it is assertively political to then name that action as queer reclamation.
8. Narrator Stodola comments about queer collectivity differing from other non-queer viewing experiences: 'I've always loved seeing horror movies in the theatre because seeing it with an audience is always so much more fun because everyone screams and everyone is really loud. And especially with the Queer Horror audience, everyone yells at the stuff that I would want to yell at, but that my mom would just be quiet through. It's the stuff where people call out jokes or will scream at certain things. It's just always so much more fun' (2020, p. 26).

9. As evidenced by my survey data, when queer spectators watch horror films in a movie theatre, they overwhelmingly go with friend(s) and/or partner(s). Conversely, when watching horror films outside of the cinemagoing experience (e.g., at home), queer horror spectators watch horror films alone. For example, 77.6 per cent (*n* = 3,162), the vast majority, of queer spectators usually watch horror films at the cinema or movie theatre with friends or partners; whereas 15.5 per cent (*n* = 630) watch alone. The breakdown of with whom queer horror fans usually watch horror films at the cinema or movie theatre is as follows: 34.7 per cent (*n* = 1,414) with a friend; 26.3 per cent (*n* = 1,074) with a partner; 7.7 per cent (*n* = 312) with an all or mostly LGBTQ+ group; 6 per cent (*n* = 244) with a mixed LGBTQ+ and heterosexual group; and 2.9 per cent (*n* = 118) with an all or mostly heterosexual group – 7 per cent (*n* = 285) of survey participants marked the question as not applicable, indicating that they do not regularly attend the cinema.
10. As noted previously, 73.5 per cent (*n* = 2,998) of queer horror fans report that horror films make them laugh, with only 8.1 per cent (*n* = 332) reporting that they do not laugh at horror films. The remaining 18.3 per cent either do not have an opinion about laughing at horror films or do not know whether or not they laugh at horror films.
11. Laughter offers queer audiences a connection and release unique to queer people. Hudson recollects: 'We did *Addams Family Values* [on 16 November 2016] and Trump had just been elected … We did a combination of the Wednesday Addams monologue about the first Thanksgiving that she does in Addams Family Values – which is amazing. We combined that with the "Cell Block Tango" from *Chicago*, and by the end of it we set Trump on fire on screen, and we all do a Stonewall kick line in front of this image of Trump on fire with an American flag. That went over well … The feedback I was getting from the queers in the audience was that that was the first time they had been able to laugh since the election' (2020c, p. 12).
12. In *Laughing Screaming: Modern Hollywood Horror and Comedy*, William Paul examines an interface of laughter and fear and states that: 'Henri Bergson has written that "laughter appears to stand in need of an echo." The same is true of screaming. We may scream watching a horror film at home on television or we may let out a real belly laugh watching a comedy, but never as much as in a theater. Horror films and comedies represent preeminently theatrical genres - movies that work best within the context of a crowded theatre – because their aesthetic aim *is* rousing rabble' (1994, p. 21).
13. Trannyshack, an inclusive queer performance art and drag show, was founded and hosted by Heklina (Stefan Grygelko) for more than twelve years (February

1996 to August 2008) at midnight on Tuesdays at the Stud, a well-known San Francisco queer bar. Starting in 1996, Grannell began developing Peaches Christ on the Trannyshack stage and 'started to find a horror family' there (2020b, p. 17). The now-legendary show was instrumental to the development of West Coast drag, yet a discussion of Trannyshack should offer historical context about the name due to the culture shifts that have eschewed usage of the term 'tranny'. Grannell, who no longer uses 'the "T" word' (2020d, p. 11) explains: 'Back then we used the word tranny – it wasn't a pejorative at the time, it hadn't become this sort of slur, this hate term – all of our non-binary- trans-identified friends, even in central Pennsylvania, used the word tranny as an inside term of endearment' (2020b, p. 15). Grygelko, in 2015, rebranded Trannyshack as Mother to respect the trans* community.

14. Mark Jancovich states that 'out' queer film-maker John Waters and the outwardly queer *Rocky Horror* 'were amongst the most prominent examples of the cult movie within the 1970s' (2008, p. 159).
15. Narrator Stacie Ponder connects the failures of hegemonic cisheteronormative culture with queer reception, stating: 'Whether it's deliberate camp or unintentional camp, there's a prism of regular, old homogenous straight white life and it's like we're seeing that life refracted – whether we're causing it to be or we just delight in a misfire' (2020, p. 29).
16. Queer audiences have infamously transformed three previously deemed disastrous films into the Hollywood camp trilogy: *Valley of the Dolls* (1967), *Mommie Dearest* (1981) and *Showgirls* (1995).
17. Greenwich Village is Manhattan's 'gay haven' neighbourhood (Gordon, 2020, p. 37) and home to the Stonewall Uprising that helped shape the queer liberation movement.
18. To date, numerous cinemas across the world continue to screen *Rocky Horror*, including long-running midnight screenings at Milwaukee, Wisconsin's Oriental Theatre and Portland, Oregon's Clinton Street Theater since 1978. When the global COVID-19 pandemic interrupted these regular cinemagoing activities, the Clinton Street Theater played *Rocky Horror* for fifty-four Saturdays in a row to an empty house to maintain the movie theatre's forty-three-year screening streak.
19. Some of the best-known mainstream horror 'flops' that have been reanimated as cult and/or horror successes by queer audiences are: *The Rocky Horror Picture Show* (1975), *Death Becomes Her* (1992), *Hocus Pocus* (1993) and *Jennifer's Body* (2009). As a survey participant writes: 'We [queers] will find movies that have tanked or that had a bad rap with the mainstream horror community and we make stars out of them' (47790815).

20. Perhaps the most well-known member of The Cockettes was singer-songwriter Sylvester who co-wrote and recorded the 1978 hit disco single 'You Make Me Feel (Mighty Real)', which was selected by the Library of Congress for preservation in the National Recording Registry in 2019.
21. This is noteworthy because the popular image of the drag queen has been 'dominated primarily by cis gay men', partially due to the international success of *RuPaul's Drag Race*, as noted by Katie Horowitz in *Drag, Interperformance, and the Trouble with Queerness* (2020, p. 2).
22. This segment of Midnight Mass was host to John Waters, Cassandra Peterson (Elvira), RuPaul Charles, Mink Stole, Tura Satana, Mary Woronov, Stephen Geoffreys, Erica Gavin and Patrick Bristow.
23. Presenting the entire history of drag is outside the scope of this study. While a single book is incapable of encapsulating all the myriad facets of drag and gender performance, see *Drag: The Complete Story* by Simon Doonan for an overview of different 'types' of drag including glamour, art, butch, Black, historical, comedy, popstar, movie and radical drag. This study does not offer a comprehensive theorisation of the gender politics of drag, nor does it engage with the limiting belief that drag is inherently misogynistic. Drag is a vast art form that encompasses much more than men performing femininity; as Meredith Heller states, the 'popular public knowledge about drag is narrow and premised on (and, I argue, bounded and limited by) a myopic vision of the genre' (2020, p. 1). However, since misogyny is a rampant socially constructed and perpetuated phenomenon, I acknowledge that some drag may be problematic (such as that which is misogynistic or racist) and that drag is not a universally accepted queer art form.
24. Narrator Michael Varrati further connects drag and horror, explaining: 'I've always said that there's a strong connection between drag queens and horror because both are art forms that take heightened reality and force you to look at things that maybe you could otherwise ignore. It's why drag queens have always been on the front lines of every great queer movement. Because if you and I are marching in front of a bar, in front of a building, on down the street with a sign, if someone chooses to look the other way, they can. And they do sometimes. But a drag queen, in that opulent, gigantic outfit, they're harder to ignore. You can't ignore something that is so in your face and so ultra. So by using the outrageous to make you look, they can then kick in a door in the same way that horror does. It's like you may be looking at the monster, but then you discover, "Oh, this is about the atomic weapon"' (2020, p. 24).
25. Narrator Estes suggests how special effects makeup and costuming can offer another connection between drag and horror: 'Drag has always been there in

horror but people don't want to call it drag, they want to call it this demon, this creature' (2020, p. 29).

26. In agreement with Dolores McElroy, this study maintains that 'at its core, camp acknowledges that "masculine" and "feminine" are merely poses and not rooted in biology or essence' (2017, p. 303).
27. The history of televised horror hosts dates back to 1954 with the debut of *The Vampira Show*, fronted by Vampira, a character created by Maila Nurmi. While the popularity and proliferation of television horror hosts since then is concentrated in localised US markets, there were numerous international horror hosts, including Deadly Earnest (Australia) and La Bruja Maldita (Mexico). Elvira, Mistress of the Dark became – and continues to be – an international pop icon based on her horror hostess debut in *Movie Macabre* (1981–6). Today, numerous horror hosts across the globe have moved from televised hosting to presenting in streaming shows online, allowing them to reach a new generation of horror fans (and horror fans in the making). For more detailed information about the robust history of television's horror hosts see Elena M. Watson's *Television Horror Movie Hosts: 68 Vampires, Mad Scientists and Other Denizens of the Late-Night Airwaves Examined and Interviewed* (1991); and Robert Michael 'Bobb' Cotter's *Vampira and Her Daughters: Women Horror Movie Hosts from the 1950s into the Internet Era* (2017).
28. The age breakdown of survey participants who have watched, on television or streaming, a horror host introduce a horror film are as follows: 36 per cent of those who are eighteen to twenty-three years old; 51.5 per cent of those who are twenty-four to twenty-nine years old; 70.6 per cent of those who are thirty to thirty-five years old; 84.5 per cent of those who are thirty-six to forty-one years old; 88.8 per cent of those who are forty-two to forty-seven years old; 80.9 per cent of those who are forty-eight to fifty-three years old; 87.5 per cent of those who are fifty-four to fifty-nine years old; 100 per cent of those who are sixty to sixty-five years old; and 66.7 per cent of those who are more than sixty-six years old.
29. Grannell further explains the transgressiveness imbued in his drag due to the traumas he sustained from growing up in a cisheteronormative society: 'Peaches Christ *had* to be born in the underground. She had to be nurtured through adversity. I don't think I would have become successful if it wasn't for those sorts of challenges and flying in the face of the establishment – and the establishment at the time could have been anything – it was anything that wasn't us' (2020c, p. 8).
30. Even though Grannell never attended a Cockettes or Sick & Twisted play, the legacy of those shows informed both the San Francisco drag culture, of which

Grannell became a vital part, and the creation of his midnight movie series. Similarly, Hudson never attended a Cockettes, Sick & Twisted or Midnight Mass event; yet the San Francisco drag culture made an impact on Portland, Oregon years later.

31. Midnight Mass existed as an occasional or international live cinema event hosted in various locations after it stopped production at the Bridge Theatre in 2009. Grannell explains: 'But, in many ways, Midnight Mass ended when we left the Bridge. And it's why I stopped calling it Midnight Mass, because I wanted to protect the legacy of those years because they were really special. What we do now is definitely born out of Midnight Mass, but it's not Midnight Mass' (2020c, p. 16).
32. The Bridge Theatre permanently closed its doors on 27 December 2012, becoming the San Francisco Baseball Academy. This closure underscores the temporary nature of the Bakhtinian carnival while simultaneously highlighting the tech-led gentrification and un-queering of San Francisco itself. Since queer spaces can exist only in the present moment, the ghosts of (temporary) queer spaces permeate and haunt the cisheteronormative landscape.
33. Grannell explains: 'It was me saying that event-based cinema was the future and that we were ahead of our time and I was right. At that time, event-based cinema was not the thing it is today. Today, Paul Reubens is going on tour with an anniversary celebration of *Pee-wee's Big Adventure*. That kind of event – *seeing* the celebrities, *seeing* a performance with cinema is now *everywhere* because it's how exhibition is competing with streaming online and people who have movie theatres in their homes. So event-based cinema now is *definitely* a thing. A *really* big thing. When I was doing it, I was calling it sort of a modern attempt at a William Castle-style screening. William Castle did event-based cinema before *anybody* else' (2020d, p. 7).
34. The final season of Midnight Mass evidences the prevalence of horror films; this season opened with an in-person tribute to Linda Blair that included screenings of *Roller Boogie* (1979) and *The Exorcist* (1973). The rest of the final season included screenings of *Heathers* (1989), *Evil Dead 2: Dead by Dawn* (1987), *Showgirls* (1995), *Pink Flamingos* (1972) and *Poltergeist* (1982). The final Midnight Mass screening was, fittingly, *Elvira: Mistress of the Dark* (1988) featuring an in-person tribute to Elvira.
35. Grannell explains how Midnight Mass framed the experience of cult films such as *Showgirls* through a horror lens: '*Showgirls* was our biggest success the entire summer of 1998. I was able to put on screen and onstage something that a handful of people – 300 people – understood and we were able to celebrate that film in a way that was horrific. We celebrated the horrors of it in

a way that was lovely. Elizabeth Berkley wasn't a terrible actress to us. She was an aggressive shitkicker who intimidated and terrified normal audiences. But we understood her, we believed in her. So I think there was horror in all of this stuff that we did' (2020c, p. 9).

36. In 2007, to celebrate the 10th Anniversary of Midnight Mass, HDnet Movie Channel produced a six-episode reality series called *Midnight Mass with Your Hostess Peaches Christ*. Also, in 2007, the M. H. de Young Memorial Museum in San Francisco hosted 'Cattychism: A Peaches Christ Retrospective'.
37. Grannell (and Peaches Christ) continues to create live horror events that entertain and impact horror-loving queers. In 2010, Grannell released his debut feature film *All About Evil* (2010), which he took on an international live cinema tour called the 'Peaches Christ 4-D Event Experience'. Grannell writes film-parody plays that he tours through Peaches Christ Productions with well-known drag queens, including Peaches Christ. These parody plays include drag horror titles such as *Sheetlejuice, The Silence of the Trans, What Ever Happened to Bianca Del Rio?, Drag Becomes Her* and *Hocum Pokem.* Recently, Grannell created Terror Vault, the first immersive haunted attraction created by queers, featuring queer performers and marketed to queers.
38. Carlo Rossi is an inexpensive ('cheap') and popular mainstream brand of wine that is often sold in jugs.
39. Queer Horror has continually sold out since 2016. *The Craft* (1996) was the first event to sell out in 2016, with nearly every screening selling out since. The event screening *Death Becomes Her* (1992) in 2017, sold out in two days and, to date, is the only event to have a second screening added.
40. This pre-show also included commentary referencing Carla Rossi having been barred from performing at Portland State University (PSU) due to Hudson's open criticism of PSU's decision to arm campus police officers. Narrator Stodola, aware of this event and aftermath, notes that 'Carla was very vocal about PSU's decision to arm their security guards, and made a point of putting that in her show, and was not asked to return' (2020, p. 10). Hudson additionally included a cheeky self-deprecating reference to Carla Rossi having lost 'Best Portland Celebrity' in the *Willamette Week* Best of Portland Readers' Poll 2017 to The Unipiper, a unicycling bagpiper who wears a kilt and sometimes a Darth Vader mask (Hudson, 'The Portland Wives', 15 March 2019).
41. As Queer Horror started to sell out the movie theatre, Hudson sought also to employ other local drag talent, stating: 'I realized that Queer Horror was now becoming a new queer drag nightlife event. And it was becoming a standby that people could depend on. As we were selling out and as we were getting more and more attention and as the *Mercury* came out and

called us "a goddamn Portland treasure" – that was nice – I realized that I also had a responsibility to bring on as many performers as I could, and as many female-assigned performers as I could, and as many trans performers as I could, to really show what I saw as the breadth of talent in the drag world in Portland. And to try to foster a space where performers could actually get paid an actual guarantee – and actually get paid something that reflects their time. Even still, what we pay now I don't think is appropriately relative to how much work they're putting in. But we're still paying much more than most shows' (2020c, p. 14).

42. Since the film's initial release in 1992, conversations about *Candyman* (directed by Bernard Rose) have included critiques of the film's racial stereotyping and centring of whiteness. Even with the film's problematic issues, *Candyman* ranks as number thirty-two on survey participants' favourite horror films list. The 2021 release of the new version of *Candyman*, directed by Nia DaCosta and produced by Jordan Peele's Monkeypaw Productions, deals directly with racial issues.
43. Carla Rossi can also be linked to the carnivalesque's tradition of the fool as a critical figure engaged in social disruption. Bakhtin, in *Rabelais and His World*, 'not only connect[s] the Fool with Carnival but also attach[es] the central concepts of ambivalence, degradation and laughter to the Fool' (Aston, 2005, p. 12).
44. This type of live cinema event is in contrast with film festivals, which tend to be based solely on business (e.g., the Cannes Film Festival), identity (e.g., the Jewish Film Festival) or genre (e.g., the DOC NYC) (2018, p. 83).
45. Even though the survey did not ask participants to name which drag artist they saw introduce a horror film, the qualitative survey responses combined with my perspective after years as participant and staff member for Midnight Mass and an active participant and observer of Queer Horror, indicate that queer live cinema events in general are imbued with a similar queer energy.
46. The Live Cinema EU Final Project Report indicates that non-normative genders are disproportionately attracted to live cinema experiences, highlighting that the queer community requires further consideration as a distinctive live cinema audience. The report states: 'Most notably in terms of gender is the 8% of audiences defining themselves as "other", indicating that live cinema events have particular appeal to a non-binary audience above the population average (1% in the UK, Gender Identity Research & Education Society)' (2018, p. 12).
47. Moreover, as discussed previously, horror fans whose queerness creates a different reaction to and taste in horror films, indeed, have the queerest relationship

to horror and are therefore more inclined to enjoy watching horror films with queer audiences. There are positive correlations with the following statement: 'I most enjoy watching horror films with queer audiences' ('different reaction' $r_s = 0.34, p < 0.000$ and queer 'taste' $r_s = 0.35, p < 0.000$), both with moderate effect.

48. Of survey participants, 65.4 per cent (n = 2,679) have watched *RuPaul's Drag Race*, with 21.7 per cent being 'Avid' fans; 21.7 per cent (n = 889) have watched *The Boulet Brothers' Dragula*, with 30.5 per cent being 'Avid' fans. The survey was released before *The Boulet Brothers' Dragula* seasons 2 and 3 were available on Netflix (31 October 2019); undeniably, the viewer and fan numbers for this show would have ranked higher after more mainstream availability.
49. Similarly, only 23 per cent (n = 941) have attended a live musical adaptation of a horror film such as *Carrie*, *Evil Dead*, *Re-Animator*, etc., yet a resounding 82 per cent (n = 2,582) would like to see a live musical adaptation of a horror film.
50. The idea of (ir)reverent worship is built into the very name of the series, Midnight Mass. Grannell grew up going to Catholic school and chose the moniker Peaches Christ directly from that childhood experience, which scarred him. Grannell directly noted the influence Catholicism had on his work, including how his live cinema series came to be known as Midnight Mass: 'I just remember Martiny [Michael Brenchley] being like, "Well, you should call it Midnight Mass because you're Peaches Christ." It was like the heavens opened up and a choir sang. I knew in that moment that that is *absolutely* what it had to be called. To this day, I'm so grateful because I've been able to use not only my own Catholic bullshit – which is a love hate relationship with the Catholic Church. I love the iconography and I'm still very into the gothic horror of the Catholic Church, but I also hate its politics and its misogyny and homophobia and all that stuff. It was this perfect way for me to exorcise that bullshit while also really being able to couch this experience correctly in a symbolic way' (2020c, p. 5).
51. While *Faster, Pussycat! Kill! Kill!* (1965) is not commonly considered a horror film, Grannell explains the 'horror' within the cult classic: 'So even if I'm doing *Faster, Pussycat! Kill! Kill!* – while not necessarily a horror film – I would argue that it's transgressive enough that it horrified straight men and it really intimidated people' (2020c, p. 9).
52. A survey participant alludes to the energy of viewing horror films with queer audiences in comparison to non-queer audiences, writing that 'heterosexual viewers are boring to watch horror films with and heterosexual men especially' (47082256).

53. Hudson maintains the importance of sharedness and liveness within Queer Horror events, noting that the live cinema event cannot exist without the queer energy from the queer horror audience: 'In this weird time of quarantine, I miss Queer Horror. People are like, "Will you do a Queer Horror livestream?" And I'm like, "No." Because the magic is when we're all together in the audience' (2020c, p. 18).
54. The Hollywood Theatre, an independent cinema in Portland, Oregon, where Queer Horror has been hosted since 2015, was closed from 14 March 2020 until 2 July 2021. My last unused cinema ticket was to celebrate Queer Horror's 5th Anniversary in March 2020 with a screening of *The Lure* (2015), a queer horror film, which was finally rescheduled and performed on 31 March 2022.

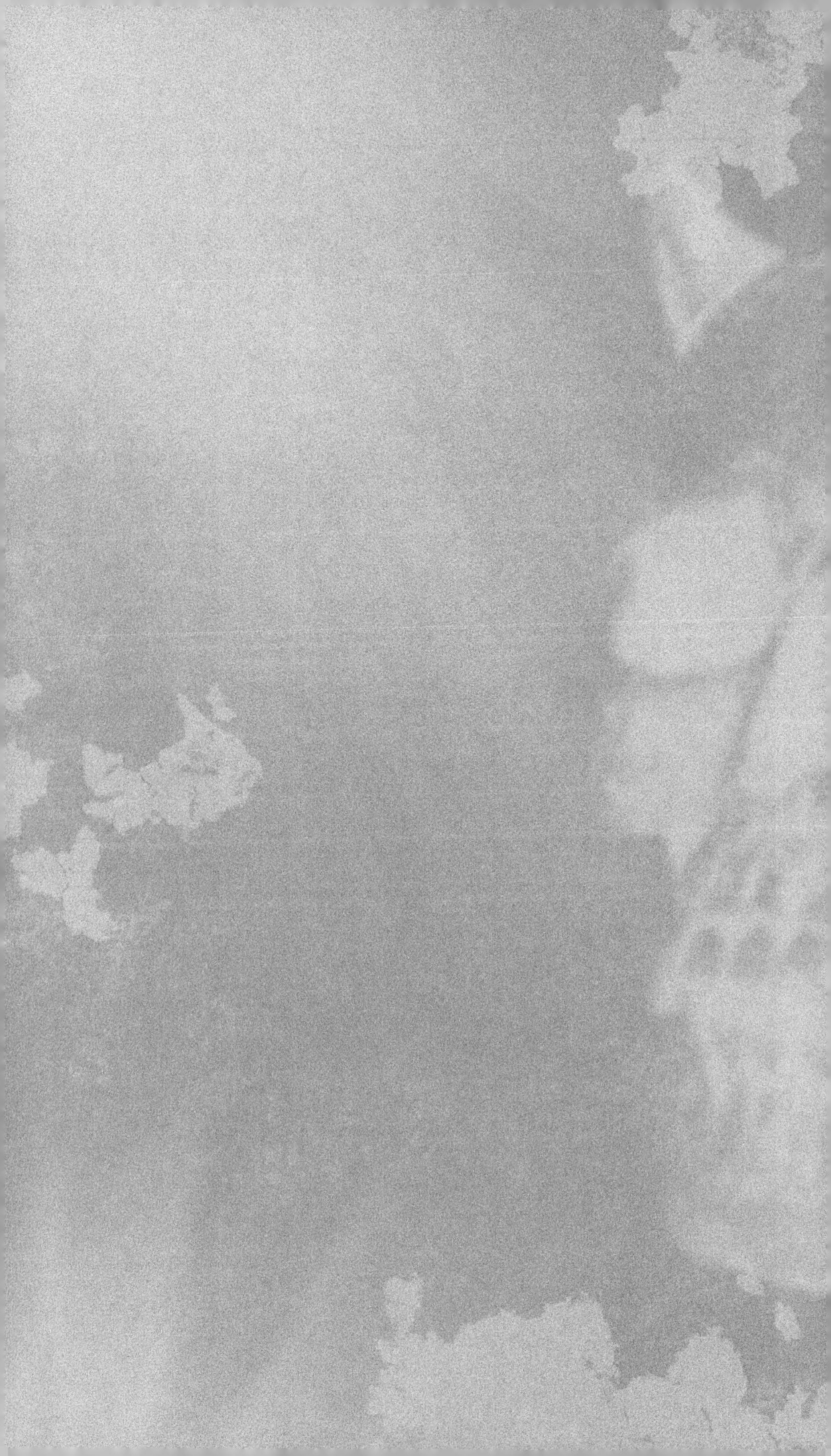

Conclusion

I wanted to be part of this research project because the face of horror or horror fans is a white man. I'm not a white man … I just want to go ahead and be like, I exist. I like horror. I understand the theories. I've read the books. My opinion is just as important as yours. Frankly, better because I've lived through oppression. I know fear. What do you know?
(Contreras, 2020, p. 15)

I think a queer audience can engage more with ideas at play in horror such as the disruption of normal life, disgust (in monster movies), physical otherness (body horror), and the sense of regaining control through the final girl.
(47336309)

I have understood that, as a queer person, I am not wanted in certain parts of society. I am feared, loathed, hated. This is similar to the narrative that horror movies get from mainstream audiences, so naturally, I think there is a connection between a queer viewer and their taste in horror.
(47100424)

THE PRIMARY OBJECTIVE of this research has been to document for the first time the opinions, habits and tastes of the queer horror spectator, ultimately arguing that queers have a distinctive spectatorial relationship with the genre unlike any other horror audience demographic. While queers statistically favour the horror genre as compared with heterosexual moviegoers (Nielsen, 2015), the queer penchant for horror film had not previously been considered empirically, and certainly not for the full spectrum of the queer community. This study's groundbreaking mixed-method dataset on the queer horror spectator challenges the disembodied theory of the academy to include the embodied queer experience, which both allows for better understanding of queer subjectivity and empirically evidences theories from fields such as queer, horror, camp, trauma and live cinema studies. Empirically engaging actual audiences is imperative since horror is, fundamentally, an affective genre. In other words, the affect of the horror genre should be understood through its lived impact on spectators, rather than only through removed theoretical hypotheses.

This research is a product of my queerness, my queer trauma and, significantly, my lifelong love of horror. As a lifelong queer horror spectator myself, this research was deeply personal and a way to establish queer visibility since 'writing is a method of rejecting invisibility; a protest statement against denial and absence; a witness statement of existence' (Smith and Molloy, 2019, p. 215). My research goal was to render visible a vital spectatorial community, the queer horror spectator, and to bring queerness to the forefront of horror studies. Therefore, directly engaging the queer horror spectator using queered methods was fundamental to this effort. The results of that spectator engagement led to this study's mixed-method dataset, which unquestionably demonstrates that queer spectators of horror distinctively engage with horror film. Narrator Joshua Grannell affirms this queer connection to horror, observing that 'the queer audience attaches to horror more deeply and takes it with them and appreciates it on a deeper level' (2020a, p. 19). When Brigid Cherry researched and theorised 'whether the female audience can be considered as a distinct entity within the horror film audience as a whole and, more importantly, whether they watch horror films differently than male viewers' (1999, p. 58), her study found that female horror fans did, indeed, engage with horror film differently than male viewers. Queer horror spectators likewise view horror film differently from heterosexual viewers, and the majority of queer spectators report that their queerness alters their reactions and tastes in horror film, which directly links queer alterity to horror. This project's 4,107 survey participants and fifteen oral history narrators enable me to establish authoritative observations about the queer horror spectator and to demonstrate that queers form a unique group of horror spectators. This study thereby contributes to the critical fields of horror, queer, trauma, camp, film and live cinema studies.

The queer spectator's connection to horror film is both theoretical *and* ontological in part due to film itself being queer. In their 'account of cinema as an inherently queer medium', Rosalind Galt and Karl Schoonover ask 'readers to think about film history as always already queer' (2016, p. 18). Building on Galt and Schoonover's deliberately and enticingly provocative declaration, this study recognises the queerness of the filmic medium and argues that horror is ontologically the queerest genre, a generic condition that is also perceived by horror's queer spectators. This queer connection to the horror genre is bolstered by the fact that a disproportionate number of early horror theorists are queer and their work, ultimately, fostered the development of horror studies as an academic discipline. Harry Benshoff and Sean Griffin posit: 'Another way to conceptualize queer film is to think about the ways that various types of films or film genres might be considered queer' (2006, p. 11). The genre is queer in part because, as they state, the 'horror film, for example, often depicts bizarre and monstrous sexualities that can be considered queer' (Benshoff and Griffin, 2006, p. 11). This study empirically documents and firmly establishes that horror *is* queer, altering the critical understandings of horror film, horror criticism, horror spectatorship and horror audiences by focusing on not the representational and allegorical, but the ontological. This research, through the elucidation of mixed-method data, demonstrates incontrovertibly that queer spectators both *think* and *feel* that the horror genre is queer and queerly relate to the genre. As the first (but hopefully not the last) empirical study on the queer relationship to the horror genre, documenting actual spectators has proven indispensable since '[a]udience research is about what people think and feel about movies. Audience research is a means for testing and verifying or refuting the scholarship on the meanings of film images' (Austin, 1989, p. ix). This study's data results ultimately indicate that both a person's queerness is the most salient aspect of identity when it comes to horror affinity, and embodied queerness affects the horror experience in return.

This is deliberately and decidedly a queer project; the queer thinking of the research participants was combined with the queer academics' work with which I engaged, both functioning to inform my own queer thinking. All scholarship is interpretation, with this study specifically being a mediated representation of the queer horror spectator and, therefore, susceptible to bias and error. Consequently, multiple steps were taken to ensure the integrity of this research project and its data. One step was to explicate and analyse transparently the research design, which simultaneously functions as a form of transparency itself. This study, the culmination of years of research, sought to eliminate, or at the very least limit, confirmation bias by being transparent, which further illustrates how transparency is fundamental to a sound methodology from beginning to end. This study employed the non-probability sampling method since the entire global population of queer spectators of horror film could not be known and, therefore, not every horror-loving queer could have had the opportunity to respond to the survey. Reliance on mutually exclusive data would have proved harmful to a significant proportion of this study's survey participants since queer embodiment is complex and fluid, with many queer people, myself included, existing beyond binaristic boundaries and across multiple labels. Queer researchers need to continually reconsider and reconceptualise normative boundaries and institutional norms to push scholarship to always be more inclusive and equitable.

This work has transmuted empirical evidence into the first cohesive and comprehensive portrait of the queer horror spectator and their opinions, habits and tastes, presenting an *inclusive* queer spectator of horror, established from 4,107 survey participants who are a full spectrum of genders, sexualities, races, ethnicities, ages, cultures, nationalities and educational levels. The overall and overwhelming consensus of the survey responses, combined with the participants' demographic data, allowed me to create the first, as well as a comprehensive, understanding of the queer spectator of the horror genre. The queer spectator is both a knowledgeable and an active horror fan who first watched horror as a child. For the queer spectator, a love of horror connects them to other queers who embrace the genre similarly, as well as functioning as a bridge to connect with non-queers (a demographic with different sensibilities and understandings). The horror-loving queer watches horror films from around the globe and enjoys positive representations of strong women and queer characters in horror. For the queer spectator, love for the entire genre takes precedence over individual films, since they love or like the majority of horror subgenres. The mixed-method data on the queer horror spectator is compared in this study with Brigid Cherry's empirical data on the female horror fan to illustrate distinction. The queer spectator connects to the monsters, the victims and the final girls of horror, finding an embodied queer connection to horror's Other and narratives of victimisation and survival. The majority of survey participants report that their queerness alters their reactions to and tastes in horror, with these queer spectators being more inclined to enjoy horror's camp aesthetics and to recognise the therapeutic and cathartic benefits of the genre because queers have 'a more intimate relationship with trauma' (47704161). The prevalence and passion of horror-loving queers is a call to makers and event organisers to include safe spaces for queer horror fans, particularly since queer spectators report feeling underrepresented on the horror screen and in horror fandom. This work, in all, evidences, illustrates and demonstrates a vehement *and* distinctive queer spectatorship of horror, transforming critical understandings of both the horror genre and the queer spectator.

I document queer trauma as being processed therapeutically through horror films and finding joyous expression through the queer spectator's camp relationship to horror. This study explicates the interwoven theoretical topics of queerness, horror, trauma and camp. This is accomplished by empirically evidencing the queer spectator's conscious therapeutic engagement with horror, finding a relationship that goes deeper than queer representation in films, and ultimately argues for horror's ability to alleviate queer suffering cathartically. This data corroborates some previously posited trauma theories in horror studies while breaking ground empirically, altogether substantiating the fundamental connections between the fields of horror, queer and trauma studies. Since all queer people suffer from the insidious trauma of living in a cisheterosexual world and since, as Laura Westengard asserts, trauma demands expression, this study found queer expression in the queer spectator's therapeutic engagement with horror and development of a camp relationship to the genre. Significantly, the survey data undeniably evidences that 'camp can be located within a system of queer praxis' (Taylor, 2012, p. 75). Queers recognise that horror and camp share an aesthetic, subtextual and transgressive foundation. For queers of all genders, camp is a key facet to engage with horror, leading to a camp relationship to the horror genre. This queer camp relationship to horror underscores that camp is felt and embodied because, as narrator Joe Fejeran explains, camp is 'something experiential' (2020, p. 37). Since queers connect to the horror genre due to its intrinsic queerness and since camp is a queer sensibility, the camp-horror nexus is fundamentally queer.

Queer embodiment is informed by insidious queer trauma, which, in turn, informs the queer camp sensibility. As such, I argue that an important queer intervention, squarely in the field of live cinema studies, is horror exhibition for queer audiences curated and hosted by drag performers. Drawing from and contributing to theories of liveness, sharedness, laughter, the carnivalesque, cult and queer failure, I have detailed and analysed the work of Peaches Christ (Joshua Grannell) and Carla Rossi (Anthony Hudson) creating the live cinema events Midnight Mass and Queer Horror (respectively), which are situated in the histories of drag and horror hosts. The mixed-method data illustrates how these queer live cinema events both represent the queer contributions to live performance and create consequential spaces for queer spectators of horror. Queers gathering together to queerly celebrate a film genre they love strengthens queer community bonds and enhances the queer spectator's connection to horror. This study's intervention in live cinema studies should signal to scholars in horror studies, queer studies and film studies that queer live cinema events are a vital area of inquiry.

While the majority of horror-loving queers will feel seen and understood by this work, others will feel as outliers to my specific research findings even though they, too, have their own distinctive relationship with the genre. I acknowledge the limits of my findings and recognise that, since there were 4,107 survey participants, there are 4,107 idiosyncratic queer relationships to the horror genre. These distinct relationships have been collected, interpreted and presented through mixed-method data in order to elucidate patterns and understandings. To be abundantly clear, this study's findings do not speak for or to the entire queer community nor, indeed, homogenise the entire horror-loving queer community. While extrapolations of statistical results are presented throughout this study and indicate percentages that would be found in the entire population of queer horror film spectators, no single question had 100 per cent consensus. Therefore, this study does not intend to collapse the *entire* community of queer horror spectators into one simplified and commodifiable archetype. Regardless, since this study is the first comprehensive empirical investigation into queer spectators of horror, as established, I have privileged presenting and understanding community similarities and consensus over differences. Future researchers from within intersectional queer communities should investigate preliminary data found in this study, such as the queer American Indian's or Alaska Native's relationship to the horror genre[1] or the transgender male spectator's love of werewolf films.[2]

The immensity of this study's mixed-method dataset means that not only do multiple avenues remain under-investigated or uninvestigated, but also researching, examining and analysing the queer spectatorial relationship to horror film continues to be relevant because neither queerness nor the horror genre are stable or ceasing. I echo Julian Hanich, who borrows from Susanne Langer in stating 'that nothing in this study is exhaustively treated and that every subject demands further analysis, research, and invention' (2018, p. 275). The cultural work of the horror genre will shift with society, while 'queer is an identity category that has no interest in consolidating or even stabilizing itself. . . . [Q]ueer is always an identity under construction' (Jagose, quoted in Doan, 2019, p. 122). Future research should investigate how the queer relationship to horror changes over time, particularly in comparison with this dataset. In other words, this study's vast mixed-method data should be compared and contrasted with future empirical studies on queer horror spectatorship. Additionally, future mixed-method research should investigate the topics that my data analysis work has determined are particularly relevant and noteworthy.[3] For example, the data demonstrates that one's queerness alters and affects the queer relationship to horror; therefore, future research should collect direct empirical data on queer spectators' attitudes and understandings of their queerness. The survey's written responses and the oral history interviews, together forming the qualitative data, reveal that a significant percentage of queer horror spectators consider the horror genre to be intrinsically queer. Future studies, therefore, should collect empirical spectator data about the intrinsic queerness of the horror genre. Relatedly, future research should collect empirical spectator data on queer attitudes regarding queer assimilation and liberation. This information could lead to a more nuanced and complex understanding of the queer spectator of horror and how a queer person's attitudes towards queer community status informs their relationship to the horror genre.

For over seven years, I have been formally submerged in queer thought – both theoretical and embodied – about the horror genre, resulting in the largest quantitative and qualitative study on the spectatorship of horror film. This queer research project has been a transformative experience for me, as well as for horror studies, queer studies, trauma cinema studies, camp studies, live cinema studies and, hopefully, for all the queer spectators of horror out there. The survey data combined with the oral histories patently demonstrate that queer people have a distinctive relationship to the horror genre. Much of queer history highlights queer trauma and/or works to rectify queer invisibility, so much so that Westengard pointedly states that 'insidiously traumatized time is haunted time is queer time' (2019, p. 21). Indeed, this study recognises and theorises our insidious queer trauma and the haunted nature of queer subjectivity – particularly having been written during a global pandemic that has exacerbated both queer trauma and the queerness of time. Yet, simultaneously, I intently and joyously focus on camp as an affirming and ebullient manifestation of queer trauma. Reading through thousands of thoughtful, informed and, many times, intimate written responses from the anonymous survey participants has reaffirmed my conviction in the potential of radical queerness. Social movements can be 'spontaneous or organized' (Luders, 2016, p. 186) or, more specifically, can be a fluid combination of proactive organisation, cultural reaction and temporal spontaneity. This work affirms my assertion that there is an ever-building movement of queers declaring horror as queer. These declarations from the queer community further confirm horror as queer, particularly when considered with expanding academic attention on queer horror, increasing production of explicitly queer horror films, growing number of explicitly queer horror podcasts and Shudder's anticipated documentary series on queer horror. While these external artefacts do not legitimise the already substantial queer horror community, they affirm what we each have known to be true about our relevance. Mathias Clasen states that the 'best works of horror have the capacity to change us for life' (2017, p. 147).[4] This study argues that queer lives have the capacity to change horror. The queer spectator, with their queer lens, engages with horror film in fundamentally queer ways and, in the process, transforms the genre into something wholly new. The conclusions of this academic study are resolutely both a political act and an intervention, seeking to move the discourse about queerness in horror beyond the textual, subtextual and representational, to bring the embodied queer spectator and queer audiences from the periphery to the centre of horror studies.

Notes

1. The American Indian or Alaska Native survey participants (n = 119) report the highest percentage of both horror fandom and knowledgeability – 97.5 per cent (n = 116) consider themselves a fan of horror film and 89.1 per cent (n = 106) consider themselves knowledgeable about horror film.
2. Trans men report loving werewolf films at the highest percentage, 36.9 per cent (n = 123), as compared to the data on cis women (25.6 per cent), cis men (24.5 per cent) and trans women (26.7 per cent).
3. There are several survey questions with which this study does not deeply engage due to limits in research breadth and relevancy. For example, the survey asked participants about which formats and with whom they usually watch horror films, but the study did not engage with that data due to space limitations.
4. Clasen directly argues for horror's ability to develop and refine the film spectator's coping skills, alertness, empathy, morality and emotionality (2017, p. 147).

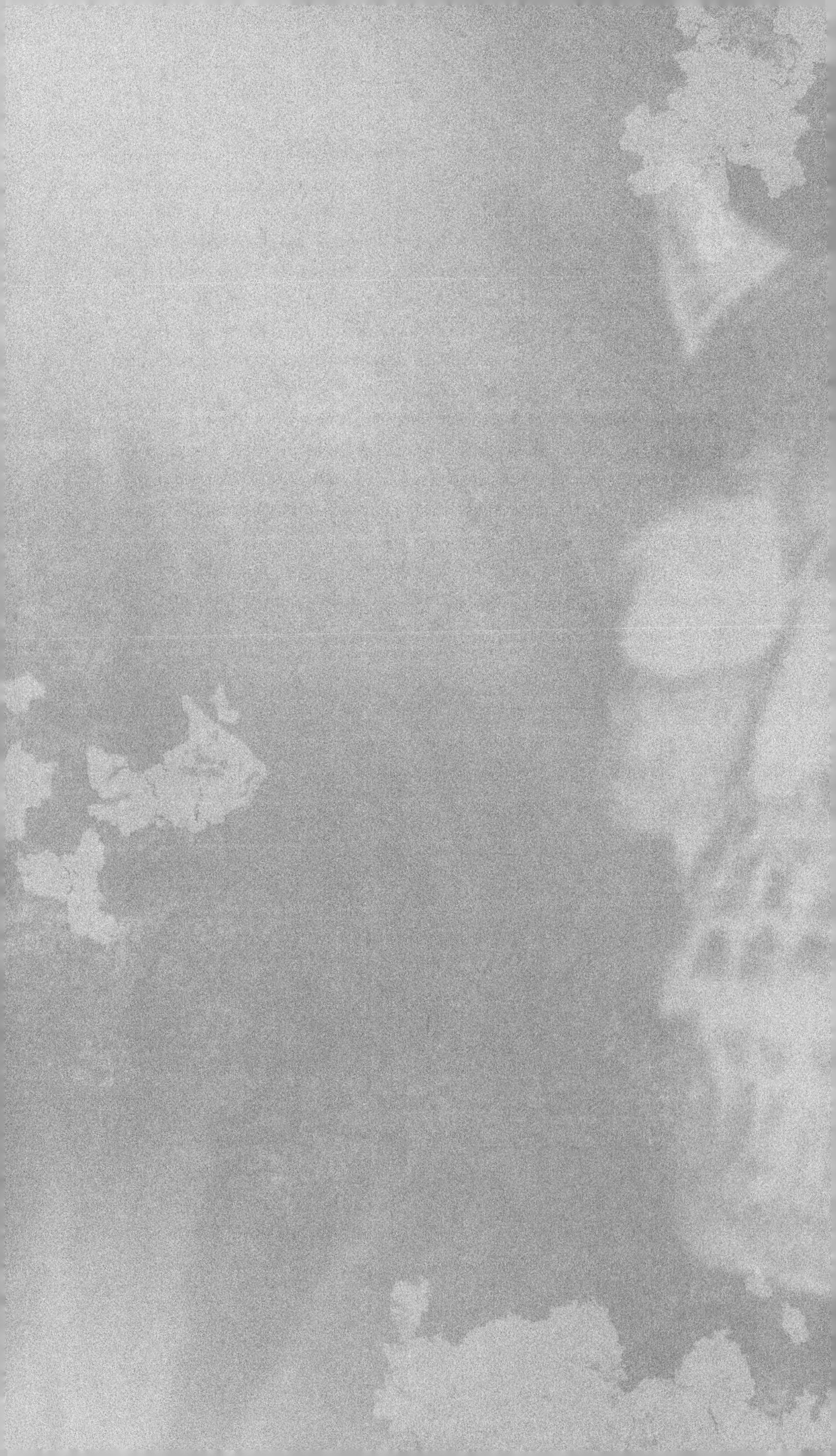

Appendix

THIS PROJECT'S METHODS and methodology are detailed in my doctoral thesis as a blueprint and explication of my research process. This appendix, however, will summarise key details about the study's design in order to provide basic methodological information to those who are interested. I designed the questionnaire to be self-selecting: potential participants needed to self-identify as both queer and a horror fan, to be eighteen years or older at the time of taking the survey, and to have the technological and linguistic abilities to take an online English-language survey. The survey was available via Online Surveys from 1 April 2019 until 1 August 2019, and protected participant privacy per the General Data Protection Regulation. I adapted and reframed select questions from surveys created by Cherry (1999) and Amy Jane Vosper (2013), who also largely repurposed Cherry's questions, for my questionnaire to establish the queer spectatorship of horror film as a distinct mode for theoretical inquiry, and thereby creating a baseline goal and set of questions for future horror audience study. I updated the methods, vocabulary and question-phrasing to achieve greater questionnaire clarity and to make the experience more relevant to twenty-first-century queer communities.

To reach as many horror-loving queer people as possible, I created the @queerforfear Instagram account before undertaking this research and built an active engagement with thousands of followers. I used this social media account both as a personal outlet to engage with horror-loving queers and as a way to build a community base for my research. I set a minimum response goal of 220 and, in order to obtain the largest *n* number (sample size) possible, I sought to reach more than 2,000 respondents since external surveys typically have a 15–20 per cent response rate (Edmonds and Kennedy, 2017, p. 134). I aimed to legitimise this community and to proactively address any possible 'positivist gatekeepers' who evaluate the significance of research in stark statistical terms. In the words of Amin Ghaziani and Matt Brim, these research gatekeepers are 'best handled by flaunting large sample sizes' (2019, p. 18). Some other comparable studies provide useful comparison sets to establish sample significance. Richard McCulloch and Virginia Crisp secured 220 responses, which is deemed 'a high volume of survey responses' (2016, p. 191), and Rosana Vivar conducted an online questionnaire with 108 respondents (2018, p. 120). Alexander Dhoest and Nele Simons received 761 survey participants, after filtering out seventy-five heterosexual respondents, which they state is a 'very well received' survey (2012, pp. 265–6). Emma Pett's 'large-scale qualitative study' obtained 709 participants (Hughes, 2016, p. 39) and Philip Schlesinger et al. in *Women Viewing Violence* obtained 546 completed surveys (1992, p. 16). The research in *Horror Films: Current Research on Audience Preferences and Reactions* feature *n* numbers such as $n = 312$ (Lawrence and Palmgreen, 1991), $n = 155$ (Tamborini and Stiff, 1987), $n = 220$ (Johnston and Dumerauf, 1990) and $n = 92$ (Edwards, 1991). The largest *n* number in *Horror Films* is $n = 1{,}573$, which does not represent human respondents but 1,573 violent acts that were coded across thirty slasher films (Molitor and Sapolsky, 1993). This research study received 4,160 total research participants, and after filtering out the thirty-one cisgender heterosexual respondents and twenty-two blank, or mostly blank, responses, my final $n = 4{,}107$. My research response rate speaks directly to the success of this survey, the increased statistical power of a large sample, and, most importantly, the desire of so many queer horror spectators to have their opinions, habits and tastes researched and known.

Due to the self-selecting design of the questionnaire, I implemented non-probability sampling, which is a sampling method often disallowed from inferential statistics because 'there is no general statistical theory of nonprobability sampling that justifies when and why accurate inferences can be expected' (Cornesse et al., 2020, p. 7). However, a researcher could not create a probability sample from the population under investigation – queer horror spectators – because the true population could never realistically be known. As well, any mathematical differences between probability and non-probability, samples are likely small enough to not actually mean much to a study such as this, a study of queer people's horror film opinions, habits and tastes (as opposed to, for example, a study determining medical treatments in which these small differences could have life or death consequences). A large international research study that investigated the accuracy of both probability and non-probability sampling concluded that 'accuracy in probability sample surveys is generally higher than in nonprobability sample surveys' (Cornesse et al., 2020, p. 22). Yet, the report never describes or speaks directly to what 'generally higher' actually means. Even if greater inaccuracies do exist, little to no evidence exists that these potentially minor inaccuracies are practically significant or cause data to be replete with bias and errors. Following the recommendation of Vasja Vehovar, Vera Toepoel and Stephanie Steinmetz 'to [be] more openly accepting [of] the reality of using a standard statistical inference approach as an approximation in non-probability settings', I present data and draw inferences from my non-probability sample (2016, p. 342). To further heed best practices in working with non-probability sampling, I provide both an acknowledgement of its limitations and research transparency, as well as following the recommendation that 'very careful planning must precede nonprobability sampling' (Meyer and Wilson, 2009, p. 25). These approaches allow for important study of the historically marginalised and excluded queer community. Heeding Meyer and Wilson's appeal to 'researchers, reviewers, and journal editors', this research involving queer community members critically evaluates sampling methodologies and does 'not adhere to such strict guidelines that would thwart progress and impede gaining important knowledge about the lives of LGB people' (2009, p. 30). With my thoughtful research planning and chosen methodologies plus my large sample size (n = 4,107), I can detect differences in my participant population, horror's queer community, which allows for more reliable conclusions and confidence that any differences found are real, even if they are not large.

I present frequency charts and graphs, a descriptive statistic, for many of the survey questions to form the foundation of my data presentation. Frequency charts will showcase collected data for each question via valid (participants who answered the selected question) and cumulative (those who answered the entire survey) percentages and hard counts (actual participant counts for the question). General confidence intervals, an inferential statistic, uses the sample survey data to calculate the estimated ± margin of error to which the analysed data is generalisable to the true population. The range of confidence intervals is determined by the sample size. The smaller the sample size (n number), the larger the given range will be. This means that I present data that shows with 99 per cent confidence that the true proportion of *all* queer horror spectators would exist within the given interval. Or, said differently, the confidence interval calculates with 99 per cent confidence the percentage range of how everyone in the queer horror population (not solely those who answered the survey) would have answered the question. As Vehovar and Manfreda remind: 'not long ago' the American Association for Public Opinion Research 'still required that confidence intervals could only be calculated with probability sample surveys. However, this strict attitude is slowly softening' (2017, p. 150). As such, I offer confidence intervals in my research analysis with the qualification that the data findings represent 'indications' and 'approximations' of the true proportion of all horror-loving queers (Vehovar, Toepoel and Steinmetz, 2016, p. 341). In summary, when I present my findings, I state that the confidence interval indicates that I can be 99 per cent confident that the true proportion of all queer horror spectators would have answered the question within the named calculated percentage range.

I have a non-probability sample that uses non-parametric statistical tests. Non-parametric tests make no assumptions about the underlying form of the distribution or sample size. I use the Spearman's non-parametric statistical procedure to show correlations and the chi-square test for independence that compares two variables to show relationships. The chi-square is a non-parametric statistic frequently used to test for a statistical significance when at least one variable is nominal/qualitative/categorical (non-numerical) and indicates whether there is a statistically significant relationship between the two variables. If the test indicates statistical significance and that there is a relationship between the two variables, there is likely to be a real pattern in the population. While the chi-square does not give correlations, it calculates and indicates a relationship between the variables via the p value. The p value itself indicates the certainty of a relationship and does not indicate the strength of relationship; the strength of relationship is indicated by the Cramér's V for effect size – 0.1 small effect size, 0.3 medium effect size, 0.5 large effect size (Gravetter and Wallnau, 2011, p. 545). In other words, the chi-square statistic value indicates the significance of a relationship, the p value (which can never be zero) indicates how likely it is that there is a relationship (whether or not to accept or reject null hypothesis) and the Cramér's V indicates the effect size. The null hypothesis is always testing that no relationship exists between the variables. The null hypothesis is only rejected if the statistical result reaches a significance level (the alpha) of unusualness, which I set at 0.01. If the *p* value is higher than 0.01 the null hypothesis is true and there is no relationship between the variables; if less than 0.01 the null hypothesis is rejected and a relationship exists between the variables. If the *p* value is under 0.01, results are considered statistically significant. If the *p* value is below 0.005, the results are considered highly statistically significant. By setting the statistical significance level at 1 per cent, I can be 99 per cent certain that the relationship between the two variables did not occur by chance. Chi-square tests are considered valid only if they contain mutually exclusive data and, as previously discussed, marginalised identities do not always fit into the tidy boxes of mutual exclusivity. As noted, none of my demographic data, with the exception of age and highest education level achieved, is mutually exclusive. In other words, overlap exists in all my demographic data. For example, a woman who selected 'lesbian', 'gay' and 'queer' as her sexual orientation identity markers is counted in the data counts for lesbian, gay and queer. Any categorical demographic data in my research cannot be tested for chi-square statistical significance. As a result, at times, I use demographic identity markers as the units of analysis, rather than the individuals. To determine if data, or variables, have an association, I employ Yule's Q, a measure of association that indicates both the strength and directionality between two variables. A result of 1 or -1 indicates a perfect association. To reiterate, the realities and validity of queer embodiment are prioritised here over the norms of cisheteropatriarchally created statistical frameworks and data analysis.

To show correlations between two ordinal variables (variables that are named and ordered such that one position can be considered higher/lower than another), I use the Spearman rank-order correlation coefficient (symbol is r_s and pronounced *rho*). For example, I test to determine a statistically significant relationship held by participants for whom horror films help them work through trauma with their preferences for each horror subgenre. The Spearman's correlation, a non-parametric statistical test, measures the strength and direction of a monotonic association between two ranked variables. All Spearman's rho correlations will exist between +1 (a perfect positive monotonic correlation) and -1 (a perfect negative monotonic correlation). A positive correlation exists when the two variables change in the same direction together (increasing or decreasing together) and a negative correlation exists when the two variables change together but in opposite directions (as one increases, the other decreases). Built into the Spearman's rho correlation is the effect size, the *r* value. The closer the *r* value is to 1 (perfect positive correlation) or to -1 (perfect negative correlation), the stronger the correlation. When the *r* value is closer to 0 the correlation is weaker (no monotonic relationship). Effect sizes for *r* values, given in absolute values, are as follows: 0.9 to 1 (almost perfect relationship); 0.7 to 0.9 (very strong relationship); 0.5 to 0.7 (strong relationship); 0.3 to 0.5 (moderate relationship); 0.1 to 0.3 (weak relationship); 0.00 to 0.1 (very weak relationship). Even though I have a large sample size and can be highly confident of the validity of any correlations found, the correlation coefficient does not speak to which variable is *causing* the other to change – in other words, correlation is not causation.

In addition, I use the independent t-test, a parametric inferential statistical test used to determine if the means of two independent groups are significantly different. Even though the t-test is a parametric test that assumes normal distribution, the central limit theorem states that if there is a sufficiently large sample size, the sampling distribution starts to approximate normal distribution. Since I have a large sample size, I can satisfy the normality assumption and, therefore, can employ the t-test to measure the difference between two means. I use the t-test with Y/N questions compared with an ordinal 1–5 Likert scale question. For example, I conduct an independent two-sample t-test to compare the mean levels of queers' enjoyment of 'camp-y' horror films with whether or not the participants report that they have a different reaction to horror films (as compared with heterosexual viewers). Once I have the SPSS t-test calculation, Cohen's *d* is calculated to get the effect size, which indicates the standardised difference between two means (0.2 is small, 0.5 is medium and 0.8 is large). The larger the effect size, the more 'impressive' or meaningful the standardised difference between the two means (Cohen, 1988, pp. 25–6). Again, because of my sizable sample, I can be confident whether a relationship exists and if that relationship is small, medium or large.

Oral History Bibliography

Castro, Gabe. Interview by Heather O. Petrocelli. 11 August 2020. Queer for Fear Oral History Collection. Philadelphia, Pennsylvania (GC) and Portland, Oregon (HOP). Transcript. Manchester Metropolitan University, Manchester, United Kingdom.

Colangelo, Harmony. Interview by Heather O. Petrocelli. 29 July 2020. Queer for Fear Oral History Collection. Cleveland, Ohio (HC) and Portland, Oregon (HOP). Transcript. Manchester Metropolitan University, Manchester, United Kingdom.

Contreras, Lana. Interview by Heather O. Petrocelli. 24 October 2020. Queer for Fear Oral History Collection. Los Angeles, California (LC) and Portland, Oregon (HOP). Transcript. Manchester Metropolitan University, Manchester, United Kingdom.

Davis, Jason Edward. Interview by Heather O. Petrocelli. 3 March 2020. Queer for Fear Oral History Collection. Portland, Oregon (JED and HOP). Transcript. Manchester Metropolitan University, Manchester, United Kingdom.

Estes, Mark O. Interview by Heather O. Petrocelli. 4 October 2020. Queer for Fear Oral History Collection. Memphis, Tennessee (MOE) and Portland, Oregon (HOP). Transcript. Manchester Metropolitan University, Manchester, United Kingdom.

Fejeran, Joe. Interview by Heather O. Petrocelli. 27 August 2020. Queer for Fear Oral History Collection. San Diego, California (JF) and Portland, Oregon (HOP). Transcript. Manchester Metropolitan University, Manchester, United Kingdom.

Grannell, Joshua. Interview by Heather O. Petrocelli. 5 May 2020a. Queer for Fear Oral History Collection. San Francisco, California (JG) and Portland, Oregon (HOP). Transcript. Manchester Metropolitan University, Manchester, United Kingdom.

— Interview by Heather O. Petrocelli. 7 May 2020b. Queer for Fear Oral History Collection. San Francisco, California (JG) and Portland, Oregon (HOP). Transcript. Manchester Metropolitan University, Manchester, United Kingdom.

— Interview by Heather O. Petrocelli. 12 May 2020c. Queer for Fear Oral History Collection. San Francisco, California (JG) and Portland, Oregon (HOP). Transcript. Manchester Metropolitan University, Manchester, United Kingdom.

— Interview by Heather O. Petrocelli. 19 May 2020d. Queer for Fear Oral History Collection. San Francisco, California (JG) and Portland, Oregon (HOP). Transcript. Manchester Metropolitan University, Manchester, United Kingdom.

Hall, Alex. Interview by Heather O. Petrocelli. 8 June 2020. Queer for Fear Oral History Collection. Toronto, Canada (AH) and Portland, Oregon (HOP). Transcript. Manchester Metropolitan University, Manchester, United Kingdom.

Hodges, CJ. Interview by Heather O. Petrocelli. 23 October 2020. Queer for Fear Oral History Collection. Portland, Oregon (CJH and HOP). Transcript. Manchester Metropolitan University, Manchester, United Kingdom.

Hudson, Anthony. Interview by Heather O. Petrocelli. 17 April 2020a. Queer for Fear Oral History Collection. Portland, Oregon (AH and HOP). Transcript. Manchester Metropolitan University, Manchester, United Kingdom.

— Interview by Heather O. Petrocelli. 23 April 2020b. Queer for Fear Oral History Collection. Portland, Oregon (AH and HOP). Transcript. Manchester Metropolitan University, Manchester, United Kingdom.

— Interview by Heather O. Petrocelli. 5 May 2020c. Queer for Fear Oral History Collection. Portland, Oregon (AH and HOP). Transcript. Manchester Metropolitan University, Manchester, United Kingdom.

— Interview by Heather O. Petrocelli. 13 May 2020d. Queer for Fear Oral History Collection. Portland, Oregon (AH and HOP). Transcript. Manchester Metropolitan University, Manchester, United Kingdom.

Ponder, Stacie. Interview by Heather O. Petrocelli. 6 May 2020. Queer for Fear Oral History Collection. Portland, Maine (SP) and Portland, Oregon (HOP). Transcript. Manchester Metropolitan University, Manchester, United Kingdom.

Stodola, Kaitlyn. Interview by Heather O. Petrocelli. 12 May 2020. Queer for Fear Oral History Collection. Newport, Oregon (KS) and Portland, Oregon (HOP). Transcript. Manchester Metropolitan University, Manchester, United Kingdom.

Thompson, Kim. Interview by Heather O. Petrocelli. 29 October 2020. Queer for Fear Oral History Collection. Nottingham, United Kingdom (KT) and Portland, Oregon (HOP). Transcript. Manchester Metropolitan University, Manchester, United Kingdom.

Varrati, Michael. Interview by Heather O. Petrocelli. 21 May 2020. Queer for Fear Oral History Collection. Los Angeles, California (MV) and Portland, Oregon (HOP). Transcript. Manchester Metropolitan University, Manchester, United Kingdom.

Velasco, Christopher. Interview by Heather O. Petrocelli. 12 July 2020. Queer for Fear Oral History Collection. Pasadena, California (CV) and Portland, Oregon (HOP). Transcript. Manchester Metropolitan University, Manchester, United Kingdom.

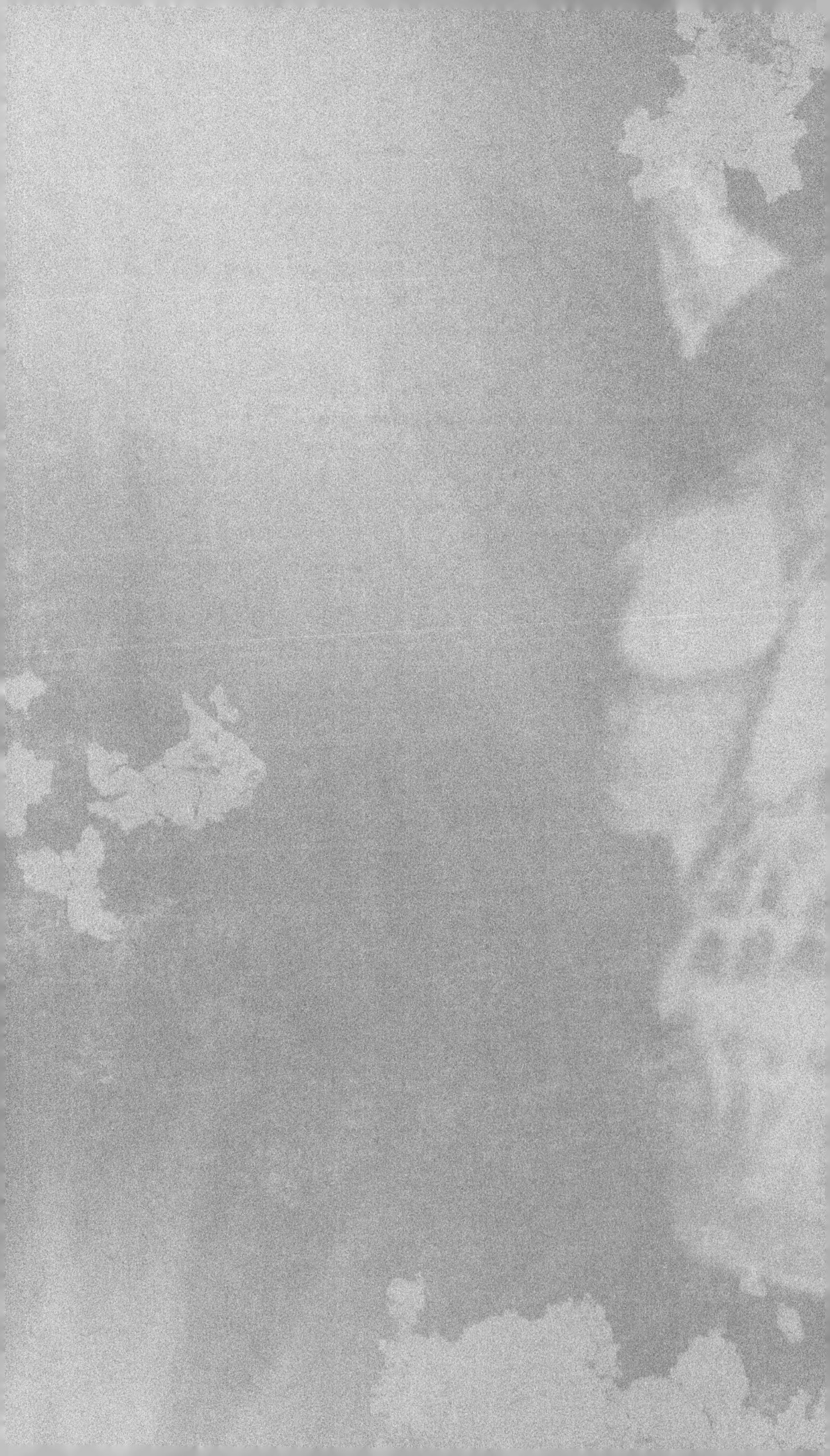

Works Cited

Aldana Reyes, Xavier. (2016) *Horror Film and Affect: Towards a Corporeal Model of Viewership*. New York: Routledge.

— (2020a) *Gothic Cinema*. London: Routledge.

— (2020b) 'Abjection and Body Horror', in Clive Bloom (ed.) *The Palgrave Handbook of Contemporary Gothic*. London: Palgrave Macmillan, pp. 393–410.

Alexander, Linda Lewis, Judith H. LaRosa, Helaine Bader, Susan Garfield and William James Alexander. (2021) *New Dimensions in Women's Health*. 8th edn. Burlington: Jones & Bartlett Learning.

Alim, H. Samy, Jooyoung Lee, Lauren Mason Carris and Quentin E. Williams. (2020) 'Language, Race, and the (Trans)Formation of Cisheteropatriarchy', in H. Samy Alim, Angela Reyes and Paul V. Kroskrity (eds) *The Oxford Handbook of Language and Race*. Oxford: Oxford University Press, pp. 291–314.

Amin, Kadji. (2019) 'Haunted by the 1990s: Queer Theory's Affective Histories', in Amin Ghaziani and Matt Brim (eds) *Imagining Queer Methods*. New York: New York University Press, pp. 277–93.

Anderson, Benedict. (2006) *Imagined Communities: Reflections on the Origin and Spread of Nationalism*. Revised edn. London: Verso.

Anzaldúa, Gloria. (1987) *Borderlands/La Frontera: The New Mestiza*. San Francisco: Aunt Lute Books.

Aston, Richard Michael. (2005) 'The Role of the Fool and the Carnivalesque in Post-1945 German Prose Fiction on the Third Reich'. Unpublished PhD thesis. University of Oxford.

Atkinson, Sarah. (2014) *Beyond the Screen: Emerging Cinema and Engaging Audiences*. New York: Bloomsbury Publishing.

Atkinson, Sarah and Helen W. Kennedy. (2016) 'Introduction – Inside-the-Scenes: The Rise of Experiential Cinema', *Participations*, 13(1), pp. 139–51.

— (2018) 'Afterword', in Sarah Atkinson and Helen W. Kennedy (eds) *Live Cinema: Cultures, Economies, Aesthetics.* London: Bloomsbury Academic, pp. 265–7.

— (2018) 'Live Cinema Presents . . . Cultures, Economies, Aesthetics', in Sarah Atkinson and Helen W. Kennedy (eds) *Live Cinema: Cultures, Economies, Aesthetics*. London: Bloomsbury Academic, pp. 1–14.

— (2018) 'Preface', in Sarah Atkinson and Helen W. Kennedy (eds) *Live Cinema: Cultures, Economies, Aesthetics*. London: Bloomsbury Academic, pp. ix–xii.

— (2018) 'Spaces: Introduction', in Sarah Atkinson and Helen W. Kennedy (eds) *Live Cinema: Cultures, Economies, Aesthetics*. London: Bloomsbury Academic, pp. 17–20.

— (2018) 'Temporalities: Introduction', in Sarah Atkinson and Helen W. Kennedy (eds) *Live Cinema: Cultures, Economies, Aesthetics.* London: Bloomsbury Academic, pp. 79–82.

— (2019) 'The Live Cinema Paradox: Continuity and Innovation in Live Film Broadcast, Exhibition and Production', in Craig Batty, Marsha Berry, Kath Dooley, Bettina Frankham and Susan Kerrigan (eds) *The Palgrave Handbook of Screen Production.* London: Palgrave Macmillan, pp. 335–46.

Auslander, Philip. (2008) *Liveness: Performance in a Mediatized Culture.* 2nd edn. New York: Routledge.

Austin, Bruce A. (1989) *Immediate Seating: A Look at Movie Audiences.* Belmont: Wadsworth.

Austin, Thomas. (2002) *Hollywood, Hype and Audiences: Selling and Watching Popular Film in the 1990s.* Manchester: Manchester University Press.

Babuscio, Jack. (1977) 'Camp and the Gay Sensibility', in Richard Dyer (ed.) *Gays and Film.* London: British Film Institute, pp. 40–57.

Bakhtin, Mikhail. (1984) *Rabelais and His World.* Translated by Hélène Iswolsky. Bloomington: Indiana University Press.

Ballon, Bruce and Molyn Leszcz. (2007) 'Horror Films: Tales to Master Terror or Shapers of Trauma?', *American Journal of Psychotherapy*, 61(2), pp. 211–30.

Barker, Martin. (2011) 'Watching Rape, Enjoying Watching Rape . . .: How Does a Study of Audience Cha(lle)nge Mainstream Film Studies Approaches?', in Tanya Horeck and Tina Kendall (eds) *The New Extremism in Cinema: From France to Europe*. Edinburgh: Edinburgh University Press, pp. 105–16.

Barker, Martin, Kate Egan, Stan Jones and Ernest Mathijs. (2008) 'Researching *The Lord of the Rings*: Audiences and Contexts', in Martin Barker and Ernest Mathijs (eds) *Watching The Lord of the Rings: Tolkien's World Audiences.* New York: Peter Lang Publishing, pp. 1–20.

Barker, Martin, Kate Egan, Tom Phillips and Sarah Ralph. (2016) *Alien Audiences: Remembering and Evaluating a Classic Movie.* New York: Palgrave Macmillan.

Barker, Martin, Ernest Mathijs and Alberto Trobia. (2008) 'Our Methodological Challenges and Solutions', in Martin Barker and Ernest Mathijs (eds) *Watching The Lord of the Rings: Tolkien's World Audiences.* New York: Peter Lang Publishing, pp. 213–39.

Barounis, Cynthia. (2018) 'Witches, Terrorists, and the Biopolitics of Camp', *GLQ*, 24(2–3), pp. 213–37.

Bazin, André. (1967) *What is Cinema? Volume I.* Translated by Hugh Gray. Berkeley: University of California Press.

Benjamin, Walter. (1999 [1929]) 'Chaplin in Retrospect', in Michael W. Jennings, Howard Eiland and Gary Smith (eds) *Walter Benjamin: Selected Writings, Volume 2, 1927–1934.* Cambridge: Belknap Press of Harvard University, pp. 222–4.

Benshoff, Harry M. (1997) *Monsters in the Closet: Homosexuality and the Horror Film.* Manchester: Manchester University Press.

— (2008) '1966: Movies and Camp', in Barry Keith Grant (ed.) *American Cinema of the 1960s: Themes and Variations.* New Brunswick: Rutgers University Press, pp. 150–71.

Benshoff, Harry M. and Sean Griffin. (2006) *Queer Images: A History of Gay and Lesbian Film in America.* Lanham: Rowman & Littlefield.

Berenstein, Rhona J. (1996) *Attack of the Leading Ladies: Gender, Sexuality, and Spectatorship in Classic Horror Cinema.* New York: Columbia University Press.

Bergman, David. (1993) 'Strategic Camp: The Art of Gay Rhetoric', in David Bergman (ed.) *Camp Grounds: Style and Homosexuality.* Amherst: University of Massachusetts Press, pp. 92–109.

— (1993) 'Introduction', in David Bergman (ed.) *Camp Grounds: Style and Homosexuality.* Amherst: University of Massachusetts Press, pp. 3–16.

Berg-Brousseau, Henry. (2022) '200+ Major U.S. Companies Oppose Anti-LGBTQ+ State Legislation'. Washington DC: Human Rights Campaign. *www.hrc.org/press-releases/200-major-u-s-companies-oppose-anti-lgbtq-state-legislation* (last accessed 5 April 2022).

Blake, Linnie. (2008) *The Wounds of Nations: Horror Cinema, Historical Trauma and National Identity.* Manchester: Manchester University Press.

Boellstorff, Tom. (2007) *A Coincidence of Desires: Anthropology, Queer Studies, Indonesia.* Durham: Duke University Press.

Bradley, Matt. (2007) 'Silenced for Their Own Protection: How the IRB Marginalizes those it Feigns to Protect', *ACME: An International Journal for Critical Geographies*, 6(3), pp. 339–49.

Brickman, Barbara Jane. (2016) '"A Strange Desire That Never Dies": Monstrous Lesbian Camp in the Age of Conformity', *Discourse*, 38(3), pp. 356–89.

— (2017) 'Voyage to Camp Lesbos: Pulp Fiction and the Shameful Lesbian "Sicko"', in Bruce E. Drushel and Brian M. Peters (eds) *Sontag and the Camp Aesthetic: Advancing New Perspectives.* Lanham: Lexington Books, pp. 3–28.

Bronski, Michael. (1984) *Culture Clash: The Making of Gay Sensibility.* Boston: South End Press.

Brooks, Daphne A. (2006) *Bodies in Dissent: Spectacular Performances of Race and Freedom, 1850–1910.* Durham: Duke University Press.

Browne, Kath. (2010) 'Queer Quantification or Queer(y)ing Quantification: Creating Lesbian, Gay, Bisexual or Heterosexual Citizens through Governmental Social Research', in Kath Browne and Catherine J. Nash (eds) *Queer Methods and Methodologies: Intersecting Queer Theories and Social Science Research.* Farnham: Ashgate, pp. 231–49.

Browne, Kath and Catherine J. Nash. (2010) 'Queer Methods and Methodologies: An Introduction', in Kath Browne and Catherine J. Nash (eds) *Queer Methods and Methodologies: Intersecting Queer Theories and Social Science Research.* Farnham: Ashgate, pp. 1–23.

Browning, John Edgar. (2017) 'Horror Criticism', in Matt Cardin (ed.) *Horror Literature through History: An Encyclopedia of the Stories That Speak to Our Deepest Fears, Volume 1.* Santa Barbara: Greenwood, pp. 97–101.

Brunt, Rosalind. (1992) 'Engaging with the Popular: Audiences for Mass Culture and What to Say about Them', in Lawrence Grossberg, Cary Nelson and Paula Treichler (eds) *Cultural Studies.* New York: Routledge, pp. 69–80.

Butler, Judith. (1994) 'Against Proper Objects: Introduction', *differences: A Journal of Feminist Cultural Studies*, 6(2+3), pp. 1–26.

Carnes, Neal. (2019) *Queer Community: Identities, Intimacies, and Ideology.* London: Routledge.

Carroll, Nöel. (1987) 'The Nature of Horror', *The Journal of Aesthetics and Art Criticism*, 46(1), pp. 51–9.

Case, Sue-Ellen. (1991) 'Tracking the Vampire', *differences: A Journal of Feminist Cultural Studies*, 3(2), pp. 1–20.

Chamberlain, Edward A. (2020) *Imagining LatinX Intimacies: Connecting Queer Stories, Spaces and Sexualities.* Lanham: Rowman & Littlefield.

Chapman, James. (2013) *Film and History.* London: Palgrave Macmillan.

Chauncey, George. (2014) 'Privacy Could Only Be Had in Public: Gay Uses of the Streets (1995)', in Jen Jack Gieseking, William Mangold with Cindi Katz, Setha Low and Susan Saegert (eds) *The People, Place, and Space Reader.* New York: Routledge, pp. 202–6.

Cherry, Brigid. (1999) 'The Female Horror Film Audience: Viewing Pleasures and Fan Practices'. Unpublished PhD thesis. University of Stirling.

— (2002) 'Screaming for Release: Femininity and Horror Film Fandom in Britain', in Steve Chibnall and Julian Petley (eds) *British Horror Cinema.* London: Routledge, pp. 42–57.

— (2009) *Horror.* New York: Routledge.

Church, David. (2021) *Post-Horror Art, Genre, and Cultural Elevation.* Edinburgh: Edinburgh University Press.

Chute, David. (1983) 'Outlaw Cinema', *Film Comment,* 19(5), pp. 9–15.

Clasen, Mathias. (2017) *Why Horror Seduces.* New York: Oxford University Press.

Clemens, Valdine. (1999) *The Return of the Repressed: Gothic Horror from The Castle of Otranto to Alien.* Albany: State University of New York Press.

Cleto, Fabio. (1999) 'Introduction: Queering the Camp', in Fabio Cleto (ed.) *Camp: Queer Aesthetics and the Performing Subject: A Reader.* Edinburgh: Edinburgh University Press, pp. 1–42.

Clover, Carol J. (1992) *Men, Women, and Chain Saws: Gender in the Modern Horror Film.* Princeton: Princeton University Press.

— (2015) *Men, Women, and Chain Saws: Gender in the Modern Horror Film.* Updated edn. Princeton: Princeton University Press.

Cohen, Jacob. (1988) *Statistical Power Analysis for the Behavioral Sciences.* 2nd edn. Mahwah: Lawrence Erlbaum.

Connor, Andrea. (2017) *The Political Afterlife of Sites of Monumental Destruction: Reconstructing Affect in Mostar and New York.* New York: Routledge.

Coppa, Francesca. (2014) 'Fuck Yeah, Fandom is Beautiful', *The Journal of Fandom Studies,* 2(1), pp. 73–82.

Core, Philip. (1984) *Camp: The Lie That Tells the Truth.* New York: Putnam Publishing Group.

Cornesse, Carina, Annelies G. Blom, David Dutwin, Jon A. Krosnick, Edith D. De Leeuw, Stéphane Legleye, Josh Pasek, Darren Pennay, Benjamin Phillips, Joseph W. Sakshaug, Bella Struminskaya and Alexander Wenz. (2020) 'A Review of Conceptual Approaches and Empirical Evidence on Probability and Nonprobability Sample Survey Research', *Journal of Survey Statistics and Methodology,* 8(1), pp. 4–36.

Cotter, Robert Michael. (2017) *Vampira and Her Daughters: Women Horror Movie Hosts from the 1950s into the Internet Era.* Jefferson: McFarland.

Coverley, Merlin. (2020) *Hauntology: Ghosts of Futures Past.* Harpenden: Oldcastle Books.

Crane, Jonathan Lake. (1994) *Terror and Everyday Life: Singular Moments in the History of the Horror Film.* London: SAGE.

Creed, Barbara. (1993) *The Monstrous-Feminine: Film, Feminism, Psychoanalysis.* London: Routledge.

Crenshaw, Kimberlé. (2018 [1989]) 'Demarginalizing the Intersection of Race and Sex: A Black Feminist Critique of Antidiscrimination Doctrine, Feminist Theory, and Antiracist Politics', in Katharine T. Bartlett and Rosanne Kennedy (eds) *Feminist Legal Theory: Readings in Law and Gender.* New York: Routledge, pp. 57–80.

Crosby, Emily Deering and Hannah Lynn. (2017) 'Authentic Artifice: Dolly Parton's Negotiations of Sontag's Camp', in Bruce E. Drushel and Brian M. Peters (eds) *Sontag and the Camp Aesthetic: Advancing New Perspectives.* Lanham: Lexington Books, pp. 47–62.

Dahl, Ulrika. (2010) 'Femme on Femme: Reflections on Collaborative Methods and Queer Femme-inist Ethnography', in Kath Browne and Catherine J. Nash (eds) *Queer Methods and Methodologies: Intersecting Queer Theories and Social Science Research.* Farnham: Ashgate, pp. 143–66.

Davis, Colin and Hanna Meretoja. (2020) 'Introduction to Literary Trauma Studies', in Colin Davis and Hanna Meretoja (eds) *The Routledge Companion to Literature and Trauma.* London: Routledge, pp. 1–8.

de Bruyn, Dirk. (2014) *The Performance of Trauma in Moving Image Art.* Newcastle upon Tyne: Cambridge Scholars Publishing.

Deleuze, Gilles and Félix Guattari. (2004) *A Thousand Plateaus: Capitalism and Schizophrenia.* Translated by Brian Massumi. London: Continuum.

Derrida, Jacques. (1994) *Specters of Marx: The State of the Debt, the Work of Mourning and the New International.* Translated by Peggy Kamuf. New York: Routledge.

Derry, Charles. (1987) 'More Dark Dreams: Some Notes on the Recent Horror Film', in Gregory A. Waller (ed.) *American Horrors: Essays on the Modern American Horror Film.* Urbana: University of Illinois Press, pp. 162–74.

Detamore, Mathias. (2010) 'Queer(y)ing the Ethics of Research Methods: Toward a Politics of Intimacy in Researcher/Researched Relations', in Kath Browne and Catherine J. Nash (eds) *Queer Methods and Methodologies: Intersecting Queer Theories and Social Science Research.* Farnham: Ashgate, pp. 167–82.

Dhoest, Alexander and Nele Simons. (2012) 'Questioning Queer Audiences: Exploring Diversity in Lesbian and Gay Men's Media Uses and Readings', in Karen Ross (ed.) *The Handbook of Gender, Sex, and Media.* Malden: Wiley-Blackwell, pp. 260–76.

Dickson, Lesley-Ann. (2018) '"Beyond Film" Experience: Festivalizing Practices and Shifting Spectatorship at Glasgow Film Festival', in Sarah Atkinson and Helen W. Kennedy (eds) *Live Cinema: Cultures, Economies, Aesthetics.* London: Bloomsbury Academic, pp. 83–100.

Dika, Vera. (1987) 'The Stalker Film, 1978–81', in Gregory A. Waller (ed.) *American Horrors: Essays on the Modern American Horror Film*. Urbana: University of Illinois Press, pp. 86–101.

Doan, Petra L. (2019) 'To Count or Not to Count: Queering Measurement the Transgender Community', in Amin Ghaziani and Matt Brim (eds) *Imagining Queer Methods*. New York: New York University Press, pp. 121–42.

Doty, Alexander. (1993) *Making Things Perfectly Queer: Interpreting Mass Culture*. Minneapolis: University of Minnesota Press.

Dyer, Richard. (1977) 'Introduction', in Richard Dyer (ed.) *Gays and Film*. London: British Film Institute, pp. 1–4.

— (1993) *The Matter of Images: Essays on Representations*. London: Routledge.

— (2002) *The Culture of Queers*. London: Routledge.

Dumas, Chris. (2014) 'Horror and Psychoanalysis: An Introductory Primer', in Harry M. Benshoff (ed.) *A Companion to the Horror Film*. Malden: Wiley-Blackwell, pp. 21–37.

Edmonds, W. Alex and Thomas D. Kennedy. (2017) *An Applied Guide to Research Designs: Quantitative, Qualitative, and Mixed Methods*. 2nd edn. Thousand Oaks: SAGE.

Elliott-Smith, Darren. (2016) *Queer Horror Film and Television: Sexuality and Masculinity at the Margins*. London: I. B. Tauris.

Eversley, Shelly and Laurie Hurson. (2019) 'Like Inciting a Riot: Queering Open Education with EqualityArchive.com', in Amin Ghaziani and Matt Brim (eds) *Imagining Queer Methods*. New York: New York University Press, pp. 248–58.

Fischer, Lucy and Marcia Landy. (1987) '*Eyes of Laura Mars*: A Binocular Critique', in Gregory A. Waller (ed.) *American Horrors: Essays on the Modern American Horror Film*. Urbana: University of Illinois Press, pp. 62–78.

Fisher, Mark. (2014) *Ghosts of My Life: Writings on Depression, Hauntology and Lost Futures*. Winchester: Zero Books.

Fiske, John. (1992) 'The Cultural Economy of Fandom', in Lisa A. Lewis (ed.) *The Adoring Audience: Fan Culture and Popular Media*. London: Routledge, pp. 30–49.

— (2003) 'Understanding Popular Culture', in Will Brooker and Deborah Jermyn (eds) *The Audience Studies Reader*. London: Routledge, pp. 112–16.

Fleming, Amanda C. (2016) 'In Search of the Child Spectator in the Late Silent Era', in CarrieLynn D. Reinhard and Christopher J. Olson (eds) *Making Sense of Cinema: Empirical Studies into Film Spectators and Spectatorship*. New York: Bloomsbury Academic, pp. 119–38.

Follows, Stephen. (2017) *The Horror Report*. *https://stephenfollows.com/horrorreport/* (last accessed 6 November 2019).

Follows, Stephen and Bruce Nash. (2016) 'The Relative Popularity of Genres Around the World'. Los Angeles: American Film Market. *https://americanfilmmarket.com/relative-popularity-genres-around-world/* (last accessed 25 March 2019).

— (2018) 'What the Data Says: Producing Low-Budget Horror Films'. Los Angeles: American Film Market. *https://americanfilmmarket.com/what-the-data-says-producing-low-budget-horror-films/* (last accessed 17 December 2019).

Foucault, Michel. (1986) Translated by Jay Miskowiec. 'Of Other Spaces', *Diacritics*, 16(1), pp. 22–7.

Frayling, Christopher. (2013) 'Foreword', in James Bell (ed.) *Gothic: The Dark Heart of Film*. London: BFI, pp. 5–7.

Freud, Sigmund. (1955 [1919]) 'The "Uncanny"'. Translated by James Strachey (ed.) *The Standard Edition of the Complete Psychological Works of Sigmund Freud, Vol. XVII, 1917–1919*. London: Hogarth Press, pp. 219–52.

Gelder, Ken. (2000) 'Introduction to Part Six', in Ken Gelder (ed.) *The Horror Reader*. New York: Routledge, pp. 187–9.

Ghaziani, Amin. (2019) 'Methodological Problems and Possibilities in Gayborhood Studies', in Amin Ghaziani and Matt Brim (eds) *Imagining Queer Methods*. New York: New York University Press, pp. 103–20.

Ghaziani, Amin and Matt Brim. (2019) 'Queer Methods: Four Provocations for an Emerging Field', in Amin Ghaziani and Matt Brim (eds) *Imagining Queer Methods*. New York: New York University Press, pp. 3–27.

Gillis, John R. (1994) 'Memory and Identity: The History of a Relationship', in John R. Gillis (ed.) *Commemorations: The Politics of National Identity*. Princeton: Princeton University Press, pp. 3–24.

Giroux, Henry A. (2021) *Race, Politics, and Pandemic Pedagogy: Education in a Time of Crisis*. London: Bloomsbury Academic.

GLAAD. (2019) 'Accelerating Acceptance Executive Summary: A Survey of American Acceptance and Attitudes Toward LGBTQ Americans Conducted by The Harris Poll'. Los Angeles: GLAAD. *www.glaad.org/publications/accelerating-acceptance-2019* (last accessed 24 June 2020).

GLAAD Media Institute. (2020) 'Studio Responsibility Index 2020'. Los Angeles: GLAAD. *www.glaad.org/sri/2020* (last accessed 24 July 2020).

Google. (2017) 'The Women Missing from the Silver Screen and the Technology Used to Find Them'. Mountain View: Google. *www.google.com/intl/en/about/main/gender-equality-films/* (last accessed 24 May 2019).

Gordon, Phillip. (2020) *Gay Faulkner: Uncovering a Homosexual Presence in Yoknapatawpha and Beyond*. Jackson: University Press of Mississippi.

Gorman-Murray, Andrew, Lynda Johnston and Gordon Waitt. (2010) 'Queer(ing) Communication in Research Relationships: A Conversation about Subjectivities, Methodologies and Ethics', in Kath Browne and Catherine J. Nash (eds) *Queer Methods and Methodologies: Intersecting Queer Theories and Social Science Research*. Farnham: Ashgate, pp. 97–112.

Grant, Barry Keith. (2008) 'Science Fiction Double Feature: Ideology in the Cult Film', in Ernest Mathijs and Xavier Mendik (eds) *The Cult Film Reader*. Berkshire: Open University Press, pp. 76–87.

— (2018) 'Foreword', in Barry Keith Grant (ed.) *Robin Wood on the Horror Film: Collected Essays and Reviews*. Detroit: Wayne State University Press, pp. vii–x.

Gravetter, Frederick J. and Larry B. Wallnau. (2011) *Essentials of Statistics for the Behavioral Sciences*. 7th edn. Belmont: Wadsworth.

Gray, Jonathan, Cornel Sandvoss and C. Lee Harrington. (2007) 'Introduction: Why Study Fans?', in Jonathan Gray, Cornel Sandvoss and C. Lee Harrington (eds) *Fandom: Identities and Communities in a Mediated World*. New York: New York University Press, pp. 1–16.

— (2017) 'Introduction: Why Still Study Fans?', in Jonathan Gray, Cornel Sandvoss and C. Lee Harrington (eds) *Fandom: Identities and Communities in a Mediated World*. 2nd edn. New York: New York University Press, pp. 1–26.

Haggerty, George E. (2006) *Queer Gothic*. Urbana: University of Illinois Press.

Halberstam, J. (1998) *Female Masculinity*. Durham: Duke University Press.

— (2000) 'Gothic', in Bonnie Zimmerman (ed.) *Lesbian Histories and Cultures: An Encyclopedia*. New York: Routledge, pp. 340–1.

— (2003) 'Reflections on Queer Studies and Queer Pedagogy', in Gust A. Yep, Karen E. Lovaas and John P. Elia (eds) *Queer Theory and Communication: From Disciplining Queers to Queering the Discipline(s)*. Binghamton: Harrington Park Press, pp. 361–4.

— (2011) *The Queer Art of Failure*. Durham: Duke University Press.

— (2018) *Trans**: *A Quick and Quirky Account of Gender Variability*. Oakland: University of California Press.

Halperin, David M. (1995) *Saint Foucault: Towards a Gay Hagiography*. New York: Oxford University Press.

— (2012) *How to be Gay*. Cambridge: Belknap Press of Harvard University Press.

Han, C. Winter. (2015) *Geisha of a Different Kind: Race and Sexuality in Gaysian America*. New York: New York University Press.

Handel, Leo A. (1950) *Hollywood Looks at Its Audience: A Report of Film Audience Research*. Urbana: University of Illinois Press.

Hanich, Julian. (2014a) 'Watching a Film with Others: Towards a Theory of Collective Spectatorship', *Screen*, 55(3), pp. 338–59.

— (2014b) 'Laughter and Collective Awareness: The Cinema Auditorium as Public Space', *NECSUS European Journal of Media Studies*, 3(2), pp. 43–62.

— (2018) *The Audience Effect: On the Collective Cinema Experience*. Edinburgh: Edinburgh University Press.

Harmetz, Aljean. (2 October 1980) 'Quick End of Low-Budget Horror-Film Cycle Seen', *The New York Times*. New York, p. C15.

Harrington, Erin. (2018) *Women, Monstrosity and Horror Film: Gynaehorror*. London: Routledge.

Hauser, Fayette. (2020) *The Cockettes: Acid Drag & Sexual Anarchy, 1969–1972*. Port Townsend: Process Media.

Heberle, Renee. (2016) 'The Personal is Political', in Lisa Disch and Mary Hawkesworth (eds) *The Oxford Handbook of Feminist Theory*. New York: Oxford University Press, pp. 593–609.

Heckert, Jamie. (2010) 'Intimacy with Strangers/Intimacy with Self: Queer Experiences of Social Research', in Kath Browne and Catherine J. Nash (eds) *Queer Methods and Methodologies: Intersecting Queer Theories and Social Science Research*. Farnham: Ashgate, pp. 41–53.

Heller, Meredith. (2020) *Queering Drag: Redefining the Discourse of Gender-Bending*. Bloomington: Indiana University Press.

Hendershot, Cyndy. (2001) *I Was a Cold War Monster: Horror Films, Eroticism, and the Cold War Imagination*. Bowling Green: Bowling Green State University Popular Press.

Herman, Judith. (2015 [1992]) *Trauma and Recovery: The Aftermath of Violence – From Domestic Abuse to Political Terror*. New York: Basic Books.

Hill, Annette. (1997) *Shocking Entertainment: Viewer Response to Violent Movies*. Luton: University of Luton Press.

Hillman, Betty Luther. (2011) '"The Most Profoundly Revolutionary Act a Homosexual Can Engage In": Drag and the Politics of Gender Presentation in the San Francisco Gay Liberation Movement, 1964–1972', *Journal of the History of Sexuality*, 20(1), pp. 153–81.

Hills, Matt. (2008) 'Media Fandom, Neoreligiosity and Cult(ural) Studies', in Ernest Mathijs and Xavier Mendik (eds) *The Cult Film Reader*. Berkshire: Open University Press, pp. 133–48.

— (2010) 'Attending Horror Film Festivals and Conventions: Liveness, Subcultural Capital and "Flesh-and-Blood Genre Communities"', in Ian Conrich (ed.) *Horror Zone: The Cultural Experience of Contemporary Horror Cinema*. London: I. B. Tauris, pp. 87–102.

— (2014) 'Horror Reception/Audiences', in Harry M. Benshoff (ed.) *A Companion to the Horror Film*. Malden: Wiley-Blackwell, pp. 90–108.

Horn, Katrin. (2017) *Women, Camp, and Popular Culture: Serious Excess.* New York: Palgrave Macmillan.

Horowitz, Katie. (2020) *Drag, Interperformance, and the Trouble with Queerness.* New York: Routledge.

Hubner, Laura. (2018) *Fairytale and Gothic Horror: Uncanny Transformations in Film.* London: Palgrave Macmillan.

Hughes, Jessica. (2016) 'The Festival Collective: Cult Audiences and Japanese Extreme Cinema', in CarrieLynn D. Reinhard and Christopher J. Olson (eds) *Making Sense of Cinema: Empirical Studies into Film Spectators and Spectatorship.* New York: Bloomsbury Academic, pp. 37–56.

Humphrey, Daniel. (2014) 'Gender and Sexuality Haunt the Horror Film', in Harry M. Benshoff (ed.) *A Companion to the Horror Film.* Malden: Wiley-Blackwell, pp. 38–55.

Humphries, Reynold. (2002) *The American Horror Film: An Introduction.* Edinburgh: Edinburgh University Press.

Isherwood, Christopher. (1999) 'From *The World in the Evening*', in Fabio Cleto (ed.) *Camp: Queer Aesthetics and the Performing Subject: A Reader.* Edinburgh: Edinburgh University Press, pp. 49–52.

Izod, John and Joanna Dovalis. (2015) *Cinema as Therapy: Grief and Transformational Film.* London: Routledge.

Jancovich, Mark. (2008) 'Cult Fictions: Cult Movies, Subcultural Capital and the Production of Cultural Distinctions', in Ernest Mathijs and Xavier Mendik (eds) *The Cult Film Reader.* Berkshire: Open University Press, pp. 149–62.

— (2019) 'Introduction', *Horror Studies*, 10(1), pp. 3–6.

Jerslev, Anne. (2008) 'Semiotics by Instinct: "Cult Film" as a Signifying Practice Between Film and Audience', in Ernest Mathijs and Xavier Mendik (eds) *The Cult Film Reader.* Berkshire: Open University Press, pp. 88–99.

Jones, Darryl. (2018) *Sleeping with the Lights On: The Unsettling Story of Horror.* Oxford: Oxford University Press.

Jones, Matthew. (2018) 'Living Cinema Memories: Restaging the Past at the Pictures', in Sarah Atkinson and Helen W. Kennedy (eds) *Live Cinema: Cultures, Economies, Aesthetics.* London: Bloomsbury Academic, pp. 185–98.

Kaplan, E. Ann. (2001) 'Melodrama, Cinema and Trauma', *Screen*, 42(2), pp. 201–5.

Kelly, Casey Ryan. (2016) 'Camp Horror and the Gendered Politics of Screen Violence: Subverting the Monstrous-Feminine in *Teeth* (2007)', *Women's Studies in Communication*, 39(1), pp. 86–106.

Kjeldsen, Jens E. (2018) 'Audience Analysis and Reception Studies of Rhetoric', in Jens E. Kjeldsen (ed.) *Rhetorical Audience Studies and Reception of Rhetoric: Exploring Audiences Empirically.* London: Palgrave Macmillan, pp. 1–42.

Klinger, Barbara. (2018) 'Foreword', in Sarah Atkinson and Helen W. Kennedy (eds) *Live Cinema: Cultures, Economies, Aesthetics.* London: Bloomsbury Academic, pp. xiii–xvii.

Lagapa, Jason. (2010) 'Parading the Undead: Camp, Horror and Reincarnation in the Poetry of Frank O'Hara and John Yau', *Journal of Modern Literature,* 33(2), pp. 92–113.

Latham, Rob. (1998) 'Phallic Mothers and Monster Queers', *Science Fiction Studies*, 25(1), pp. 87–101.

Laurie, Charles and Eric Jensen. (2016) *Doing Real Research: A Practical Guide to Social Research.* London: SAGE.

Levin, Nina Jackson, Shanna K. Kattari, Emily K. Piellusch and Erica Watson. (2020) '"We Just Take Care of Each Other": Navigating "Chosen Family" in the Context of Health, Illness, and the Mutual Provision of Care amongst Queer and Transgender Young Adults', *International Journal of Environmental Research and Public Health,* 17(19), pp. 1–20.

Levitt, Lauren. (2017) '*Batman* and the Aesthetics of Camp', in Bruce E. Drushel and Brian M. Peters (eds) *Sontag and the Camp Aesthetic: Advancing New Perspectives.* Lanham: Lexington Books, pp. 171–88.

— (2018) 'Nostalgia and Placemaking at Los Angeles' Outdoor Movies', in Sarah Atkinson and Helen W. Kennedy (eds) *Live Cinema: Cultures, Economies, Aesthetics.* London: Bloomsbury Academic, pp. 21–32.

Lloyd, Moya. (2007) *Judith Butler: From Norms to Politics.* Cambridge: Polity Press.

Lorde, Audre. (1983) 'There Is No Hierarchy of Oppressions', *Interracial Books for Children Bulletin: Homophobia and Education,* 14(3–4), p. 9.

Love, Heather. (2019) '"How the Other Half Thinks": An Introduction to the Volume', in Amin Ghaziani and Matt Brim (eds) *Imagining Queer Methods.* New York: New York University Press, pp. 28–44.

Lowenstein, Adam. (2005) *Shocking Representation: Historical Trauma, National Cinema, and the Modern Horror Film.* New York: Columbia University Press.

Luders, Joseph E. (2016) 'Feminist Mobilization and the Politics of Rights', in Lorenzo Bosi, Marco Giugni and Katrin Uba (eds) *The Consequences of Social Movements.* Cambridge: Cambridge University Press, pp. 185–214.

Ludlam, Charles. (1992) *Ridiculous Theatre: Scourge of Human Folly: The Essays and Opinions of Charles Ludlam.* Edited by Steven Samuels. New York: Theatre Communications Group.

Lynskey, John. (2020) 'Queer Cult Performance: Recreating *Rocky Horror* in the Twenty-First Century', in Darren Elliott-Smith and John Edgar Browning (eds) *New Queer Horror Film and Television.* Cardiff: University of Wales Press, pp. 31–42.

Mai, Nadin. (2015) 'The Aesthetics of Absence and Duration in the Post-Trauma Cinema of Lav Diaz'. Unpublished PhD thesis. University of Stirling.

Maltby, Richard. (2006) 'On the Prospect of Writing Cinema History from Below', *TMG Journal for Media History*, 9(2), pp. 74–96.

Marchetti, Gina. (2008) 'Subcultural Studies and the Film Audience: Rethinking the Film Viewing Context', in Ernest Mathijs and Xavier Mendik (eds) *The Cult Film Reader*. Berkshire: Open University Press, pp. 403–18.

Mathijs, Ernest and Xavier Mendik. (2008) 'Editorial Introduction: What is Cult Film?', in Ernest Mathijs and Xavier Mendik (eds) *The Cult Film Reader*. Berkshire: Open University Press, pp. 1–11.

— (2008) 'The Concepts of Cult: Introduction', in Ernest Mathijs and Xavier Mendik (eds) *The Cult Film Reader*. Berkshire: Open University Press, pp. 15–24.

— (2008) 'Cult Consumption: Introduction', in Ernest Mathijs and Xavier Mendik (eds) T*he Cult Film Reader*. Berkshire: Open University Press, pp. 369–79.

McCulloch, Richard and Virginia Crisp. (2016) '"Watch like a grown up … enjoy like a child": Exhibition, Authenticity, and Film Audiences at the Prince Charles Cinema', *Participations*, 13(1), pp. 188–217.

McElroy, Dolores. (2017) 'Camp', in Bettina Papenburg (ed.) *Gender: Laughter*. Farmington Hills: Macmillan Reference USA, pp. 293–310.

Meyer, Ilan H. and Patrick A. Wilson (2009) 'Sampling Lesbian, Gay, and Bisexual Populations', *Journal of Counseling Psychology*, 56(1), pp. 23–31.

Meyer, Moe. (1994) 'Introduction: Reclaiming the Discourse of Camp', in Moe Meyer (ed.) *The Politics and Poetics of Camp*. London: Routledge, pp. 1–22.

Miller, Sam J. (2011) 'Assimilation and the Queer Monster', in Aviva Briefel and Sam J. Miller (eds) *Horror After 9/11: World of Fear, Cinema of Terror*. Austin: University of Texas Press, pp. 220–33.

Mooney, Linda A., Molly Clever and Marieke Van Willigen. (2021) *Understanding Social Problems*. 11th edn. Boston: Cengage.

Morrison, Ken. (2006) *Marx, Durkheim, Weber: Formations of Modern Social Thought*. 2nd edn. London: SAGE.

Moser, Robert H. (2008) *The Carnivalesque Defunto: Death and the Dead in Modern Brazilian Literature*. Athens: Ohio University Press.

Motion Picture Association. (2020) 'Theatrical Home Entertainment Market Environment (THEME) Report: A Comprehensive Analysis and Survey of the Theatrical and Home/Mobile Entertainment Market Environment for 2019'. Washington DC: Motion Picture Association. *www.mpa-apac.org/wp-content/uploads/2020/03/MPA-THEME-2019.pdf* (last accessed 3 May 2020).

Muñoz, José Esteban. (1996) 'Ephemera as Evidence: Introductory Notes to Queer Acts', *Women & Performance: A Journal of Feminist Theory*, 8(2), pp. 5–16.

— (1999) *Disidentifications: Queers of Color and the Performance of Politics*. Minneapolis: University of Minnesota Press.

— (2009) *Cruising Utopia: The Then and There of Queer Futurity*. New York: New York University Press.

Nadal, Kevin Leo Yabut. (2020) *Queering Law and Order: LGBTQ Communities and the Criminal Justice System*. Lanham: Lexington Books.

Neale, Steve. (2000) *Genre and Hollywood*. London: Routledge.

Newton, Esther. (1979 [1972]) *Mother Camp: Female Impersonators in America*. Chicago: University of Chicago Press.

Newton, Michael. (2019) *Show People: A History of the Film Star*. London: Reaktion Books.

Nielsen. (2014) 'Lights, Camera, Action! State of the LGBT Moviegoer'. New York: Nielsen. *www.nielsen.com/us/en/insights/report/2014/lights-camera-action-state-of-the-lgbt-moviegoer/#* (last accessed 17 October 2018).

— (2015) 'Proudly Setting Trends: The 2015 LGBT Consumer Report'. New York: Nielsen. *www.nielsen.com/us/en/insights/report/2015/proudly-setting-trends-the-2015-lgbt-consumer-report/* (last accessed 17 October 2018).

Nielsen, Elly-Jean. (2016) 'Lesbian Camp: An Unearthing', *Journal of Lesbian Studies*, 20(1), pp. 116–35.

Niles, Richard. (2004) 'Wigs, Laughter, and Subversion: Charles Busch and Strategies of Drag Performance', *Journal of Homosexuality*, 46(3–4), pp. 35–53.

Nowell, Richard. (2011) '"There's More Than One Way to Lose Your Heart": The American Film Industry, Early Teen Slasher Films, and Female Youth', *Cinema Journal*, 51(1), pp. 115–40.

Oliver-Hopkins, Olivia. (2017) '"I's Got to Get Me Some Education!": Class and the Camp-Horror Nexus in *House of 1000 Corpses*', in Bruce E. Drushel and Brian M. Peters (eds) *Sontag and the Camp Aesthetic: Advancing New Perspectives*. Lanham: Lexington Books, pp. 151–68.

Orloff, Alvin. (2019) *Disasterama!: Adventures in the Queer Underground, 1977–1997*. New York: Three Rooms Press.

Paul, William. (1994) *Laughing, Screaming: Modern Hollywood Horror and Comedy*. New York: Columbia University Press.

Pellegrini, Ann. (2015) 'After Sontag: Future Notes on Camp', in George E. Haggerty and Molly McGarry (eds) *A Companion to Lesbian, Gay, Bisexual, Transgender, and Queer Studies*. Malden: Wiley-Blackwell, pp. 168–93.

Pine II, B. Joseph and James H. Gilmore. (1998) 'Welcome to the Experience Economy', *Harvard Business Review*, 76(4), pp. 97–105.

Pinedo, Isabel Cristina. (1997) *Recreational Terror: Women and the Pleasures of Horror Film Viewing*. Albany: State University of New York Press.

— (2020) '*Get Out*: Moral Monsters at the Intersection of Racism and the Horror Film', in Katarzyna Paszkiewicz and Stacy Rusnak (eds) *Final Girls, Feminism and Popular Culture*. London: Palgrave Macmillan, pp. 95–114.

Radstone, Susannah. (2001) 'Trauma and Screen Studies: Opening the Debate', *Screen*, 42(2), pp. 188–93.

Ramírez, Horacio N. Roque. (2008) 'Memory and Mourning: Living Oral History with Queer Latinos and Latinas in San Francisco', in Paula Hamilton and Linda Shopes (eds) *Oral History and Public Memories*. Philadelphia: Temple University Press, pp. 165–86.

Reinhard, CarrieLynn D. and Christopher J. Olson. (2016) 'Introduction: Empirical Approaches to Film Spectators and Spectatorship', in CarrieLynn D. Reinhard and Christopher J. Olson (eds) *Making Sense of Cinema: Empirical Studies into Film Spectators and Spectatorship*. New York: Bloomsbury Academic, pp. 1–16.

Reisner, Sari L. and Jaclyn M. W. Hughto. (2019) 'Comparing the Health of Non-Binary and Binary Transgender Adults in a Statewide Non-Probability Sample', *PLOS ONE*, 14(8), pp. 1–20. *https://doi.org/10.1371/journal.pone.0221583* (last accessed 7 March 2021).

Rich, Adrienne. (1980) 'Compulsory Heterosexuality and Lesbian Existence', *Signs: Journal of Women in Culture and Society*, 5(4), pp. 631–60.

Rich, B. Ruby. (2013) *New Queer Cinema: The Director's Cut*. Durham: Duke University Press.

Rivera, David P. and Kevin L. Nadal. (2019) 'The Intersection of Queer Theory and Empirical Methods', in Amin Ghaziani and Matt Brim (eds) *Imagining Queer Methods*. New York: New York University Press, pp. 191–206.

Robinson, Zandria F. and Marcus Anthony Hunter. (2019) 'Measurement, Interrupted: Queer Possibilities for Social Scientific Methods', in Amin Ghaziani and Matt Brim (eds) *Imagining Queer Methods*. New York: New York University Press, pp. 163–90.

Rogers, Jillian C. (2021) *Resonant Recoveries: French Music and Trauma Between the World Wars*. New York: Oxford University Press.

Rooke, Alison. (2010) 'Queer in the Field: On Emotions, Temporality and Performativity in Ethnography', in Kath Browne and Catherine J. Nash (eds) *Queer Methods and Methodologies: Intersecting Queer Theories and Social Science Research*. Farnham: Ashgate, pp. 25–39.

Root, Maria P. P. (1992) 'Reconstructing the Impact of Trauma on Personality', in Laura S. Brown and Mary Ballou (eds) *Personality and Psychopathology: Feminist Reappraisals*. New York: Guilford Press, pp. 229–66.

Ross, Andrew. (2008) 'Uses of Camp', in Ernest Mathijs and Xavier Mendik (eds) *The Cult Film Reader*. Berkshire: Open University Press, pp. 53–66.

— (2014 [1989]) *No Respect: Intellectuals and Popular Culture*. London: Routledge.

Royle, Nicholas. (2003) *The Uncanny*. Manchester: Manchester University Press.

Rubin, Herbert J. and Irene S. Rubin. (2012) *Qualitative Interviewing: The Art of Hearing Data*. 3rd edn. Los Angeles: SAGE.

Russo, Vito. (1987) *The Celluloid Closet: Homosexuality in the Movies*. Revised edn. New York: Harper & Row.

Rutherford, Anne. (2013) 'Film, Trauma and the Enunciative Present', in Meera Atkinson and Michael Richardson (eds) *Traumatic Affect*. Newcastle upon Tyne: Cambridge Scholars, pp. 80–102.

Scahill, Andrew. (2015) *The Revolting Child in Horror Cinema: Youth Rebellion and Queer Spectatorship*. New York: Palgrave Macmillan.

Scales, Adam Christopher. (2015) 'Logging into Horror's Closet: Gay Fans, the Horror Film and Online Culture'. Unpublished PhD thesis. University of East Anglia.

Schäfer, Mirko Tobias. (2011) *Bastard Culture!: How User Participation Transforms Cultural Production*. Amsterdam: Amsterdam University Press.

Scheff, Thomas J. and Don D. Bushnell. (1984) 'A Theory of Catharsis', *Journal of Research in Personality*, 18(2), pp. 238–64.

Scheibel, Will. (2017) *American Stranger: Modernisms, Hollywood, and the Cinema of Nicholas Ray*. Albany: State University of New York Press.

Schlesinger, Philip, R. Emerson Dobash, Russell P. Dobash and C. Kay Weaver. (1992) *Women Viewing Violence*. London: BFI.

Schoonover, Karl and Rosalind Galt. (2016) *Queer Cinema in the World*. Durham: Duke University Press.

Schottmiller, Carl. (29 March 2018) 'A Drag Primer: Situating *RuPaul's Drag Race* Within Academic Drag Studies', Presentation at the Popular Culture Association/American Culture Association National Conference. Indianapolis.

Scott, Suzanne. (2019) *Fake Geek Girls: Fandom, Gender, and the Convergence Culture Industry*. New York: New York University Press.

Scrivner, Coltan, John A. Johnson, Jens Kjeldgaard-Christiansen and Mathias Clasen. (2021) 'Pandemic Practice: Horror Fans and Morbidly Curious Individuals Are More Psychologically Resilient During the COVID-19 Pandemic', *Personality and Individual Differences*, 168, pp. 1–6.

Shaviro, Steven. (1993) *The Cinematic Body*. Minneapolis: University of Minnesota Press.

Sher, Ben Raphael. (2015) 'Fraught Pleasures: Domestic Trauma and Cinephilia in American Culture'. Unpublished PhD thesis. University of California, Los Angeles.

Skakov, Nariman. (2012) *The Cinema of Tarkovsky: Labyrinths of Space and Time.* London: I. B. Tauris.

Skal, David J. (2016) *Halloween: The History of America's Darkest Holiday.* Mineola: Dover.

Smith, Rommi and Jenni Molloy. (2019) 'The Map Where We Meet and Other Queer-Quare Stories', in Amin Ghaziani and Matt Brim (eds) *Imagining Queer Methods.* New York: New York University Press, pp. 207–29.

Sontag, Susan. (2008 [1964]) 'Notes on "Camp"', in Ernest Mathijs and Xavier Mendik (eds) *The Cult Film Reader.* Berkshire: Open University Press, pp. 41–52.

Staiger, Janet. (1992) *Interpreting Films: Studies in the Historical Reception of American Cinema.* Princeton: Princeton University Press.

Stam, Robert. (1989) *Subversive Pleasures: Bakhtin, Cultural Criticism, and Film.* Baltimore: Johns Hopkins University Press.

Stark, Ian. (2021) 'Response: "You Dropped Your Butter" – Laughing the Pain Away: The Cathartic Value of Relief Humor in Health Communication', in Michael K. Cundall Jr. and Stephanie Kelly (eds) *Cases on Applied and Therapeutic Humor.* Hershey: IGI Global, pp. 3–10.

Stokes, DaShanne. (2020) 'The LGBT Medical and Political Crisis in the Wake of COVID-19', in Glenn W. Muschert, Kristen M. Budd, Michelle Christian, David C. Lane and Jason A. Smith (eds) *Social Problems in the Age of COVID-19, Volume 1: US Perspectives.* Bristol: Bristol University Press, pp. 81–90.

Tamborini, Ron and James B. Weaver. (1996) 'Frightening Entertainment: A Historical Perspective of Fictional Horror', in James B. Weaver and Ron Tamborini (eds) *Horror Films: Current Research on Audience Preferences and Reactions.* Mahwah: Lawrence Erlbaum, pp. 1–13.

Tamborini, Ron and James Stiff. (1987) 'Predictors of Horror Film Attendance and Appeal: An Analysis of the Audience for Frightening Films', *Communication Research*, 14(4), pp. 415–36.

Tamborini, Ron and Kristen Salomonson. (1996) 'Horror's Effect on Social Perceptions and Behaviors', in James B. Weaver and Ron Tamborini (eds) *Horror Films: Current Research on Audience Preferences and Reactions.* Mahwah: Lawrence Erlbaum, pp. 179–97.

Taylor, Jodie. (2012) *Playing it Queer: Popular Music, Identity and Queer World-Making.* Bern: Peter Lang.

Taylor, Leila. (2019) *Darkly: Black History and America's Gothic Soul.* London: Repeater Books.

Thornton, Sarah. (1995) *Club Cultures: Music, Media, and Subcultural Capital.* Cambridge: Polity Press.

Tudor, Andrew. (1989) *Monsters and Mad Scientists: A Cultural History of the Horror Movie.* Oxford: Basil Blackwell.

— (2003) 'Genre', in Barry Keith Grant (ed.) *Film Genre Reader III.* Austin: University of Texas Press, pp. 3–11.

Tulloch, John and Henry Jenkins. (1995) *Science Fiction Audiences: Watching Doctor Who and Star Trek.* London: Routledge.

Van Iquity, Sister Dana. (27 June 1996) 'A Linda Blair Affair to Remember', *San Francisco Bay Times.* San Francisco.

Veeder, William. (1998) 'The Nurture of the Gothic, or How Can a Text Be Both Popular and Subversive?', in Robert K. Martin and Eric Savoy (eds) *American Gothic: New Interventions in a National Narrative.* Iowa City: University of Iowa Press, pp. 20–39.

Vehovar, Vasja and Katja Lozar Manfreda. (2017) 'Overview: Online Surveys', in Nigel G. Fielding, Raymond M. Lee and Grant Blank (eds) *The SAGE Handbook of Online Research Methods.* 2nd edn. London: SAGE, pp. 143–61.

Vehovar, Vasja, Vera Toepoel and Stephanie Steinmetz. (2016) 'Non-Probability Sampling', in Christof Wolf, Dominique Joye, Tom W. Smith and Yang-chih Fu (eds) *The SAGE Handbook of Survey Methodology.* London: SAGE, pp. 329–45.

Vivar, Rosana. (2018) 'Never Seen a Shot Like that Before! Playfulness and Participatory Audiences in San Sebastian Horror and Fantasy Film Festival', in Sarah Atkinson and Helen W. Kennedy (eds) *Live Cinema: Cultures, Economies, Aesthetics.* London: Bloomsbury Academic, pp. 117–32.

Waldron, Darren. (2016) 'Transnational Investments: Aging in *Les Invisibles* (Sébastien Lifshitz, 2012) and Its Reception', in CarrieLynn D. Reinhard and Christopher J. Olson (eds) *Making Sense of Cinema: Empirical Studies into Film Spectators and Spectatorship.* New York: Bloomsbury Academic, pp. 57–76.

Walker, Janet. (2005) *Trauma Cinema: Documenting Incest and the Holocaust.* Berkeley: University of California Press.

Waller, Gregory A. (1987) 'Made-for-Television Horror Films', in Gregory A. Waller (ed.) *American Horrors: Essays on the Modern American Horror Film.* Urbana: University of Illinois Press, pp. 145–61.

Watson, Elena M. (1991) *Television Horror Movie Hosts: 68 Vampires, Mad Scientists and Other Denizens of the Late-Night Airwaves Examined and Interviewed.* Jefferson: McFarland.

Weaver III, James B. and Ron Tamborini. (1996) 'Preface', in James B. Weaver and Ron Tamborini (eds) *Horror Films: Current Research on Audience Preferences and Reactions.* Mahwah: Lawrence Erlbaum, pp. ix–x.

Weiss, Andrea. (1992) *Vampires and Violets: Lesbians in Film*. New York: Penguin Books.

Westengard, Laura. (2019) *Gothic Queer Culture: Marginalized Communities and the Ghosts of Insidious*. Lincoln: University of Nebraska Press.

Whatling, Clare. (1997) *Screen Dreams: Fantasising Lesbians in Film*. Manchester: Manchester University Press.

Wilcox, Melissa M. (2021) *Queer Religiosities: An Introduction to Queer and Transgender Studies in Religion*. Lanham: Rowman & Littlefield.

Williams, Linda. (1991) 'Film Bodies: Gender, Genre, and Excess', *Film Quarterly*, 44(4), pp. 2–13.

Winter, Jay. (1998) *Sites of Memory, Sites of Mourning: The Great War in European Cultural History*. Cambridge: Cambridge University Press.

Wood, Robin. (1984) 'An Introduction to the American Horror Film', in Barry Keith Grant (ed.) *Planks of Reason: Essays on the Horror Film*. Metuchen: Scarecrow Press, pp. 164–200.

— (1995) 'Responsibilities of a Gay Film Critic', in Corey K. Creekmur and Alexander Doty (eds) *Out in Culture: Gay, Lesbian and Queer Essays on Popular Culture*. Durham: Duke University Press, pp. 12–24.

— (2002) *Hitchcock's Films Revisited*. Revised edn. New York: Columbia University Press.

— (2003) *Hollywood from Vietnam to Reagan … and Beyond*. Expanded and revised edn. New York: Columbia University Press.

Yep, Gust A. (2003) 'The Violence of Heteronormativity in Communication Studies: Notes on Injury, Healing, and Queer World-making', *Journal of Homosexuality*, 45(2–4), pp. 11–59.

Yep, Gust A., Karen E. Lovaas and John P. Elia. (2003) 'Reflections on Queer Theory: Disparate Points of View', in Gust A. Yep, Karen Lovaas and John P. Elia (eds) *Queer Theory and Communication: From Disciplining Queers to Queering the Discipline(s)*. Binghamton: Harrington Park Press, pp. 335–8.

Zillmann, Dolf and James B. Weaver. (1996) 'Gender-Socialization Theory of Reactions to Horror', in James B. Weaver and Ron Tamborini (eds) *Horror Films: Current Research on Audience Preferences and Reactions*. Mahwah: Lawrence Erlbaum, pp. 81–101.

Zillmann, Dolf and Rhonda Gibson. (1996) 'Evolution of the Horror Genre', in James B. Weaver and Ron Tamborini (eds) *Horror Films: Current Research on Audience Preferences and Reactions*. Mahwah: Lawrence Erlbaum, pp. 15–31.

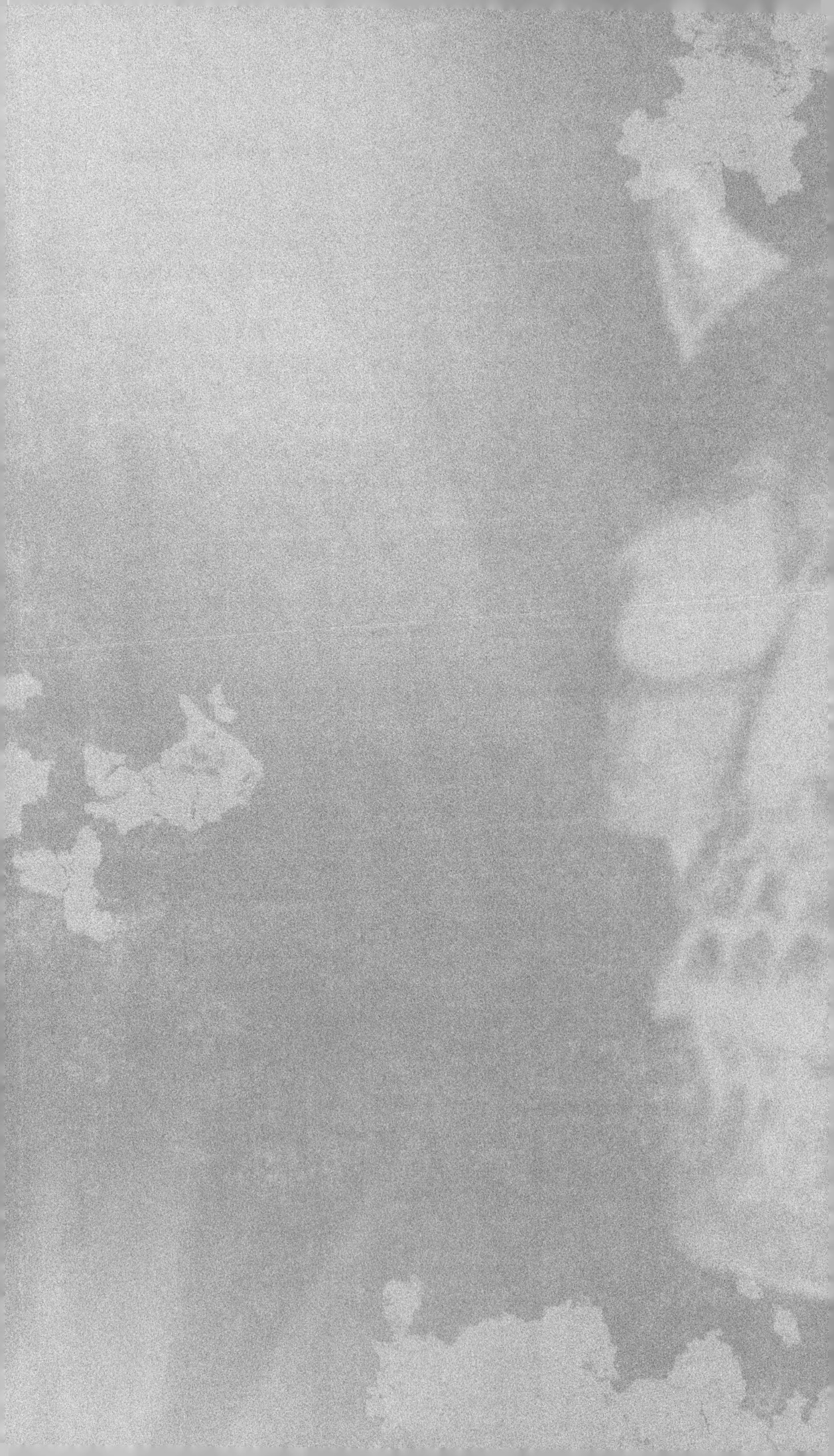

Index

abject 9, 29, 130–1, 146
ableism xiii, 9, 166n5, 189
academics 3, 17, 21–3, 31, 130, 235–6
ACT UP 20, 206
Adam All 220n3
Ahmed, Sara 19
AIDS epidemic 15, 20, 219
Alberta Arts District 205
Aldana Reyes, Xavier 2, 26, 29, 30–1, 91, 105, 137, 139, 142, 168n17
Alexander, Linda Lewis (et al.) 127–8
Alim, H. Samy (et al.) 47n8
American Psychiatric Association (APA) 118n46
Amin, Kadji 15
Anderson, Benedict 6
Anzaldúa, Gloria 8, 18
apparatus theory (Baudry) 36
Apparitional Lesbian, The (Castle) 22
Aristotle 123
Arrow Films 111
asexual *see* queer
Atkinson, Sarah 5, 38, 42, 177, 180, 190, 195, 209–10, 212, 219
Attack of the Leading Ladies (Berenstein) 24
audience
  and the co-presence with performers 182
  queer 2, 5, 19, 25, 27, 33, 52, 93, 97, 100, 111, 122, 149, 152, 159–60, 163, 175–230 *passim*
  research / study 2, 31–2, 37–8, 59, 61, 107, 153, 235
  studies 2, 32, 36, 38, 122, 243
Audience Effect, The (Hanich) 183
audience reception studies 37–8, 40
Auslander, Philip 182
Austin, Bruce A. 2–3, 32, 37–8, 191, 194, 235
Austin, Thomas 61
Australia 8, 58, 63f, 64, 66, 98–9, 99f, 113n5, 169n26, 200, 225n27
Aylion, David (photo credit) 179

Babuscio, Jack 119n56, 145–6, 147, 163
Bacon-Smith, Camille 38
Bakhtin, Mikhail 186–90, 226n32, 228n43
  see also carnivalesque
Ballon, Bruce 131–2, 138
Barker, Martin 31, 48n14 (et al.), 58–9
Barounis, Cynthia 105, 145, 156, 162, 172n40
Barthes, Roland 32, 36, 191
Baudry, Jean-Louis 36
Bazin, André 14
Benjamin, Walter 185
Benshoff, Harry M. 5, 12, 22, 26–7, 32, 49n20, 57–9, 67, 105, 145, 147, 149–50, 155–7, 165, 235
Berenstein, Rhona J. 22, 24–6, 32, 49–50n21, 60
Bergman, David 159, 204
Bergson, Henri 222n12
binary 15, 19, 32
BIPOC (Black, Indigenous and People of Colour)
  connection to horror 48n13
  disidentificatory practices 147–8
  discrimination and violence 9–10, 43, 46n3, 127, 161, 166n3, 166n6, 219
  feminist theory 18
  inclusivity in filmmaking 4
  meaning of the term 47n6
  quantitative data on 62–4, 63f, 68, 79–80
  trauma 127, 161, 166n3, 166nn5–6
bisexual *see* queer
Blair, Linda 196, 226n34
Blake, Linnie 29, 122–3, 130–1, 133, 135
body horror
  and camp 171n36
  and the therapeutic effects 141–3
  and trans* people 118n45, 142–3, 168n18
  defined 168n17
Boellstorff, Tom 14
Boulet Brothers' Dragula, The 198, 229n48
Bourdieu, Pierre 88
Bowery, Leigh 196
Bradley, Matt 46n3
Brenchley, Michael 202, 229n50
  see also Martiny Downsize
Brickman, Barbara Jane 144–5, 147, 151
Bridge Theatre 202–3, 226nn31–2
Brim, Matt 5, 18, 42, 244
Bronski, Michael 145, 161
Brooks, Daphne 168n21
Browne, Kath 16–17, 19–20, 56
Browning, John Edgar 21–2
Brunt, Rosalind 2
Bunny Galore 220n3
Bushnell, Don D. 124
Butler, Judith 17–18, 198–9

camp
  aesthetic 94, 144–6, 237
  and age 155–6
  and gender 153–5
  and shared attributes with horror 149–52
  and the Other 156, 160, 162, 164
  and trauma 124, 144, 146, 161–3, 165, 237–8, 240

as a lens 112, 145, 150
as a political tool of disidentificatory practice 147–8
as a relationship 41, 145–6, 148, 151, 153, 156–9, 163, 165, 237–8
as a survival strategy 156, 161, 165
as an aspect of queer identity 148
as embodied 143, 146–9 *passim*, 151, 155, 157, 161–2, 238
as joyous rage 112, 240
as opposition to hegemonic normativity 156
as queer code 149, 151–2
as vulnerable resistance 144
camp-horror nexus 41, 148–53, 161, 165, 169n24, 237
is a truth in the lie 157
laughter 144, 147, 159–64, 171n39, 185
performance 113, 176, 198–201, 204, 206, 219
quantitative data on 93, 96, 146, 152–5, 153f, 158–60, 160f, 169–70nn26–9, 170–1nn31–6
transgressiveness of 150–1
Canada 58, 63f, 66, 98–9, 99f, 100, 113n5, 169n26, 178, 200
Canyon Cinema 202
capitalism 6, 8, 43, 78, 166n5, 220n4
Carla Rossi 6, 42, 165, 176, 178, 180, 182, 194, 201, 205–7 *passim*, 217, 227n40, 228n43, 238
portrait of 181
see also Hudson, Anthony
Carnes, Neal 3
carnivalesque 186–90, 201, 218–19, 226n32, 228n43, 238
Carroll, Nöel 12, 29
Caruth, Cathy 126, 130
Case, Sue-Ellen 7, 13, 16, 22, 49–50n21, 105, 155
Castle, Terry 22–3, 50
Castle, William 226n33
Castro, Gabe 4, 11, 46n3, 82, 84, 86, 129
catharsis 12, 92–3, 123–4, 126, 129, 132, 134–44 *passim*, 160–4, 167n7, 167n12, 171n37, 204, 209, 237
quantitative data on 92–3, 139–40, 140f
censorship 10, 167n11
Chamberlain, Edward A. 154
Chapman, James 21
Charcot, Jean-Martin 126
Chauncey, George 214
Cherry, Brigid 3, 5, 9, 32–3, 50n23, 57, 60–1, 64–5, 87, 94–112 *passim*, 116n26, 116nn32–3, 150, 153, 187, 234, 236–7, 243
chi-square test 45, 77, 118n48, 246–7
'Children of the Night' (Dyer) 22
chosen family 8, 88, 115n24
Church, David 115n15
Chute, David 192, 203
cinema as church 143–4, 217–18
Cinema as Therapy (Izod and Dovalis) 143
cinematic apparatus theory 36
cisheteronormativity 7–9, 14–19 *passim*, 24, 47nn8–9, 56, 59, 75, 126–9, 140–64 *passim*, 176, 183–94 *passim*, 207–26 *passim*

cisheteropatriarchy 6, 8, 12, 15, 17, 24, 29–30, 44, 47n8, 80–3, 124–5, 150, 156, 178, 247
cisheterosexism 190
heterocentrism 33–4
queer transgression of cisheterosexual norms 7, 16–17, 150–1, 162, 213
Clasen, Mathias 29, 124, 137, 240, 241n4
classism xiii, 4, 9, 64–6, 166n5
Clemens, Valdine 31
Cleto, Fabio 145
Clever, Molly 166–7n6
Clover, Carol J. 23–4, 29, 32, 49n20, 49–50nn21–2, 76, 106, 142
Cockettes, The 180, 195–6, 201–2, 224n20, 225–6n30
Cohen's *d* 248
Colangelo, Harmony 46n3, 84, 116n29, 167n8
Collins, Patricia Hill 18
colonialism 17, 47n10
compulsory heterosexuality 127
Confederated Tribes of Grand Ronde 207
confidence intervals 52n34, 57, 67, 75, 115n17, 115n20, 245–6
Connor, Andrea 15
Contreras, Lana 1, 46n3, 70, 82, 84, 214, 233
Coppa, Francesca 38, 40
Core, Philip 145, 157
Cornesse, Carina (et al.) 44, 244–5
Cotter, Robert Michael 193, 225n27
see also horror hosts
counter-hegemonic 156, 165, 187–8, 193
Coverley, Merlin 14
see also hauntology
COVID-19 pandemic xiv, 138, 166n3, 167n7, 218–19, 220n3, 223n18, 240
Cramér's V 69, 91, 246
Crane, Jonathan Lake 28
Crawford, Joan 172n43
Creed, Barbara 22, 26, 28–9, 32, 50
Crenshaw, Kimberlé 18, 47n7
Crisp, Quentin 193
Crisp, Virginia 244
Crypticon 82
cult film 187, 190–2, 204, 221n5, 226n35
The Rocky Horror Picture Show (1975) as a 113, 151, 166n1, 180, 194–5, 202, 223n14, 223nn18–19
cultural and subcultural capital 88–9, 220n4
Cvetkovich, Ann 144

Dahl, Ulrika 217
Davis, Angela 18
Davis, Bette 172n43
Davis, Colin 125, 143
Davis, Jason Edward 9, 11, 46n3, 84, 89, 121, 157–8, 178, 180, 181 (photo credit), 188–9, 193, 207
de Bruyn, Dirk 128, 133
Deleuze, Gilles 20
demographics of survey participants
age 64–7, 66f
country of residence 58
educational attainment 64–7, 65f
gender 59–61, 60f

race/ethnicity 62–4, 63f
sexual orientation 59–62, 62f
Derrida, Jacques 14
see also hauntology
Derry, Charles 134
Detamore, Mathias 42, 46n3
Dhoest, Alexander 33, 41, 114n8, 153, 244
Dickson, Lesley-Ann 208
digital divide 64
Dika, Vera 86
disidentification 147–8
Divine 201, 203–4, 221n5
Doonan, Simon 224n23
Doty, Alexander 27, 45n1, 67, 164, 191
Dovalis, Joanna 143–4
drag
as a queer art form 176, 188, 197–201
as an umbrella term 220n1
at the forefront of live cinema 180
booger *see* Martiny Downsize
clown *see* Carla Rossi
queen *see* Peaches Christ
scene 170n30
types of 224n23
see also horror hosts
Duffett, Mark 38
Dumas, Chris 23, 130
Durkheim, Émile 218
Dyer, Richard 8, 22–3, 49–50nn20–1, 75, 105, 145, 154

Edelman, Lee 15
Edmonds, W. Alex 244
Egan, Kate 58
elevated horror 3–4
Elia, John P. 17
Elliott-Smith, Darren 24, 27–8, 32, 49n20, 59
Elvira 200–1, 203, 224n22, 225n27, 226n34
see also horror hosts
Estes, Mark O. 1, 9, 46n3, 48n13, 69–70, 85, 194–5, 214–15, 224n25
Eversley, Shelly 20–1

fairy tales 138
Fake Geek Girls (Scott) 82
family of origin 87–8, 115n22
fandom (queer horror) 16, 38–40, 52n35, 61, 89, 111–12, 148, 193, 209, 237, 241n1
international horror films and 98–9, 99f
liminal position of 3
quantitative data on 81–6, 81f, 83f, 88–9, 158–9, 170n33, 241n1
white supremacist structures within 9
Fangoria's Weekend of Horrors 82
Fantastic Fest 82
favourite horror films of survey participants 107–11, 109f, 110f, 118n50, 228n42
Fejeran, Joe 9, 11–12, 46n3, 47n10, 82–3, 86, 88, 90, 162, 237
Felman, Shoshana 126
'Female Horror Film Audience, The' (Cherry) 33
film
and expressions of trauma 133
as haunted 13–14
as queer 10, 12, 21, 235

as uncanny 13
as the cathedral of the arts 217
ontological nature of 10, 12–14
temporality of 13–14
film studies (development of) 21, 36–7
final girl 23–4, 76, 78, 92–3, 96, 142, 161, 233, 237
see also Clover, Carol J.
Fischer, Lucy 28
Fisher, Mark 15, 110–11, 119n54
see also hauntology
Fiske, John 38, 88–9, 178, 189
Follows, Stephen 60, 65–6, 99, 114n9, 115n15, 116n34
Foucault, Michel 193
heterotopias 212
France 98–9, 99f
Frayling, Christopher 13
Freud, Sigmund
and catharsis 123–4, 128
and the uncanny 13
see also psychoanalysis
Fright School podcast 88

Galt, Rosalind 8, 10, 13, 16–18, 27, 113n6, 176, 212, 235
gay *see* queer
Gelder, Ken 30
gender binary 107, 199, 220n1
gender performativity 104, 198–9
see also Butler, Judith
General Data Protection Regulation (GDPR) 243
Ghaziani, Amin 5, 8, 18, 42, 244
ghosts 13–15, 34, 105, 226n32
Gibson, Rhonda 35
Gillis, John R. 6
Gilmore, James H. 180
Giroux, Henry A. 6–7
GLAAD 79, 100, 115n18
Google 80
Gordon, Phillip 223n17
gore 90, 92–4, 102, 104, 116n30, 117n39, 149, 160, 163, 210
Gorky, Maxim 13
Gorman-Murray, Andrew 72
Gothic
and queer culture 12, 29–30, 43, 51n31, 125
and trauma 124–5
fiction 30, 73, 101, 129
horror (tropes and motifs) 26, 51n31, 124, 148, 229n50
literature 30, 51n30
mode (affective and aesthetic) 30–1, 51n29
theory 31
Gothic Queer Culture (Westengard) 43, 51n31, 125
gothicism 43, 51n31, 125
Grande Dame Guignol 172n43
Grannell, Joshua 46n3, 85, 89, 145, 180, 182, 188, 196–209 *passim*, 216–18, 221n5, 222–3n13, 225–6nn29–31, 226n33, 226n35, 227n37, 229nn50–1, 234, 238
see also Peaches Christ
Grant, Barry K. 21, 192
Gravetter, Frederick 45, 246
Gray, Jonathan 38–9, 41
Greenwich Village 194, 223n17
Griffin, Sean 5, 57–8, 67, 105, 149, 155–6, 165, 235
Grotjahn, Martin 132
Guattari, Félix 20

Haggerty, George E. 30
Halberstam, Jack xiii, 6, 17, 19, 22, 24, 30, 49n17, 49n20, 51n32, 187, 193, 197, 208
Hall, Alex 11, 46n3, 134, 136–7, 167n9, 168n19, 210–11
Hall, Stuart 36–7
Halloween (holiday) 101–2, 195–6, 203
Halperin, David 7, 18, 162–3
Han, C. Winter 197
Handel, Leo A. 32, 37, 86
Hanich, Julian 29, 163, 183–6, 217, 239
Hanson, Ellis 22–3, 49–50nn20–1
Harmetz, Aljean 106
Harrington, C. Lee 38–9, 41
Harrington, Erin 12, 19, 32, 79
haunted attraction / haunts 87f, 89, 102, 227n37
haunted places 101
haunting
  and historical trauma 16, 130, 240
  and queer theory 14–15, 51n31
hauntology 14–15
Hauser, Fayette 195–6
  see also Cockettes, The
Heberle, Renee 20
Heckert, Jamie 20
Heklina (Stefan Grygelko) 222–3n13
  see also Trannyshack
Heller, Meredith 224n23
Hendershot, Cyndy 10, 151
Henkin, Bill 194
Herman, Judith 126
heteronormativity *see* cisheteronormativity
Hill, Annette 132
Hillman, Betty Luther 197
Hills, Matt 31–2, 38, 192, 220n4
Hodges, CJ 4, 46n3, 186, 206–8, 211, 214
Hollywood Theatre 205, 230n54
homonormativity 15, 43, 72
homophobia xiii, 8, 15, 29, 47n10, 49n19, 82, 126, 128, 136–8, 146, 157, 166n3, 229n50
homosexuality *see* queer
hooks, bell 18
Horn, Katrin 152
Horowitz, Katie 220n1, 224n21
horror
  and affect (psychophysiological) 29–31, 91, 136–7, 139, 167n10, 234
  and female horror fans 3, 25, 33, 57, 60–1, 64, 87, 94–7, 101, 103f, 103–7 *passim*, 111, 116n32, 234, 236; *see also* Cherry, Brigid
  as a trauma processor 93, 122, 136
  as heirloom 86–8
  as non-normative 10, 30, 142; *see also* Other, the
  as the queerest genre 10, 235
  as transgressive 5, 10, 12, 29–31, 129, 149–52, 198, 237
  audiences 32, 34, 56, 59–61, 64–6, 85–6, 201, 209, 216, 234–5, 243
  censorship of 10
  critical disapproval of 21
  empirical studies on 32–6, 60, 85
  escapism in 93, 96, 136, 167n8
  heterocentrism in 34

inclusivity in 3–4
is queer 1, 9–12 *passim*, 21, 28, 48n13, 235
queer gateway into 87–8, 87f
queer kinship with 10, 132
representation of women in 4, 26, 79–80, 236
studies 21–34, 40–2, 59, 61, 111, 118n45, 122, 130, 132, 134, 137, 234–5, 239–40
subgenres 24, 103–8, 103f, 117–18nn43–5, 118n47, 118n49, 141–3, 160, 168n15, 168n18, 171nn35–7, 236, 241n2
the generic language of 5
the Gothic and 12, 29–31, 51nn29–30
therapeutic function of 41, 94, 97–8, 117n42, 123, 129–43 *passim*, 167n7, 237
see also fandom (queer horror); film
'Horror and the Monstrous-Feminine' (Creed) 22
horror bros 1, 82
Horror Film and Affect (Aldana Reyes) 137
Horror Films (Weaver and Tamborini) 32–6 *passim*, 244
horror hosts 176, 180–3, 185, 194, 197–201 *passim*, 204, 214, 220n3, 225nn27–8, 238
horror is queer 1, 9–12 *passim*, 21, 28, 48n13, 235
Horror Report, The (Follows) 114n9
Horror Studies (journal) 28
Hubner, Laura 13–14, 21
Hudson, Anthony 11, 46n3, 84, 156, 178–92 *passim*, 196, 205–10 *passim*, 217, 222n11, 225–6n30, 227nn40–1, 230n53, 238
see also Carla Rossi
Hughes, Jessica 185–6, 191, 203, 244
Hughto, Jaclyn M. W. 41
Humphrey, Daniel 26, 61, 154, 169n26, 172n40
Humphries, Reynold 28, 119n53, 142
Hunter, Marcus Anthony 20, 45
Hurson, Laurie 20–1

imagined community 6, 40, 217
Imagining Queer Methods (Ghaziani and Brim) 14, 17
International Imperial Court System 201
intersectionality 7, 9, 16, 18, 41, 47n7, 47n10, 48n13, 49n16, 49–50n21, 56–9 *passim*, 68–70 *passim*, 72, 79, 90, 111, 125, 127, 147–8, 238
intersex *see* queer
Ireland 58, 63f, 66, 113n5, 169n26, 200
Isherwood, Christopher 146
Izod, John 143–4

Jagose, Annamarie 239
Jancovich, Mark 28, 223n14
Janet, Pierre 126
Japan 98–9, 99f, 116n34
Jenkins, Henry 38
Jensen, Eric 44
Jerslev, Anne 191
Johnston, Lynda 72

Jones, Darryl 10, 13, 105, 139–40, 142
Jones, Matthew 213
Jones, Stan 58
jump scares 90–2, 102, 116n29

Kaplan, E. Ann 133
Kelly, Casey Ryan 149
Kennedy, Helen W. 5, 38, 42, 177, 180, 190, 195, 209–10, 212, 219
Kennedy, Thomas D. 244
Kjeldsen Jens E. 2
Klinger, Barbara 164, 177, 195
Klubstitute 196
Kristeva, Julia 28
Kuchar Brothers 202

Lacan, Jacques 23, 28, 36
Lagapa, Jason 148–9
Landy, Marcia 28
Langer, Susanne 239
Latham, Rob 25–6
Laub, Dori 126
Laurie, Charles 44
lesbian *see* queer
'Lesbian Vampire on Film, The' (Zimmerman) 22
Leszcz, Molyn 131–2, 138
Levin, Nina Jackson (et al.) 115n24
Levitt, Lauren 147, 168n20, 211
Linda Blair Affair 196
Lippe, Richard 21
live cinema
    and community formation 184–5, 190, 204, 207, 209, 195, 218–19
    and queer performance 176–82
    as a celebration of queerness and horror 184–8, 194
    as a term 5
    as an academic field 5–6, 42, 176–7, 212, 216, 238
    as cult 190–1, 195
    definition of 177
    historical overview of 177, 180, 194–6
    liveness and sharedness of 176–7, 182–3, 204, 209, 219, 220n4, 230n53
    quantitative data on 212–14, 220n2
    queer 176–8, 180, 186–8, 190–1, 195, 200, 204, 209–10, 219, 220n4, 221n6, 238
Live Cinema (Atkinson and Kennedy) 177, 182
Lloyd, Moya 199
'Logging into Horror's Closet' (Scales) 28
Lorde, Audre 18, 69
Lovaas, Karen E. 17
Love, Heather 44
Lowenstein, Adam 122, 126, 130–1
Lozar Manfreda, Katja 246
Luckhurst, Roger 130
Luders, Joseph E. 240
Ludlam, Charles 145, 171nn38–9, 207
Lumière Cinématographe 13
Lynskey, John 187, 194, 209, 215

Mai, Nadin 144
Make A Scene 178, 221n6
Making Sense of Cinema (Reinhard and Olson) 36
Maltby, Richard 177, 184
Marchetti, Gina 20, 178
Martiny Downsize 193, 229n50
    see also Brenchley, Michael

Mathijs, Ernest 58–9, 190–1, 195
McCulloch, Richard 244
McElroy, Dolores 151, 161, 164, 225n26
Men, Women, and Chain Saws (Clover) 23, 49n21
Mendik, Xavier 190–1, 195
Meretoja, Hanna 125, 143
methodology and methods 17, 19, 21, 28–33 *passim*, 38–44 *passim*, 56, 59, 64, 113n2, 212, 234, 236, 243, 245
Meyer, Ilan H. 64, 245
Midnight Mass 6, 42, 176–30 *passim*, 238
Miller, Sam J. 19, 27, 42–3, 59, 75
misogyny xiii, 9, 29, 49n19, 82, 123, 126, 146, 166nn2–3, 166n5, 172n43, 189, 224n23, 229n50
Miss McGee's Creature Feature 178, 221n6
Mitchell, Alice M. 107
mixed-method data 2, 41
Molloy, Jenni 166n4, 234
'Mommie Dearest' (Berenstein) 22
monster, the
  as queer 14, 24, 26–7, 42–3, 59, 71, 73, 75–9, 92, 132, 151, 237
  figure of 23, 26
  quantitative data on queer identifications with 75–9, 76f, 77f, 92–4, 172n42
Monsters in the Closet (Benshoff) 22, 26
monstrous-feminine 22
  see also Creed, Barbara
Mooney, Linda A. 166–7n6
Moraga, Cherríe 18
Moser, Robert H. 188
Mother Camp (Newton) 198
Motion Picture Association 37, 100
Mr Wesley Dykes 220n3
Muñoz, José Esteban 15, 17, 19, 147–8, 156
Murnau, F. W. 119n55
Musser, Charles 177
mutual exclusivity in statistics 44, 108, 113n2, 236, 247
'My Words to Victor Frankenstein' (Stryker) 22

n number (sample size) 33, 244–5
Nadal, Kevin Leo Yabut 9, 15, 19, 21, 126–7
Nash, Bruce 65, 116n34
Nash, Catherine J. 16–17, 56
Neale, Steve 5
Necrology (Russo) 167n9
neoliberalism
  and identity politics xiii, 6, 20, 47n7, 131, 168–9n21
  and individualism 6–7
  and the anti-neoliberal praxis 6–7
neurocinematics 29
New Zealand 58, 63f, 66, 113n5, 169n26, 200
Newman, Kim 112
Newton, Esther 144, 161, 163–4, 198
Newton, Michael 13, 38
Ní Fhlainn, Sorcha 105
Nielsen 2, 117n35, 234
Nielsen, Elly-Jean 153, 164
Niles, Richard 172n41, 198
non-normative gender
  and the live cinema experience 228n46

defined 7
expression 197
of author 21
of survey participants 59–61, 113n7
non-normative sexuality
defined 7
of author 21
of survey participants 61–2
non-probability sampling 44, 236, 244–6
'Notes on "Camp"' (Sontag) 145
Nowell, Richard 61

Oliver-Hopkins, Olivia 146–9, 165, 190
Olson, Christopher J. 36–7
ontology 10, 12, 14, 19, 28, 30, 80, 102, 122, 131, 133–4, 150, 168–9n21, 191, 209, 235
Oppenheim, Hermann 126
oral history (methodology) 39–40, 46n3
Orloff, Alvin 196
Other, the 1, 8–12 *passim*, 23, 30, 48n13, 48n15, 51n26, 67–71, 74, 78, 80, 112, 133, 152, 156, 160, 162, 164, 190–3 *passim*, 199, 211, 215, 218, 237
see also queer alterity

pagan religions 102
Pagoda Palace 195
Palmer, Paulina 13
Patton, Mark 2
Paul, William 86, 172n44, 186, 222n12
Peaches Christ 5, 42, 165, 176, 178, 180, 193–205 *passim*, 221n5, 222–3n13, 225n29, 227nn36–7, 229n50, 238
portrait of 179
and sidekick Martiny 193, 229n50
see also Grannell, Joshua
Peele, Jordan 4, 228n42
personal is political 20, 23, 39
Peterson, Cassandra 224n22
see also Elvira
phenomenology 19, 28–30 *passim*, 133, 176, 182–6, 191–2, 217
Pine II, B. Joseph 180
Pinedo, Isabel 3, 32, 132
Piro, Sal 194
Ponder, Stacie 7, 46n3, 82, 85, 223n15
Portland, Oregon 42, 176, 180, 205, 207, 214, 223n18, 225–6n30, 227–8nn40–1, 230n54
'Portrait of a Cult Film Audience' (Austin) 37
post-binary 19
praxis 7, 25, 237
counter- 153
psychoanalysis 23, 28–9, 36, 51nn26–8
misogyny and homophobia of 29, 51nn26–7, 123, 126
Putanesca (José Guzmán Colón) 203

queer
alterity 7, 131, 162, 235
anger 1, 15, 132
as a permanent minority 8
as haunted and haunting 14–16, 30, 226n32, 240
as monstrous *see* Other, the
as societal spectre 14

assimilation 15, 27, 42–3, 153, 239; *see also* homonormativity
characters 72–5, 79–80, 93, 95, 115n17, 136, 150–1, 220n2, 236
cinemagoing 100, 143–4, 184–6, 194, 208–19 *passim*, 220n2, 222n9, 228n46
collectivity 183, 187, 221n8
community xiii, 3, 8–9, 15–16, 20, 27, 41–4, 57, 69, 127, 148, 152, 161, 164–5, 166n3, 166n6, 189, 195, 218–19, 238, 245
dehumanisation 76, 127
disassociation 137
elders 18, 22, 27
failure 193, 206, 219, 238
gaze 27, 75, 152
history as spectre 15
-ing 6, 17, 113n2, 125–6, 199, 214, 226n32
invisibility 15–16, 137, 234, 240
joy 16, 112, 144, 149, 156–7, 161, 188, 192–3, 210–11, 218, 237, 240
lens 48n13, 52n36, 67–75, 80, 90–4, 111, 126, 147, 171n38, 189, 208, 240
liberation 17, 185, 188–9, 193, 239
liberation movement 223n17
liminal precarity 15, 27, 43
liminality 3, 43
meaning of term 7, 16
reclamation 7, 15, 20, 42, 79, 164, 192–3, 213–14, 218, 221n7
representation and identification in horror 4, 10, 12, 24, 27, 67, 72–80 *passim*, 76f, 77f, 92–3, 97, 126, 132, 142, 151, 236–7; *see also* final girl; monster, the; Other, the; victim; victimised survivor
researchers 44, 236
self-reflective subjectivity 19–20, 166n3, 234
solidarity 7, 16, 38–9, 208, 212
space 39–40, 176, 178, 187–90, 203, 207, 212, 214, 218–19, 221n7, 226n32
temporality 15, 43, 105
theory 8, 14–19, 29–31, 33, 45, 49n21, 51n31, 72, 154
transgression 7, 10, 12, 30–1, 74, 150–62, 187, 195, 213, 215
visibility 3, 19, 73, 153, 209, 234
voice 2–3, 19, 31, 39, 46n3
see also trauma
Queer Art of Failure, The (Halberstam) 193
Queer Cinema in the World (Schoonover and Galt) 16
queer embodiment (non-normative) 7, 16, 57–9, 61, 69, 98, 123, 140, 143, 148–9, 157, 161, 201, 236, 238
as haunted 14–15
as necessary when studying the queer community 20
in drag performance 207
in statistics 44, 247
Queer Fear 178, 184, 210–11, 221n6

Queer for Fear Oral History
Collection 3, 39, 46n3, 88
narrators (collectively) 3, 5, 9–10, 19, 21, 34, 39–40, 45n1, 46n3, 49n19, 58–9, 72, 83, 89–90, 101, 113–14n7, 235
Queer Horror 6, 20, 42, 176–30 *passim*, 238
Queer Horror Film and Television (Elliott-Smith) 27, 49n20
Queer Images (Benshoff and Griffin) 155
Queer Methods and Methodologies (Browne and Nash) 17
Queer Theory and Communication (Yep, Lovaas and Elia) 17
queerness 9, 25–7, 33–4, 56–7, 59, 105, 147, 158, 169n25, 176, 185, 198, 213–14, 217, 234, 237, 239–40
and BIPOC feminist theory 18
and camp 148–51
and trauma 112, 123–4, 129–31, 134–6, 141
as a shared language 58
as a unifying identity marker 6, 8
as an existence created outside the norm 7–8, 192, 219
as both an identity and a methodological tool 19–20, 23, 25
as haunted 14–15
as societal transgression 10–12, 31, 195
as uncanny 12–14
of film and the horror genre 10–16, 21, 28, 43, 48n13, 80, 235
quantitative data on 67–9, 71–2, 90–3, 213, 228n47
'Questioning Queer Audiences' (Dhoest and Simons) 33, 114n8
questionnaire *see* survey

racism xiii, 9, 46n3, 49n19, 69–70, 146, 166n2, 189, 206, 224n23
Radstone, Susannah 128
Ramírez, Horacio N. Roque 39–40
Reinhard, CarrieLynn D. 36–7
Reisner, Sari L. 41
research transparency 49, 236, 245
return of the repressed 23–3
Reubens, Paul (Pee-wee Herman) 226n33
Rich, Adrienne 127
Rich, B. Ruby 186
Rivera, David P. 19, 21
Robinson, Zandria F. 20, 45
Rogers, Jillian C. 125–6
Rooke, Alison 31
Root, Maria P. P. 127
Ross, Andrew 145, 154, 165, 178, 194
Royle, Nicholas 13
Rubin, Herbert J. 39
Rubin, Irene S. 39
Russian River Massacre 203
Russo, Vito 27, 67, 167n9
RuPaul's Drag Race 170n30, 197–8, 224n21, 229n48
Rutherford, Anne 127

Salomonson, Kristen 35
San Francisco, California 42, 155, 176, 193, 195–6, 201–4 *passim*, 214, 218, 221n5, 222–3n13, 225n30, 226n32, 227n36

Sandvoss, Cornel 38–9, 41
Satana, Tura 216, 221n5, 224n22
Scahill, Andrew 17–18, 59
Scales, Adam Christopher 3, 27–8, 32, 59, 104, 132–3, 169n22
scavenger methodology 17–18, 37, 176
  see also Halberstam, Jack
Schäfer, Mirko Tobias 101
Scheff, Thomas J. 124
Scheibel, Will 217
Schelling, F. W. J. 13
Schlesinger, Philip (et al.) 244
Schoonover, Karl 8, 10, 13, 16–18, 27, 113n6, 176, 212, 235
Schottmiller, Carl 21
Scott, Suzanne 82
ScreamQueenz podcast 52n36
Scrivner, Coltan (et al.) 137–8, 167n7
Sedgwick, Eve Kosofsky 8, 17
Shaviro, Steven 28, 51n27
Sher, Ben 128, 139, 167n11, 168n16
Shocking Entertainment (Hill) 132
Shocking Representation (Lowenstein) 122
Sick & Twisted Players, The 195–6, 201, 225n30
Simons, Nele 33, 41, 114n8, 153, 244
Sisters of Perpetual Indulgence, The 201
Skal, David J. 32, 101
Skin Shows (Halberstam) 22
slasher films
  and camp 160
  and queer spectatorship 106
  therapeutic effects of 141–3
Smith, Rommi 14, 166n4, 234
social media 64, 100–2, 189, 243
societal institutions and systems
  dismantling of xiii
  white supremacy in 6, 9, 47n6, 47n8, 47n10, 48n13, 69–70, 78, 166n5, 207
  see also ableism; classism; homophobia; misogyny; racism; transphobia
Sontag, Susan 145–7, 154, 161
South Korea 98–9, 99f
Spearman's rho 91, 116n27, 141, 246–7
spectator
  imagined community of the queer horror 6, 40, 217
  largest study of the horror 2, 239
spectatorship
  and centring queerness 33–4, 57, 240
  and queer code-switching 86–7
  as a cultural historical artefact and a psychic function 25
  as active and embodied 19, 28, 31, 36–7, 42, 56–7, 67, 72, 90, 111, 123–4, 126, 128–34 *passim*, 147, 149, 151, 161, 171n38, 192, 240
  as context-activated 37
  as creative 124–5
  theoretical development of 36–7
spectatorship-as-drag 25
Spines, Christine 61
Staiger, Janet 37, 57
Stam, Robert 187
Stark, Ian 124
statistics
  chi-square test 45, 77, 118n48, 246–7

Cohen's *d* 248
confidence intervals 52n34, 57, 67, 75, 115n17, 115n20, 245–6
Cramér's V 69, 91, 246
mutual exclusivity in statistics 44, 108, 113n2, 236, 247
n number (sample size) 33, 244–5
non-probability sampling 44, 236, 244–6
Spearman's rho 91, 116n27, 141, 246–7
t-test 45, 141, 158, 168nn13–14, 170–1nn32–4, 248
Yule's Q 45, 68, 79, 80, 115n25, 247
Steinmetz, Stephanie 245, 246
Stiff, James 85–6, 115n21, 244
Stodola, Kaitlyn 46n3, 48n15, 85, 180, 187, 193, 207–8, 214–15, 217–18, 221n8, 227n40
Stokes, DaShanne 219
Stryker, Susan 19, 22, 49–50n21
subcultural analyst 20
subcultural capital 220–1n4
survey 9, 19, 39–40, 44, 48n14, 56–8, 112–13nn1–2, 235–6, 238, 243–6
design 2, 41, 44, 81, 167n12, 243–4, 113nn5–6, 114n12, 118n50, 167n12, 243
marketing of 64, 81, 243–4
respondents as active participants 46n2
response rate 2, 118n50, 243–4
see also demographics of survey participants
t-test 45, 141, 158, 168nn13–14, 170–1nn32–4, 248
Tamborini, Ron 32, 34–5, 85–6, 115n21, 138, 244
Tampon Troupe 196
tarot 102
Taylor, Jodie 145, 154, 162, 237
Taylor, Leila 76, 171n39
television 25, 27, 87f, 101–2, 170n30, 200–1, 222n12, 225nn27–8
Terror Vault 227n37
Thompson, Kim 4, 46n3, 49n16, 84, 121, 159–60, 211
Thornton, Sarah 220n4
Toepoel, Vera 245–6
Toronto, Canada 21, 178, 210, 214
'Tracking the Vampire' (Case) 22
Trannyshack (rebranded as Mother) 108, 197, 201–2, 222n13
trans*
explanation of 51n32
see also queer
transdisciplinary 17, 29, 44
transgender / trans* people
and body horror 142–3, 168n18
and the art of becoming 197
and trauma 127–8, 166n3, 166n6
discrimination and violence against 15, 43, 46n3, 50n24, 161, 166n6, 219
quantitative data on 68, 105–6, 108, 110f, 118n45, 170n28, 241n2
see also queer
transphobia xiii, 46n3, 166n2, 167n8
trauma
and creativity 124–5, 166nn3–4

- and laughter 144, 147, 161–4, 188
- and queer alterity 131
- and queer embodiment 112, 126, 129, 132, 140, 143, 166n3, 199, 238
- and the BIPOC and/or trans* community 9, 43, 127–8, 161, 166n3, 166n6, 219
- as haunting 14–16, 130, 240
- collective queer 14, 125, 127, 143
- etymology of the word 130
- filmic representation of 122, 126, 129, 131, 133
- historical 112, 125, 127, 129–31 *passim*
- insidious queer 112, 124–9 *passim*, 134, 162, 188, 237
- loop 127, 136
- quantitative data on 92–3, 135, 135f, 141–2, 168nn13–15
- sexual or sexuality-related 103, 117n42, 157
- studies 126, 130

Trobia, Alberto 58–9
true crime and serial killers 102
Tudor, Andrew 5
Tulloch, John 38
two-spirit *see* queer
typological representativeness 58

uncanny, the 7, 12–14, 43, 130–1, 148, 151, 178, 199
'Undead' (Hanson) 22
Uninvited (White) 22
United Kingdom (UK) 58, 60, 63f, 65–6, 98–9, 99f, 113n5, 114n13, 169n26, 178, 200, 228n46
United States (US) 48n11, 50n24, 58, 63f, 66, 68, 80, 84, 98–9, 99f, 100, 108, 113n4, 114n13, 116n34, 169n26, 178, 200, 218, 221n6, 225n27

Vaguely, Tony 196
Vampira (Maila Nurmi) 200–1, 225n27
- *see also* horror hosts

Vampires and Violets (Weiss) 22
Van Iquity, Sister Dana 196
Van Willigen, Marieke 166–7n6
Varrati, Michael 1, 11–12, 46n3, 85, 112, 138–9, 156–7, 175, 224n24
Veeder, William 129
Vehovar, Vasja 245–6
Velasco, Christopher 46n3, 82, 84, 117n42, 143
victim (representational) 26–7, 75–9, 92, 132, 161, 237
- quantitative data on 76f, 77f, 172n42

victimised survivor 76
Vinegar Syndrome 111
Vinsantos (Vinsantos DeFonte) 203
Vivar, Rosana 176, 212, 216, 244
Vosper, Amy Jane 243

Waitt, Gordon 72
Waldron, Darren 36
Walker, Janet 130, 133–4, 144
Waller, Gregory 150
Wallnau, Larry 45, 246
Walsh, Patrick K. 52n36
Waters, John 202, 204, 223n14, 224n22
Watson, Elena M. 200, 225n27
- *see also* horror hosts

Waverly (theatre) 194
Weaver, James B. 32, 34–5, 138, 140
Weiss, Andrea 22, 32, 50, 155
Weiss, R. H. 35, 52n34
Westengard, Laura 14, 29, 30–1, 43, 51n31, 76, 124–5, 127, 237, 240
Whale, James 2, 12, 119n55
Whatling, Clare 9
White, Patricia 22, 23, 26
whiteface 207
Wilcox, Melissa M. 154
Williams, Linda 76
Wilson, Patrick A. 64, 245
Winter, Jay 14
witchcraft 102
Women Viewing Violence (Schlesinger et al.) 244
Wood, Robin 10, 21–3, 42, 49n20, 51n30
Wounds of Nations, The (Blake) 122

Xenomorph 1809246(09)

Yep, Gust 7–8, 17, 47n9, 127
Yule's Q 45, 68, 79–80, 115n25, 247

Zillmann, Dolph 35, 140
Zimmerman, Bonnie 22, 32, 49–50n21, 105

also in series

Lindsey Decker, *Transnationalism and Genre Hybridity in New British Horror Cinema* (2021)

Stacey Abbott and Lorna Jowett (eds), *Global TV Horror* (2021)

Michael J. Blouin, *Stephen King and American Politics* (2021)

Eddie Falvey, Joe Hickinbottom and Jonathan Wroot (eds), *New Blood: Critical Approaches to Contemporary Horror* (2020)

Darren Elliott-Smith and John Edgar Browning (eds), *New Queer Horror Film and Television* (2020)

Jonathan Newell, *A Century of Weird Fiction, 1832–1937* (2020)

Alexandra Heller-Nicholas, *Masks in Horror Cinema: Eyes Without Faces* (2019)

Eleanor Beal and Jonathan Greenaway (eds), *Horror and Religion: New literary approaches to Theology, Race and Sexuality* (2019)

Dawn Stobbart, *Videogames and Horror: From Amnesia to Zombies, Run!* (2019)

David Annwn Jones, *Re-envisaging the First Age of Cinematic Horror, 1896–1934: Quanta of Fear* (2018)